The American
Community College

Arthur M. Cohen

Florence B. Brawer

The American
Community College

 Jossey-Bass Publishers

San Francisco • Washington • London • 1982

THE AMERICAN COMMUNITY COLLEGE
By Arthur M. Cohen and Florence B. Brawer

Library of Congress Cataloging in Publication Data

Cohen, Arthur M.
　　The American community college.

　　Bibliography: p. 367
　　Includes index.
　　1. Community colleges—United States.
I. Brawer, Florence B., 1922-　　. II. Title.
LB2328.C55　　　378'.052　　　81-19319
ISBN 0-87589-511-5　　　AACR2

Manufactured in the United States of America

JACKET DESIGN BY WILLI BAUM

FIRST EDITION

Code 8201

The Jossey-Bass
Series in Higher Education

A publication of the

EDUCATIONAL RESOURCES INFORMATION CENTER

Clearinghouse For Junior Colleges

UNIVERSITY OF CALIFORNIA, LOS ANGELES

This publication was prepared with funding from the National Institute of Education, U.S. Department of Health, Education, and Welfare under contract no. 400780038. The opinions expressed in this report do not necessarily reflect the positions or policies of NIE or HEW.

Foreword

This book appears at a time of great significance to the community college. The decade of the eighties will mark a turning point in its history. It is already evident that the community college is experiencing the effects of lean years following an unusually long succession of fat years when a new college appeared each week and double-digit enrollment increases were announced annually. Especially threatening are the public's efforts to curtail spending by propositions such as 13 (California) and 2½ (Massachusetts) and by caps on enrollment. Significant for the future may be the end of the campaign to transmute the community college into a new kind of institution, neither college nor high school—an idea espoused by Edmund J. Gleazer, who recently retired as president of the American Association of Community and Junior Colleges. These developments and many others mentioned by Cohen and Brawer may denote for the community college maturity, as well as the end of the Golden Age.

Cohen and Brawer's book will take its place alongside

books by such community college giants as Koos, Eells, Bogue, and Medsker. Their comprehensive, incisive, interpretive analysis of the community colleges covers nearly all facets of the college. They start with a historical analysis of the origins and development of the college and end with a critique of the college's critics. In between, chapters are devoted to administrators, students, and faculty. Four chapters, almost one third of the book, are devoted to the curriculum functions. Chapter One offers the rationale used throughout most of the book. The authors state that their function is to present information and examine the many viewpoints that have been advanced. From this approach, they do not expect to find ultimate answers but hope that better questions will result.

Those acquainted with the authors will not be surprised that they undertook this formidable task. They know that Cohen and Brawer have been immersed in community college research for more than two decades. During that time they have visited hundreds of community colleges, associated with nearly all those who have written on the college, reviewed thousands of documents sent for inclusion in the collection of the ERIC Clearinghouse for Junior Colleges since it was organized in 1966, edited the quarterly *New Directions for Community Colleges* series from its origin in 1973, and conducted major research in the humanities and sciences through the Center for the Study of Community Colleges. There is hardly a subject or topic on community college education that does not appear in one or more publications that have been written by them or produced under their guidance. Their book is a distillation of this vast experience and knowledge and is a capstone to the many articles and books they have written individually and as coauthors.

The thirteen chapters describe, probe, and dissect every facet of the institution, sometimes sympathetically, at other times critically, although seldom superficially. Despite the kaleidoscopic nature of the community college, the authors' comprehensive, incisive treatment brings into focus the changes it has undergone since its modest beginnings as a liberal arts junior college to the multifaceted giant community college of the sixties and seventies. Now, the incipient reform movement calls into question the sacrosanct principles of the open door and equal opportunity. Instead of the new institution, neither high school nor college, the authors see a return to an expanded version of the college of the postwar era of the 1940s and 1950s.

In chapter after chapter the authors make clear that research as often as not raises more questions than answers. In the areas of teaching and especially learning, the profession has made very little progress in evaluating its efforts. A historical survey of the research in these two areas would, if presented graphically, look much like graphs depicting the course of the economy, with cyclical changes representing the rise and fall of particular theories. One would like to see the trend line in community college learning slope upward; but, as Cohen and Brawer intimate, the trend line here, as in nearly all segments of education, would have a downward slope. Despite all the labors, the results, except as reported by those in charge of the experiments, are of minor significance unless one gains some comfort that the educators have learned which ideas and theories do not produce results.

Although the authors modestly assert that answers to current problems will not be found, one wonders whether it is possible for two of the most prominent students of the community college, with strong convictions expressed in many publications, to submerge these convictions in questions in such a comprehensive, wide-ranging book. Their strategy of wondering, offering information, and examining many viewpoints has enabled them to range farther afield speculatively, seemingly without committing themselves. Yet questions, no matter how carefully worded, often suggest the answers the authors would have given if they had been taking the test instead of administering it. It is noteworthy that in the four curriculum chapters the authors dispense with questions; they substitute their convictions. How could it be otherwise with authors who have been immersed in the study of the community college for two decades?

The reader will be confronted with the many paradoxes

surrounding the community college. The most nettlesome is, as
the authors point out, that it is called a college, but elementary-
grade subjects—arithmetic, reading, writing—rank high in terms
of courses offered and students enrolled. Another: Although it
has been the fastest-growing segment of education, it seems to
be the least known. After seventy-five years it has yet to adopt
a name that describes its functions. "Identity" or "image" remains one of the most serious concerns of community college
educators—a concern that has been with them almost from the
beginning. It will, the authors imply, remain with them as long
as the community college remains for students a second or
lower choice rather than equal choice with other higher education institutions and as long as educators and leaders of their
professional organizations continue to emulate chameleons in
adopting and dropping one educational fad after another, all in
the name of innovation.

One of the most intriguing chapters is "The Social Role."
The reader will find here the arguments of the leading critics
that the community college has failed to provide upward mobility or access to higher education. Briefly, the authors describe
the criticisms and, at times, raise questions of their validity.
They resist the temptation to be apologists, pointing out that
the persistence of doubts concerning the community college's
role in furthering upward mobility derives "from a gap in perception" of the educators.

In their chapters "Collegiate Function" and "General
Education" the authors make a strong plea for "liberal education for the informed citizen." The community colleges, they
maintain, must "provide some portions of the education for the
masses that tends toward encouraging exercise of the intellect."
They offer a "model for effecting general education for a free
people in a free society."

Because this book records the many changes that affect
the community college and, more important, the way educational leaders react to them, it will appeal to those who seek
only the "facts." How many? What courses and curricula?
Where from? At the other extreme it will help those seeking to
understand the philosophy—philosophies perhaps—that has pro-

pelled this institution to its present status. The critics—the community college personnel and the authors' colleagues who are involved in research on the institution—will find much to applaud and probably more to contend with. Although the authors will welcome the plaudits, they will not be disappointed if they elicit disagreement. They have strong beliefs and they are critics. So they will welcome the opportunity to be on the receiving end for the sake of starting a dialogue that they believe is urgently needed as educational leaders struggle to find solutions in the new, unfamiliar environment of zero growth and fiscal retrenchment.

September 1981   John Lombardi
Former President
Los Angeles City College

Preface

This book is about the American community colleges, institutions that offer associate degrees and occupational certificates to their students and a variety of other services to the communities in which they are located. These 1,250 colleges range in size from less than 100 to more than 30,000 students. Around one fifth of them, mostly the smaller institutions, are privately supported. The others, the larger comprehensive structures, are found in every state.

The purpose of our book is to present a comprehensive study useful for everyone concerned with higher education: college staff members, graduate students, trustees, and state-level policy makers. The descriptions and analyses of each of the institution's functions can be used by administrators wishing to learn about practices that have proved effective in other colleges, by curriculum planners involved in program revision, by faculty members seeking ideas for modifying their courses, and by trustees and policy makers enacting financial and administrative guidelines.

The book focuses mainly on the period from 1965 to 1980, when the community colleges underwent several major changes. During that time the number of public two-year institutions nearly doubled, and their enrollments quadrupled. The relations between administrators and faculty changed as multicampus districts were formed and as contracts negotiated through collective bargaining became common. Institutional financing was affected both by tax limitations and by a continuing trend toward state-level funding. The proportion of students transferring to universities fell from one in three to less than one in ten, outnumbered now by those transferring from universities to community colleges. The collegiate function was shaken as career and community education made tremendous strides and as the colleges grappled with problems of teaching the functionally illiterate.

The book is written in the style of an interpretive analysis. It includes data summaries on students, faculty, curriculum, and many other quantifiable dimensions of the institutions. It explores the inversion of institutional purpose that resulted in the career programs serving as the basis for transfer and the transfer programs becoming areas of terminal study. It explains how students' pattern of college attendance forced a conversion from a linear to a lateral curriculum pattern, from students taking courses in sequence to students dropping into and out of classes almost at will. It shows how general education can be reconciled with the career, compensatory, community, and collegiate education functions and how counseling and other auxiliary services can be integrated into the instructional program. And it examines some of the criticism that has been leveled at the community college by those who feel it is doing a disservice to most of its matriculants, especially the ethnic minorities.

Chapter One, "Background," recounts the social forces that contributed to the expansion and contemporary development of the community colleges. It examines the ever-changing institutional purposes, showing how their changes come in conflict with funding patterns and structures. It traces the reasons that local funding and control have given way to state-level management and questions what the shape of American higher education would be if there had been no community colleges.

Chapter Two, "Students," displays the changing patterns of students from the point of view of their age, ethnicity, and goals. The reasons for part-time attendance patterns are explored. There is a particular emphasis on minority students. The chapter also examines attrition, showing how the concept is an institutional artifact masking students' true achievements.

Chapter Three, "Faculty," draws on national data to show how the full-time and part-time faculty differ. It examines tenure, salary, work load, modes of faculty evaluation, professional associations, and faculty preparation. It discusses the relations between moonlighting and burnout and the conflict between instructors' desires for better students and the realities of the institutions in which they work.

Chapter Four, "Governance and Administration," reviews how management has changed in accord with institutional size, collective bargaining, available funds, and locus of control. Examples of varying modes of college organization and the role of each administrator within them are presented.

Chapter Five, "Finances," describes the various funding patterns, showing how they have followed shifts in mode of organization. Relations between the level of tuition and equity and efficiency in institutional operations are explored. The chapter also details the effects of Proposition 13 and similar fiscal limitation measures and shows how various cost-saving practices have been installed.

Chapter Six, "Instruction," discusses learning resource centers and the stability in instructional forms that has been maintained despite the introduction of mastery learning, computer-assisted instruction, and a host of reproducible media. Data are presented from surveys of more than 2,000 instructors in 175 colleges regarding their teaching practices, their goals, and the types of support services they use.

Chapter Seven, "Student Services," traces the student personnel functions, including counseling and guidance, recruitment and orientation, and extracurriculars. It also considers financial aid and the shifting patterns of articulation, detailing the efforts to enhance student flow from community colleges to senior institutions.

Chapter Eight, "Career Education," considers the rise of

occupational education as it moved from a peripheral to a central position within the institutions, from a terminal function for a few students to a set of well-articulated programs serving people seeking new jobs and upgrading within jobs they already had, relicensure candidates, hobbyists, and professional trainees.

Chapter Nine, "Compensatory Education," traces the decline in student literacy at all levels of education and shows how community colleges are bearing the brunt of ill-prepared students. It reviews specific college programs to enhance students' basic skills, and it questions whether the community colleges can maintain their credibility as institutions of higher education in the face of the massive effort in compensatory education that will be required in the coming decade. The chapter examines the controversies surrounding student mainstreaming and restrictive programming, and it explores the options of screening students at entry on a course-by-course basis or, instead, allowing students to enter any course of their choice but requiring simultaneous remedial assistance.

Chapter Ten, "Community Education," considers adult and continuing education, lifelong learning, and community services as they now operate. It recounts numerous examples of cooperative arrangements between colleges and community agencies, asks how funding can be maintained for this function, and explores how the major institutional associations promoted community education in the 1970s. The chapter also describes how the definitions of community education can be strengthened by a reclassification on the basis of students' intent.

Chapter Eleven, "Collegiate Function," considers the rise and fall of the liberal arts. It reports national survey data on enrollment trends in all subject fields and shows that the decline of the liberal arts has resulted not only from students' intent to use the two-year college as an entry to the workplace but also from the failure of the lower schools to prepare students to read, write, and think. The effects of this decline on instructors, degrees awarded, and percentage of students transferring to senior institutions are also noted.

Chapter Twelve, "General Education," traces the ebb and flow of general education through interdisciplinary courses and shows how the concept has suffered from failure of consistent definition. An upswing in general education is predicted because history shows that excesses in curriculum cannot long be maintained. The chapter offers a plan for reviving general education in each of the colleges' dominant curricula.

Chapter Thirteen, "The Social Role," examines the philosophical and practical questions that have been raised about the community college's role in leveling the social-class structure in America in general and in enhancing student progress toward higher degrees in particular. It shows how the same data can be used to reach different conclusions when the critics do not properly consider the differences between social equalization and equal access for individuals. The chapter poses alternative organizational forms within existing community colleges so that both equity and access and an avenue for individuals to attain higher degrees can be maintained.

An annotated bibliography cites the major books, journals, and monograph series published since 1967.

The information included in this book derives from many sources but predominantly from published observations and findings. The major books and journals and the Educational Resources Information Center files have been searched for documents pertaining to each topic.

We have also used our own research for information about curriculum and instructional practices. Between 1974 and 1980 the Center for the Study of Community Colleges, Los Angeles, conducted a series of studies of the liberal arts in community colleges nationwide. Funded by the National Endowment for the Humanities and the National Science Foundation, these studies examined the humanities, sciences, social sciences, and technologies by surveying faculty members, scanning college catalogues, class schedules, and enrollment figures, gaining data from administrators, and visiting twenty colleges and interviewing staff members to determine trends in and support for the collegiate function in those institutions.

Although we have relied primarily on printed sources and on our own research studies, we have also sought counsel from the many community college staff members around the country whom we meet during their visits to the ERIC Clearinghouse for Junior Colleges at UCLA, at conferences, and during our visits to their own institutions. However, even though we have drawn on all these sources and tried to present an evenhanded treatment, we must admit that we have our prejudices. We are advocates for the community colleges, believing that they have an essential role to play in the fabric of American education. We are advocates for their educative dimension, that portion of their effort that affects human learning. And we favor especially the collegiate and general education functions, feeling that they must be maintained if community colleges are to continue as comprehensive institutions.

Above all, we are critical analysts, concerned more with the ideas undergirding the community colleges' functions than with describing the operations themselves. We wonder about the interrelations of funding, management, curriculum, and teaching. And we are concerned about the shape that the institutions have taken as increasing percentages of their students attend part-time and as their curriculum has taken more a lateral than a linear form.

This latter point deserves elaboration. Which college serves best? One with 10,000 students, each taking one class? One with 5,000 students, each taking two classes? Or one with 2,500 students, each taking four classes? In all cases the cost is about the same, but the institutions are quite different. In the first example, the college has a broad base of clients, and its curriculum has a lateral form composed of disparate courses like those offered through university extension or adult education centers. In the second, the curriculum has taken a more linear shape, and the implication is that students are expected to progress toward a certificate or degree. The third type of college has apparently restricted admission to those who can attend full-time, and its courses are arrayed in sequential fashion, each of them demanding prerequisites.

The shape that an institution takes is not derived accidentally. Deliberate measures can be effected to bring about an emphasis in one or another direction. The policy makers who would serve the broadest base of clients would offer courses at night and in off-campus locations, allow students to enter and withdraw from classes without penalty at any time, and engage in vigorous marketing campaigns to attract people who might not otherwise consider attending college. Those who see their college as serving best if it enrolls full-time students would offer courses on campus only, install strict academic probation and suspension standards, demand advance registration, and enforce course prerequisites. The point is that either extreme, or any position between, could be taken by officials operating colleges within the same state, under the same sets of regulations.

We believe that the function of the analyst is to bring these types of options to the attention of people within the colleges so that they become aware that their institutions can be changed and that these changes need not be undertaken haphazardly. Broad-scale social forces and so-called community needs may act on colleges, but the institutions are propelled more by their internal dynamics, a point that can be demonstrated readily by viewing the differences between institutions in the same types of communities.

No long-sustained project ever operates in isolation, nor is it ever the work of its authors alone. For this book and the research on which it is based, many people provided assistance. We are especially grateful to Stanley Turesky of the Office of Planning and Analysis, National Endowment for the Humanities, which sponsored the research dealing with the humanities. His interest and critical analysis are very much appreciated. Raymond Hannapel of the National Science Foundation, who oversaw the science projects conducted by the Center for the Study of Community Colleges, was also helpful and deserves our thanks.

Several staff members of the ERIC Clearinghouse for Junior Colleges at UCLA helped put the book together. Gayle Byock, associate director, guided the typists and bibliographers and participated throughout. Anita Colby and Donna W. Dzierlenga provided references. James Palmer prepared the annotated bibliography. Pamela Inaba of ERIC and Christine Carrillo of the UCLA Graduate School of Education did much of the typing. Center for the Study of Community Colleges staff members

Donna Sillman and Nancy Zajac helped prepare the tables and the bibliography, and Linda Smith assisted in the typing. UCLA provided a two-quarter sabbatical leave.

John Lombardi's willingness to review the manuscript and prepare the Foreword is appreciated. As a colleague of long standing, he taught us much. Many of his ideas are reflected in this work. Thelma C. Altshuler, Norman C. Harris, Richard C. Richardson, Jr., and John N. Terrey also critiqued the manuscript and shared their thinking with us.

And because people help in different ways, sometimes just by being there, this book is dedicated to: Thelma C. Altshuler, Edward I. Blum, Morton A. Blum, Edward P. Cohen, and Martin J. Cohen.

Los Angeles, California   Arthur M. Cohen
December 1981   Florence B. Brawer

Contents

The Authors

Arthur M. Cohen has been a professor of higher education at the University of California at Los Angeles since 1964. His teaching emphasizes curriculum and instruction in higher education and the community college as an institution. Cohen's bachelor's and master's degrees were in history at the University of Miami. His doctorate was taken in higher education at Florida State University.

As director of the ERIC Clearinghouse for Junior Colleges since 1966, Cohen has been involved with the literature about community colleges, stimulating writing in the field and disseminating information analysis papers to all practitioners. As president of the Center for the Study of Community Colleges since 1974, he has conducted several national research studies of faculty, curriculum, and instruction.

Cohen has been involved with numerous journals and professional associations and has written extensively. His books include *Dateline '79: Heretical Concepts for the Community College* and *Objectives for College Courses*.

Florence B. Brawer is research director of the Center for the Study of Community Colleges and a research educationist at the ERIC Clearinghouse for Junior Colleges. A former psychometrist and counselor, she received her bachelor's in psychology from the University of Michigan. Her master's and doctorate were in educational psychology from UCLA. She is the author of *New Perspectives on Personality Development in College Students* and the coeditor of *Developments in the Rorschach Technique, Volume Three*.

Cohen and Brawer together wrote *Confronting Identity: The Community College Instructor* and *The Two-Year College Instructor Today*. They have also edited several series of monographs published by the Center for the Study of Community Colleges and the ERIC Clearinghouse for Junior Colleges. Since 1973 they have been editor-in-chief and associate editor, respectively, of the Jossey-Bass sourcebook series *New Directions for Community Colleges*. Together with other ERIC staff members they wrote *A Constant Variable: New Perspectives on the Community College* and *College Responses to Community Demands*.

The American
Community College

1

Background

*The Expanding
Role of the
Community College*

The American community college dates from the early years
of the twentieth century. Several social forces contributed to
its rise. The most prominent were the need for workers trained
to operate the nation's expanding industries; the lengthened
period of adolescence, which mandated custodial care of the
young for a longer time; and the drive for social equality, which
was enhanced by opening more schools and encouraging everyone to attend. Community colleges seemed also to reflect the
growing power of external authority over everyone's life, the
peculiarly American belief that people cannot be legitimately
educated, employed, religiously observant, ill or healthy unless
some institution sanctions that aspect of their being.

Across the country, the ideas permeating higher education early in the century fostered the development of these new
colleges. Science was seen as enhancing progress; the more people who would learn its principles, the more rapid the development of the society. The new technologies demanded skilled
operators. Individual mobility was held in the highest esteem,
and the notion was widespread that people who applied themselves most diligently would advance most rapidly. Social institutions of practical value to society were being formed. This
was the era of the Chautauqua, the settlement house, the Popu-
lists. And in the colleges, the question "What knowledge is of
most worth?" was rarely asked; the belief in learning for its own
sake was in retreat. The more likely question was "What knowledge yields the greatest tangible benefit to individuals or to society?" The public perceived schooling as an avenue of upward
mobility and as a contributor to the community's wealth. Veblen's (1918) and Sinclair's (1923) diatribes against domination
of the universities by industrialists were ineffectual outcries
against what had become a reality.

Publicly supported universities, given impetus by the
Morrill Acts of 1862 and 1890, had been established in every
state. Although many of them were agricultural institutes or
teacher training colleges little resembling modern universities,
they did provide a lower-cost alternative to private colleges. The
universities were also pioneering the idea of service to the
broader community through their agricultural and their general
extension divisions. Access for a wider range of the population
was increasing as programs to teach an ever-increasing number
of subjects and occupations were introduced. It was then that
schools of business, forestry, journalism, and social work became widespread. People with more diverse goals led to more
diverse programs; the newer programs attracted greater varieties
of people.

Probably the simplest overarching reason for the growth
of community colleges is that this century has seen a plethora
of demands placed on the schools at every level. Whatever the
social or personal problem, schools were supposed to solve it.
As a society, we have looked to the schools for racial integra-

tion. The courts and legislatures have struck down all forms of discrimination in housing; one cannot refuse to sell a home on the grounds that the potential buyers are undesirable because of their ethnicity. But the courts and legislatures have not taken the next step and said that a certain proportion of a community's homes *must* be sold to people of various races in order to effect ethnic balance. Instead, they have insisted that the schools mitigate discrimination by merging students across ethnic lines in their various programs. Similarly, the schools are expected to solve problems of unemployment by preparing students for jobs. Subsidies awarded to businesses that train their own workers might be a more direct approach, but we have preferred paying public funds to support career education in the schools. The list could be extended to show how the charge to do something about drug abuse, alcoholism, inequitable incomes, and other individual and societal ills has been assigned to the schools soon after the problems were identified. Cremin summed up the phenomenon well: "Fifty thousand people a year are being killed on the highways; obviously, traditional forms of driving instruction are not working; some new institution must assume the responsibility; the school must do it. It is a curious solution, requiring courses instead of seat belts, but typically American" (1965, p. 11).

Despite periodic disillusionment with the schools, the pervasive belief has been that education, defined as more years of schooling, is beneficial. It was not always that way. Earlier centuries, other societies, did not ascribe such power to or make such demands of their schools. Illich has said, "We often forget that the word *education* is of recent coinage. . . . Education of children is first mentioned in French in a document of 1498. . . . In the English language the word *education* first appeared in 1530. . . . In Spanish lands another century passed before the word and idea of education acquired some currency" (1971, p. 8). But the easily accessible, publicly supported school became an article of American faith, first in the nineteenth century, when responsibility for educating the individual shifted from the family to the school, then in the twentieth, when the schools were unwarrantedly expected to relieve society's ills.

The community colleges thrived on the new responsibilities, grown large because they had no traditions to defend, no alumni to question their role, no autonomous professional staff to be moved aside, no statements of philosophy that would militate against their taking on responsibility for everything.

The principle that free, public secondary education should extend to grades 13 and 14 dominated the rationale for organizing and extending the community colleges. As Bogue put it at midcentury, "It is expected that greater fluidity and a more continuous educational process will be accomplished without the sharp break at the end of the traditional twelfth year" (1950, p. 14). The 1947 President's Commission on Higher Education also articulated the value to be derived from a populace with free access to two years more of study than the secondary schools could provide. Because, as the commission put it, around half the young people could benefit from formal studies through grade 14, the community colleges had an important role to play.

Definitions of the Two-Year College

Two generic names have been applied to two-year colleges. From their beginnings until the 1940s they were known most commonly as junior colleges. Eells's (1931) definition of the junior college included the university branch campuses offering lower-division work either on the parent campus or operated at a distance; state junior colleges supported by state funds and controlled by state boards; district junior colleges, usually organized by a secondary school district; and local colleges formed by a group acting without legal authority. Bogue reported that at the second annual meeting of the American Association of Junior Colleges, in 1922, the definition of *junior college* was "an institution offering two years of instruction of strictly collegiate grade" (1950, p. xvii). In 1925 this definition was modified slightly to include the statement "The junior college may, and is likely to, develop a different type of curriculum suited to the larger and ever-changing civic, social, religious, and vocational needs of the entire community in which the college is located. It is understood that in this case, also, the work offered shall be on a level appropriate for high-school graduates" (Bogue, 1950, p. xvii). But the association also stuck with its original declaration of "strictly collegiate grade" and said that where the colleges offered courses usually offered in the first two years by the senior institutions, "these courses must be identical, in scope and thoroughness, with corresponding courses of the standard four-year college" (p. xvii). Bogue was careful to point out that skill training alone was not sufficient to qualify an institution for the appellation *community college*; a general education component must be included in the occupational programs: "General-education and vocation training make the soundest and most stable progress toward personal competence when they are thoroughly integrated" (p. 22).

During the 1950s and 1960s, the term *junior college* was applied more often to the lower-division branches of private universities and to two-year colleges supported by churches or organized independently, while *community college* came gradually to be used for the comprehensive, publicly supported institutions. By the 1970s, the term *community college* was usually applied to both types.

Several names in addition to *community* and *junior* have been advanced, but none has taken hold. The institutions have been called "Two-Year College" and "City College" and nicknamed "People's College," "Democracy's College," and "Anti-University College"—the last by Jencks and Riesman (1968), who saw them as negating the principles of scholarship on which the universities had been founded.

And there have been concerted attempts to blur the definition—for example, the continuing efforts of the American Association of Community and Junior Colleges (AACJC) during the 1970s to identify the institutions as community education centers standing entirely outside the mainstream of graded education. In 1980 the AACJC began listing "regionally accredited proprietary institutions" in addition to the nonprofit colleges in its annual *Community, Junior, and Technical College Directory*.

It has seemed most accurate to define the community college as *any institution accredited to award the associate in arts or science as its highest degree.* That definition includes the comprehensive two-year colleges as well as many of the technical institutes, both public and private. It eliminates most of the publicly supported area vocational schools and adult education centers and most of the proprietary business colleges. But that definition may not suffice for long; each year a smaller proportion of the student body obtains associate degrees. By 1980 the freshman and sophomore studies for which the colleges originally had been founded represented a minority of their efforts.

Development of Community Colleges

Although community colleges now operate in every state and enroll half the students who begin college in America, they found their most compatible climate early on in the West, most notably in California. One reason may have been that many of the ideals of democracy first took form in the western states, where women's suffrage and other major reforms in the electoral process were first seen. But the western expansion of the community college must also be attributed to the fact that during the eighteenth century and the first half of the nineteenth, while colleges sponsored by religious institutions and private philanthropists grew strong elsewhere, the West had not yet been settled. In the twentieth century it was much easier for publicly supported institutions to advance where there was little competition from the private sector. Bogue saw California as the leader in community college development because of support from the University of California and Stanford University, a paucity of small denominational colleges, and strong support for public education at all levels. Further, he said, the admission requirement of the university automatically disqualified "from half to two thirds of all high school graduates in the state" (1950, p. 88).

The junior college's purpose of relieving the university of freshman and sophomore studies dates to proposals made in 1851 by Henry Tappan, president of the University of Michigan, and in 1896 by William Folwell, president of the University of Minnesota. Both called for institutions that would take students to the point of entry to university studies in the professions and higher learning. Later, William Rainey Harper, of the University of Chicago, Edmund J. James, of the University of Illinois, and Stanford's president, David Starr Jordan, all cited the experience of European universities and secondary schools in which the curricula, students, and instructional forms had the effect of reserving to the universities the higher-order scholarship while relegating to the lower schools those functions designed to take students to their nineteenth or twentieth year. At the turn of the century, Harper also believed that the weaker four-year colleges might better become junior colleges and spend the money they were wasting on doing the higher work superficially on doing the lower work more thoroughly. And, indeed, Eells (1941a) reported that by 1940, of 203 colleges with enrollments in 1900 of 150 or fewer students, 40 percent had perished, but 15 percent had become junior colleges.

Bogue (1950, p. 82) cited the universities' attempts to drop off the lower division: "Proposals to discontinue the first two college years were made at the University of Georgia in 1859, the University of Michigan in 1852 and again in 1883, at Leland Stanford in 1907 and again in 1927, and at the Johns Hopkins University in 1926." Cubberly, in his introduction to Eells's book, commented that the senior colleges had feared that if they abolished their preparatory departments and depended on high schools for preparing their students, their standards would be lowered. But the departments were abolished, and both high schools and colleges thrived. He was hopeful that "within the next decade or two a similar step upward would be attended with equally happy results" (Eells, 1931, p. xi).

From an educational point of view, it probably would have been feasible to limit Stanford and the University of California to upper-division and graduate and professional studies because of the early, widespread development of junior colleges in California. Such proposals were made several times but never successfully implemented. But grades 13 and 14 were not given over to community colleges in any state. Instead, those schools developed outside the channel of graded education that reaches from kindergarten to graduate school. The organization of formal education in America had been undertaken originally from both ends of the continuum. Dating from the eighteenth century, the four-year colleges and the elementary schools were first. And during the nineteenth century, the middle years were accommodated as the colleges organized their own preparatory schools and as public secondary schools were built. By the turn of the twentieth century, the gap had been filled. If the universities had shut down their lower divisions and surrendered their freshmen and sophomores to the two-year colleges, these newly formed institutions would have been part of the mainstream. But they did not, and the community colleges remained adjunctive.

Their standing outside the tradition of higher education, first with its exclusivity of students, then with its scholarship and academic freedom for professors, was both good and bad for the community colleges. Initially it gained them support from influential university leaders who sought a buffer institution that would cull the poorly prepared students and send only the best on to the upper division. Later it enabled them to capitalize on the sizable amounts of money available for programs in occupational education, to accept the less well-prepared students who nonetheless sought further education, and to organize continuing education activities for people of all ages. But it also meant that they were doomed to the status of alternative institutions. In some states, notably Florida and Illinois, upper-division universities were built so that the community colleges could feed students through at the junior level. But even there the older publicly supported universities clung to their freshman and sophomore classes, and the community colleges remained on the periphery. Realization of this fact served as a major impetus to many community college leaders who sought four-year college status for their institutions. Successful in some instances, this movement had virtually subsided by the late 1960s.

Arguments in favor of a new institution to accommodate students through their freshman and sophomore years were fueled by the belief that the transition from adolescence to adulthood typically occurred at the end of a person's teens. Koos (1924, p. 343) quoted Folwell on the importance of letting youths reside in their homes until they had "reached a point, say, somewhere near the end of the sophomore year." Eells, too, posited that the junior colleges allowed students who were not fit to take the higher work to stop "naturally and honorably at the end of the sophomore year" (1931, p. 91). He said, "As a matter of record, the end of the second year of college marks the completion of formal education for the majority of students who continue post-high school studies" (p. 84). They would be better off remaining in their home communities until greater maturity enabled a few of them to go to the university in a distant region; the pretense of the higher learning for all could be set aside. Bogue (1950, p. 32) quoted Conant as saying that the community college can be seen as a terminal education institution: "By and large, the educational road should fork at the end of the high school, though an occasional transfer of a student from a two-year college to a university should not be barred."

Junior colleges were widespread in their early years. Koos reported 20 in 1909 and 170 ten years later. By 1922 thirty-seven of the forty-eight states contained junior colleges, this within two decades of their founding. Of the 207 institutions operating in that year, 137 were privately supported. Private colleges were most likely to be in the southern states, publicly supported institutions in the West and Midwest. Most of the colleges were quite small, although even in that era the public colleges tended to be the larger type. In 1922, the total enrollment for all institutions was around 20,000; the average was around 150 students in the public colleges and 60 in the private.

By 1930 there were 450 junior colleges, found in all but five states. Total enrollment was around 70,000, an average of about 160 students per institution. California had 20 percent of the public institutions and one third of the students, and although the percentages have dropped, California never relinquished this early lead. Other big public junior college states at the time were Illinois, Texas, and Missouri, with sizable numbers of private junior colleges also found in the latter two states. By 1940 there were 610 colleges, still small, averaging about 400 students each.

The high point for the private junior colleges came in 1949, when there were 322 privately controlled two-year colleges, 180 of them affiliated with churches, 108 independent nonprofit, and 34 proprietary. As Table 1 shows, they then

Table 1. Numbers of Public and Private Two-Year Colleges, 1900-1978

Year	Total	Public		Private	
		Number	Percentage	Number	Percentage
1900-01	8	0	0	8	100
1915-16	74	19	26	55	74
1921-22	207	70	34	137	66
1925-26	325	136	42	189	58
1929-30	436	178	41	258	59
1933-34	521	219	42	302	58
1938-39	575	258	45	317	55
1947-48	650	328	50	322	50
1952-53	594	327	55	267	45
1954-55	596	336	56	260	44
1956-57	652	377	58	275	42
1958-59	677	400	59	277	41
1960-61	678	405	60	273	40
1962-63	704	426	61	278	39
1964-65	719	452	63	267	37
1966-67	837	565	68	272	32
1968-69	993	739	74	254	26
1970-71	1,091	847	78	244	22
1972-73	1,141	910	80	231	20
1974-75	1,203	981	82	222	18
1976-77	1,233	1,030	84	203	16
1978-79	1,234	1,047	85	187	15
1980-81	1,231	1,049	85	182	15

Source: American Association of Community and Junior Colleges (1960, 1976, 1979, 1980).

began a steady decline. By 1980 the median private college had fewer than 500 students; only three had more than 5,000. By contrast, the median public college enrolled more than 2,000 students, and forty-four had more than 15,000. Figure 1 charts the enrollment trend since 1900.

More than any other single factor, access depends on proximity. In 1980 even the highly selective University of California's urban campuses drew at least three quarters of their entering freshmen from within a fifty-mile radius. Hence, the

Figure 1. Average Two-Year College Enrollments, 1900-1980

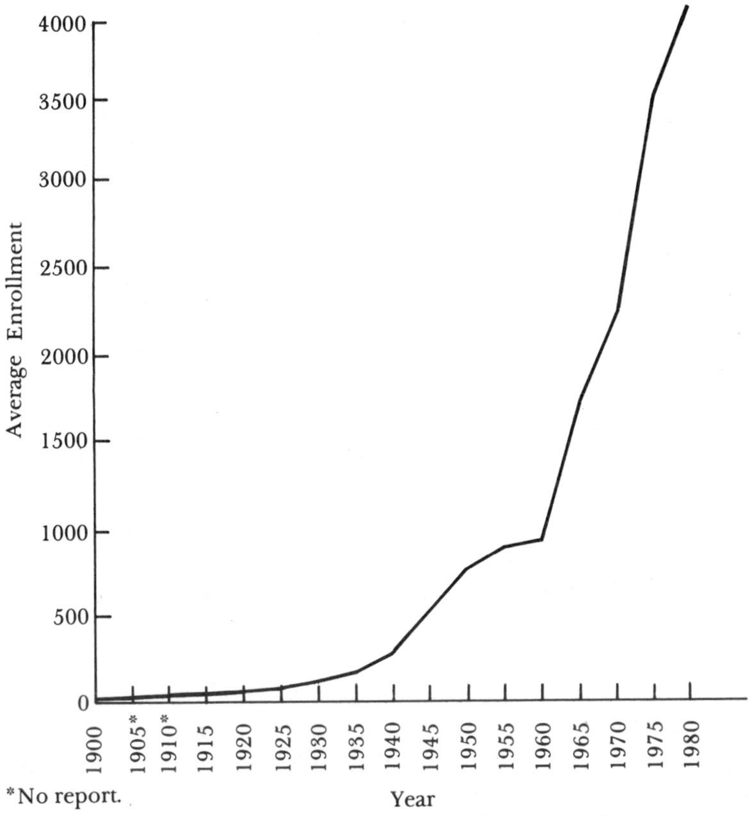

*No report.

Source: American Association of Community and Junior Colleges (1973, 1980).

advent of the community college as a neighborhood institution did more to open higher education to broader segments of the population than did its policy of accepting even those students who had not done well in high school. Throughout the nation, in city after city, as community colleges opened their doors, the percentage of students beginning college expanded dramatically. During the 1950s and 1960s, whenever a community college was established in a locale where there had been no publicly supported college, the proportion of high school graduates in that area who began college immediately increased, sometimes by as much as 50 percent.

Fueled by the high birthrates of the 1940s, this rapid expansion of community colleges led their advocates to take an obsessive view of growth. Growth in budgets, staff, students was considered good; stasis or decline was bad. It is a peculiar, but readily understandable, view. When budgets, enrollments, and staff are on an upswing, anything is possible; new programs can be launched, new staff members can be found to operate them. It is much easier to hire a new composition teacher than to get a history instructor whose course enrollments have declined to teach remedial English. Small wonder that the college leaders made growth their touchstone. It is a position of convenience that is easier than change. The philosophy is that new programs serve new clients; the conclusion is that the institution that grows fastest serves its district best.

Obviously, though, expansion cannot continue forever. In 1972 M. J. Cohen traced the relations among the number of community colleges in a state, the state's population density, and its area. He found that community colleges tended to be built so that 90-95 percent of the state's population lived within reasonable commuting distance, about 25 miles. When the colleges reached this ratio, the state had a mature community college system, and few additional colleges were built. As that state's population grew larger, the colleges expanded in enrollments, but it was no longer necessary to add new campuses. Cohen identified seven states that in the early 1970s had mature systems: California, Florida, Illinois, New York, Ohio, Michigan, and Washington. In these states, the denser the population, the smaller the area served by each college, and the higher the per-campus enrollment. Applying his formula of the relations among numbers of colleges, state population, and population density, he showed that 1,074 public community colleges would effectively serve the nation. (By 1980, 1,050 such colleges were in operation.)

Diversity marked the organization, control, and financing of colleges in the various states. Like the original four-year colleges and universities, the junior colleges grew without being coordinated at the state level. Bogue wrote, "Without doubt, the weakest link in the chain of cooperation for junior colleges is in the lack of authority for leadership and supervision at the state level. . . . By and large, the junior college in the United States has been growing without plan, general support, or supervision, and in some states almost as an extralegal institution" (1950, pp. 137-138). As Blocker, Plummer, and Richardson saw it, the colleges were "a direct outgrowth of customs, tradition, and legislation," with the institutions' "confused image . . . related to state and regional differences and legislation and to the historical development of the institution" (1965, p. 76).

Various organizing principles dictated construction of the private junior colleges. The Educational Commission of the Baptist Church coordinated the Baptist junior college development in Texas. Elsewhere, four-year private colleges struggling to maintain their accreditation, student body, and fiscal support might abandon their upper-division specialized classes to concentrate on freshman and sophomore work and thus become junior colleges. The University of Missouri helped several struggling four-year colleges in that state to decapitate themselves and become private junior colleges. In other southern states where weak four-year colleges were prevalent, this dropping of the upper division also took place, accounting for the sizable number of private junior colleges in that region. Originally, over half the private colleges were single-sex institutions, with colleges for women found most widely in New England, the Middle West, and the South.

Junior colleges were organized also by public universities wanting to expand their feeder institutions. The first two-year colleges in Pennsylvania were established as branch campuses of the Pennsylvania State College. The state universities of Kentucky, Alaska, and Hawaii also organized community colleges under their egis. Some public universities established two-year colleges on their own campuses. A University Center System gave rise to several two-year institutions in Wisconsin. And the University of South Carolina founded several regional campuses.

Many community colleges in California, in Texas, and elsewhere grew out of secondary schools. In Mississippi they were spawned by the county agricultural high schools. But many were founded without legal sanction. Eells reported public colleges operating in eleven states not authorized by general legislation or special legislation; most had been organized as extensions of public school systems "on the theory that since they were not expressly forbidden by law, they were allowed" (1931, p. 40).

The 1907 California law authorizing secondary school boards to offer postgraduate courses "which shall approximate the studies prescribed in the first two years of university courses," together with several subsequent amendments, served as a model for enabling legislation in numerous states. Anthony Caminetti, the senator who introduced the legislation, had been responsible twenty years earlier for the act authorizing the establishment of high schools as upward extensions of grammar schools. The extent of the influence, if any, of Alexis Lange, a University of California advocate of community colleges, or President Jordan of Stanford on Senator Caminetti is not certain. Lange had been a student at the University of Michigan and was aware of attempts there to truncate the university. By chance he moved to California in 1890 and brought the idea with him, writing about it extensively.

Actually the law of 1907 only sanctioned a practice in which many of the high schools in California were already engaged. Those located at some distance from the state university had been offering lower-division studies to assist their students who could not readily leave their home towns at the completion of high school. When Fresno took advantage of the law to establish a junior college in 1910, one of its presenting arguments was that there was no institution of higher education within nearly 200 miles of the city; such justifications for two-year colleges have been used throughout the history of the development of those institutions. Subsequent laws in California authorized junior colleges to open as districts entirely independent of the secondary schools, and this form of parallel development continued for decades. By 1980 nearly all the junior college districts had been separated from the lower school districts.

The beginnings of the two-year college in other states that have well-developed systems followed similar patterns but with some variations. Arizona in 1927 authorized local school districts to organize junior colleges. In 1917 a Kansas law allowed local elections to establish junior colleges and to create special taxing districts to support them. Michigan's authorizing legislation was passed the same year. Public junior colleges had already begun in Minnesota before a law was passed in 1925 providing for local elections to organize districts. Missouri's legislation permitting secondary schools to offer junior college courses dates from 1927, although junior colleges were established there earlier. Most of the community colleges in New York followed a 1949 state appropriation to establish a system of colleges to "provide two-year programs of post-high-school nature combining general education with technical education, special courses in extension work, and general education that would enable students to transfer" (Bogue, 1950, p. 34). Each state's laws were amended numerous times, usually to accommodate changed funding formulas and patterns of governance.

Curricular Functions

The various curricular functions noted in each state's legislation usually include academic transfer preparation, vocational-technical education, continuing education, remedial education, and community service. All have been present in community colleges from the start. In 1936 Hollinshead wrote that "the junior college should be a community college meeting community needs" (p. 111), providing adult education and educational, recreational, and vocational activities and placing its cultural facilities at the disposal of the community. Every book written about the institution since has also articulated these elements.

The academic transfer, or collegiate, studies were meant to fulfill several institutional purposes: a popularizing function, a democratizing pursuit, and a function of conducting the lower division for the universities. The popularizing activity was to have the effect of advertising higher education, showing what it could do for the individual, encouraging people to attend. The democratizing function was realized as the community colleges became the point of first access for people entering higher education; by the late 1970s, 40 percent of all first-time-in-college, full-time freshmen and around two thirds of all ethnic minority students were in the two-year institutions. The function of relieving the universities from having to deal with freshmen and sophomores was less pronounced, although colleges beginning at the junior year were opened in the 1960s in Florida and Illinois to take the flow from the two-year colleges of those states. Instead, community colleges made it possible for universities everywhere to maintain selective admissions requirements and thus to take only those freshmen and sophomores that they wanted.

In 1930 Eells surveyed 279 junior colleges to determine, among other things, the types of curricula offered (Eells, 1931). He found that 69 percent of the semester hours were presented in academic subjects, with modern foreign languages, social sciences, and natural sciences predominating. The 31 percent left for nonacademic subjects included sizable offerings in music, education, home economics, and extension-division-type presentations. At that time there was little difference between the curricula presented in public colleges, whether state-controlled or locally controlled, and in private denominational or independent institutions, but the older the institution, the more likely it was to be engaged in building a set of nonacademic studies. The universities accepted the collegiate function and readily admitted the transferring students to advanced standing, most universities granting credit on an hour-for-hour basis for freshman and sophomore courses. Bogue reported that "60 percent of the students in the upper division of the University of California at Berkeley, according to the registrar, are graduates of other institutions, largely junior colleges" (1950, p. 73).

Vocational-technical education was written into the plans in most states from the earliest days. In the 1970s, the U.S. Office of Education popularized *career education,* which is used throughout this book as a collective term for all occupational, vocational, and technical studies. Originally conceived as an essential component of "terminal study," education for students who would not go on to further studies, career education in the two-year colleges was designed to teach skills more complicated than those taught in high schools. Whereas secondary schools in the 1930s were teaching agriculture, bookkeeping, automobile repair, and printing, for example, junior colleges taught radio repair, secretarial services, and laboratory technical work. Teacher preparation, a function of the junior college in the 1920s, had died out as the baccalaureate became the requirement for teaching, but a sizable proportion of the occupational curriculum in the 1930s was still preprofessional training: prelaw, premedicine, pre-engineering. According to Eells (1931), in 1929 the proportional enrollment in California public junior colleges was 80 to 20 in favor of the collegiate, and in Texas municipal junior colleges it was 77 to 23. By the 1970s, the percentage of students in career education had reached parity with that in the collegiate programs and was climbing.

The continuing education function arose early, and the percentage of adults enrolled increased dramatically in the 1940s. The 1947 President's Commission on Higher Education noted the importance of this function, and Bogue noted with approval a Texas college's slogan, "We will teach anyone, anywhere, anything, at any time whenever there are enough people interested in the program to justify its offering" (1950, p. 215). He reported also that "out of the 500,536 students reported in the 1949 [AACJC] *Directory,* nearly 185,000 are specials or adults" (p. 35).

Remedial education, also known as developmental, preparatory, or compensatory studies, grew as the percentage of students poorly prepared in secondary schools swelled community college rolls. Although some compensatory work had been offered early on, the disparity in ability between students entering community colleges and those in the senior institutions was not nearly as great in the 1920s as in the 1970s. Koos (1924) reported only slightly higher entering test scores by the senior college matriculants. The apparent breakdown of basic academic education in secondary schools in the 1970s, coupled with the expanded percentage of people entering college, brought compensatory education to the fore. By the mid 1970s, one third of the mathematics taught in community colleges was at a level lower than beginning algebra. And Morrison and Ferrante (1973) found separate compensatory programs in 59 percent of public colleges.

The community service function was pioneered by private

junior colleges and by rural colleges, which often served as the cultural centers for their communities. Early books on two-year colleges display a wide range of cultural and recreational events that institutions of the time were presenting for the enlightenment of their communities. Public two-year colleges adopted the idea as a useful aspect of their relations with the public, and in some states special funds were set aside for this function. By 1980 the AACJC *Directory* listed nearly 4 million community education participants, predominantly people enrolled in short courses, workshops, and noncredit courses. The community service function also included spectator events sponsored by the colleges but open to the public as well as to students.

This book presents separate chapters on each curricular function: collegiate (academic transfer), career (vocational-technical), and compensatory (remedial) education. Community service and continuing education are merged, and general education is accorded treatment on its own. Student guidance, often mentioned as a major function, is covered in the chapter on student services. Yet all the functions overlap, because education is rarely discrete. Community college programs do not stay in neat categories when the concepts underlying them and the purposes for which students enroll in them are scrutinized. Although courses in the humanities are almost always listed as part of the collegiate program, they are career education for students who will work in museums. A course in auto mechanics is for the general education of students who learn to repair their own cars even though it is part of the offerings in a career program. Collegiate, career, continuing education—all are intertwined. Who can say when one or another is occurring?

The definitions are pertinent primarily for funding agents and accreditation associations and for those who need categories and classification systems as a way of understanding events. "Career" education is that which is supported by Vocational Education Act monies and/or which is supposed to lead to direct employment. When a course or program is approved for transfer credit to a senior institution, it becomes part of the "collegiate" function. When it cannot be used for associate degree credit, it is "compensatory" or "community" education. That is why community college presidents may say honestly that their institutions perform all tasks with great facility. When confronted with the charge that their school is not doing enough in one or another curriculum area, they can counter that it is, if the courses and students were only examined more closely. All education is general education. All is potentially career-enhancing. All is for the sake of the broader community.

Changing Purposes

Community colleges have effected notable changes in American education, especially by expanding access. Well into the middle of the twentieth century, higher education had elements of mystery within it. Only one young person in seven went to college, and most students were from the middle and upper classes. To the public at large, which really had little idea of what went on behind the walls, higher education was a clandestine process, steeped in ritual. The demystification of higher education, occasioned by the democratization of access, has taken place steadily. Given marked impetus after World War II by the GI Bill, when the first large-scale financial aid packages were made available and people could be reimbursed not only for their tuition but also for their living expenses while attending college, college going increased rapidly, so that by the 1970s three in every eight persons attended.

The increase in enrollments was accompanied by a major change in the composition of the student body. No longer sequestered enclaves operated apparently for the sons of the wealthy and educated on their way to positions in the professions and for the daughters of the same groups, who would be marked with the manners of a cultured class, the colleges were opened to ethnic minorities, to lower-income groups, and to those whose prior academic performance had been marginal. And of all higher education institutions, the community colleges contributed most to opening the system. Established in every metropolitan area, they were available to all comers, attracting the "new students," the minorities, the women, the people who had done poorly in high school, those who would otherwise never have considered further education.

During this same era community colleges contributed also

to certain shifts in institutional purpose. They had always been an avenue of individual mobility; that purpose became highlighted as greater percentages of the populace began using colleges as a step up in class. And the emphasis in higher education on providing trained personnel for the professions, business, and industry also became more distinct. Identifying the students who sought learning for its own sake or who went to college to gain the manners that would mark them as ladies or gentlemen is a precarious exercise; perhaps students whose purposes were purely nonvocational were rare even before 1900. But by the last third of the twentieth century few commentators on higher education were even articulating those purposes. Vocationalism had gained the day. College going was for job getting, job certifying, job training. The old values of a liberal education became supplemental—adjuncts to be picked up incidentally, if at all, along the way to higher-paying employment.

Other shifts in institutional purpose have been dictated not by the pronouncements of educational philosophers but by the exigencies of financing, the state-level coordinating bodies, the availability of new media, and the new student groups. There has been a steady increase in the public funds available to all types of educational institutions, the community colleges most profoundly affected by the sizable increases in federal appropriations for occupational education. Beginning with the Smith-Hughes Act in 1917 and continuing through the Vocational Education Acts of the 1960s and 1970s, federal dollars have poured into the education sector. Community colleges have not been remiss in obtaining their share. Their national lobbyists have worked diligently to have the community college named in set-asides, and the colleges have obtained funds for special occupational programs. The career education cast of contemporary colleges is due in no small measure to the availability of these funds.

State-level coordinating agencies have affected institutional role. Coordinating councils and postsecondary education commissions, along with boards of regents for all higher education in some states, have attempted to assign programs to the different types of institutions. These bodies may restrict lower-division offerings in community colleges. In some states, continuing education has been assigned; in others, it has been taken away from the colleges.

The new media have had their own effect. Electronic gadgetry has been adopted, and elaborate learning resource centers have been opened on campus. Because learning laboratories can be made available at any time, it becomes less necessary for students to attend courses in sequence or at fixed times of day. The new media, particularly television, have made it possible for institutions to present sizable proportions of their offerings over open circuit. The colleges have burst their campus bounds.

But the new students have had the most pronounced effect. The community colleges reached out to attract those who were not being served by traditional higher education, who could not afford the tuition, who could not take the time to attend a college on a full-time basis, whose ethnic background had constrained them from participating, who had inadequate preparation in the lower schools, whose educational progress had been interrupted by some temporary condition, who had become obsolete in their jobs or who had never been trained to work at any job, who needed a connection to obtain a job, who were confined in prisons, physically handicapped, or otherwise unable to attend classes on a campus, or who were faced with increased leisure time. Their success in enrolling these new students has affected what they can offer. Students who are unable to read, write, and compute at a level that would enable them to pursue a collegiate program satisfactorily must be provided with different curricula. As these students become a sizable minority—or, indeed, a majority—the college's philosophy is affected. Gradually the institution's spokespersons stop talking about its collegiate character and speak more of the compensatory work in which it engages. Gradually the faculty stops demanding the same standards of student achievement. Part-time students similarly affect the colleges as new grading policies are adopted to accommodate students who drop in and out, and new types of support systems and learning laboratories are installed for those who do not respond to traditional classroom-centered instruction.

Overall, the community colleges have suffered less from goal displacement than have most other higher education institutions. They had less to displace; their goals were to serve the people with whatever the people wanted. Standing outside the tradition, they offered access. They had to instruct; they could not offer the excuse that they were advancing the frontiers of scholarship. Because they expanded so rapidly, their permanent staffs had not been in place so long that they had become fixed. As an example, it was relatively easy to convert their libraries to learning resource centers because the libraries did not have a heritage of the elaborate routines accompanying maintenance and preservation of large collections. They could be fit to the instructional programs.

In 1924 Koos was sanguine about the role of the junior college in clarifying and differentiating the aims of both the universities and the secondary schools. He anticipated an allocation of function "that would be certain to bring order out of the current educational chaos. . . . By extending the acknowledged period of secondary education to include two more years . . . allocation of purpose to each unit and differentiation among them should take care of themselves" (p. 374). He saw most of the aims and functions of the secondary school rising to the new level and giving to the first two years of college work a new significance. These aims included occupational efficiency, civic and social responsibility, and the recreational and esthetic aspects of life. The universities would be freed for research and professional training. Further, the college entrance controversy would be reduced, and preprofessional training could be better defined. Duplication of offerings between secondary schools and universities would also be reduced by the expansion of a system of junior colleges.

Clearly, not many of Koos' expectations were borne out. He could not have anticipated the massive increase in enrollments, the growth of universities and colleges and the competition among them, the breakdown in curriculum fostered, on the one hand, by part-time students who dropped in and out of college and, on the other, by the institutions' eagerness to offer short courses, workshops, and spectator events. His scheme did not allow for the students who demanded higher degrees as a right, crying that the colleges had discriminated against them when the degrees were not awarded as a matter of form. And he was unaware of the importance that students and educators alike would place on programs related to job attainment.

Current Issues

The revolution in American education in which the two-year college played a leading role is almost over. Two years of postsecondary education is within reach—financially, geographically, practically—of virtually every American. It has been one third of a century since President Truman's Commission on Higher Education recommended that the door to higher education be swung open. Now community colleges are everywhere. There are systems with branches in inner cities and rural districts and with programs in prisons and on military bases. Classes are offered on open-circuit television, on Saturdays, and at all hours of the night. Open-admissions policies and programs for everyone ensure that no member of the community need miss the chance to attend.

But the question remains, "Access to what?" Should community colleges educate for further studies, or should they be the capstone for graded education? Can they be both? Those who would make the community college the elementary school for further learning have been in headlong retreat. Capstone, or terminal, education currently takes the form of so-called compensatory studies, in which students are given one last chance to learn minimal language and computational competencies. Occupational education stands like a colossus on its own.

To Bogue in 1950, the critical problems of the community colleges were these: devising a consistent type of organization, maintaining local or state control, developing an adequate general education program integrated with the occupational, finding the right kind of teachers, maintaining adequate student guidance services, and getting the states to appropriate sufficient funds. These problems have never been satisfactorily resolved.

Fifteen years later, Blocker and his coauthors (1965) identified nine issues: maintaining comprehensive programs, serving equally well the wide variety of unselected students, adapting to changes in society or becoming static, giving the community anything that anyone wants while continuing to maintain educational integrity, maintaining fiscal support, finding sufficient educational leaders to staff the institutions, adopting the best patterns of administration and organization, avoiding division into vocational schools, on the one hand, and college transfer institutions, on the other, and getting society to accept the notion that all individuals have a right to education as far as they want to go. Most of these problems have also persisted.

Recent changes in both intra- and extramural perceptions of community colleges have led to further issues. Some of these shifts are due to educational leadership at the state and the institutional level, but more are due to changing demographic patterns and public perceptions of institutional purposes. First, there has been an inversion in the uses of career and collegiate education. Career education was formerly considered terminal. Students were expected to complete their formal schooling by learning a trade and going to work. Students who entered career programs and failed to complete them and then to work in the field for which they were trained were considered to have been misguided. Collegiate programs were designed to serve as a bridge between secondary school and baccalaureate studies. Students who entered the programs and failed to progress to the level of the baccalaureate were considered dropouts.

By 1980 more students who completed career programs were transferring to universities than those who completed collegiate programs. Career programs typically maintained curricula in which the courses were sequential. Many of these programs, especially those in the technologies and the health fields, had selective admissions policies. Students were forced to make an early commitment, be admitted to the programs, and make satisfactory progress through them. This pattern of schooling reinforced the serious students, leading them to enroll in further studies at a university. The collegiate courses, in contrast, were more likely to be taken by students who had not made a commitment to a definite line of study, who already had degrees and were taking courses for personal interest, or who were trying to build up their prerequisites or grade-point averages so that they could enter a selective admissions program at the community college or at another institution. Thus, for most students enrolled in them, the collegiate courses had become the catchall, the "terminal education" program.

A second issue is that the linear aspect of community colleges, the idea that the institution assists students in bridging the freshman and sophomore years, had been severely reduced as a proportion of the community colleges' total effort. The number of students transferring was reasonably constant, but most of the expansion in community college enrollments in the 1970s was in the areas of career and continuing education. The collegiate programs remained in the catalogues, but students used them for completely different purposes. They dropped in and out, taking the courses at will. In 1978 the mean number of credit hours completed by California community college students per term was between seven and eight, but the mode was three—in other words, one course (Hunter and Sheldon, 1979). The course array in the collegiate programs was more accurately viewed as lateral than as linear. Not more than one in ten course sections enforced course prerequisites; not more than one course in ten was a sophomore-level course. What had happened was that the students were using the institution in one way whereas the institution's modes of functioning suggested another. Catalogues displayed recommended courses, semester by semester, for students planning to major in one or another of a hundred fields. But the students took those courses that fit a preferred time of day or those that seemed potentially useful. By 1980 colleges in several states had taken deliberate steps to quell that pattern of course attendance, but nationwide it was still the norm.

Third, a trend toward less-than-college-level instruction has accelerated. Not only have compensatory courses gained as a proportion of the curriculum, expectations in collegiate courses have changed. To take one example, students in community college English literature courses in 1977 were expected to read 560 pages per term, on average, whereas, according to Koos, the average was three times that in *high school* literature courses of 1922. These figures are offered not to derogate community colleges but only to point out that the institutions cannot be understood in traditional terms. They are struggling to find ways of educating students whose prior learning has been dominated by nonprint images. The belief that a person unschooled in the classics was not sufficiently educated died hard in the nineteenth century; the ability to read *anything* is suffering a similar fate in an era when most messages are carried by wires and waves.

But all questions of curriculum, students, and institutional mission pale in light of funding issues. Are the community colleges—any schools—worth what they cost? Have the colleges overextended themselves? Do their outcomes justify the public resources they consume? Can they, should they, be called to account for their outcomes? Those questions have appeared with increasing frequency as public disaffection with the schools has grown. Whether the community colleges stand alone or whether they are cast with the higher or lower schools, their advocates will be forced to respond.

Several other current issues may also be phrased as questions. How much more than access and the illusory benefits of credits and degrees without concomitant learning do the colleges provide? Are they in or out of higher education? How much of their effort is dedicated to the higher learning, to developing rationality and advancing knowledge through the disciplines? How much leads students to form habits of reflection? How much tends toward public and private virtue?

Is it moral to sort and grade students, sending the more capable to the university while encouraging the rest into other pursuits? Eells commented on the terminal programs, the commercial and general education courses that did not transfer to the universities, saying, "Students cannot be forced to take them, it is true, but perhaps they can be led, enticed, attracted" (1931, p. 310). And in his chapter on the guidance function he noted that "it is essential that many students be guided into terminal curricula" (p. 330). The "cooling out" function (so named by Clark in 1960), convincing the students they should not aspire to the higher learning, yielded an unending stream of commentary—for example, an issue of *New Directions for Community Colleges* entitled *Questioning the Community College Role* (Vaughan, 1980). But the question is still unanswered.

What would the shape of American education have been if the community colleges had never been established? Where would people be learning the trades and occupations? Apprenticeships were the common mode in earlier times. Would they still dominate? Would the less-than-college-level regional occupational centers and area vocational schools be larger and more handsomely funded? Would different configurations have developed?

What would have happened to the collegiate function? How many fewer students would be attending college? Would the universities have expanded to accommodate all who sought entry? Community colleges certainly performed an essential service in the 1960s and 1970s when a mass of people demanded access. By offering an inexpensive, accessible alternative, these colleges allowed the universities to maintain at least a semblance of their own integrity. How many universities would have been shattered if community colleges to which the petitioners could be shunted had not been available?

If there had been no community colleges, what agencies would be performing their community services? How many of the services they have provided would be missed? Would secondary schools have better maintained their own curricular and instructional integrity if community colleges had not been there to grant students absolution for all past educational sins? Would other institutions have assumed the compensatory function?

Although such questions have been asked from time to time, they have rarely been examined, mainly because during most of its history the community college has been unnoticed, ignored by writers about higher education. The books on higher education published from the turn of the century, when the first community colleges appeared, through the 1960s rarely gave even a nod to the community college; one searches in vain for a reference to them in the index. In 1950 Bogue deplored the lack of attention paid to the junior colleges, saying that he had examined twenty-seven authoritative histories of American education and found only a superficial treatment of junior colleges or none at all. Rudolph's major history of the higher education curriculum, published in 1977, gave them a scant two pages. And seldom have the questions been answered or even considered by community college leaders and their counterparts in those four-year institutions that did not develop traditions of scholarship. Instead the leaders have seized on a new term, *post-secondary education,* which they felt allowed the colleges engaged primarily in basic instruction to be fit in the same tent with the research universities.

It may be best to characterize community colleges merely as untraditional. They do not follow the tradition of higher education as it developed from the colonial colleges through the universities. They do not typically provide the students with new value structures, as residential liberal arts colleges aspire to do. Nor do they further the frontiers of knowledge through scholarship and research training, as in the finest traditions of the universities. Community colleges do not even follow their own traditions. They change frequently, seeking ever-new programs and clients. Community colleges are indeed untraditional, but they are truly American because, at their best, they represent the United States at its best. Never satisfied with resting on what has been done before, they try new approaches to old problems. They maintain open channels for individuals, enhancing the social mobility that has so characterized America. And they accept the idea that society can be better, just as individuals can better their lot within it.

Students

Greater Numbers,
More Diversity,
Varied Purposes

Two words sum up the students: *number* and *variety*. To college leaders, the spectacular growth in student population, sometimes as much as 15 percent a year, has been the most impressive feature of community colleges. The numbers are notable: enrollment increased from just over ½ million in 1960 to more than 2 million by 1970, more than 4 million by 1980. During the 1960s much of the increase was due to the expanded proportion of eighteen- to twenty-four-year-olds in the population—the result of the World War II baby boom. Not only were there more people in the college-age cohort, more of them were going to college. Table 2 shows the percentage of the age group in all types of colleges and Table 3 the percentage of high

Table 2. Enrollment of College-Age Population in Institutions of
Higher Education, 1899-1900 to 1980

Year	College-Age Population (in thousands)[a]	Enrollment (in thousands)[b]	Percentage
1899-1900	14,951	232	1.6
1909-10	18,212	346	1.9
1919-20	18,821	582	3.1
1929-30	22,487	1,054	4.7
1939-40	24,033	1,389	5.8
1950	16,076	2,281	14.2
1960	16,128	3,583	22.2
1970	24,687	8,581	34.8
1980	29,463[c]	12,376[c]	42.0

[a]Includes armed forces; 15-24-year-olds through 1940, 18-24-year-olds from 1950 through 1980.

[b]Degree-credit enrollment through 1960; degree-credit and nondegree-credit enrollment 1970-1980.

[c]Estimated.

Sources: U.S. Department of Health, Education, and Welfare, National Center for Education Statistics, Opening (Fall) Enrollment in Higher Education; U.S. Department of Commerce, Bureau of the Census, Current Population Reports.

Table 3. First-Time Students Enrolled in Higher Education Institutions
as a Percentage of High School Graduates, 1950-1978

Year	High School Graduates (in thousands)[a]	First-Time Students (in thousands)	Percentage
1950	1,200	517	43.1
1955	1,415	675	47.7
1960	1,971	930	47.2
1966	2,679	1,566	58.5
1968	2,829	1,908	67.4
1970	2,944	2,080	70.7
1972	3,043	2,171	71.3
1974	3,140	2,393	76.2
1976	3,149	2,377	75.5
1978	3,144	2,422	77.0

[a]Includes graduates of public and nonpublic schools.

Source: "Twenty-Year Trends in Higher Education" (1978).

school graduates starting college. Whereas around half the high school graduates went to college in the early 1960s, by the late 1970s three fourths of them were entering some postsecondary school, an increase occasioned in large measure by the community colleges' availability. Community colleges also recruited students aggressively; to an institution that tries to offer something for everyone in the community, everyone is potentially a student.

Reasons for the Increase in Numbers

The increase in community college enrollments may be attributed to several conditions: older students' participation; physical accessibility; financial aid; part-time attendance; the reclassification of institutions; the redefinition of students and courses; and high attendance by low-ability, women, and minority students.

The colleges often sought out certain constituencies. Older students, particularly, were recruited. Butcher (1980) found tuition waivers for seniors a typical practice nationwide, although simplified registration, special counseling, and supplemental transportation were rare. Dib (1978) reviewed the catalogues of fifty-five southern California community colleges and found nineteen noting special programs for older adults. Charles (1979) surveyed the 106 California community colleges and found 43 percent with special classes or programs for retired persons and 60 percent that were trying to recruit older people through special publicity and cooperation with other community agencies.

Accordingly, older students swelled enrollments during the 1970s. According to the AACJC, the mean age of students enrolled for credit in 1980 was twenty-seven; the median age was twenty-three; the modal age was nineteen. Note the discrepancy among these three measures. The mean is most sensitive to extremes; hence a program for even a few senior citizens in a retirement community affects that measure dramatically. The median suggests that the students just out of high school and those in their early twenties who either delayed beginning college or entered community colleges after dropping out of other institutions accounted for half the student population. This 50 percent of the student body that was composed of students aged eighteen to twenty-three was matched on the other side of the median by students ranging in age all the way out to their sixties and seventies. The mode reflects the greatest number, and although the percentage of students under twenty dropped from 53 in 1970 to 37 in 1977, nineteen-year-olds were still the dominant single age group in the institutions. Thus, a graph depicting the age of community college students would show a bulge at the low end of the scale and a long tail reaching out toward the high end.

Physical accessibility also enhanced enrollments. The effect of campus proximity on the rate of college going has been well documented. As an example, Tinto (1973) found the presence of local colleges affecting the rate of attendance among high school graduates in Illinois and North Carolina, especially among students of lower ability. Most of the high-ability students would have attended college anyway, even if it meant leaving their hometown, but the rate of college going among lower-ability students increased dramatically when a public community college became readily available to them.

The availability of financial aid brought additional students as state and federal payments, loans, and work-study grants rose markedly. Nearly all the types of aid were categorical, designed to assist particular groups of students. The largest group of beneficiaries was the war veterans; in California in 1973, veterans made up more than 13 percent of the total enrollment. Students from economically disadvantaged and minority groups were also large beneficiaries of financial aid; more than 30,000 such students in Illinois received state and local funds in 1974. Student assistance programs were found in twelve states in 1964, in twenty-two in 1970, and by 1980, in nearly every state.

As the age of the students went up, the number of credit hours each student attempted went down. The percentage of part-timers grew from 48 at the beginning of the 1970s to 63 at the end (see Table 4). And these figures do not include noncredit students enrolled in community continuing education, high

Table 4. Part-Time Enrollments as a Percentage of Total Enrollments,
1963-1980

Year	Opening Fall Enrollment	Part-Time Enrollment	Percentage
1963	914,494	488,976	53
1968	1,909,118	888,458	47
1969	2,234,669	1,064,187	48
1970	2,447,401	1,164,797	48
1971	2,678,171	1,290,964	48
1972	2,863,780	1,473,947	51
1973	3,100,951	1,702,886	55
1974	3,528,727	1,974,534	56
1975	4,069,279	2,222,269	55
1976	4,084,976	2,219,605	54
1977	4,309,984	2,501,789	58
1978	4,304,058	2,606,804	61
1979	4,487,872	2,788,880	62
1980	4,825,931	2,996,264	62

Source: American Association of Community and Junior Colleges (1965-1981).

school completion courses, and short-cycle occupational studies. As can be seen in Table 5 (New York and North Carolina not shown), in all states with community college enrollments greater than 50,000, part-time students outnumbered full-timers.

The rise in the number of part-time students can be attributed to many factors—a decline in eighteen-year-olds as a percentage of the total population, an increase in the number of students combining work and study, and an increase in the number of women attending college, to name but a few. However, the colleges made deliberate efforts to attract part-timers by making it easy for them to attend. Senior citizens' institutes, weekend colleges, courses offered at off-campus centers, in workplaces, and in rented and donated housing around the district, and countless other strategems have been employed. The noncampus colleges that sprang up in the 1970s present a good example of institutional efforts to attract part-timers; few of them counted any full-timers among their enrollees.

The rise in part-time attendance has lowered the percentage of students attending community colleges past their first

Table 5. Part-Time Enrollments as a Percentage of Total Enrollments
in Selected States, 1979

State	Opening Fall Enrollment	Part-Time Enrollment	Percentage
Alabama	160,171	128,102	80
Arizona	106,923	78,834	74
California	1,101,648	777,477	71
Virginia	106,565	74,855	70
Illinois	336,240	226,941	67
Texas	262,236	165,001	63
Florida	201,626	122,204	61
Ohio	140,691	85,689	61
New Jersey	102,319	60,246	59
Wisconsin	137,670	79,963	58
Massachusetts	81,134	43,595	54
Pennsylvania	88,268	47,226	54

Source: American Association of Community and Junior Colleges (1980).

year. Although AACJC data for 1963-1973 (Table 6) showed a relatively constant ratio of about 2.4 freshmen to one sophomore, by the end of the decade, the proportion of students *completing* two years had dropped to less than one in five. Part of this decrease may be attributed to certificate programs that could be completed in one year, part to the massive increase in students without degree aspirations taking only a course or two

Table 6. Ratio of Freshman to Sophomore Enrollments,
1953-54 to 1973-74

Year	Number of Freshmen	Number of Sophomores	Ratio of Freshmen to Sophomores
1953-54	172,566	83,138	2.1:1
1963-64	541,946	214,082	2.5:1
1968-69	1,106,558	444,427	2.5:1
1969-70	1,274,633	515,179	2.5:1
1970-71	1,370,668	561,868	2.4:1
1971-72	1,593,586	636,277	2.5:1
1972-73	1,659,094	690,024	2.4:1
1973-74[a]	1,827,012	771,742	2.4:1

[a]Last year for which the figures were published.
Source: American Association of Community and Junior Colleges (1955-1975).

for their own interest. The AACJC's dropping "freshman" and "sophomore" categories from its *Directory* after 1975 reflected the tendency of most colleges to avoid referring to their students' year of attendance. The preferred mode of classification was to designate those who wanted credits for transfer to a baccalaureate institution, those who sought occupational training, and "other." Not necessarily more accurate, at least this type of information differentiated students according to major funding sources: degree credit, occupational studies, and adult or continuing education.

The growth in total enrollments did not result alone from the colleges' attracting students who might not otherwise have participated in education beyond high school. Two other factors played a part—the different ways of classifying institutions and a redefinition of the term *student*. Changes in the classification of colleges are common: Private colleges become public; two-year colleges become four-year (and vice versa); adult education centers and proprietary trade schools enter the category, especially as they begin awarding degrees. The universe of community and junior colleges is especially fluid. From time to time, entire sets of institutions, such as trade and vocational schools and adult education centers, have been added to the list. As examples, in the mid 1960s four vocational-technical schools became the first colleges in the University of Hawaii community college system, and in the mid 1970s the community colleges in Iowa became area schools responsible for the adult education in their districts. Sometimes institutional reclassification is made by an agency that gathers statistics; in 1980 the American Association of Community and Junior Colleges began adding proprietary trade schools to its *Directory*. All these changes add to the number of students tabulated each year.

Reclassification of students within colleges has had an even greater effect on enrollment figures. As an example, when the category "defined adult" was removed from the California system, students of all ages could be counted as equivalents for funding purposes. In most states the trend has been toward including college-sponsored events, whether or not such activities demand evidence of learning attained, as "courses" and hence the people attending them as "students." Further, the community colleges have taken under their egis numerous instructional programs formerly offered by public and private agencies, including police academies, hospitals, banks, and religious centers. These practices swell the enrollment figures and blur the definition of *student,* making it possible for community college leaders to point with pride to the enhanced enrollments and to gain augmented funding when enrollments are used as the basis for accounting. They also heighten imprecision in counting students and make it difficult to compare enrollments from one year to another.

Student Ability

Classification of students by academic ability revealed increasing numbers of lower-ability students. As Cross pointed out, three major philosophies about who should go to college have dominated the history of higher education in this country: the *aristocratic,* suggesting that white males from the upper socioeconomic classes would attend; the *meritocratic,* holding that college admission should be based on ability; and the *egalitarian,* which "means that everyone should have equality of access to educational opportunities, regardless of socioeconomic background, race, sex, *or ability*" (1971, p. 6). By the time the community colleges were developed, most young people from the higher socioeconomic groups and most of the high-aptitude aspirants were going to college. Cross concluded: "The groups new to higher education in the decade of the 1970s will be those of low socioeconomic status and those with low measured ability. The movement is already underway; the majority of students entering open-door community colleges come from the lower half of the high school classes, academically and socioeconomically" (p. 7).

The Cooperative Institutional Research Program (CIRP) annual freshman survey data reveal the number of students with low prior school achievement in community colleges. Table 7 indicates the academic rank in high school for students enrolling in 1979.

Table 7. High School Academic Performance of College Freshmen, 1979

Measure of Academic Performance	Percentage of Enrollment	
	All Institutions	All Two-Year Colleges
Rank in high school		
Top 20 %	38	23
Second 20%	23	23
Middle 20%	32	45
Fourth 20%	6	8
Lowest 20%	1	1
Average grade in high school		
A or A+	9	4
A—	12	7
B+	19	17
B	27	30
B—	14	16
C+	12	15
C	7	10
D	less than 1	1

Source: Astin and others (1979).

Other data also reveal the lower academic skill level of entering freshmen. The American College Testing Program's entering test means for community colleges were considerably lower than the norm for all college students. In Illinois the mean for entering community college freshmen in 1978 was 16.6, down from 18.0 in 1973. This compares with a 1978 national norm of 18.7 (Lach and others, 1979).

Although these data provide an overall view, they tend to obscure differences among sets of institutions. In states where public institutions of higher education are arrayed in hierarchical systems, most of the students begin in a community college, and the proportion of lower-ability students is greatest in such colleges. But where the publicly supported universities maintain open admissions, the prior school attainment of their entering freshmen differs little from that of two-year college matriculants.

Comparisons of entering students who said they would need remedial help in their studies suggest these different patterns. The CIRP data showed that, nationally, the proportion of students indicating they would probably need remedial work while in college was 13 percent for English and 23 percent for mathematics. (The percentages saying they would need help differed little between matriculants in two-year and four-year colleges.) But nearly half the 12,789 entering freshmen who took the American College Testing Program battery in Illinois (where state universities have relatively open admissions) in 1978 said they would need help in mathematics or in study skills (Lach and others, 1979). And Combs (1978) reported that 33 percent of the students at Maricopa Technical Community College (Arizona) indicated a need for more basic English and math courses.

Community colleges have also matriculated a number of high-ability students. Like most other institutions of higher education, they have always sought out those students and made special benefits available to them. Olivas (1975) found that 47 of the 644 public and private colleges responding to a national survey had established formal honors programs. Most of the others indicated that they had honors classes, honors societies, provisions for independent study, and/or scholarships available for high-ability students; fewer than 20 percent indicated that they had no special provisions. White (1975) surveyed 225 colleges in the North Central region and found around 10 percent with formalized honors programs and nearly half of the others with some provision for superior students. The honors programs were most likely to be in rural community colleges, least likely in the newer suburban institutions.

How do the high-ability students fare? Schultz (1967-1968) studied the initiates of Phi Theta Kappa, an organization for full-time students ranking in the upper 10 percent of their class, and found that they spoke favorably of their time in the community colleges. However, Astin (1977) argued that although community colleges brought expanded opportunities for students of low ability who had been denied access to higher education, they had a negative effect among the more highly able. He pointed out that fewer students who had graduated in the top 20 percent of their high school classes were attending four-year colleges in 1977 than fifteen years earlier; the decline was 16 percent for males, 9 percent for females. In contrast, the proportion of highly able males who were attending two-year colleges had increased by 10 percent, and the proportion of females had increased by 12 percent.

According to Astin, this shift away from four-year college attendance that was occasioned by the easily accessible two-year colleges was proving detrimental to the higher-ability students, who, by virtue of attending community colleges, were reducing their chances for obtaining baccalaureate degrees. Astin has presented a serious indictment, contending that although community colleges provide important services to a number of part-time students and to adults and students pursuing technical courses, they may not really serve the students who come directly from high school seeking baccalaureate degrees. He concludes that these students' chances of persisting to the baccalaureate are simply less at a two-year college than at a four-year college, public or private (1977, p. 247).

Women

Differences between male and female college students have long been documented because, as Cross (1968, pp. 12-13) pointed out, "the computer (which is neuter) seems to recognize differences between the sexes on all manner of educational variables." She indicated that, historically, among students of questionable ability, fewer women than men attended college, and when funds were limited, more male than female high-ability students from low-income families entered college. Further, the women who went to college were more likely to be dependent on their families for support, and college women had better high school records. Some of Cross's contentions were corroborated by the CIRP data on community college entrants. Table 8, showing the distribution of high school grades and academic ranks among men and women entering community colleges, points up the difference.

Notable differences between the family income of students entering two-year and four-year colleges have been well documented. The CIRP data showed the persistence of these differences through the 1970s (see Table 9). However, by the end of the 1970s, the difference in sources for educational ex-

Table 8. High School Academic Performance of Entering Community
College Freshmen by Sex, 1979

Measure of	Percentage of Enrollment	
Academic Performance	Men	Women
Rank in high school		
Top 20%	19	27
Second 20%	24	22
Middle 20%	46	43
Fourth 20%	9	7
Lowest 20%	2	1
Average grade in high school		
A	7	14
B+	15	20
B	28	32
B—	19	14
C+	19	12
C	12	8

Source: Astin and others (1979).

penses indicated by men and women had disappeared. In fact, 57 percent of entering women were from families whose estimated parental income was less than $20,000, whereas only 52 percent of the men were from the same group. And nearly equal numbers of men and women entering community colleges indicated they would be receiving no parental aid or working part-time while in school.

Table 9. Parental Income of Entering College Freshmen, 1970 and 1979

Estimated Parental Income	Percentage of Enrollment			
	All Institutions		All Two-Year Colleges	
	1979	1970	1979	1970
Less than $6,000	8	13	10	20
$6,000-9,999	8	24	10	29
$10,000-14,999	15	31	18	30
$15,000-19,999	14	13	16	10
$20,000-24,999	17	7	17	5
$25,000-29,999	10	4	9	3
$30,000-34,999	8	2	7	2
$35,000-39,999	6	1	4	1
$40,000 or more	14	4	9	2

Source: Astin and others (1979).

The feminist movement seemed to have had little effect on the types of programs that community college students entered. Women still went into the traditionally female allied health and office fields, men into the traditionally male fields of construction and transportation. A study of California students found only around 3 percent of matriculants in occupational programs to be in nontraditional areas; that is, only around 3 percent of students in the welding and automotive programs were female, and only around 3 percent of students in the nursing and secretarial programs were male (Hunter and Sheldon, 1979).

Ethnic Minorities

Community colleges' diligence in recruiting students from segments of the population that had not previously attended college yielded sizable increases in college attendance by members of ethnic minorities. By the end of the 1970s, community colleges were enrolling nearly 40 percent of the ethnic minority students attending college in the United States. Naturally, the pattern differed from state to state, depending on the minority group population. The states with the highest percentages of minorities among their community college students were Alabama, Alaska, California, Hawaii, Louisiana, Maryland, Mississippi, South Carolina, and Texas. However, minorities were also enrolled in significant numbers in those other states that had well-developed community college systems.

More so than in the universities, the community college student population tends to reflect the ethnic composition of its surroundings. By 1977, minority group students formed more than 60 percent of the enrollment in the Los Angeles Community College District, the largest district in the country. Community colleges in other cities with high proportions of minorities—Cleveland, El Paso, and New York, to name a few—also enrolled sizable numbers of minority students who commuted from the neighborhood. However, the urban colleges were not alone in attracting the minorities; Chicano students made up 30 percent of the enrollment in Reedley College, located in a small California town where fewer than half of the high school students are Mexican-American (Clark, 1975). Several community colleges were established especially to serve minorities. Oglala Sioux Community College (North Dakota), Haskell Indian Junior College (Kansas), Navajo Community College (Arizona), and Bacone Community College (Oklahoma) are notable examples of institutions for American Indian students. Los Angeles Southwest College, Malcolm X College (Chicago), Hostos Community College (New York), and several other urban-based institutions, though not designed officially for minorities, are segregated de facto.

Nationwide, minority group students constitute approximately one fourth of all community college enrollments. During the 1970s, black students nearly achieved parity with their proportion of the population; in fact, in half the states, the proportion of blacks in two-year colleges was higher than their proportion in the eighteen-to-twenty-four age group. Students of Hispanic origin had not achieved this parity, but their numbers increased markedly during the 1970s. Tables 10 and 11 provide detailed information on minority group enrollments.

Table 10. Representation of Blacks and Hispanics in Two-Year Colleges and in the Eighteen- to Twenty-Four-Year-Old Population by State, 1976

	Blacks		Hispanics	
State	Percentage of Enrollment	Percentage of Population Aged 18-24	Percentage of Enrollment	Percentage of Population Aged 18-24
Alabama	20.8	29.3	0.1	0.4
Alaska	4.2	4.7	1.7	1.8
Arizona	3.6	2.3	11.4	15.3
Arkansas	15.9	20.5	0.3	0.0
California	9.3	9.5	9.9	15.9
Colorado	4.6	3.6	8.5	10.8
Connecticut	8.4	7.6	2.5	3.0
Delaware	15.9	13.9	1.2	1.9
Florida	12.7	17.9	6.7	6.7
Georgia	16.6	31.3	0.4	0.4
Hawaii	1.2	1.1	3.8	2.2
Idaho	0.2	0.2	0.9	4.9
Illinois	15.2	16.4	2.4	3.9
Indiana	9.4	6.3	0.6	1.8
Iowa	2.1	1.6	0.5	1.0
Kansas	6.2	4.8	2.1	2.8
Kentucky	13.8	10.5	0.2	0.6

Table 10. Representation of Blacks and Hispanics in Two-Year Colleges
and in the Eighteen- to Twenty-Four-Year-Old Population by State, 1976
(Continued)

	Blacks		Hispanics	
State	Percentage of Enrollment	Percentage of Population Aged 18-24	Percentage of Enrollment	Percentage of Population Aged 18-24
Louisiana	31.6	27.5	1.4	1.5
Maine	0.3	0.5	0.0	0.5
Maryland	20.0	20.9	0.6	0.5
Massachusetts	3.5	2.6	1.8	0.8
Michigan	13.9	12.5	0.9	1.3
Minnesota	1.2	0.8	0.2	0.7
Mississippi	27.4	37.3	0.1	0.4
Missouri	18.5	14.0	0.5	1.0
Montana	0.0	1.0	0.0	1.0
Nebraska	5.1	3.5	0.8	1.4
Nevada	6.0	7.2	2.4	5.9
New Hampshire	0.4	0.3	0.2	0.5
New Jersey	13.7	10.3	3.3	5.5
New Mexico	2.7	1.6	15.7	34.1
New York	12.7	13.5	6.1	7.2
North Carolina	20.1	25.5	0.4	0.0
North Dakota	0.2	0.4	0.1	0.4
Ohio	14.2	10.1	0.7	1.3
Oklahoma	9.1	8.1	0.8	1.8
Oregon	1.3	1.5	1.1	2.1
Pennsylvania	10.6	9.3	0.9	1.0
Rhode Island	2.0	3.4	0.3	0.6
South Carolina	28.6	32.2	0.1	0.7
South Dakota	0.2	0.4	0.2	0.9
Tennessee	20.6	17.9	0.3	0.5
Texas	11.6	11.7	16.9	20.1
Utah	0.4	1.1	2.5	3.5
Vermont	0.0	0.2	0.4	1.3
Virginia	14.4	15.6	0.5	0.7
Washington	3.0	2.5	1.6	2.7
West Virginia	3.0	2.3	0.1	0.2
Wisconsin	5.3	3.4	0.8	0.9
Wyoming	1.3	1.1	3.2	5.7
Total	11.0	12.0	8.2	5.3

Source: Population data, Policy Analysis Service, American Council on Education. Based on unpublished data from the Bureau of the Census. Survey of Income and Enrollment Data, Fall 1976, Higher Education General Information Survey. Reprinted in Gilbert (1979, p. 16).

Because the issue of minority students' progress in college has been so charged politically, the question whether the community colleges have enhanced or retarded progress for minority

Table 11. Racial/Ethnic Composition of Enrollments in Two-Year Colleges by State, 1978 (Percentages)

State	Non-resident Alien	Black Non-Hispanic	American Indian and Alaskan Native	Asian and Pacific Islander	Hispanic	White Non-Hispanic	Minority Sub-Total
Alabama	1.3	27.8	0.1	0.1	0.1	70.2	29.8
Alaska	0.2	0.2	42.3	1.2	0.7	55.1	44.9
Arizona	0.9	3.0	4.9	0.7	8.9	81.3	18.7
Arkansas	0.5	20.7	0.8	0.4	0.4	77.0	23.0
California	1.0	9.6	1.5	5.9	10.3	71.4	28.6
Colorado	2.3	3.8	0.9	0.9	8.4	83.5	16.5
Connecticut	0.4	8.7	0.2	0.5	2.5	87.3	12.7
Delaware	0.1	15.2	0.1	0.4	0.9	82.9	17.1
Florida	2.0	11.5	0.3	0.6	8.6	76.7	23.3
Georgia	1.5	18.9	0.2	0.5	0.6	78.0	22.0
Hawaii	3.1	1.2	0.2	70.1	3.8	21.2	78.8
Idaho	0.8	0.5	0.4	0.9	1.8	95.3	4.7
Illinois	5.0	14.4	0.3	1.2	2.2	76.6	23.4
Indiana	0.8	11.2	0.7	0.6	0.8	85.7	14.3
Iowa	0.9	1.6	0.4	0.4	4.8	91.6	8.4
Kansas	1.5	5.6	3.2	0.2	1.5	87.7	12.3
Kentucky	1.7	11.4	0.1	0.2	0.2	86.2	13.8
Louisiana	2.4	32.5	0.3	0.8	2.1	61.6	38.4
Maine	0.0	0.0	6.0	0.0	0.0	93.6	6.4
Maryland	3.0	19.6	0.3	1.3	1.1	74.5	25.5
Massachusetts	1.3	3.7	0.2	0.3	1.8	92.4	7.6
Michigan	0.7	13.1	0.7	0.5	1.6	83.0	17.0
Minnesota	1.5	0.7	0.4	0.2	0.3	96.6	3.4
Mississippi	0.3	23.3	0.3	0.3	0.5	75.0	25.0
Missouri	0.3	6.3	0.4	0.3	1.7	90.7	9.3
Montana	0.3	0.1	8.3	0.0	0.6	90.4	9.6

Nebraska	0.1	2.1	0.3	0.3	1.0	95.9	4.1
Nevada	0.3	6.5	1.8	1.3	2.4	87.7	12.3
New Hampshire	0.2	0.4	0.1	0.2	0.4	98.5	1.5
New Jersey	0.9	14.0	0.2	0.9	2.8	81.0	19.0
New Mexico	0.0	1.7	13.5	0.3	34.5	49.6	50.4
New York	0.4	10.3	0.5	0.8	4.5	83.2	16.8
North Carolina	0.5	20.5	0.9	0.3	0.3	77.1	22.9
North Dakota	0.7	0.3	18.1	0.0	0.2	80.6	19.4
Ohio	0.2	14.6	0.2	0.4	0.7	83.6	16.4
Oklahoma	4.7	8.0	4.5	0.9	1.0	80.6	19.4
Oregon	1.5	1.1	1.1	1.8	1.3	92.9	7.1
Pennsylvania	0.2	13.2	0.1	0.8	0.8	84.5	15.5
Rhode Island	0.2	5.1	0.1	0.3	0.3	93.7	6.3
South Carolina	0.4	29.9	0.1	0.3	0.2	68.7	31.3
South Dakota	0.2	0.2	2.6	0.6	0.0	96.2	3.8
Tennessee	0.7	18.6	0.1	0.2	0.3	79.8	20.2
Texas	1.7	10.8	0.3	1.0	12.0	73.9	26.1
Utah	0.2	0.4	1.4	1.0	3.1	93.6	6.4
Vermont	0.3	0.3	0.1	0.1	0.1	98.8	1.2
Virginia	0.2	13.0	0.2	1.7	0.8	83.8	16.2
Washington	3.4	2.6	1.3	1.9	1.2	89.3	10.7
West Virginia	0.0	4.0	0.2	0.4	0.2	94.9	5.1
Wisconsin	0.2	7.0	0.7	0.4	1.1	90.3	9.7
Wyoming	1.0	0.7	1.3	0.3	1.7	94.7	5.3
American Samoa	0.0	0.0	0.0	98.5	0.0	1.4	98.6
Puerto Rico	0.0	0.0	0.0	0.0	100.0	0.0	100.0
Micronesia	0.0	0.0	0.0	100.0	0.0	0.0	100.0
Total	1.4	10.7	1.0	2.4	6.6	77.6	22.4

Source: Gilbert (1979, p. 11).

students has been debated at length. Those who say that the community colleges have assisted minority students point to their ease of access, low tuition, and minimal entrance requirements. They note the numerous programs that provide special services to minority students, and they applaud the efforts made to recruit them. Their most telling argument is that a sizable percentage of those students would not be in college at all were it not for the community colleges. Detractors have taken the position that because students who begin at a community college are less likely to obtain baccalaureate degrees, minorities are actually harmed by two-year institutions.

The question whether community colleges are beneficial to minority students is, thus, unresolved. If sizable percentages of minority students would not attend any college unless there were a community college available, and if the act of attending college to take even a few classes is beneficial, then community colleges have certainly helped in the education of minority students. But if the presence of a convenient community college discourages minority students from attending senior institutions, thus reducing the probability of their completing the baccalaureate, then for those students who wanted degrees the college has been detrimental. The CIRP data on which Astin based his contentions certainly suggest that most students want higher degrees: among full-time freshmen entering two-year institutions in fall 1979, around 80 percent aspired to at least a bachelor's degree. (When *all* entering students are considered, as in studies done in Virginia [Adams and Roesler, 1977], Maryland [Tschechtelin, 1979], California [Hunter and Sheldon, 1979], and Washington [Meier, 1980], the proportion of bachelor's degree aspirants drops to 15-33 percent.)

Still, these findings obscure as much as they reveal. The question is not whether minority students tend to be concentrated in two-year colleges; they are. The question is not whether they tend to go through to the level of the associate degree and then transfer to the university; as a group they do not. The question is what effect the community colleges have on *all* their students. And the answer is that they have a similar effect on all their students, minority and majority. They tend not to be designed primarily for the purpose of passing students through to the baccalaureate. The issue must be seen in its total context; it does not merely affect the minorities.

The poor record of minority groups in community colleges must also be viewed in association with their record in other levels and types of institutions. Around 3 million pupils began the first grade each year during the 1950s, and twenty years later, around 35,000 doctoral degrees were awarded annually. Obviously, most of the students left the school system somewhere along the way, but where? The progress made by these 3 million students in graded education was different for minority and majority students. As a group, minority students began at a point of lower academic achievement, and the difference between them and the majority students increased through the grades toward graduate school. Similarly, the number of minorities dropping out of graded education was greater at each year along the way.

Those who would understand the effect of community colleges should visualize two lines representing continuance in school. If one line shows majority students' persistence and the other minorities', the two will not be parallel; the line representing the majorities will show the lesser attrition. The lines will be farther apart (the difference between minority and majority students will be greater) at grade 14 than at grade 12; fewer of the minorities are in college. Those who argue that the community college does a disservice to minorities will point to the gap between minority and majority students' persistence in college. But they usually fail to note that a comparison between the groups for *any* two years of graded education, from kindergarten through the doctorate, would show a similar difference. Thus, because minority students tend to be clustered more in community colleges, the charge is made that they do less well in those institutions.

The reasons that minority students drop out are not as clear. It does seem that college policies encourage dropping out —and dropping in, too. Minority students are more likely to delay entry into college after completing high school; the community colleges will take them at any time. Minority students are more likely to attend school part-time; the community colleges encourage part-time attendance. Minority students are more likely to be from low-income families, and although community colleges have low tuition, the financial aid offered to students at senior institutions reduces the tuition differential.

If the purpose of the collegiate enterprise is to pass most students through to the baccalaureate degree, then the community college is a failure by design. Its place in the total scheme of higher education assures that a small number of its matriculants will transfer to universities and obtain the baccalaureate. It draws poorly prepared students and encourages part-time and commuter status. Its students perceive the institution as being readily accessible for dropping in and out without penalty. They know they need not complete a program soon after leaving secondary school; the institution will be there to accept them later.

Astin has charged that minority students who begin in community colleges will do less well than those of equal ability who begin in the senior institution and that this differential is greater for them than it is for majority students. However, the question must be put more broadly: "The community college or what?" For most students in two-year institutions, *the choice is not between the community college and a senior residential institution; it is between the community college and nothing.*

Whom do the community colleges best serve? Egalitarians would say that the institutions should maintain parity in the percentage of each ethnic group attaining each of the following goals: entering college, enrolling in transfer-credit courses, persisting in any courses, gaining the associate degree, gaining admittance to a high-level technological program, graduating from such a program, transferring to the university at any point, and transferring to the university at the junior level. In practice, however, this level of equivalence is impossible to attain, short of imposing strict quotas at every step.

Who Is Being Served?

The classification of students into special groups is more politically inspired than educationally pertinent. Women, ethnic minorities, and the handicapped were able to have their concerns translated into special programs only after they became politically astute. In the later 1960s and early 1970s, ethnic and women's studies courses were widely adopted, and in the late 1970s, programs for the handicapped, complete with their own funds, were established. However, the educative dimension of these programs—the desired learning outcomes—still rested on traditional academic forms. Where it did not, the students, however classified, were not well served.

Similarly, the program classifications—transfer, credit, evening, and so on—were hardly justifiable from the standpoint of education. They related to funding channels, not to teaching forms. The temptation to place a course or a student in a category for which special additional funds were available was always present. The mature woman with a bachelor's degree, taking an art class for credit that happened to be taught by someone with whom she wanted to paint at a time of day that was convenient for her, was not deserving of the special treatment accorded to "returning women," "the aged," or "students intending to transfer." She was there for her personal interest. Yet the politically and institutionally inspired definitions resulted in her being counted each time the institution reported its numbers of women, aged, and transfer students.

The temptation to classify students has always been present. Assessments of community college students have been made from perspectives that span the social sciences: psychological, sociological, economic, and political. To the psychologist, community college students are pragmatic, little concerned with learning for its own sake. They are not self-directed or self-motivated; they need to be instructed. To the sociologist, the students are struggling to escape from their lower-class backgrounds; some do, but many are inhibited by a bias against leaving family and friends that a move in class would engender. To the economist, students from low-income families p⁻y more in the form of forgone earnings as a percentage of total family income than their counterparts from higher-income groups, a differential that more than offsets the savings gained by attending a low-tuition institution. To the political scientist, students attending community colleges are given short shrift because the institutions are funded at a lower per capita level than the universities, and hence the students do not have equivalent libraries, laboratories, or faculty-student ratios available to them.

All these characterizations are correct, even though they mean little to institutional planners. Certainly the students are realistic, because they use the institutions for their own purposes. But what students do not, in schools where attendance is not mandated? Certainly many are from lower social classes than those attending the universities, but their class base is higher than that represented by the majority of Americans who do not attend college at all. Certainly many are from the lower-income groups, but their attendance usually leads to higher earnings. Certainly they welcome an instantly responsive institution; whether they are harmed by the college's failure to maintain standards in curriculum and a consistent philosophical base is less certain. And they do respond favorably to the variety of instructional media available to them, although the effects of nonpunitive grading and forgiveness for past educational sins on their proclivities for learning have not yet been traced.

Unaware of all these analyses, the students continue attending the community colleges for their own purposes. Those just out of high school may matriculate merely because they have been conditioned to go to school every time September appears on the calendar. Students of any age wanting a better job may attend because the career programs are connected to the employers. Those who have jobs but want additional skills may hope to find a short-term program that will teach them to use the new equipment that has been introduced in their industry. Many begin at the introductory level and learn complete sets of job skills enabling them to qualify for trades that they might have known nothing about before entering the programs. Some students seek out special-interest courses ranging from "The Great Books" to "Poodle Grooming," taking a course or two whenever one that strikes their fancy appears in the class schedule. Some use the community colleges as stepping stones to other schools, finding them convenient and economical entry points to higher education and the professions.

Determining the reasons that students attend college has

never been easy. They come for a variety of reasons, and the same person may have a half-dozen reasons for attending. Much depends on the way the questions are asked and the interpretations that the respondents make. But there can be little doubt that although most students attend community colleges to better themselves financially, a sizable percentage are there for reasons of personal interest having nothing to do with direct fiscal benefit. Gold (1979) surveyed students at Los Angeles City College in 1976 and again in 1978, asking their "most important reason for attending college." The 1978 survey found 52 percent attending "to acquire or improve occupational or technical skills" or "to help choose a career," up from 46 percent that had given those occupationally related responses two years earlier. But the main attraction of the college itself was that it was close to home and charged no tuition. And Hunter and Sheldon's study of students who had matriculated at fourteen California community colleges in 1978 found 37 percent interested primarily in finding a job or improving job skills and 26 percent who were attending for their own interest or as a leisure-time pursuit.

The conventional belief is that community college students are less interested in academic studies and in learning for its own sake, more interested in the practical, which to them means earning more money. Although some research evidence supports that belief, the perception that higher education is particularly to be used for occupational training seems to be pervasive among students in all types of institutions. According to CIRP data (Astin and others, 1979), 80 percent of the entering freshmen in two-year colleges studied noted "get a better job" as a very important reason in deciding to go to college; but 76 percent of matriculants in four-year colleges and 77 percent of those in universities gave the same reason. Similarly, although 67 percent of two-year college entrants gave as an important reason "make more money," 61 percent of freshmen at four-year colleges and 64 percent of freshmen at universities said the same thing.

Several studies conducted in the 1960s and 1970s did identify practicality among two-year college students. On the

Omnibus Personality Inventory, a multiphasic test standardized on two-year and four-year college and university students in the early 1960s, the one scale on which two-year college students typically exceeded the others was Practical Orientation. Drawing on his lengthy experience as a community college administrator, Monroe asserted that "community college students tend to place more emphasis on receiving immediate goals and rewards than on postponing the possibility of winning greater rewards at some future date. . . . A relevant education means practical, occupationally oriented education" (1972, pp. 199-200). Cross (1971) also noted that students who graduated in the lower third of their high school classes and subsequently attended two-year colleges were positively attracted to careers. She found them presenting a more pragmatic, less questioning system of values than traditional students. Brawer (1973) corroborated many of these findings but also assessed students on different measures. Her concept of "functional potential" addresses the question of ego strength and provides a basis for placing students in particular learning environments.

Studies comparing students at a single community college and its neighboring university often report similar differences. As an example, more Montgomery College students gave job preparation and job improvement as major reasons for their interest in higher education than University of Maryland students (Montgomery College, 1974). Trent (1972) reported that 70 percent of the students in fifteen California community colleges indicated vocational training as their most important reason for attending. But once again, it is important to note that during the 1970s similar, although perhaps not quite so pronounced, tendencies were found by researchers studying students in four-year colleges and universities. And large numbers of community college students attend for reasons having nothing to do with jobs.

Some information is available on what percentage of each of various groups in the population is served. Lucas (1978) compared the student body of an Illinois college with the population of the district it served and found that 3 percent of the district's female population over age seventeen was enrolled, double the percentage for males. Most of the women were enrolled in continuing education; credit-course enrollments accounted for less than one third of the total head count at the college. Students' family income was considerably less than the median income for the district: 13 percent less for credit students and 28 percent less for students in continuing education. And 60 percent of the continuing education students and 43 percent of the students enrolled for transfer credit had had some prior education; a high proportion already had bachelor's degrees. The college was serving lower-income people, more women than men, and people who had already had prior college experience. If it were designed for people seeking higher degrees, it would either have to seek a different clientele or run the risk of doing a disservice to those it had enrolled.

Transfer and Attrition

Reliable data on students intending to transfer are difficult to obtain. Many colleges have maintained policies of counting as a transfer student everyone who is taking a credit course but who is not enrolled in an occupational program, a procedure that throughout the history of the community college has undoubtedly contributed to inflated figures on the number of students intending to transfer. Students can be asked about their intentions. Except for those who already have higher degrees and those who are enrolled in occupational programs with a license to practice available at the end of their community college work, however, few students are willing to forgo their options for a higher degree. Hence, few will say that they never intend to transfer to a senior institution. The community colleges have fostered the idea that periodic college attendance is not only available but also desirable. Their matriculants cannot reasonably be expected to say that they plan no further education. Accordingly, all studies of first-time-in-college, full-time students have found a majority saying they plan on obtaining the baccalaureate or higher degree.

The decline in the percentage of students who transfer from community colleges to baccalaureate institutions has been well documented. The absolute number of transferring students has actually increased, but when compared with the much greater increases in students interested in programs that lead to immediate employment, courses that enhance job skills, and courses that students take only for their personal interest, the number of traditional baccalaureate-bound transfer students has shrunk as a percentage of the whole. Not more than one in twenty enrollees completes a two-year program and transfers in the succeeding term. The main problem with the data is that no one keeps records on the students who attend a community college for a semester or two, drop out, and eventually enroll at a university.

Several studies have pointed out the difficulties experienced by students who transfer. Kissler (1980a) reported on the high and increasing failure rate of students transferring into the University of California, a rate that had reached 30 percent by 1980. This compares with the 31 percent rate reported for Arizona university transfers (Richardson and Doucette, 1980). Many of the students lose credits. Of those who graduated from Montgomery College (Maryland) in 1976 and transferred to senior institutions, 56 percent said they lost some credits (Gell, 1977). Many suffer a loss in grades earned. Head (1971) reported that English majors transferring to the University of Mississippi did poorly, compared with native students. Tucker (1969) noted that a large percentage of English majors transferring to East Texas State University needed remedial work in composition, and Belford (1967) found transfer music majors also needing remedial work.

Russell and Perez (1980) explained the attrition among community college students transferring to UCLA as being associated primarily with academic difficulties. The attrition was especially severe in the physical sciences, mathematics, and engineering. In separate studies done at the University of Illinois (Anderson, 1977) and at UCLA (Menke, 1980), the average GPA of two-year college transfer students was found to be lower than that of students who had begun postsecondary education at the university. Transfers to physical science, math, and engineering were found to have the most difficulty, and transfers in those fields often changed their majors.

Even when community college transfers do succeed in obtaining baccalaureate degrees, it seems to take them longer. Moughamian (1972) reported that among students transferring from the City Colleges of Chicago to senior institutions and eventually graduating, only 44 percent completed their upper-division work in two and one-half years or less; 29 percent took three years; and 11 percent took four years. Menke's (1980) study of baccalaureate recipients at UCLA found that those who had transferred from community college took 1.4 years longer than natives did to earn the degrees.

The reasons that students transferring to universities have had a difficult time there can only be surmised. It is possible that native students were tied into an informal network that advised them on which professors and courses were most likely to yield favorable results. Transfers may have taken their distribution requirements at the community colleges and, when they entered the specialized courses at the universities, done worse in them. Community colleges may have been passing through the students who would have failed or dropped out of the freshman and sophomore classes in the senior institutions. And, as a group, the community college students were undoubtedly less able at the beginning. All these variables probably operated to some degree and tend to confound the reasons for junior-level dropout and failure.

Astin (1977) has said that "even after controlling for the student's social background [and] ability and motivation at college entrance, the chances of persisting to the baccalaureate degree are substantially reduced" (p. 234). His finding that residence on campus, a high degree of interaction with the peer group, the presence of good students on the campus, and full-time student status lead to the attainment of degrees is useful in describing the factors relating to both individuals and institutions that interact to yield success as measured by degree attainment. But he was describing the polar opposite of community colleges. Few two-year institutions have residence halls; in most states, especially those with a hierarchical public higher education system, the community college students are of lesser ability; most are part-timers, and most have jobs off campus. Thus, the combination of individual and institutional factors at the community college level operates distinctly to reduce the probability that any student will complete the two years and transfer to a baccalaureate-granting institution.

Determining the institutional procedures that affect dropout tells only part of the story. The institution's efforts to recruit and enroll sizable numbers of students must also be considered. In the 1970s, community colleges made tremendous efforts to bring in a variety of students. They established off-campus recruitment centers and sent vans staffed with counselors into shopping centers and parks. They advertised in newspapers and conducted telephone solicitations. Some of the advertising campaigns were planned as carefully as sophisticated marketing plans used by private business enterprises. These efforts certainly contributed to the swelling of enrollments, but they also tended to attract sizable numbers of students with only a casual commitment to college-level studies.

The admissions procedures alone that allowed students to enter classes almost at will certainly contributed to the dropout rate. Studies of the reasons that students drop out of college rarely considered the strength of their initial commitment, but it seems likely that a student who petitions for admission, takes a battery of entrance tests, and signs up for classes six months in advance of the term is more genuinely committed to attend than one who appears on the first day of classes without any preliminary planning. Data on students' ethnicity, prior academic achievement, and degree aspirations pale in comparison with the essential component, the degree of their personal commitment.

Studies of student dropout may be only marginally relevant to an institution that holds accessibility as its greatest virtue. The community colleges have organized themselves around the theme of ease in entrance, exit, and reentry. Their admissions procedures, patterns of courses without prerequisites, non-punitive marking systems, modular courses allowing entrance at biweekly or monthly intervals, and procedures for recruiting students without regard to prior educational attainment all reveal an institution dedicated to ease of access. In that context, the concept of dropout loses its importance.

However, dropout was still a matter of concern. Having made all effort to recruit students and to offer them something useful, most faculty members and administrators did want to keep them enrolled, at least until degree or program objectives had been fulfilled. College reimbursements were usually provided on the basis of student attendance, and each withdrawal meant a loss of income. Accordingly, several efforts to maintain student attendance were undertaken, with systems for telephoning students who were absent for more than two classes in a row a favorite active approach, and allowing students to withdraw at any time and return without penalty the most prevalent passive technique. Still, the divergence was obvious between the massive recruiting efforts and ease of entry and exit, on the one hand, and, on the other, the attempts to keep students enrolled. It was difficult for an institution built on the theme of easy access to limit easy exit.

Those who deplore the high attrition rates at community colleges because of the waste they represent rarely take into account the students who realize their goals short of completing a program. Programs and sequential curricula are institutionally determined, certainly for the good of the students, who will learn more if they maintain continuous enrollment in a curriculum designed to lead them to sophisticated knowledge of a subject. However, students use community colleges for their own purposes and frequently achieve those purposes short of program completion.

Goal Attainment and Dropout

How many students achieve their goals in community colleges? The information given by students on matriculation is typically flawed, representing a forced choice not often congruent with the students' actual purposes. Students usually have more than one reason for attending college, and the importance of one or another may shift over time. Students may enter because there are few attractive alternative pursuits and because they think it would be nice to have a college degree and, along the way, to be prepared for some type of higher-level employment. Few information-gathering forms force students to search themselves for the dominant purposes, and even if they did, few students could make those distinctions.

Most studies analyzing persistence in college in relation to student goal attainment have found little correspondence. Kessman (1975) reported that two thirds of a sample of students who had withdrawn from a Midwestern community college stated that they had achieved their purposes. Knoell and others (1976) studied a large sample of California community college students and concluded that many who terminated their enrollments during the first year were, in fact, "completers" who needed only a course or two to satisfy their objectives. Other studies have reported higher attrition rates for part-time students, suggesting that people who have made only a partial commitment to college readily withdraw when employment or some other activity proves more attractive. However, part-time students are usually those who attend college intermittently, and the institution may be counting them as dropouts when they fail to maintain enrollments in successive terms. Part-timers are also likely to be those who find only a few courses necessary for satisfying their personal interests, teaching them the skills they need for job entry or promotion, or connecting them with employers.

This pattern of ad hoc attendance seems to fit the desires expressed and demonstrated by students who are using the colleges for their own purposes. Follow-up studies have tended to confirm the institution's value for students with short-term goals. A West Los Angeles College study found retention high only among those students stating an intention to transfer; the nonreturning students tended to be older, to have limited or specific objectives, and to have planned on taking only selected courses (Garber, 1979). A Montgomery College (Maryland) follow-up study found two thirds of the respondents indicating they had achieved their goals (Wenckowski and others, 1979). In a Macomb County Community College (Michigan) study, 89 percent of the respondents indicated they had met or surpassed their educational goals (Stankovich, 1978). Retention and dropout seem to be concerns for the institution, not the individual.

Follow-up studies often ask students why they withdrew, but the evidence is inconclusive because students who cannot state accurately why they entered college in the first place may have equally vague reasons for withdrawing. Stine (1976) listed the reasons that students had given for withdrawing from one California community college, and Hunter and Sheldon (1980) did the same for fourteen others. The students offered job conflicts, insufficient funds, personal problems, no study time, transfer to another school, lack of preparation, indefinite motivation, dislike of class or instructor, transportation, poor grades, and entry into armed services. The notable characteristics of the list are that jobs and finances presented problems to students in California, where there is no tuition, and that few of the problems stated by the students were amenable to amelioration by the college. Student withdrawal is most often for reasons that are beyond college control.

The question whether minority group students are more likely than majority students to withdraw cannot readily be answered. However, several studies have addressed it, many revealing no difference and others suggesting that blacks and Hispanics were overrepresented in the groups that withdrew. Knoell and others (1976) found slightly higher withdrawal rates among minorities in California community colleges during the term than after the term. And Tschechtelin (1979) found that in Maryland community colleges, after three and one-half years, black students had completed twenty-seven units, on average, compared with thirty-three for Anglos.

The students who attend community colleges for only a short time and then leave without receiving a degree or certificate of completion may be the pragmatic ones. The value of the degree itself is based, in large measure, on its scarcity. When few people had college degrees, those who had them were usually considered more desirable employees and more highly educated citizens. But the value of a general studies degree as an entry to employment diminished to the extent that college enrollments increased.

When a large pool of job applicants have degrees, employers must select among them on bases other than the level of schooling attained. As Richardson stated, the possession of a degree was highly valued by employers, "but with the advent of mass higher education, which community colleges helped to bring about more than any other segment of higher education, it is now possible for almost anyone to earn a college degree if he is sufficiently persistent" (1972-1973, p. 40A). It thereupon became necessary to demonstrate values for the degrees other than their ability to impress prospective employers. Since those values had not been well articulated by community college educators or, if articulated, were not well accepted by students and their families, the students began attending intermittently, using the institution only for their personal interest or to obtain skills for job entry or promotion. It became common for students to leave without obtaining the associate degree even though they lacked only one or two courses required for it.

Community colleges awarded associate degrees and occupational certificates to only around 9 percent of their students during the 1970s. According to the National Center for Education Statistics, the figures for 1976 were 368,335 degrees and certificates awarded, out of 4,001,970 students. Some commentators found these figures distressing, saying that an institution ostensibly dedicated to human development should not deliberately encourage part-time, nonsequential attendance. Sanford and others (1971) said that along with millions of people who work in large organizations, students suffer from the impersonality of their surroundings. Our colleges and universities, which could be models of human communities, tend to go the way of other bureaucracies. But with rare exceptions the community colleges had dedicated themselves to attracting commuters who could drive to the campus, park, attend a class, and leave immediately for work or other pursuits.

Tracking

Curriculum tracking within the colleges has risen and fallen with the times. Throughout their early years the community colleges typically administered achievement tests to matriculants and attempted to place students in courses presumed consonant with their abilities. Students were shunted from transfer to remedial or occupational programs, a practice that gave rise to the "cooling out" thesis. A 1968 report is instructive. The authors recommended putting together a profile for each student before the counseling interview, and then—

1. Students whose total profile presents a picture of being at or above the mean for college freshmen (on national norms) may be encouraged to enter a college-parallel program. . . .
2. Students whose total profile places them in the middle 50 percent could be expected to succeed in an associate degree collegiate-technical-level occupational education program.
3. Students in the top half of the lower quartile could be encouraged to enroll for a vocational-level program where the emphasis would be on specialized manipulative skills, rather than on further academic and cognitive work. It is unlikely that students in the lower quartile of academic ability will succeed in collegiate-technical-level programs.
4. Finally, those students whose profiles indicate that they are at or below the 10th percentile should be required to enroll in one or more developmental courses or clinics [*A Developmental Program* . . . , 1968, p. 55].

Most institutions of the time also maintained academic probation, F grades, one-term dismissal of students not making satisfactory progress, transcripts required for admission, entrance tests, midterm grades, penalties for dropping classes after the eighth week, mandatory exit interview, required class attendance, and mandatory orientation courses. However, during the early 1970s these practices fell into disfavor as many students demanded the right to enter courses of their own choosing. Further, measuring students' abilities has never been an exact science; a student deficient in one area of knowledge may be well qualified in another, and stories of abuses in program tracking are common. Educators rationalized their inability to assess their students accurately by saying that anyone had the right to try anything, even if it meant failure. The 1970s saw an erosion of course prerequisites as surely as the dress codes had been abandoned in an earlier day.

By the end of the decade, the pendulum had swung back,

propelled more by the students than by changes in institutional philosophy. The career programs were being reserved for the favored few, while the transfer curricula were entered by those unqualified for the technologies or uncertain of their direction. This use of the collegiate courses by the less able, by those waiting for billets in the more desirable programs to open, and by those trying to make up deficiencies in prior preparation may have contributed to the high dropout rates. Subtly, but decisively, the collegiate programs were being transformed into catchalls for the unable and/or uncommitted students.

During the 1970s, the community colleges groped for a middle ground between linear, forced-choice, sequential curricula and the lateral laissez faire approach of letting students drop in and take any course they wanted. Recognizing that neither of the extremes was feasible and that neither best served the clients, the staff in most institutions attempted to maintain some semblance of counseling, orientation, and testing to determine why the students had appeared and how they could best be helped. But students were using the college for purposes other than those anticipated by the program planners. Except for those who enrolled in the selective-admissions high-technology and allied health fields, few students attended courses in the sequence envisaged by program planners. The drop-in and drop-out approach had gained the day. The pattern of sequential attendance through first introductory, then advanced courses was in decisive retreat.

Even though the planned programs were often out of phase with students' course-taking patterns, the students seemed remarkably well satisfied with their experiences at community colleges. In study after study, graduates and nongraduates alike reported that the colleges had provided them with what they were looking for. The vagaries of data collection, especially differences in the way the questions were asked, made it impossible to obtain precise information on student satisfaction, but information about student satisfaction was tucked in among the reports of the pertinence of job training and transfer success. In studies of Hawaii community college graduates, between 45 and 75 percent felt that the colleges had been very helpful to them in attaining their goals (University of Hawaii, 1977, 1978, 1979). Many students enrolled with short-duration objectives that could be met by completing a few courses, and they were the ones who usually indicated that their objectives had been achieved. These findings were reported in Illinois (Illinois Community College Board, 1979a) and in California (Hunter and Sheldon, 1980). Even Astin found community college students more satisfied than their university counterparts with the quality of their programs and mentioned, "It is also somewhat surprising that students at community colleges are relatively satisfied with the social life" (1977, p. 235).

But students entering the specialized and general education courses in the collegiate curricula were displaying less ability to comprehend the instruction. This not only dismayed instructors who remembered better students from their earlier years and deplored a reduction in their academic standards, it also seemed to discredit the community colleges as those students who passed through the collegiate courses and went on to senior institutions began failing in great numbers. By 1980 a move toward once again assessing students at entrance was underway. Miami-Dade Community College had established a policy of assessing students, mandating certain courses, and placing on probation or suspending students who were not making satisfactory progress toward completing a program—in short, reinstating the policies under which most institutions had operated fifteen years earlier (Middleton, 1981). Whether this policy presaged a widespread move toward curricular sequence was not certain. What is certain is that the first two years of that policy resulted in several thousand students being dropped from the rolls at Miami-Dade.

Any institution needs to demonstrate its usefulness to society if it is to continue to be supported. A school which people are not obliged to attend but which continually enrolls greater segments of the population may be justified with the argument that it must be offering something of value to those who are investing their own time and money. It may be argued that enrolling ever-greater percentages of the population is a social good because the more people who are exposed to schooling, the more likely it is that intellectual leaders will emerge from among them. If intellectual ability in the population is distributed on a probability basis, intelligent people will come forth if more are given access to schooling. By that line of reasoning, any restricted educational system runs counter to social policy, whether the restriction is by wealth, sex, race, or scholastic test.

Questions of dropout and transfer pale in that light. The better question to ask is *"Of what value is the community college even to those people who do not graduate or transfer to a baccalaureate degree-granting institution?"* By their nature, by deliberate intent, the community colleges sought to become open-access institutions. They vigorously recruited the part-timers, the commuting students, the students who were working off-campus. To attract these students, they abandoned most of the punitive grading, academic probation, class attendance requirements, and other policies designed for the more traditional students. Who can estimate the extent of the social need they were fulfilling?

Issues

Issues of the number and types of students properly enrolled in community colleges will concern institutional planners during coming years. One set of questions that must be faced includes these: How separate the people attending merely for the financial benefits from the serious students? How prevent them from abusing the system without jeopardizing open access?

Questions of finances will also impinge. Should the colleges continue marketing their programs and attempting to recruit students from every source? Faced with limited finances and enrollment caps, they may have to reduce those efforts. What would static enrollments mean to an institution that has prided itself on growth?

Which groups have first claim on the institution? If enrollment limitations mean some students must be turned away, who shall they be? Those of lesser ability? Those with indistinct goals? Lists placing the categories of potential students in order from highest to lowest priority may have to be developed.

The designations "transfer," "remedial," and "occupational" are institutionally inspired. They do not accurately describe the students' intentions. What more realistic categories might be defined?

Colleges can control the types of students they attract by expanding or contracting off-campus classes and by enforcing student probation and suspension procedures more or less stringently, to name but two obvious means. Who should decide on the policies and hence the student types?

Historically the community college student has been defined as one who is enrolled in a course. Yet some colleges have recently taken steps to purge their rolls of those who were not making satisfactory progress toward completing a program. Must the definition of *student* rest on sequential attendance? Can colleges find some other way of classifying people who want only to use the campus for the social interaction it provides?

And the broadest questions of all: Which people benefit most from, and which are harmed by, an institution that allows all to attend at their pleasure? For which students should society pay full fare? The personal and social implications of these questions give way rapidly to the political and fiscal as soon as they are put to the test.

3

Faculty

Coping with
Changing
Conditions

Although it is possible only to generalize in the grossest way when describing 200,000 people, demographically the community college faculty differs from instructors in other types of schools. The proportion of men is lower than in universities, higher than in secondary schools. Most of the faculty members hold academic master's degrees or equivalent experience in the occupations they teach; they are less likely to hold advanced graduate degrees than university professors. Their primary responsibility is to teach. They rarely conduct research or scholarly inquiry, and they have only a modest formal connection with institutional management. They are more concerned with subject matter than are their counterparts in the secondary

66

schools, less so than university professors. On a full-time basis they conduct four or five classes per term, twelve to sixteen hours a week. Many have prior or concurrent experience teaching at other types of institutions; more than half are part-time employees at their colleges.

The Workplace

Behind the demographics stand the people: how they function, what they do, and how they feel about their work. In an issue of *New Directions for Community Colleges* on the theme "Responding to New Missions," one instructor began an article, "Let's be candid about the major issue in the community college today: the low academic achievement of its students" (Slutsky, 1978, p. 9). She discussed the demoralization of faculty members who had expected to be teaching college-level students but who found few able students in their classes. She reported the concern felt by instructors who believed that the decline in student ability was encouraged by institutional policies over which the instructors themselves had no control. And she deplored the colleges' practice of recruiting students with offers of financial aid, remediation, and inappropriate occupational programs—and especially their attempts to retain on the rolls even those students who would not show up for class, let alone keep up with their course work.

Community college instructors rarely write for publication, but when they do, and when they speak at conferences, they often reveal similar attitudes. In reviewing their writings together with other commentaries on the institutions, it is possible to trace the current degree of faculty professionalization, the origins and directions of collective bargaining, and the extent to which the community college is a personally satisfying workplace. Even though cause and effect among these variables cannot be determined, they are certainly associated.

People willingly endure incredible levels of discomfort when they feel they are striving for a higher cause. The history of saints and soldiers, monks and missionaries reveals that when superordinate goals are dominant, participants relinquish the tangible rewards that they might otherwise think are their due. But when faith or patriotism wanes, demands for more immediate benefits increase, and the group must provide extrinsic incentives to sustain its members' allegiance. Eventually, a formal organization evolves with ever stricter rules of conduct guiding the lives of its people, who themselves have since been transformed from participants into workers.

Many two-year colleges began as small adjuncts to public secondary schools, and their organizational forms resembled the lower schools more than they did the universities. Their work rules and curricula stemmed from the state education codes. Mandated on-campus hours for faculty members, assigned teaching schedules, textbooks selected by committees, and obligatory attendance at college events were common. Institutional size fostered close contact among instructors and administrators. The administrators held the power, but at least they were accessible, and face-to-face bargains could be struck regarding teaching and committee assignments. And as long as the institution enrolled students fresh from high school, the faculty could maintain consistent expectations.

The major transformation in the community college as a workplace came when it increased in size and scope. Size led to distance between staff members; rules begat rules; layers of bureaucracy insulated people between levels. Decision making shifted from the person to the collectivity, decisions made by committees defusing responsibility for the results. The staff became isolates—faculty members in their academic-freedom-protected classrooms, administrators behind their rulebook-adorned desks.

As the colleges broadened their scope, the transformation was furthered. First, career education, then adult basic studies, compensatory programs, and—unkindest of all from the faculty viewpoint—the drive to recruit and retain apathetic students. Numerous instructors, who may have felt themselves members of a noble calling contributing to society by assisting the development of its young, reacted first with dismay, then with apathy or antagonism to the new missions articulated by college spokespersons. Feeling betrayed by an organization that had shifted its priorities, they shrank from participation, choosing instead to form collectivities that would protect their right to maintain their own goals. The *Gemeinschaft* had become a *Gesellschaft*.

Whether or not collective bargaining in community colleges resulted from this transformation, it did affect faculty well-being, although not nearly as much as its proponents had hoped or as much as its detractors had feared. The working conditions most obviously affected were class size, the provision of aides or assistants to the faculty, the number of hours instructors must spend on campus, the out-of-class responsibilities that may be assigned to them, the number of students they must teach per week, and the funds available for professional development opportunities. Because all these elements were associated with contractual requirements, informal agreements between instructors and administrators about switching classes, trading certain tasks for others, released time in one term in return for an additional class in another, were rendered more difficult to effect. Work rules often specified the time that could be spent on committee service, media development, and preparing new courses. In brief, the contracts solidified the activities associated with teaching, binding them by rules that had to be consulted each time a staff member considered any change, and hence they impinged on the instructors as though they had been mandated by an autocratic administration.

Part-Time Instructors

Community colleges have always employed numerous part-time instructors, although over the years the rationale for doing so has changed. When most of the colleges were small, Eells (1931) said it was better to have secondary school instructors of physics, chemistry, and biology offer individual courses in their disciplines in the community college than to have a single instructor present all the college courses in the sciences. (He also suggested that employing part-time faculty members would enable junior colleges to obtain the services of university professors, making for closer coordination of the curriculum between the two institutions.) When the community colleges grew large, the argument favoring the part-timers continued to be that the institutions could offer specialized courses in areas that could not support full-time instructors. This proved true in the foreign languages, for example, where few institutions could afford to employ a full-time teacher skilled in presenting esoteric languages, whereas a part-timer could usually be found for a single course in Norwegian or Gaelic. Part-time instructors also represented a high proportion of the faculty in art, religion, and the numerous career programs that had been established.

Part-time faculty members presented college administrators with several additional advantages. They were willing to teach at odd times and locations. Most significant for cost-conscious administrators, their compensation per class was between one-third and two-thirds as much as the institution would have to pay a full-timer. Moreover, their right to their job was weaker, and hence they could be dismissed more readily when enrollments fell. The 1970s saw a tendency toward pro rata pay and continuing contracts for part-timers, but for most of the part-time faculty, pay at a lesser rate and the threat of discontinuance at the end of each term was the norm.

The ratio of part-time to full-time instructors has changed during various stages of community college development. In the early years, sizable percentages of the instructors were part-timers. Eells (1931) reported that more than half the instructors in Texas community colleges in the late 1920s were part-time. He also reported a 1921 finding that in eight California junior colleges, more than 90 percent of the staff were part-timers. Nationwide the ratio of part-timers showed a steady increase throughout the 1970s; by 1976 they had reached 56 percent of the total (see Table 12).

The sources of part-time teachers have shifted too. The early junior colleges sought secondary school instructors because they were qualified teachers and university professors because they lent an aura of prestige. However, by the mid 1970s only two thirds of the part-timers working in community college academic programs were employed elsewhere. Instead, many retired people were teaching a course or two, and young

Table 12. Numbers of Full-Time and Part-Time Two-Year
College Instructors, 1953-1980

Year	Total Instructors	Full-Time		Part-Time	
		Number	Percentage	Number	Percentage
1953	23,762	12,473	52	11,289	48
1958	33,396	20,003	60	13,393	40
1963[a]	44,405	25,438	57	18,967	43
1968	97,443	63,864	66	33,579	34
1973	151,947	89,958	59	61,989	41
1974	162,530	81,658	50	80,872	50
1975	181,549	84,851	47	96,698	53
1976	199,655	88,277	44	111,378	56
1977	205,528	89,089	43	116,439	57
1978	213,712	95,461	45	118,251	55
1979	212,874	92,881	44	119,993	56
1980	238,841	104,777	44	134,064	56

[a]Includes administrators.
Source: American Association of Community and Junior Colleges (1955-1981).

people completing their graduate studies at nearby universities were teaching part-time for the compensation it afforded and because it provided potential access to full-time positions. Nearly half the part-timers were age thirty-five or younger.

Are the part-time instructors qualified? Do they teach as well as full-timers? Numerous studies have attempted to answer those questions, but the findings are inconclusive. Cohen and Brawer (1977) reported studies showing that the part-timers are less experienced. They have spent fewer years in their current institutions, they are less likely to hold memberships in professional associations, they read fewer scholarly and professional journals, and they are less concerned with the broader aspects of curriculum and instruction and of the disciplines they represent. However, where they are working in the field—for example, when the local minister teaches a course in religious studies or when a realtor teaches courses in real estate—they may be more directly connected to the practical aspects of their work, and they may have a greater fund of knowledge than most full-time instructors. As for the routine aspects of the job, part-timers certainly seem to present few problems; they are just as likely to turn in their grade sheets on time, and their students rate them as highly as they do the full-timers.

Although part-timers hold the same credentials as full-timers, they occupy a different status. They are employed less carefully, the rationale being that because the institution is making no long-term commitment to them, there is no need to spend a great deal of time and money in selection. They may be evaluated differently; a California study found that numerous colleges had no evaluation policy for part-timers, and most that did used different procedures for them. Only half as many of the California colleges conducted in-service faculty development programs for part-timers as for full-timers. Three fourths of the colleges failed to provide part-timers with office space (Sewell and others, 1976). Marsh and Lamb (1975) found that part-timers rarely participated in campus activities and had little contact with students out of class and practically no contact with their peers, a finding corroborated by two other studies (California Community and Junior College Association, 1978b; Friedlander, 1979).

Salary, Tenure, Work Load

Comparisons of faculty salary, tenure, and work load also shed light on the profession and the workplace. Except for the part-timers paid at an hourly rate, salary ranges for community college instructors have tended to be higher than in secondary schools, lower than in universities. Eells reported that the median salary of the best-paid instructors in the 1920s was about the same as that of a starting professor in the universities. But most community college instructors were able to reach the top of the salary scale in twelve or fifteen years, whereas in the universities, more steps intervened although a higher ceiling was available. The ratio shifted somewhat in the 1970s when collective bargaining made deep inroads, and the tops of the salary schedules were lifted, but the university ranges remained greater. The American Council on Education survey of university and community college faculty members found the greatest percentage of the two-year college group receiving more money than the mode at the university. However, when salaries rose toward the top of the scale, more university people were represented (Bayer, 1973).

Community college faculty salaries typically have been related to degrees earned: the higher the degree, the higher the salary. Thus, although people with doctoral degrees were welcomed in the early community colleges because of the prestige they lent, they tended less to be sought by the well-established institutions because of the higher salaries they commanded. The higher salaries paid doctoral degree holders also accounted in large measure for the tendency for two-year college instructors to seek graduate degrees even while they were employed. In the mid 1970s, nearly one fourth of the humanities instructors who responded to a survey by the Center for the Study of Community Colleges (CSCC) said they were working on a higher degree.

Tenure patterns in community colleges more closely resembled those in the lower schools than they did the procedures in universities. Tenure was awarded after a single year or, in many cases, after a probation of two or three years; the practice rarely approximated the seven-year standard common in universities. Although tenure rules varied from state to state, by the 1960s in some states tenure was awarded simultaneously with the award of a full-time teaching contract. That is, after a one-year contract had been tendered and the instructors had fulfilled their responsibilities, a contract for the succeeding year could be demanded unless the institution could show cause that the instructor was not deserving of it. During the 1970s, unless tenure was included in the state laws governing community colleges, it became a negotiable item in contract bargaining. In Illinois, for example, of the thirty-nine community college districts established under the 1965 Community College Act, nine failed to adopt a tenure policy, and two that did subsequently abandoned it (Swenson, 1980). However, in 1970 the Illinois legislature passed a bill that included due process rights and other procedures that, in effect, reinstated tenure throughout the system.

Faculty work load, usually defined as the number of hours an instructor spends in the classroom and/or the number of students met per week, varies somewhat among teaching fields, but it has been relatively consistent over time. Koos (1925) reported 13.5 hours taught weekly by the full-time faculty in the public colleges of the 1920s, 14.9 hours in the private institutions. Kent (1971) found 25 percent of the English instructors with a fifteen-hour teaching load and 37 percent with more than fifteen hours a week, with a median of fourteen to seventeen. The CSCC surveys found thirteen to fifteen hours the norm for all academic instructors in the mid 1970s.

The full-time faculty member of the 1920s met about 250 students a week. By the 1970s, the average had increased to around 450, owing mainly to the increased class size in the larger community colleges. Instructors of physical education, music, studio courses in the arts, and courses with laboratory sections usually had the highest number of teaching hours. It was difficult to maintain high weekly student contact hours in the small colleges even when each instructor taught a number of subjects.

Evaluation

The intent of faculty evaluation has been to make instructors aware of their strengths and shortcomings, with the expectation that they would modify their behavior. Because of community colleges' roots in the lower schools, early evaluations were often conducted by administrators who visited classrooms and recorded their perception of instructors' mannerisms, appearance, attitude, and performance. As the colleges broke away from the lower schools, and as the faculty gained more power, evaluation plans became more complex. Peers and students were brought into the process, and guidelines were established for every step. These procedures often gained labyrinthine complexity; rules specified the frequency and duration of evaluations, who was to be involved, at what point the instructors were to be notified of the results and which people or committees would notify them, the duration of file maintenance and who had access, and the appeal process.

Superficially, the procedures gave the appearance of attempting to improve instruction. Practically, they had little effect. If an instructor was to be censured, dismissed, or rewarded for exceptional merit, the evaluation records provided essential documentation. But only a minuscule percentage of the staff was affected. Instructors who wanted to improve could act on the commentary of peers, administrators, and students. Those who chose instead to ignore the feedback could do so. Only the instructors who were far distant from any semblance of good teaching—for example, those who failed to meet their classes regularly—could be called to task. In general, the most minimal evidence of classroom performance or student achievement satisfied evaluators.

Faculty associations' intrusion into the evaluation process proved a mixed blessing. Frequently the contracts mandated that the whole faculty be involved in evaluation at every step of the way. This involvement would be a step toward professionalization because, by definition, a profession should police its own ranks, set standards of conduct, and exercise sanctions. However, faculty bargaining units leaned considerably more in the direction of protecting their members than toward enhancing professional performance.

The types of faculty evaluation in vogue at the time the contracts were negotiated tend to be written into the rules. The forms, checklists, and observations remain the same. Instructors may feel that their chairpersons are less likely to exercise capricious standards and more likely to make informed judgments, but that is all that has been gained. Evaluation procedures that depend primarily on viewing teacher performance rather than the learning gains effected among the students do little to advance the profession (see Cohen and Brawer, 1972).

Preparation

When the size and number of community colleges were expanding rapidly, the question of the proper training and experience for instructors was frequently debated. Should instructors have prior experience in the lower schools? Should they hold the doctorate? What qualities were needed? The answers varied, but the flow of instructors into the community colleges can be readily traced.

Beginning with the earliest two-year colleges and continuing well into the 1960s, instructors tended to have prior teaching experience in the secondary schools. Eells reported a study done in the 1920s showing that 80 percent of junior college instructors had previous high school experience. In the 1950s Medsker (1960) found 64 percent with previous secondary or elementary school experience. Around 44 percent of new teachers of academic subjects entering two-year colleges in California in 1963 moved in directly from secondary schools, and others had had prior experience with them (California State Department of Education, 1963-1964). However, as the number of newly employed instructors declined in the 1970s, the proportion of instructors with prior secondary school experience declined with it. More were coming from graduate programs, from the trades, and from other community colleges.

The master's degree obtained in a traditional academic department was the typical preparation. The doctorate has never been seen as the most desirable degree; arguments against it may be found from Eells in 1931 (pp. 403-404) to Cohen and Brawer in 1977 (pp. 119-120). During the 1920s, fewer than 4 percent of two-year college instructors held the doctorate. By the 1950s, the proportion had climbed to between 6 and 10 percent, and there it remained for two decades; Blocker (1965-1966) reported 7 percent; Bayer (1973), 6.5 percent; Medsker and Tillery (1971), 9 percent. By the mid 1970s, it had reached 14 percent as fewer new instructors without the degree were being employed, and many of those already on the job were concurrently receiving advanced degrees. Table 13 shows the proportions of instructors holding bachelor's, master's, and doctor's degrees from 1930 through 1979. Graduate degrees were rarely found among teachers in career programs, where experience in the occupations along with some pedagogical training was considered the best preparation.

Few community college instructors were prepared in programs especially designed for that level of teaching. Few had even taken a single course describing the institution before they

Table 13. Highest Degree Held by Two-Year College Instructors
(Percentages)

Year and Source	Less than B.A.	Bache-lor's	Mas-ter's	Doctor-ate
1930 Wahlquist (cited in Eels, 1941a, p. 103)	7	29	59	5
1941 Koos (cited in Monroe, 1972, p. 248)	3	27	64	6
1957 Medsker (includes admin.; cited in Monroe, 1972, p. 248)	7	17	65	10
1969 National Center for Education Statistics	17 (includes both)		75	7
1972 National Center for Education Statistics	3	13	74	10
1979 Brawer and Friedlander	3	8	74	15

Sources: Eels (1941a); Monroe (1972); U.S. Department of Health, Education, and Welfare (1970, 1980); Brawer and Friedlander (1979).

assumed responsibilities in it; a 1949 survey found that less than a tenth of practicing instructors had taken such a course (Koos, 1950). Eells (1931) had recommended that people entering two-year college instruction after having secondary school experience take intervening work at the university, but not many took that route. By the late 1960s, several well-integrated graduate-school-based programs for preparing community college instructors had been established, but they never became a major source of two-year college teachers (Cohen, 1968).

Degrees especially tailored for college instructors have been introduced on numerous occasions. The Master of Arts in Teaching received some support during the late 1960s, when colleges were expanding rapidly and seeking well-qualified staff, and the Doctor of Arts was promoted by the Council of Graduate Schools and the Carnegie Commission on Higher Education

(Dressel and Thompson, 1977). Both these degrees continued to be offered, some at the more prestigious universities, throughout the 1970s. The programs usually included a base of subject matter preparation in an academic department, some pedagogical preparation, and a period of practice teaching or internship. Some were especially designed for people who were already teaching in community colleges but who wanted additional preparation in pedagogy and/or in academic areas outside their own disciplines.

Periodically, such programs have been given impetus by government and foundation support. The Education Professions Development Act in the late 1960s and early 1970s helped to support more than fifty such programs; the Carnegie Foundation for the Advancement of Teaching and the Ford Foundation also provided funds for community college programs at the master's degree level and for the Doctor of Arts curriculum. Support for programs in particular disciplines has also been forthcoming: for science instructors from the National Science Foundation, for humanities instructors from the National Endowment for the Humanities and the Danforth and Mellon foundations. O'Banion (1971) summarized the status of preservice staff preparation and made numerous recommendations for expansion of such programs. However, the need for new staff to teach academic subjects declined during the 1970s, and none of the programs developed as a major source of teachers in its area for community colleges.

Regardless of the degree titles and types of programs, an emphasis on breadth of preparation and on people sensitive to the goals of the community colleges and the concerns of their students has been a standard recommendation. Calls for these types of people have been made not only by community college administrators but also by the major professional and disciplinary associations. Shugrue concluded that "the teacher of English at any level should have personal qualities which will contribute to his success as a classroom teacher and should have a broad background in the liberal arts and sciences" (1968, p. 111). A survey sponsored by the National Council on the Teaching of English deplored the university programs that trained English majors rather than teachers (Worthen, 1968). Interdisciplinary programs that would draw from the various education departments as well as from speech, psychology, philosophy, and English have been recommended (Huff and others, 1974).

Although formal in-service training had been a feature of the community colleges throughout their history, calls for expanding that activity reached a peak in the 1970s as institutional expansion subsided, and relatively few new staff members were employed. Who would teach the new students and handle the different technologies? Faculty members already there had their own priorities, based on their expectations when they entered the college and their subsequent experience within it. Administrators had found it much easier to employ new instructors to perform different functions than to retrain old instructors, a procedure that worked well as long as expansion was rapid. But when the rate of change exceeded the rate of expansion, when new priorities were enunciated more rapidly than new funds could be found, the residue of out-of-phase staff members increased—hence the calls for staff development.

Several types of in-service preparation programs have been established. The most common have been discipline-based institutes, released time, sabbatical leaves, and tuition reimbursements for instructors to spend time in a university-based program, as well as short courses or workshops on pedagogy sponsored by single institutions or by institutional consortia. A 1970 survey revealed 276 in-service programs conducted that year—37 percent in academic areas, 10 percent in occupational areas, 33 percent in education, 13 percent in administration, 7 percent in student services (O'Banion, 1971, pp. 141-142).

Instructors preferred courses and programs in their teaching field, offered by universities close at hand, that enabled them to gain further knowledge in their sphere of interest, degrees and credits that would enable them to rise on the salary schedule, and time off from their teaching responsibilities. Administrators, in contrast, preferred workshops and seminars offered on campus for the instructors, with the content centering on pedagogy and community college-related concerns. The Center for the Study of Community Colleges (CSCC) found paid sabbatical leaves and similar opportunities to earn higher degrees the faculty's preferred form of professional development; 86 percent of the instructors in academic areas favored further professional development, but fewer than 10 percent of them wanted workshops on their own campuses. Paid leaves for professional development were written into many negotiated agreements between faculty associations and their institutions (Cohen and Brawer, 1977).

Burnout and Satisfaction

The term *teacher burnout* entered the literature in the 1970s. It referred to instructors who were weary of performing the same tasks with few apparent successes and a lack of appreciation for their efforts. The term supplanted *dissatisfaction,* which connoted a malcontent. *Burnout* more suggested people whose fatigue was caused by environmental pressures beyond their control. A reduced rate of institutional expansion had led to an aging faculty and, because most colleges paid increments for years of service, a faculty crowded toward the top of the salary schedules. Many members of that group found few new challenges in their work and despaired of facing a succession of years doing the same tasks for the same pay. They turned to other jobs on their off hours. Always present in some measure, moonlighting became more prevalent.

Actually, except for the terms used, faculty satisfaction and dissatisfaction have been traced for some time. For the first half century of community college history, when most faculty members were recruited from the secondary schools, positive attitudes among the faculty were the norm. Moving from a secondary school to a college faculty position offered both higher status and a reduced teaching load. And so it was that most studies of faculty satisfaction found the concept related to the conditions under which the person entered the institution. Older faculty members, those who were appointed from secondary school positions, who entered teaching after retiring from a different type of job, who had made a midlife career change, or who were teaching in career programs after being affiliated with an occupation, showed up as the more satisfied groups. The younger instructors, who may not have thought of themselves as career teachers but who found themselves performing the same tasks year after year with little opportunity for the revitalization that accompanies a new challenge, were the dissatisfied ones.

Teacher burnout may well be more related to age and stages of adult development than to the workplace. Cohen and Brawer (1977) surveyed 1,998 instructors in 156 two-year colleges in 1975 and applied their construct of satisfaction to the responses. They found a high positive correlation between faculty age and satisfaction (in Table 14, compare the percentage

Table 14. Satisfaction Among Community College Faculty Members
by Age, 1975

Age	N	Percentage of Total Sample	Satisfaction (Percent)		
			High	Medium	Low
Under 26	19	1.3	0.8	1.5	1.1
26-30	181	12.1	6.7	12.4	15.3
31-35	303	20.3	11.4	20.4	26.4
36-40	242	16.2	18.1	15.6	16.4
41-45	195	13.1	11.0	13.0	14.7
46-50	206	13.8	18.1	14.3	9.4
51-55	142	9.5	11.0	9.9	7.5
56-60	113	7.6	14.2	6.1	6.4
Over 60	92	6.2	8.7	6.8	2.8

Source: Cohen and Brawer (1977, p. 27).

of instructors in each age group with their percentage in the high-, medium-, and low-satisfaction columns). Lee (1977) traced adult development in that same sample of instructors and found satisfaction related to distinct developmental stages. Faculty members in their twenties and thirties were less satisfied, while those in their early forties seemed to be experiencing stress as they encountered a middle-age transition. Instructors fifty-six and older had a high level of satisfaction. Women of all ages revealed a greater concern for students. Lee recommended that colleges begin providing mentors (older adults working with younger staff members) and in-service programs that would work with instructors during their transition stages.

However, burnout may be a more complex phenomenon. Organizational or external demands have often been related to dissatisfaction, whereas intrinsic attitudes have been considered responsible for satisfaction. Herzberg postulated this as his "two-factor theory": those elements leading to personal satisfaction are related to the content of the work, whereas the environment surrounding the worker leads to dissatisfaction (Herzberg, Mausner, and Snyderman, 1959). Several studies of community college instructors have traced this duality. Cohen (1973) found that feedback from students was most likely to lead to feelings of satisfaction, whereas characteristics of the workplace, such as lack of support from administrators and colleagues or institutional red tape, led to dissatisfaction. Wozniak (1973) also identified interpersonal relations with students and a sense of accomplishment in teaching as determinants of satisfaction among the instructors he studied, whereas dissatisfaction stemmed from institutional policies, administrative demands, and similar extrinsic characteristics. But the CSCC studies of faculty members lent support to the view that satisfaction is not related to number of hours taught or to institutional conditions; it seemed to be more a personality trait that transcends the working environment.

The demands of the institution did shift somewhat during the 1970s, making the workplace less attractive for people whose image of teaching was that it is a private activity, a transaction that takes place in isolation between an instructor and one or more students. Purdy (1973) found that perception among instructors, with many of them resisting any teaching method that would require sharing responsibility with other people: "Deciding what will go on in a course and then enacting that plan is seen as a personal challenge to each teacher" (p. 177). Purdy traced the need for hands-on involvement, which instructors found important so that they could get personal feedback from their students, and related it to the reluctance of many instructors to become involved with team teaching, reproducible media, or any form of instruction that reduced their contact with individual students. The instructors tended to see themselves as uniquely qualified to associate with their students.

This attitude of satisfaction coming from personal interaction with students and privacy within the classroom also found its way into the contracts negotiated by faculty representatives and the community college districts. In fact, it may have been one of the bases of the drive toward unionization. If a faculty member's feeling of self-worth depends in great measure on being left alone to fuse content and style of teaching, it follows that faculty members as a group are uniquely qualified to make decisions concerning what and how they shall teach. Thus, one reason for the polarization between the faculty and the administrators and trustees that accompanied the rise in collective bargaining may have been that the faculty sensed that only people who were currently engaged in instruction could understand the way instructors feel. Purdy related how "recommendations about a new teaching method coming from faculty members are more likely to be considered by teachers while information presented by administrators . . . can be ignored" (1973, p. 181). The CSCC studies found faculty members rating their colleagues highest as potential sources of advice on teaching. Their students were second in a list of eight sources, their administrators a distant last.

Many of the changes occurring in the 1970s might have been expected to lead to dissatisfaction. An increase in the number of ill-prepared students made it more difficult for instructors to find satisfaction in effecting student achievement. A reduction in the number of specialized courses made it less likely that an instructor would be able to teach in an area of special interest. More students tended to be part-timers, dropping in and out of school and making faculty relationships with students over more than one term less probable. The percentage of students completing courses fell sharply, so that instructor satisfaction in seeing individual students through even a single course was reduced. More formal requests for measures of productivity were installed, along with demands that instructors present evidence of student achievement. And the feasibility of moving from community college to university teaching, or even from one college to another, was reduced as the demand for full-time instructors fell.

London (1978) discussed the effects of one community college on its instructors, noting that faculty members did not have a voice in determining the policy of admitting marginal students; they questioned the open-door policies, and the teaching of poorly prepared students adversely affected their morale. He identified three groups of instructors: The first felt that students are solely responsible for their fates, rising or falling on their own merit independent of teacher intervention. The second believed that students were products of their society and needed special care to help them rise above their deprived backgrounds. The third group also put the blame on society and in addition wanted to politicize the students so they could compensate for what society had done to them. London admitted that for all three kinds of teachers the results of their efforts were modest, thus leading to faculty demoralization.

More detailed information was reported from the CSCC's nationwide studies in the mid 1970s, when some distinct shifts in faculty members' perception of their role and working conditions seem to have occurred. Instructors seemed generally satisfied with their jobs, seeing community college teaching as a worthy career in its own right. Few of them aspired to teach in senior institutions. Bushnell had reported that 80 percent of the faculty expected to be teaching in a community college five years from the date of his report (1973), and 78 percent of the CSCC's respondents said that "doing what I'm doing now" in five years would be quite attractive. In fact, that statement was the most popular of nine choices, including "faculty position at a four-year college or university."

But details of the work situation revealed sources of satisfaction and dissatisfaction. Three characteristics of the environment and three areas of the faculty's professional concerns seemed to summarize the situation: Instructors wanted more time, more interaction with their colleagues, and better professional development opportunities, and they wanted better support services, students, and media and materials.

Most of the instructors interviewed by Garrison (1967) cited lack of time to perform their jobs effectively as their over-riding professional concern. Many reported that they did not have enough time to keep up in their field, to develop new teaching approaches, to do a good job of preparing for their classes, to discuss educational matters with their colleagues, to give adequate attention to individual students, or to participate effectively on faculty committees. Concern over lack of time available for instructors to perform their teaching and other as-signed duties properly while keeping informed in their academic field was also identified by Kurth and Mills (1968).

Desires

What would make the workplace more gratifying? The CSCC surveys found that faculty members would prefer spend-ing more time on research or professional writing, their own graduate education, interacting with students outside class, plan-ning instruction, and conferring with colleagues. They wanted to devote less time to administrative activities, reading student papers or tests, classroom instruction, and professional-associa-tion work. Just over 40 percent indicated that their courses could be improved if they had smaller classes and more time for preparation. Few felt that their colleagues and administrators were interfering with their courses, and only 10 percent wanted more autonomy in choosing instructional materials. Not sur-prisingly, this latter group was mostly part-time faculty mem-bers.

Like members of any professional group, most instructors would like to improve their working conditions. They want more professional development opportunities, sabbatical leaves, grants for summer study, provisions for released time, and al-lowances for travel. They also want more secretarial services, laboratory assistance, readers and paraprofessional aides, and other support services. They would like better students, too, more highly motivated and with stronger academic backgrounds. They would like better instructional materials. Many of them are not satisfied with the textbooks, laboratory materials, or collections of readings that they are using in their classes. Many want more and better laboratory facilities (Brawer and Fried-lander, 1979).

Thus, faculty desires seemed to stabilize during the 1970s. Despite the rhetoric surrounding collective bargaining and contract negotiations, instructors were generally satisfied. They wanted to better their working conditions, but they tended not to aspire to positions at other levels of schooling. Some of their desires were much like those articulated by employees in other enterprises: security and a living wage. Continuity of employment and periodic salary increases were the minimum. The faculty felt threatened when enrollment declines or declining budgets boded to strike at those essentials.

But beyond the basics, the instructors seem unrealistic. They want better working conditions, but that translates into shorter working hours, better-prepared students, and smaller classes. Desirable as these might be, they are difficult to obtain because they run counter to college policies and budgetary realities. As long as colleges are reimbursed on the basis of the number of students attending, instructors will have a difficult time achieving more pay for fewer student contact hours. As long as colleges are pledged to maintain a door open to all regardless of prior academic achievement or innate ability, instructors will be unable to satisfy their desire for students who are better prepared.

Even when the desired changes in the workplace are more realistic, one goal is often in conflict with another. To illustrate: Faculty members, in general, want more participation in institutional decision making, but they dislike administrative and committee work. They do not aspire to be administrators; they resent the time spent on committees; they see their classroom activities and their meeting with students outside class as the portion of their workday that brings the greatest satisfaction. But administrative decisions are made in the context of committees, memorandums, and persuasion that suggest a political arena. Instructors will not easily attain their goal of participation in decision making as long as they shun the mechanisms through which decisions are made.

The matter of support services offers a second illustration

of conflict between instructor desires. A relatively small percentage of instructors has paraprofessional aides or instructional assistants available to them. However, only about one in eight expresses a desire for more of these types of assistants. Apparently, the ideal of the instructor in close proximity to the students remains a paramount virtue. Instructors seem unable to perceive themselves as professional practitioners functioning with a corps of aides. They want to do it all: interact with students, dispense information, stimulate, inspire, tutor—all the elements of teaching—through personal interaction. They do not realize the magnification of influence that they might obtain through relinquishing some portions of their work to paraprofessionals or assistants.

Through negotiated contracts, instructors have tried to mitigate the untoward conditions of the environment and attendant feelings of dissatisfaction. Provisions for released time to work on course revisions or other projects related to teaching are often written into the contracts. Tuition reimbursement plans that pay instructors to study at universities have been included. Some contracts allow the faculty-student ratio to be spread across the academic department, making it possible to compensate for low enrollments in specialized courses with high enrollments in the department's introductory classes. Funds for travel and for sabbatical leave have also been negotiated. Negotiated contracts often make it possible for instructors to be relieved of routine responsibilities and to change their milieu.

However, the contracts may not offer enough. No contract can substitute for the feelings of self-worth engendered by the knowledge that one can always escape the current workplace by moving to a different institution. At the start of the 1980s, new full-time positions were scarce, and although faculty exchange programs were in place in some institutions, they were not widespread. Nor could the contracts ameliorate the faculty's feeling that students were poorly prepared or that the traditional programs in which the instructors taught when they entered the institutions were on the decline. Telling instructors that their jobs were protected through tenure and elaborate procedures for due process proved of minimal value to people who found themselves forced to teach subjects not of their choosing. The attempts to recruit students to the institution rang like false coin on the ears of instructors who suspected, with good reason, that these students would be even less interested in affairs of the mind than those with whom they were already confronted. Administrative pleas for retaining students were hardly welcomed by instructors who felt that students had a responsibility either to pursue the course work satisfactorily or to leave. And few instructors took kindly to calls for grading practices that would not penalize students for failing to perform course work adequately.

Professionalism

The faculty's professional status presents yet another issue. Some commentators have reasoned that the community college is best served by a group of instructors with minimal allegiance to a profession. They contend that professionalism invariably leads to a form of cosmopolitanism that ill suits a community-centered institution, that once faculty members find common cause with their counterparts in other institutions, they lose their loyalty to their own colleges. This argument stems from a view of professionalism among university faculties that has ill suited teaching in the senior institutions, where, as faculty allegiance turned more to research, scholarship, and academic disciplinary concerns, interest in teaching waned.

However, that argument suggests that a professionalized community college faculty would necessarily take a form similar to that taken by the university faculty. It need not. It more likely would develop in a different direction entirely, tending neither toward the esoterica of the disciplines nor toward research and scholarship on disciplinary concerns. The community college faculty disciplinary affiliation is too weak, the institutions' demands for scholarship are practically nonexistent, and the teaching loads are too heavy for that form of professionalism to occur.

A professionalized community college faculty organized around the discipline of instruction might well suit a teaching institution. The faculty is already engaged in course modification, the production of reproducible teaching media, and a variety of related activities centered on translating knowledge into more understandable forms. A profession that supported its members in these activities would well suit the community college. Teaching has always been the hallmark of that institution; a corps of professionalized instructors could do nothing but enhance it. This form of professionalism might also be applied to curriculum construction. Whereas instructional concerns have been left to the faculty, the propagation of curriculum has been more an administrative charge. A professionalized faculty might well direct much of its attention to designing a curriculum to fit an institution that shifts priorities rapidly.

A professional faculty in charge of the essential conditions of its work could also reconceptualize the academic disciplines themselves to fit the realities of the community colleges. As an example, the traditional humanities courses are ill suited to the students in the career and compensatory programs that constitute most of the community college effort. With the use of concepts stemming from the disciplines in the humanities, instructional sequences could be designed for those students. Whether a professionalized community college faculty could succeed in the necessary curriculum reformation is not certain; it is certain that a disparate set of instructors cannot do so and that university professors or community college administrators will not lead in this essential reconstruction. Such disciplinary reconceptualization takes stimulation from peers, the contribution of individuals acting as proselytizers, and the application of thought about the core principles in each discipline as they pertain to the variant teaching roles that must be adopted for the different clients. These activities require a professionalized faculty. The future of both the collegiate and the general education functions in community colleges may hang in the balance.

Several attempts have been made to assist faculty professionalization. Journals directed toward two-year college instructors in mathematics, journalism, and English have been established. Professional associations, including the Community College Social Science Association and the Community

College Humanities Association, have been formed. Within some institutions, professionalism has been fostered by supporting individual instructors through internal grants for course revision and media preparation. And in colleges that employ instructional aides and paraprofessionals, the faculty plays a managerial role. Part-time faculty members, too, are sometimes supervised by department or division chairpersons. During the 1970s, the number of foundation and federal grants available to community college instructors increased, thus offering those faculty members with considerable professional commitment the opportunity to magnify their influence by managing curriculum development projects.

However, the road to professionalization is a long one, and some might say it should not be traveled anyway. All professions have been attacked for their unresponsiveness to clients and their overspecialization. Among faculty members a loss of confidence to prescribe what people should learn reveals a loss of faith in their own vocation. Some of their own professional associations have cautioned them against specifying the outcomes toward which they are teaching, lest they be held accountable. And if the colleges are to be only for the immediate gratification of their clients, it is difficult to make a case for a professionalized faculty within them.

As for "burnout," a feasible short-term solution might be to keep the faculty engaged in fulfilling the responsibilities of teaching that reach beyond the classroom. The phenomenon of instructors' saying, "I won't do it if it isn't in the contract," has already been heard as they refuse committee work and other non-classroom-related activities. Management has countered with demands that instructors spend specified numbers of hours on campus, but in many colleges, neither group is satisfied with the result. Faculty attention to tasks might better be stimulated by providing funds and released time to those who would build better instructional materials and media. This might also reduce the widespread incidence of instructors' working on jobs unrelated to their teaching.

Other changes seem imminent as instructors realize the importance of program support. Humanities instructors at a few colleges have organized lay advisory committees to provide links between campus and community. Composed of influential citizens, such groups have functions far beyond advising on the curriculum in particular programs. They help recruit students to the programs, assist with extracurricular presentations, act as guests in the courses, and, most important, support the programs. These committees provide a new set of peers for instructors to relate to, and they offer the college a community connection. They seem destined to expand.

Instructors may well expand their role beyond that of classroom teachers to become presenters of information through colloquia, seminars, lectures, recitals, and exhibitions offered for both students and the lay public. Most faculty members in the academic areas feel there are too few such presentations at their own colleges and want to devote more time to them. The more sophisticated contracts make provision for instructors to act in such capacities and also to manage learning laboratories, prepare reproducible media, or coordinate the work of the part-time faculty.

Some instructors understand the value of presenting information in large lecture sections. Departments that can generate sizable ratios of student contact hours have often taken advantage of large lectures to support their more specialized courses. Similarly, flexibility in instruction can be enhanced by paying instructors from one department to teach short portions of courses in another or using community service funds to augment instructional budgets. These types of funding arrangements have proved difficult to effect, but formulas that run to total programmatic emphases might make them more feasible.

Although two-year college instructors may be moving toward the development of a profession, its lines are as yet indistinct. The teaching loads take their toll, but as long as instructors insist on moonlighting and on having close personal contact with students in classes—the smaller the better—the attendant high cost of instruction makes it difficult for colleges to fund the alternatives that could be pursued. The most positive note is that the community college has become a well-known, visible workplace not only among its own staff but also among the legislators and agency officials who make decisions affecting its directions. And, as a group, faculty members no longer look to the universities for their ideas on curriculum and instruction, nor do they see the community colleges only as stations on their way to university careers. Community college instruction has become a career in its own right. Its flowering but awaits a more fully developed professional consciousness on the part of its practitioners.

Issues

Some of the key issues surrounding the faculty can be feasibly managed; others will persevere because of the nature of the profession and the institution.

Will the adversarial relations between the faculty and boards and administrators subside? Are they related primarily to contract negotiations, or are they based in the essence of the institution?

Can teacher burnout be mitigated through deliberate modification of the working environment? Or are moonlighting and psychic early retirement to be permanent conditions?

Will faculties engage in the necessary reconceptualization of their academic disciplines to fit the realities of their colleges? Or will the collegiate programs survive primarily as intellectual colonies of the universities?

Will instructors realize that paraprofessional aides are important for their well-being over the long term? That funds for new media can enhance their satisfaction?

Will administrators continue employing part-timers for the short-term salary savings that accrue? Or will they allow the faculty to build its profession and help it by minimizing the annual influx of teachers?

All these questions relate to the history of the colleges, to the funds available, and, above all, to whether college leaders perceive their institutions as labile structures responding readily to the whims of all comers or as centers of teaching and learning with an ethos of their own.

4

Governance and Administration

Managing the
Contemporary
College

More has been written about governance and administration than about any other aspect of the community college. Why? Perhaps institutional management is more important or more complex than curriculum, instruction, or student services. Perhaps it presents more options. Perhaps the writers think it more feasible to persuade administrators to change organizational charts than instructors to change teaching practices. It may be that they are on a Sisyphean quest for the one best management form. Or it may be simply that people concerned with managing institutions write more than those whose prime interest is teaching students.

Regardless of the reasons, the literature is filled with

plans for alternative governance structures, advice to administrators, and new administrative models. College administration is not a responsibility assigned to a faculty member temporarily on leave from teaching responsibilities; it is more akin to the management of a large business corporation, which indeed the community college is. As Friedenberg said in speaking of secondary school administrators, they are "not professional educators in the sense that a physician, an attorney, or a tax accountant are professionals. . . . They are specialists in keeping an essentially political enterprise from being strangled by conflicting community attitudes and pressures" (1965, p. 92).

The changes assailing community college administrators seem to have accelerated. Koltai (1980, p. 1) wrote, "The luxury of long-range planning is simply not available to us. . . . The status quo is no longer an option." He noted that as the 1980s began, more frequent accommodation was demanded of community colleges than at any other period in their history: "Enrollment slumps, collective bargaining agreements, redefined taxpayer priorities, legislative scrutiny, declining academic performance, and the advent of student consumerism" (p. 1) were contributing to the pace of change. Koltai saw the uncertainty about the funds that would be available as more difficult to deal with than even the reduced funding itself.

Yet the forces for prescriptive planning seemed almost as strong as the uncertainties. Trow (1973) described the burden being placed on administrative structures designed for smaller, simpler systems by central governmental agencies desirous of controlled planning and predictable development. Kintzer (1980a) similarly saw the problems occasioned by increasing state government surveillance superimposed on organizational structures designed to serve smaller, more autonomous institutions. He traced the organizational and administrative changes resulting from the power struggles of collective bargaining, the demands for more sophisticated data to be reported to external agencies, the pressures for budget and personnel accountability, and the new forms of services for students who no longer fit the traditional college-going pattern. The decisions to expand or contract, the rules for admission, and the definition of who should be served and in what way had become governed almost entirely by external forces.

Governance is complex under the best of circumstances. Monroe defined it as encompassing all aspects of the control and direction of the college, "including the state constitution, statutes, state boards of education or higher education, local boards of control, the administration, and in some institutions, the faculty and the student body. It includes both the policy-making mechanisms and the agencies through which the policies are executed or administered" (1972, p. 303). Thornton offered a less diffuse definition: "Locally controlled community junior colleges are governed in much the same way as other elements of the public schools. A locally elected board of trustees establishes policies for the college or colleges in its district, under the laws enacted by the legislature and the regulations of a state board" (1972, p. 116). And Corson defined governance as though the college itself were a government: "the process or art with which scholars, students, teachers, administrators, and trustees associated together in a college or university establish and carry out the rules and regulations that minimize conflict, facilitate their collaboration, and preserve essential individual freedom" (1960, pp. 12-13). However, all the writers noted the difficulty of separating the established policies from the practices maintained on their behalf; the act of administering a policy is as much a part of that policy as is the statement of rules or laws on which it is based.

It is understandable that contemporary administrators and trustees, embroiled in the complexities of the moment, would hearken to a golden era when rules were few and administration was simple. In its early years, when the junior college was often an adjunct of the local secondary school, the institution was usually administered by the high school principal or by a designate responsible to the principal. The local school board took up junior college affairs as part of its regular responsibilities. As the colleges separated themselves from the local school districts, the newly established boards of trustees similarly concerned themselves with budgetary matters and the selection of presidents who would keep the staff content and the college running smoothly, or at least keep the problems from becoming apparent to the public. Yet as long ago as 1931, when Eells wrote his book on the junior college, he noted that the areas of organization and administration were too varied and comprehensive to be treated completely. And although boards of trustees and administrators may have been able to govern without apparent conflict, issues of financing, staff morale, and conformity with state laws have always been present.

Different forms of college control have been more or less popular at one or another time. In the 1970s, the number of private junior colleges declined, multiunit college groupings increased, and nearly all colleges affiliated with local public school districts severed that connection. The public colleges were arrayed in single independent districts, multiunit independent districts, state university systems and branch colleges, and state systems with innovative patterns, including noncampus colleges and cluster colleges scattered among them.

Independent two-year colleges, a category that includes church-related institutions, private nonprofit colleges, and proprietary schools operated for profit, have varying patterns of control. The ultimate control of church-related colleges is the governing board of the church itself. Boards of control for other independents may be associated with the occupations emphasized, or they may be self-perpetuating bodies composed of concerned philanthropists. In private colleges that retain affiliation with a sponsoring church, religious studies may be a separate division headed by a minister. Directors of development, also known as fund raisers, are also usually prominent in the college's organizational chart. And because many private colleges still maintain residence halls, there may also be a director in charge of campus life.

Regardless of organizational form, size seems to be the most important variable. In study after study, whether the topic of concern is students, curriculum, library holdings, or unit costs, institutional size, more than any other characteristic, differentiates publicly supported institutions from one another. In fact, it has even been difficult to discern the differences between private and public institutions, because the private junior colleges are almost all quite small, and the significant differences between them and the public institutions appear to be related as much to size as to control.

The Local District

Most colleges in the nation are organized within single districts. A board of trustees, elected locally, establishes policy for the institution and employs a chief executive officer. Vicepresidents or deans manage business affairs, student personnel, academic instruction, and technical education. In most colleges the department chairpersons report to the dean of instruction or vice-president for instruction. However, in larger institutions, as shown in Figure 2, associate deans or assistant vice-presidents are sometimes added to manage detailed operations under each of the main functions.

The multiunit independent district dates from the 1930s, with Chicago and Los Angeles as early examples. There were ten such districts in 1964, forty in 1968, and by 1980, sixty-six in twenty-two states (Kintzer, 1980a). As shown in Figure 3, these multicollege districts operate with a central district organization headed by a president or chancellor and staffed with research coordinators, personnel administrators, business managers, and numerous others responsible for overall academic, fiscal, and student services.

The multiunit districts typically arose when a college opened a branch campus that eventually grew to a size that warranted an independent administration. However, the trend has not been solely in the direction of single-district, multicollege operation. Some districts, with St. Louis a notable example, have converted to a single-college, multicampus format.

Multiunit districts are far more complex, structured, and formalized than single-college districts. Those who advocate centralizing administration generally stress greater economy and uniformity of decisions. After examining forty-five colleges within multiunit districts, Kintzer, Jensen, and Hansen (1969) concluded that highly centralized colleges were characterized by maximum uniformity, impartiality, and efficiency; however, the

Figure 2. Traditional Organization Chart for a Large Community College

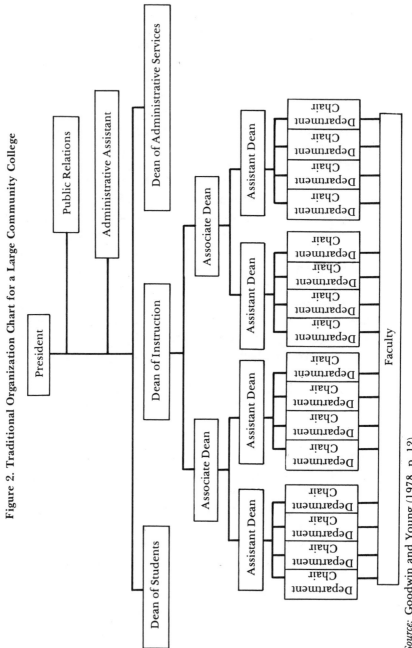

Source: Goodwin and Young (1978, p. 12).

Figure 3. Organizational Chart for a Multicollege District

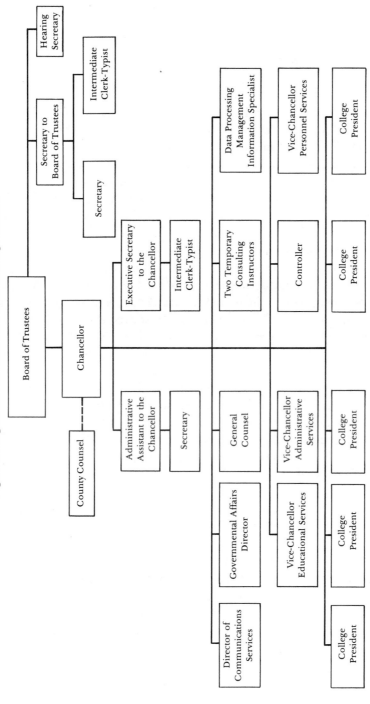

risk of depersonalization and low morale increased. Lander
(1977) showed that when multiunit districts in Arizona were
formed, another stratum of administrators was inserted between
the first-line administrators at each college and the district's
chief administrator. He concluded that increased size—the major
factor contributing to structural differences—forced increases in
complexity of function, formality in communication, delega-
tion of responsibility, and centralization of ultimate authority.

Chang's 1978 summary of the differences between centralization and decentralization points to the merits of each. A
centralized structure is supposed to eliminate duplication of
purchasing, data processing, facilities planning, personnel research, finance, physical plant, and contracting; standardize recruiting, fringe benefits, and payroll and affirmative action procedures; provide specialized personnel for collective bargaining
purposes; foster the equal treatment of support services, salaries, promotions, grievances, and resource allocation; minimize
rivalry and competition between campuses at the same time
that it enhances recruitment campaigns, publicity, grantsman-
ship, community service, and coordination; facilitate educational program coordination and staff development; and permit
the formation of vocational advisory committees for each vocational field rather than one area on separate campuses. At its
best, a decentralized structure encourages campus initiative and
creativity, allows each campus to respond to the community
and students more rapidly, fixes responsibility at a lower structural level, fosters the development of leadership among campus
administrators, and enhances staff morale by a greater degree of
local participation in decision making.

In their examination of twelve urban multicampus districts, Jenkins and Rossmeier (1974) found that neither a centralized nor a decentralized distribution of authority necessarily
related to the way faculty members and administrators perceived administrative effectiveness. According to their respondents, the most effective organization was one in which participation in decision making was maximized for staff members at
all levels, regardless of the nature of the hierarchy. Thus, although decision making occurred with increasing frequency at

district headquarters, the characteristics of multicampus districts did not preclude participation by staff members in all the units.

However, in multiunit districts, decision-making power has tended to gravitate toward the central district administration. Although many chancellors have attempted to share authority with the campus heads, it has been difficult to maintain a decentralized decision-making process when nearly all the factors affecting any unit affect them all. As an example, in nearly all multiunit districts, budget requests may be generated on each campus but only within the guidelines and limitations set down by the central authority. The central district offices often also maintain separate legal affairs offices to assure that all decisions on personnel selection and assignments are made in accordance with the terms of the contracts and laws governing the institution.

State Systems

Placing all publicly supported colleges under the control of a single authority has been effected in numerous states. In 1965 Blocker, Plummer, and Richardson identified twenty states with the community colleges under a state board of education and six where the colleges reported to a state department or superintendent of education. Separate state junior college boards or commissions existed in only six states; in thirteen others the colleges were under a state board of higher education or the board of a four-year state university. The trend toward state control accelerated with the Higher Education Amendments of 1972, which led to the creation of commissions to coordinate higher education in each state, and by 1980 Kintzer (1980a) found fifteen states with boards responsible for community colleges only, five with a university system including two-year colleges, and ten with boards for all of higher education. In addition, fifteen states had boards coordinating all levels of education. Where the state boards had coordinating authority only, they tended to act primarily in fact-finding and advisory capacities. But where they were legally defined governing boards, they recommended budgets and the allocation of state funds, salary schedules, articulation agreements, and the establishment of new institutions.

In states where the public community colleges are under state board control, decisions of funding and operation have become maximally centralized. Connecticut, Delaware, and Minnesota, for example, each seem to have one community college with several branches. Statewide bargaining and budgeting are the norm, although some autonomy in curriculum planning has been reserved for the individual colleges. Figure 4 shows the organization pattern typical of such states.

Figure 4. Administrative Organization Pattern for State Junior Colleges—a Composite

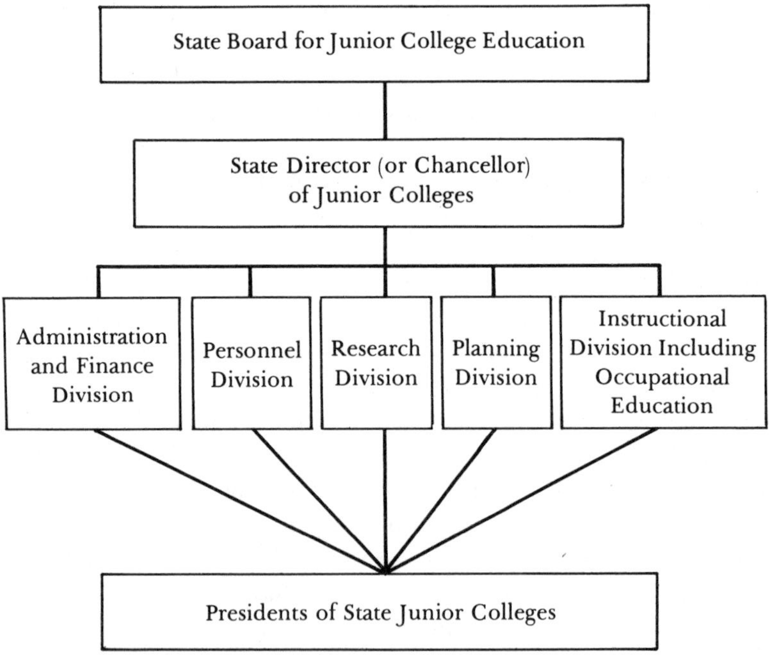

```
┌─────────────────────────────────────────────────┐
│       State Board for Junior College Education    │
└─────────────────────────────────────────────────┘
                        │
┌─────────────────────────────────────────────────┐
│            State Director (or Chancellor)         │
│                  of Junior Colleges               │
└─────────────────────────────────────────────────┘
```

| Administration and Finance Division | Personnel Division | Research Division | Planning Division | Instructional Division Including Occupational Education |

```
┌─────────────────────────────────────────────────┐
│         Presidents of State Junior Colleges       │
└─────────────────────────────────────────────────┘
```

Source: Kintzer, Jensen, and Hansen (1969, p. 43).

The combined state university and community college system has been one way of implementing state-level management. Thirty parent institutions and 103 two-year colleges, campuses, or institutes affiliated with state universities have been established in sixteen states. Such institutions are prevalent in Ohio and Wisconsin. All community colleges in Alaska, Hawaii, Kentucky, and Nevada are under the state university system. The university president is the chief executive officer, and the presidents of the colleges answer to the university executives rather than to their own governing boards (see Figure 5). The uni-

Figure 5. Administrative Organization Pattern for the
Hawaii Community College System

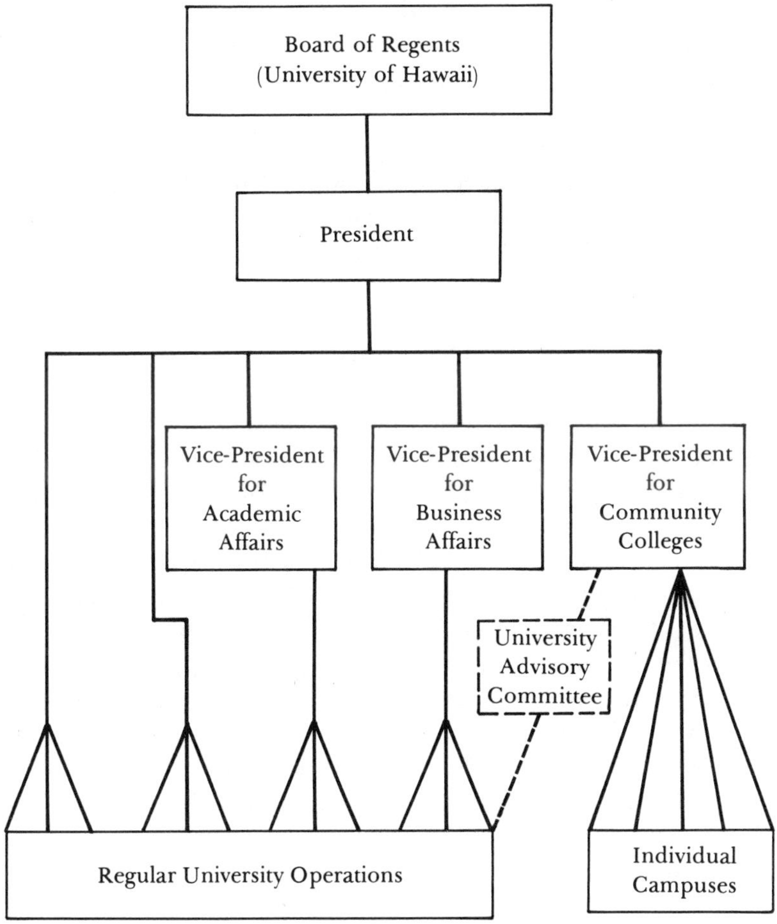

Source: Kintzer, Jensen, and Hansen (1969, p. 45).

versity boards of regents establish policy. The University of Wisconsin system operates more like a statewide multicampus district, with a chancellor heading the system and each campus under the direction of a dean.

A single state community college board that can exert influence on the state legislature, compete with the university for funding, assure quality education and equal treatment of faculty, and coordinate a statewide college-development system seems appealing. If the boards responsible for community colleges were also responsible for all of higher education, a thoroughly coordinated, economical, and articulated pattern of higher education for the state might result. Ideal in theory, this practice has not been universally adopted, and where it has, its benefits have not been uniformly realized.

Control of expenditures, program planning, and rules for nearly all aspects of college functioning, from the employment of personnel to the space a college should allocate for different functions, have moved steadily to the state agency level. Nonetheless, it is difficult to make a case for the greater efficiency that a trend toward larger units was supposed to bring. In fact, numerous authors have documented complaints about duplication, contradictory regulations, and the mass of approvals that must be garnered from regulatory agencies before college leaders can make a move. Darnowski (1978) sketched the number of agencies that had to be consulted before the simplest decision could be made by a Connecticut community college. Koehnline (1978) acknowledged that in Illinois the local community college board hired the president and adopted the budget, but "the state coordinating body adopts more official policies, procedures, and guidelines each year" (p. 44).

In states where most of the funds running to community colleges are allocated through a state board for community colleges, yet attempts to retain local autonomy are still being made, the strains are evident. The problem, however, is not merely one of decision-making authority shared between the local governing board and the state board; it relates also to other state agencies. Mundt (1978) offered several examples of "intervening interest outside the state board and the twenty-two district boards whose impact must be taken into account in the decision-making process and in the actual operation of the colleges" (p. 51). In the state of Washington he listed executive orders coming from the governor, directives from the Office of Financial Management, and contractual controls, legal opinions, and audits stemming from numerous state agencies. Information demands alone were high: "Recently the president of Highline Community College . . . found the college was reporting to twenty-nine outside, third-party agencies in one way or another" (p. 53). And Owen (1978) listed a group of state regulations and agencies impinging on the operation of community colleges in Florida, including state laws providing for public hearings to precede any "rule, fee, degree program, or major catalogue change" (p. 26).

However, the advantages of greater state-level coordination have also been documented. Funding has been made more equitable than it was when community college districts depended on local tax revenues and the gap between richer and poorer districts was pronounced. Some states have developed sophisticated management information systems and student information systems wherein all colleges provide data in uniform fashion, data that may then be cross-tabulated for the benefit of planners at individual institutions and may be used to generate reports for other state and federal agencies. Articulation between community colleges and public universities in the same state has also been enhanced when statewide coordination is evident. And a state board is more able to speak to the legislature with a single voice.

Richardson, Blocker, and Bender (1972) analyzed the trend toward state-level coordination and concluded that under such plans community colleges had the most to gain and the least to lose. But the line between statewide coordination and state control is fine. Many educators would prefer that the resources be provided with no strings attached, fearing that state mandates regarding programs and types of services that may be provided within specific categories would unduly restrict their efforts to provide the proper services for their constituents. State-level coordination has certainly magnified the sets of regulations under which community colleges operate, moved decision making to broader political arenas, and fostered the development of administrators whose chief skill and responsibility is to interpret the codes. But it has also yielded more stable funding, the augmentation of services for certain groups of students, such as the handicapped, and the strengthening of minimal standards of operation, and it has helped to minimize program duplication. The question whether it has been of general benefit or detriment cannot be answered; best only to say that it has changed the ground rules for institutional operation, the professional outlook of the staff, and the way the colleges are perceived by the public.

State-level coordination has certainly made starting a new community college a more complex undertaking. In the 1920s, the local school may have done little more to start a college than to get the state board of education's approval to offer some postsecondary classes. The 1907 California enabling act had said merely that the board of trustees might charge tuition for such classes. Gradually the criteria expanded to include minimum enrollments, minimum district population, and tax support.

By 1960 the general guidelines for establishing community colleges included "(1) general legislative authorization of two-year colleges, (2) local action by petition, election, or action by local board of control, (3) approval by a state agency, (4) a minimum assessed valuation considered adequate for sound fiscal support of the college, (5) a state or local survey to demonstrate the need for the college, (6) a minimum population of school age, (7) a minimum total population of the district, (8) a minimum potential college enrollment, (9) types of educational programs (curricula) to be offered, (10) availability and adequacy of physical facilities, (11) compliance with state operating policies, (12) proximity of other institutions" (Morrison and Martorana, 1960, cited in Blocker, Plummer, and Richardson, 1965, pp. 80-81).

And by the 1970s Evans and Neagley (1973) had offered an entire book showing the various patterns of college establishment. They included chapters on state regulations, conducting local needs studies and securing local support, spelled out guidelines for appointing and organizing the board of trustees, and presented sample organizational charts and recruiting and selection procedures for staff.

Nontraditional Organizations

Regardless of the form of institutional control, different organizational patterns have been tried. The "noncampus" college became popular in the 1970s, and because such institutions typically employed few full-time instructors and offered much of their program through reproducible media, often including open-circuit television, their administrative patterns differed. A president would report to a districtwide chancellor, but program directors or associate deans would take responsibility for separate geographical service areas. Further, because of the emphasis on rapid change in course design, instructional planners rather than department or division chairpersons would be more prominent. Whatcom (Washington), Coastline (California), Rio Salado (Arizona), and the Community College of Vermont were notable examples of "colleges without walls."

At the other extreme, the continuing search for ways of bringing the decision-making process closer to the faculty and students led to the development of cluster colleges. As Anthony noted, "The basic idea is to break up the college . . . into small, semiautonomous units or subcolleges, all of which share institutional resources to some extent" (1976, p. 13). The more freedom the smaller unit has to design its own academic program and to set its own rules of conduct for staff and students, the more it fits the ideal of a small unit operating under the umbrella of a parent organization that provides budgets, legal authority, and a general structure. Advocates of cluster colleges have put them forth as the best for bringing students and staff into the process of making decisions about the types of programs that should be presented. These subcolleges may effect their own distinctive patterns, focusing, for example, on the humanities or on a group of related technologies while sharing access to a central library, auditorium, gymnasium, and general administrative support services.

Cluster units have been organized in around twenty-five
to thirty colleges. The units in Cypress College and the Indian
Valley Colleges, in California, centered on academic disciplines.
At Oakton Community College (Illinois) transfer, occupational,
and general education were merged within each cluster. Small
units within Los Medanos College (California) were dedicated to
a core of general education based on interdisciplinary studies.
Management was effected through a coordinating committee,
which included a director of learning resources, a business services officer, a director of admissions and records, a public information officer, and a professional development facilitator.
Deans of the four major areas in general education (behavioral
science, humanities, social science, and natural science) managed the programs in their areas. Traditional academic departments have been conspicuously absent in most cluster college
plans. Student services are decentralized, each cluster having its
own set of counselors.

Governing Boards

The idea of a lay governing board that represents the people is an old concept in American education, and public education has used elected boards to reflect the collective will and
wisdom of the people since earliest times. Ideally, the board is
the bridge between college and community, translating community needs for education into college policies and protecting the
college from untoward external demands. The degree to which
boards do so has always been questioned, some observers saying
their composition was too homogeneous. Bernd (1973), for
example, argued that since the typical trustee was a Protestant,
Republican, business or professional man over age forty-five, he
could not represent all his constituents adequately. But such a
contention has always been difficult to document.

Community college boards usually consist of from five to
nine members elected from the district at large for four-year
terms. They may meet once or twice a month or, in some cases,
weekly. According to the Association of Community College
Trustees, their responsibilities include selecting, evaluating, and

terminating the president; ensuring professional management of the institution; purchasing, constructing, and maintaining facilities; defining the role and mission of the college; engaging in public relations; preserving institutional independence; evaluating institutional performance; creating a climate for change; insisting on being informed; engaging in planning; and assessing board performance (Potter, 1977).

Because the boards are public corporations, they are legally responsible for all college affairs. This status involves them in legal actions on everything from personnel matters to issues of purchasing materials. Potter (1976) has discussed the importance of the board's understanding of the law as it affects the governance of the college, saying it must have a working knowledge of educational law and be able to recognize potential legal problems before they develop into actual litigation. He offered examples of litigation brought on by students, by faculty members, and by other parties—for example, suits by students in relation to tuition or over disruption on campus that they felt interfered with their education, and suits by faculty members, who have usually engaged in litigation because of dismissal from their job.

State associations for community college presidents and trustees have been prominent in around two thirds of the states. These voluntary organizations typically coordinate statewide conferences and meetings, conduct professional development workshops for various types of administrators, arrange orientation sessions for newly appointed trustees, prepare and distribute newsletters, and monitor legislation. They provide an avenue for chief administrators and trustees from the colleges within a state to meet and discuss topics of common interest. Active associations that cross state lines, such as the New England Junior College Council, operate in similar fashion. Support for these associations most often comes from members' dues, but some have received funds from the state or a philanthropic institution.

The Association of Community College Trustees (ACCT) has also been active in apprising board members of their need to take a prominent role in college affairs. Since ACCT was organized in 1972, its publications and conferences have been directed toward moving board members away from a "rubber stamp" mentality that approves everything the college administration presents. It has also stressed the importance of the board's monitoring the college's fiscal affairs and public relations and the necessity of open communication between the board and the college president.

Administration

All colleges must have administration, although the way this function is organized and staffed differs from one college to another. In the medieval university, even though the students were powerful, often fixing tuition charges and determining the curriculum, the faculty was the controlling wheel of the institution. During the nineteenth century a system of centralized control developed in the United States, and faculty power diminished as the administration took over the university. Teachers concentrated on their research, scholarship, and teaching, and professional managers controlled the affairs of administration, thus dividing the ranks between administrators and teachers.

With their roots in the secondary schools, the community colleges were managed usually by former instructors who had become first part-time, then full-time administrators. Monroe described many of them as autocrats who had freed "themselves from the control of their superiors and the general public. They assumed a paternalistic, superior attitude toward the teachers. Administrative decisions of the past have often gone unquestioned by governing boards. The members of the boards rubber stamp administrative policies and decisions so that in practice the college's administrators become the decision makers of the college" (1972, p. 305). But he was speaking of a time gone by; the all-powerful president had disappeared from all but the smallest colleges by the 1970s.

The role of the president changed as colleges grew larger. And as faculty and community advocate groups grew stronger, it became ever more circumscribed. Still, the president was the spokesperson for the college, interpreting it to the public on ceremonial occasions. The president was also the scapegoat when staff morale or funds for a favored program diminished. The average presidential tenure during the 1970s was eight or nine years, lower than faculty tenure but certainly sufficiently high to suggest that the job was not particularly precarious.

The president's duties include primarily general administration and meeting with the board. To a lesser extent, the president is also involved with coordinating the college program with other institutions, public relations, attending state and national meetings, relations with state agencies, recruiting and selecting faculty members, and coordinating with other community groups. Fund raising and student personnel issues occupy little of the public college president's time; however, they are high on the list of responsibilities assumed by presidents of private colleges.

The college deans are usually line officers in charge of planning and supervising one or a combination of college programs concerned with instruction, student personnel services, evening division, or community services. The larger colleges may also have deans for college development and for admissions, but deans of men and women, prominent in the early colleges, had become rare in the public colleges of 1980. Like the president, each dean becomes involved with legal issues, public relations, intrainstitutional administration and personnel matters, budgeting, and liaison with state and federal agencies. Most deans serve as part of a president's council or cabinet.

Departmental Structure. The structure of the academic program within community colleges has usually rested on the department or the division organized around a cluster of academic disciplines or related teaching fields. The primary objective in creating academic departments, inherited from the universities, was to create manageable organizational units, not necessarily to interrelate the teaching of certain subjects or to build interdisciplinary courses. The number of departments is often related to institutional size; in small colleges where not more than one or two instructors may be teaching in any subject field, the combination of teaching fields within a single department may be quite broad. But in the larger institutions, the number of departments has often increased as the number of instructors teaching a single discipline has grown. As Lombardi put it, "Tradition, pride, logic, and number of instructors are all factors in determining whether a department comprised of several disciplines will remain intact or be divided into separate departments" (1973a, p. 3).

The academic department has been a basic building block in the organizational structure in nearly all community colleges. Its influence has been quite marked. As an example, the administration may organize collegewide orientation sessions for new instructors, but true indoctrination takes place when the neophytes begin maintaining their offices in the suite assigned to the academic department of which they are members. And inservice faculty development workshops conducted on an institution-wide scale pale in comparison with the influence exerted by a senior departmental colleague's pointed comment, "That's not the way we do it around here!"

Departments may have responsibility for constructing class schedules, assigning instructors, allocating funds for auxiliary employees and services—in short, for acting as miniature governmental units within the larger college structure. For this reason, many senior administrators have sought to retain control by minimizing departmental power; hence the move toward the larger organizational unit of the division. Other administrators have attempted to minimize the power of the department by having faculty members from different departments share office space or otherwise mixing the staff. But the departments have survived in most institutions, probably because the affinity among instructors teaching the same courses or courses in the same academic fields remains strong. Further, some department chairpersons have served the administration well by maintaining certain records, supervising staff, screening applicants for positions, and reconciling conflicts among staff members and between staff members and students that might have been blown out of proportion if they had reached higher levels of arbitration.

Until the spread of collective bargaining in community colleges, the academic department remained the most popular organizational unit. However, as bargaining units were established, the chairpersons with managerial responsibilities were often designated as administrators, thus removing them from the bargaining unit. And at that point the move toward organizing larger units or divisions accelerated, lest a college have thirty or forty administrators, each supervising only a few instructors. However, the distinction was not clear, and department chairpersons were considered faculty members in some contracts, administrators in others.

In general, administrators would prefer that chairpersons be excluded from the bargaining unit, whereas the faculty would want them to be included. Nearly all department chairpersons still teach courses, albeit on a reduced load; hence, it is difficult to assign them universally to the ranks of the administrator. However, chairpersons do have certain supervisory responsibilities. This divided status leads to an indeterminate role. In some colleges the department chairperson might be a faculty member whose responsibilities are severely circumscribed; in others the chairperson might be an administrator with far-reaching supervisory powers who also happens to be teaching a class or two.

Lombardi (1974) reports studies showing lengthy lists of responsibilities for department chairpersons: sixty-nine discrete items in one statement, fifty-one in another. However, he suggests that the duty statements appearing in collective bargaining agreements seldom contained more than fifteen items. The essential minimum seemed to be orientation for new faculty members, involving faculty members in making departmental decisions, encouraging faculty participation in professional activities, reporting departmental accomplishments, developing long-range departmental goals, ascertaining the needs for equipment, preparing the department budget and overseeing the allocation of funds, planning curriculum changes with the faculty, reviewing trends in student characteristics, and reviewing new developments in similar departments in other community colleges.

Administrative Patterns. So many administrative patterns have been advocated that it is impossible to describe an ideal form. The line-staff organization recommended by Blocker,

Plummer, and Richardson (1965) had the president reporting to the board of control, with a business manager and a director of community relations reporting to the president (see Figure 6). Underneath the president on the organization chart was a dean of liberal arts and sciences, a dean of technological science, a dean of students for vocational education, and a dean of continuing education. Under the deans were department or division chairs and guidance personnel, and under those appeared the faculty. Blocker and his coauthors posed such an organization as better than the conventional model because it placed more emphasis on college functions. To them the typical organization of the time had the dean of student personnel and the business manager reporting to the academic dean, who reported to the president.

Their recommendation was to split the educational functions, making them the responsibility of deans of the major service areas: "Student affairs, technical and vocational sciences, and community services are as important as the college-parallel program; if these segments of the comprehensive educational program of the college are to prosper, they must have status equal to that of the transfer program" (p. 179).

Numerous variations on this traditional administrative chart have been postulated. As a way of bringing administration into a flatter profile, as opposed to the hierarchy or pyramid represented by president, dean, and associate dean, some colleges have built management teams in which a president works with several administrators of equal rank. In others, the major institutional divisions—learning resources, business services, academic programs, and so on—operate as autonomous units within a model of decentralization.

Richardson (1975) suggested that models must be constructed in order to understand complex institutions and offered three major models to explain why colleges appear as they do. The bureaucratic model presents the college as a formal structure with defined patterns of activity that are related to the functions spelled out in law and policy decisions. The positions are arranged in the shape of a pyramid, and each series of positions has specified responsibilities, competencies, and privileges.

Figure 6. Line-Staff Organization Plan

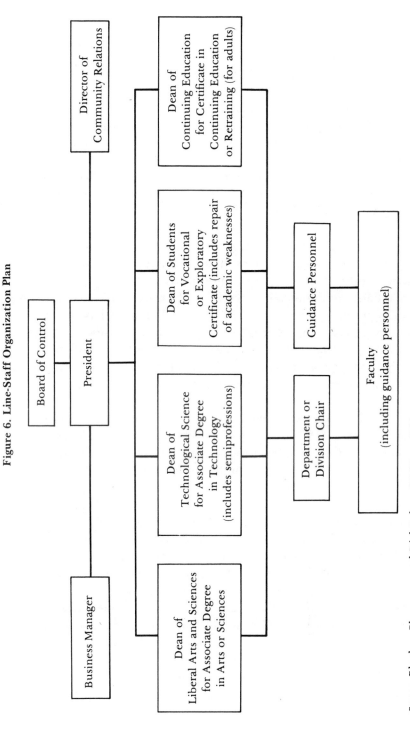

Source: Blocker, Plummer, and Richardson (1965, p. 178).

This organization is held together by authority delegated from the top down, with persons at the top receiving greater benefits than those at the bottom; the lowest levels of the triangle are occupied by faculty and students.

In the political model, the interests of students, faculty, administrators, and trustees are seen as different, thus leading to conflict.

Richardson favored a *shared authority,* or collegial, model intended to reduce status symbols and increase morale and communication: "Instead of being at the bottom of a pyramid, faculty and students are part of a community of equal partners. Authority is not delegated downward as in the bureaucratic model; rather, trustees share their authority with students and faculty as well as with administrators. Students and faculty members communicate directly with the board rather than through the president" (1975, p. ix). The model is based on group process, the concept of community, the sharing of authority, and the making of decisions within a framework of participation and consensus. However, the notion that students have much voice in college administration has little basis in reality.

In a book addressed to academic administrators, Richman and Farmer (1974) discussed several models of governance. They found the bureaucratic model, the traditional formal organization plan focusing on hierarchies, rules, and predetermined procedures, a closed system and saw the collegial model, based on the notion of a community of scholars, "a rather ambiguous concept that favors full participation in decision making, especially by the faculty" (p. 28). Baldridge's (1971) political model seemed to explain most accurately the current status of college governance and administration because it took conflict among contending forces as a natural phenomenon. And Richman and Farmer added a fourth model to the list, organized anarchy, described by Cohen and March in 1974 as a collection of choices looking for problems in which they might be aired, solutions looking for issues to which they might be the answers; people whose dispositions were for or against open admissions, liberal education, higher pay for teaching assistants, or whatever, would weigh each issue as it affected their own concerns.

Richman and Farmer asserted that conflict stemmed from the differences in views of goals held by the various groups within the institution and by the constituencies being served. Although their case studies were predominantly of universities, the implications applied to community colleges, in which the need to refine and accommodate conflicting and ambiguous goals was no less apparent. As an example, they listed the goal "protect the faculty" as the highest among the thirty-one goals being pursued in American colleges (p. 119), a goal certainly evident to anyone who perceives that despite all the rhetoric of satisfying student and community needs, the procedures maintained within community colleges tend toward protecting the staff's rights, satisfaction, and welfare.

Administrative theories notwithstanding, administrators are people, more or less effective in their relations with other people. Walker (1979) characterized the less effective administrators as those who need to "defend the sanctity of their office" and who react with "counteraggressive behavior when under attack." They believe that they are supposed to make decisions, even unpopular ones, and that their responsibilities are to see that their orders are obeyed and the rules enforced. "They view decision making as a series of personal acts of courage, will, and purpose. . . . Over a period of time, because faculty members and students entertain a different notion of leadership, their activities come to be regarded by the administrator as perverse" (pp. 2-3).

The more effective administrators are those who "accept the privileges and status of their office, but wear them lightly. They separate themselves, as individuals, from their office. . . . They regard themselves as working with faculty colleagues who deserve respect as fellow professionals" (p. 4). They work to reconcile the differences among the constituencies on campus, and they may even consider themselves expendable if the welfare of the institution requires that they leave. They consider administration a process, not a series of discrete events, and they tend to be good politicians. "Their assurance apparently derives from an intuitive knowledge of the organization and appropriate administrative roles rather than from naked self-confidence in the egotistical sense" (p. 5).

Is the form of administration important to anyone but administrators? Heermann (1976) felt that college organization had "an indirect but important relationship" to student learning, that education was "the result of a unique blending of a diverse constituency: administrators, students, support staff, and teachers" (p. vii). But the person of the administrator still seems the most important ingredient. Some administrators have succeeded admirably, others failed terribly, even while adhering to ostensibly similar administrative styles within the same type of organization.

Collective Bargaining

Collective bargaining swept into higher education on the coattails of legislation authorizing public employees to negotiate. As these laws were passed in various states in the 1960s and 1970s, employee groups ranging from refuse collectors to prison guards gained union representation and began negotiating contracts.

Within education, elementary and secondary school teachers were first to take advantage of the legislation. Kemerer and Baldridge (1975) attributed this to their being the furthest from professional autonomy. Community college faculties were next most likely to be represented by a bargaining agent, with the National Education Association and the American Federation of Teachers their two most prominent agents. By 1980, authorizing legislation had been passed in more than half the states, and around half of community college instructors were covered under negotiated contracts (see Table 15).

The expansion of collective bargaining effected a shift in administrative roles. In general, it marked the demise of the concept of paternalism, with the president as authority figure, and opened an era of political accommodation among contending forces. These changes were difficult for many administrators whose experience had not prepared them for their different roles, but the realities of management within the confines of a negotiated contract so confronted them that they either learned to do it or left the practice.

Table 15. Total Two-Year College Faculty Collective
Bargaining Contracts by Agents, 1966-1979

Year	National Education Association	American Federation of Teachers	American Association of University Professors	Inde-pendent	AAUP/ NEA
1966	1	1	0	0	0
1967	3	4	0	1	1
1968	5	6	0	2	2
1969	9	10	1	11	7
1970	15	13	2	21	14
1971	32	22	3	30	25
1972	67	43	4	41	36
1973	90	55	5	46	38
1974	90	56	5	46	38
1975	102	69	3	26	31
1976	133	77	2	38	7
1977	166	114	4	45	7
1978	185	125	6	47	7
1979	228	129	7	33	7

Sources: Hankin (1975); *Chronicle of Higher Education,* 1966-1979.

Collective bargaining not only drew a legal line between members of the bargaining unit and those outside it—between faculty, on the one side, and administrators and trustees, on the other—but it expanded the number of detailed rules of procedure. It prevented administrators from making ad hoc decisions about class size or scheduling, faculty assignments, committee structures, budget allocations, funding of special projects, and a myriad of other matters, both great and small. It forced a more formalized, impersonal pattern of interaction, denying whatever vestige of collegiality the staff in community colleges might have aspired to. It brought the role of the legal expert to the fore and magnified the number of people who must be consulted each time a decision is considered.

Swift (1979) studied the effects of the negotiated contract on Minnesota community colleges and found that although job security and fringe benefits were enhanced, faculty involvement in institutional decision making, managerial authority, and campus communication were impaired. Armstrong (1978) reported that the administrators at a California community college felt collective bargaining to have reduced their flexibility in assigning tasks. And some faculty members (Worthen, 1979, for example) have deplored the effect of collective bargaining in limiting the dialogue among instructors, administrators, and trustees.

Collective bargaining seems also to have accelerated a move to larger institutional units. In multicampus districts where the faculty bargains as a districtwide unit, the district-level administration aggregates power, weakening the autonomy of the individual campuses. In states where the faculty bargaining unit negotiates a master contract for all the colleges, power gravitates toward the state level. At best, this may result in a federal system with certain powers reserved for the individual colleges; at worst, the colleges become single statewide institutions, with branch campuses in the different localities.

In many institutions where contracts have been negotiated, administrators have adopted a practice of interpreting the rules and administering them in accordance with their best determination. This has proved a boon to those who welcomed the opportunity to avoid responsibility for their decisions. The more skilled administrators have been able to maneuver through the thicket of regulations and make decisions beneficial to the institution's educational programs. And as colleges gain experience with collective bargaining, more of this latter group will come to the fore.

Lombardi (1979a), who traced the effects of collective bargaining on administrators, showed that most accepted it reluctantly, while some actually welcomed it, allowing the union bureaucracy to become an arm of administration by providing for more control of the faculty. Most administrators, however, recognized that collective bargaining reduced them to ministerial functionaries carrying out the decisions made during the negotiations. Lombardi detailed the restrictions made on administrators who could no longer arbitrarily assign summer or evening classes, reduce staff size, change salaries, fringe benefits, or work loads, or devise their own procedures for selecting chairpersons and new faculty members. He also noted the move toward bargaining for administrators, detailing how in Michigan and New York some agreements involving administrators had been negotiated. But the handbook compiled by administrators and formally approved by the governing board has been the more common approach, serving the administrators as the contracts had served the faculties.

More difficult to document is the contention that distrust between faculty and administrators increased. Freligh argued that "the disheartening consequence of collective bargaining is that it fails to do what it was created to do: it precludes the creation of any position that by definition combines teaching and administration, removes faculty-administration liaison as a primary function of the departmental/divisional leader; compels adversary positions; cuts off debate; disallows independence of judgment; imposes the industrial model (management/labor) on academic institutions . . . and presumes that differences of opinion and perception can be reconciled only through negotiation of contractual agreements rather than by the exercise of reason among professional people" (1976, p. 65).

Under collective bargaining, the faculty gained prerogatives in establishing the conditions of the workplace up to and including a say in institutional governance. Administrators lost the freedom to act according to general principles and were forced to attend to the procedures specified in the contracts. Both parties were restrained from reaching private agreements. In general, an informal relationship of faculty and administration as unequal parties became a formal compact of near equals.

Attempts at Efficiency

Various efforts to make community colleges more efficient were undertaken during the 1970s. First was "increasing the quantity and quality of learning and personal growth while being cost effective" (Goodwin and Young, 1978, p. 4). Operationally this meant lowering costs, increasing student learning and staff efficiency, making the college accessible to more students, cutting student attrition, and managing the physical plant more effectively. However, increased productivity in one area might lead to a decrease in another, for example, success in attracting different types of students to community colleges might increase the costs of instruction. Further, measuring productivity by the number of students processed through a class in a given time equates the outputs of education with those of a factory. But Goodwin and Young did note that productivity would be enhanced if communication channels among staff members remained relatively open, bureaucratic approvals required for changes were kept to a minimum, flexibility in the academic calendar was maintained, differentiated staffing was introduced (providing paraprofessional aides as support for the faculty), and a variety of instructional forms were used. Berchin (1972) also traced community college productivity, finding it related in large measure to class size and to reproducible media.

Second, the concept of management by objectives (MBO), first popularized by Drucker (1954), made inroads in college administration. The advantages of MBO seemed to center on its demanding that all staff members define in measurable terms what they intended to accomplish. It thus formed a base for staff accountability and helped the staff coordinate their activities around common goals. Critics of MBO found it too time-consuming and too mechanistic, but its proponents, including Lahti (1979), concluded that it brought college processes out from behind what the public perceived as a curtain of secrecy designed to conceal waste and inefficiency.

And third, the changes in student composition occasioned by the reduced expansion of the traditional college population led to the introduction of marketing. Always alert to new programs to attract different types of students, administrators in many colleges began accelerating their promotional activities and coordinating them with particular programs. The arguments for so doing ranged from a belief that the college that promoted its wares most extensively served its community best to the importance of college officials' protecting their programs against the incursions of senior colleges and proprietary schools that themselves had stepped up efforts to attract students long considered the proper clients for the community colleges. Johnson (1979) defined marketing as an integration of promotional activities with programs designed particularly for certain population segments offered at times and places convenient to those groups. He considered it important for college managers to understand marketing, convince other staff members of its importance, and put all elements of the college into a marketing stance, and he advocated organizing marketing task forces to work with instructors and other staff members in devising and promoting new programs.

Institutional Research

Every increase in federal- and state-level categorical programs has led to an increased need for data to be provided by the campuses. In many cases responsibility for gathering the data has been assigned to the offices of admissions and records, but because of the flood of requests, institutional research received a boost. As extramural grants and contracts were opened to community colleges, institutional research offices became more involved in proposal writing. And as the computer became ubiquitous, more sophisticated data tabulations could be made.

A study coordinated by the ERIC Clearinghouse for Junior College Information at UCLA (Roueche and Boggs, 1968) assessed the status of institutional research in community colleges in the 1960s, tracing its scope, the number and type of studies completed, and the number of institutions with research coordinators. Full-time research coordinators were found in only about one in five community colleges, usually the larger institutions. In two of five colleges, responsibility for institutional research was assigned to an administrator who also had other duties, and in two of five, no regular staff member had responsibility for coordinating institutional studies. Institutional research studies addressed students, programs, and institutional operations, with a few studies of faculty and student personnel services also underway. The authors concluded that the key to running a successful research office was a commitment by the president, who insisted on good data on which to base educational decisions.

Subsequent studies of institutional research in community

colleges revealed that institutional research offices were established in increasing proportion during the 1970s but that they operated on small budgets, in no case exceeding 1 percent of the total operating budget. Knapp (1979) found institutional research offices typically staffed with only one or two persons. Those offices were seen as arms of the administration, providing data to the top administrators while conducting few, if any, studies on behalf of the faculty. Cherdack (1979) suggested a broadened role for institutional research, urging that researchers engage in institutional cost-effectiveness studies, studies of marketing strategies to recruit students, assessments of needed programs, and program evaluation.

The highest priority for institutional research has been topics concerned with students, including enrollment trends, student characteristics, and follow-up studies. According to Wattenbarger (Educational Testing Service, 1976), data gathering can be properly focused by asking certain questions—for example, "What effect does probation status have on students? What teaching procedures are most cost-effective? What schedule provides the most effective use of facilities?" Wattenbarger recommended that institutional research responsibilities be assigned to one person who would coordinate all the college's research activities. He also recommended establishing an institution-wide advisory committee; providing adequate financial support for the research office; urging instructors to participate by suggesting studies and taking an active role in collecting and interpreting data; having meetings of research coordinators with their counterparts in other institutions; maintaining proper filing systems; publishing and distributing findings; and enlisting the aid of as many people as possible in interpreting and acting on the results.

Alfred (Educational Testing Service, 1976) urged that community college institutional research shift to future-oriented studies: enrollment projections, career program outcomes, economic impacts of the college on the community, and the plotting of curricular needs. As such, it could help the staff establish institutional goals, furnish information for planning, and provide the means for appraising the effects of the practices adopted. According to Alfred's plan, goal setting, program development, cost effectiveness, and program review are the basic components of research, whereas data on students, programs, communities, facilities, finance, staff, and organization are the raw materials from which research is conceptualized.

Several other researchers reported upon their activities at the national meeting coordinated by the Educational Testing Service. Selgas described a lengthy research project undertaken at Harrisburg Area Community College (Pennsylvania) that provided information on the educational and occupational plans of high school students in the college's service area, the educational desires and intentions of adults, and the training needs expressed by employers (Educational Testing Service, 1976). Lightfield discussed procedures for sampling and processing data, noting particularly the importance of preparing different types of reports for the different audiences. Gell similarly noted the importance of easily interpreted reports so that the findings would have a chance to be interpreted and used by people relatively unsophisticated in statistics. Lombardi showed how research directors must use the definitions in place in their own institutions to avoid misinterpretation.

The importance of institutional researchers' collecting information of use to institutional planners was stated by Knoell and by Lach. Knoell's point was that limitations on funds for community colleges make it imperative that plans be devised to accommodate an era in which growth can be undertaken only in predictable areas. Lach argued in favor of statewide coordination of community college institutional research so that uniform data will be made available. Statewide coordination seems likely, as several states are building student and management information systems, using common data drawn from all institutions; Illinois, Hawaii, Washington, and Maryland offer the best examples of statewide information systems.

Issues

Several issues swirl around the concepts of governance and administration. What elements of control should be maintained by state agencies? What should be reserved for the local institutions? What further changes in institutional management will result from the trend toward placing more control at the state level?

Similar moves toward larger organizations have been made within districts since single colleges opened branch campuses that had to be coordinated by some form of central administration. What is the effect of the additional levels of bureaucracy that have been set in place? Is multicollege or multicampus the better form?

The college as a learning enterprise does not operate well when it is managed as a factory with inputs, process, and outputs as the model. Can the anarchical elements of collegiality coexist with contracts negotiated by distant representatives? Is management by objectives feasible?

Vague and often conflicting aspirations affect every classroom and administrative office. How can the college maintain consistent direction when numerous organized groups within and outside the institution all demand to participate in governance? Can participatory management survive in an era of collective bargaining?

Issues of productivity and accountability have been raised continually. How can staff members be held responsible for their actions when most of the decisions that affect them are beyond their control? Does the larger bureaucracy protect the staff from external scrutiny? Do formalized grievance procedures enhance or retard individual responsibility and creativity?

Institutional research coordinators spend most of their time gathering data to fill out reports requested by external agencies. How can they expand their efforts to serve the college by gathering information necessary for program construction, accurate enrollment projections, and college efficiency and accountability?

As the colleges have grown larger and more complex, administrators, faculty members, and trustees all have had to adjust. The only certainty is that regardless of the form of governance and the models of administration adopted, these adjustments will have to be made with increasing frequency.

5

Finances

Maintaining
Fiscal Support

Trends in financing community colleges have followed shifts in institutional purpose and mode of organization. The colleges have expanded so that they enroll half of all people who begin college; they can no longer be considered merely alternative institutions for students who do not wish to leave their home town to go to a university. They have become large enterprises, some with budgets exceeding the $100 million mark.

When the colleges were small, they made modest demands on public funds. Few people outside the institutions cared where these colleges' money came from or how they spent it. But when they and their budgets grew large and began competing for sizable funds with other public agencies, they gained prominence in the public eye. Thus, when most of the public felt that the colleges were contributing to the welfare of the community and its individuals, the colleges were handsomely supported. But when the public became disaffected, and inflation and rapidly increasing enrollments drove costs upward at a phenomenal rate, the colleges' support base was shaken.

Supporters of the public colleges have always had to operate in a political arena. Since 1907, when the first junior college enabling legislation was passed in California, there has been continual legislative activity on their behalf. The colleges had been organized as extensions of the secondary schools, deriving their support through the public school budgets, but that changed as soon as independent community college districts were organized. Even so, their support continued to come predominantly from local tax funds. The usual pattern was for the local district to provide a fixed sum of money per student in attendance, with state aid minimizing the differences among districts of varying wealth. The proportion of state aid was quite small: Augenblick (1978) reported it at an average of less than 5 percent of all public college revenues in the 1920s. And during most of the pre-World War II era, student tuition and fees provided more funds to the community colleges than the states did. Richardson and Leslie (1980) noted that in 1934, local districts provided 84 percent of the colleges' support, with student fees accounting for most of the remainder. But even in those early years there was much variation among states: Eells (1931) showed that student tuition made up 77 percent of the financial support for the Texas colleges, whereas in California, taxpayers from the students' home districts provided the colleges with 81 percent of their operating funds.

Although community college funding over the years has been marked by shifting proportions coming from tuition, local taxes, and state revenues, the trend has been for the states to pick up an increasingly larger share of the support. State financing arrangements have done more than merely minimize the differences in wealth among community college districts; they have reflected the growing importance of the community college as a resource for all the people. Attendance has become in-

Finances 129

creasingly probable as higher percentages of the population have gone to some form of postsecondary education. The state funds have provided incentives for the institutions to broaden access by encouraging program variety and by reimbursing institutions on the basis of the number of students enrolled.

There is so much variation among the states that support patterns in general cannot be considered indicative of any one of them. As an example, by the end of the 1970s, community colleges in Arizona were still deriving about half their support from the local tax base, while in at least ten states, none of the revenues came from that source. And whereas students in California paid practically nothing, community colleges in seven states derived more than one fourth of their revenue from their students. The overall proportions are shown in Table 16, which also displays the changing sources during the past several decades.

Table 16. Percentages of Income from Various Sources for
Public Two-Year Colleges, 1918-1980

Source	1918[a]	1930[a]	1942[a]	1950[a]	1959	1965	1975	1977	1980
Tuition and fees	6	14	11	9	11	13	15	18	15
Federal aid	0	0	2	1	1	4	8	5	5
State aid	0	0	28	26	29	34	45	59	60
Local aid	94	85	57	49	44	33	24	15	11
Private gifts and grants	0	0	0	0	0	3	1	0	1
Auxiliary services	N.A.	N.A.	N.A.	N.A.	12	6	6	0	3
Other	0	2	2	2	2	7	1	3	3

[a]Includes local junior colleges only.
Sources: Starrak and Hughes (1954, p. 28); Medsker and Tillery (1971, p. 115); Olivas (1979, p. 20); Richardson and Leslie (1980, p. 20); Chronicle of Higher Education (June 8, 1981, p. 8).

Capital-outlay projects have usually been funded differently from operating budgets. Some states require the colleges to present long-term plans on the need for buildings and facilities, plans that have been difficult to defend in an era of rapidly shifting enrollments. And when appropriations become hard to obtain, capital-outlay projects are among the first to be curtailed. Some states require a bond issue to finance college buildings. Although the community colleges in many states occupy handsome quarters, their policies of reaching out to offer classes in a variety of off-campus localities have reduced their need for new buildings.

Funding Patterns

Increased complexity in patterns of state reimbursement has accompanied the increased proportion of funds coming from the state. Wattenbarger and Starnes (1976) listed four typical models for state support: negotiated budget, unit-rate formula, minimum foundation, and cost-based program funding. Negotiated budget funding is arranged annually with the state legislature or a state board. Used especially in states where all or nearly all the community college funds come from the state, negotiated budgets demand a high level of institutional accountability for funds expended. Budgets tend to be incremental; one year's support reflects the prior year's, with increments or reductions based on funds available, changing costs, and the introduction or suspension of various programs.

Under the unit-rate formula, the state allocates funds to colleges on the basis of a formula that specifies a certain number of dollars per unit of measure. The unit of measure may be a full-time equivalent student (FTE), the number of students in certain programs, the credit hours generated, or some combination of measures.

The minimum foundation plan is a modification of the unit-rate formula. State allocations are made at a variable rate that depends on the amount of local tax funding available to the institution. The allocation may be expressed either as a set dollar amount minus the local funds available per student or as a proportion of the approved district budget minus the amount provided by the local contributions. In either case the intent is to provide more state funds to colleges where local support is less. Inequities in local support among community college districts are smaller than those among lower school districts because community college districts tend to be larger and therefore more likely to include both wealthy and poor neighborhoods, and their students come from a broader range of the population. Still, considerable variation exists because community college attendance is not mandatory, so that districts can differ widely in the proportion of the population they serve.

The cost-based funding model provides state allocations based on actual expenditures. In this model state funds are allocated on the basis of program functions, specifically budgeted objectives, and detailed instructional categories. Local tax funds may or may not be factored into the formulas, and the appropriations vary greatly among institutions, depending on the costs of the programs they offer.

The funding formulas are often complex, and whatever formula is adopted benefits certain institutions, certain programs, and certain classes of students while penalizing others. The common practice of reimbursing colleges on the basis of full-time equivalent student attendance may penalize institutions with higher proportions of part-timers. Although reimbursement for occupational students is made at a different rate than for those enrolled in the lower-cost academic programs, costs vary among all the programs. And because of the differences in facilities used, staff salaries, types of students enrolled, and so on, absolute parity among institutions can never be achieved.

Breneman and Nelson (1981) examined community college funding patterns from the point of view of the economist and concluded that no one system can possibly accommodate all purposes. They found that the various taxonomies purporting to describe community college funding patterns were not based on mutually exclusive categories. They categorized the several choices that must be made in defining financing plans: funding from the state only or a combination of state and local funding; tuition as a fixed percentage of costs or on some other basis; budgets negotiated or following statutory formulas; financing credit courses only or funds for noncredit; treating community colleges in isolation or making their support relative to other segments of higher education; deriving a proper formula based on recovery costs, average daily attendance, student credit hours, or other measures.

Breneman and Nelson summarized as follows: Remedial education should be tuition-free because it is a true extension of lower-school work, which is tuition-free; occupational programs providing training for particular industries should receive at least partial support from the industries that benefit; community education primarily for personal enrichment should be self-supporting; community college students do not necessarily receive less support than their counterparts in public universities, because university costs for lower-division instruction alone cannot be accurately calculated; student aid should be restricted to students enrolled at least half-time; and finance formulas should be devised to reflect differences in program costs and differences in unit costs associated with college size.

Tuition and Student Aid

Questions of the proper balance between local and state funding are no more controversial than the issues surrounding the tuition and fees paid by students. Many two-year college leaders have advocated a no-tuition or a low-tuition policy for their institutions, which they felt were natural extensions of the free public schools. However, their views were not shared by many outside the institutions. Even in California, where no tuition was charged, only 56 percent of the respondents to a 1979 survey of the public were aware that credit courses could be taken free (Field Research Corporation, 1979, p. 20). (However, 65 percent of respondents said the courses *should* be tuition-free, after being told that they were.)

After studying the history of tuition charges, Lombardi (1976) concluded that the issue was not whether tuition should be charged but how much. He reported a 1941 survey of a national sample of educators, editors, and other officials that found only a small majority affirming free tuition for public junior colleges. And although the 1947 President's Commission on Higher Education stressed the importance of making public education free through grade 14, nearly all the community colleges organized in the 1950s and 1960s charged tuition. By the 1970s, the Carnegie Commission on Higher Education urged that students pay a larger share of instructional costs as a way of saving the private sector of higher education. As Lombardi (1976) put it, the concept of no tuition was destined to abort early in its development. Perhaps Eells anticipated what was coming when he quoted a speaker at the 1928 annual meeting of the American Association of Junior Colleges who said, "Many people, including those who are careful students of education finance, share the opinion that when the student has monetary investment, he is going to attack the problem of education more seriously than . . . when it is handed to him for the asking" (1931, p. 123).

Well into the 1930s, the difference between tuition costs in two-year colleges and in public universities was not large. Between 28 and 37 percent of two-year colleges were charging less than $50 tuition during the 1920s and 1930s, and most others charged less than $150; the highest was $200. During the 1970s, a student in the typical state saved only around $200-400 in tuition per year by attending a community college rather than a state university. The greater savings accrued to the students who commuted, living at home and working part-time.

During the 1970s community college tuition increased at a higher annual rate than tuition at four-year colleges. By the end of the 1970s, two-year college tuition averaged around 60 percent of the tuition charged in four-year colleges. And whereas the median tuition stayed between $1 and $99 from the beginnings of the community colleges through the 1950s, it moved to $100-199 in the 1960s and $200-299 in the 1970s. By the end of the decade, it was over $300, and 15 percent of colleges were charging $500 or more. Although private colleges still relied heavily on tuition, in public institutions it ranked third, behind state and local tax revenues, as a source of support (Lombardi, 1976).

The pressure for increasing tuition has usually come from state legislators seeking ways of holding down appropriations. Their argument has been that the people who benefit from going to college should pay and that students will take their education more seriously if their own money is at stake. The counterarguments are that the entire population benefits when more of its members have been educated and that equity demands that low-income students not be forced to pay the same tuition as the sons and daughters of wealthy parents, because such charges represent a higher percentage of family income for the former group.

The most common type of tuition is a fixed rate for full-time students and a uniform credit hour rate for all others. When full-time rates are charged, they act as an incentive for students to enroll in more courses per term. Where rates per credit hour are charged, they usually eventuate in the part-timers paying a higher per-course rate.

Whereas tuition usually represents a portion of the costs of instruction, student fees are for special services that may not be required for all students. Optional fees may include use of laboratories or special equipment for certain courses, parking fees, library fines, and special fees for late registration or for changes of program. Some states limit the total amount or the types of fees that colleges may charge, but in others the colleges attempt to collect reimbursements for a wide array of services.

Variations in tuition are wide, depending on the college, the state, and the classification of student. Colleges that derive much of their support locally are usually permitted to establish their own tuition, within certain limits. Out-of-state and foreign students usually pay at a higher rate, as do certain categories of part-time, adult, and evening-division students. In some states at least a minimum tuition must be charged; in others the legislature establishes a maximum. But state policy almost invariably fixes community college tuition at a lower rate than for the public senior institutions because legislators usually want the community colleges to serve as a low-cost alternative for beginning college students.

In the early years, tuition and fees represented a major source of institutional income, but they declined as a percentage of total revenues in the 1950s and 1960s. More recently they have provided a conduit for federal aid that might not otherwise run to the community colleges. And even though mechanisms for distributing state financial aid to students are imperfect because of the limitations on part-time attendance, problems of assessing the financial condition of students' families, and the difficulty in accommodating adult, independent students—all three conditions more prevalent in community colleges than in other sectors—the states have been able to enhance equity by providing funds to the lower-income groups. This has proved a significant method of equalizing opportunity.

In reviewing the issues of equity and efficiency in tuition charges, Breneman and Nelson (1981) argued for a higher-tuition/higher-aid strategy. It is possible for tuition to be set at a level that reflects the balance between private and public benefits and still maintain equity by running financial aid to low-income students. The problem of aid systems that penalize students who enroll for only one or two courses can be offset by a state's paying the tuition for anyone taking a course considered of prime use, as, for example, a person on welfare who takes a course in an occupational program. Increased student aid should properly be used for tuition payments lest the incentive for students to enroll in college and receive financial aid to pay living costs lead to the system's being viewed as an adjunct to welfare. Breneman and Nelson concluded that community college students receive adequate aid, considering that more of them live at home and work while attending school and hence their overall costs are much lower. Questions of students not applying for aid because they are unaware that it is available or because they are overwhelmed by the paperwork involved, and of community college financial aid officers who do not bend all effort to obtain financial aid for their students, cannot readily be tested. Aid offices tend to differ more by institutional size than by type, the smaller colleges having less experienced aid administrators and smaller staffs.

Richardson and Leslie (1980) favored charging different tuition rates for different programs, contending that students in the high-cost, high-demand programs (such as the allied health fields) should pay more. This would not discriminate against low-income groups, since full-time students receive assistance based on the costs of the programs they attend. Richardson and

Leslie also recommended tuition waivers for needy students who are ineligible for outside aid and the elimination of tuition waivers for "the more affluent senior citizen who takes advantage of continuing education or community services" (p. 40).

Problems in Funding

The increases in tuition and financial aid to students and the shifting of the major source of support from local to state tax revenues took place in the context of what numerous commentators called a "financial crisis." Lombardi's (1973c) issue of *New Directions for Community Colleges,* entitled *Meeting the Financial Crisis,* and Richardson and Leslie's 1980 monograph, *The Impossible Dream? Financing Community College's Evolving Mission,* were but two of the many analyses coming from a time when changes in support patterns, coupled with rapidly escalating costs, put community colleges under severe pressure. However, no college was closed for lack of finances. Quite the contrary: 250 new public colleges were opened during the 1970s, and enrollments more than doubled during that decade.

The colleges did experience several fiscal shocks, most notably the well-publicized "taxpayer revolt." Tax-limitation laws were passed in twenty states during the 1970s, some designed to limit the growth of governmental expenditures, others setting ceilings on property tax rates. Both types affected community college support expectations.

California's "Proposition 13," adopted in 1978, was the most highly publicized tax initiative, limiting the property tax to 1 percent of the 1975-1976 assessed valuation, with a maximum of a 2 percent annual increase. Local community college districts found their major sources of funds effectually capped. Their losing $465 million was not as catastrophic as it might have been because the state, having a large surplus in its treasury at the time, bailed them out. But some of the seventy California districts had to make deep cuts in programs and personnel. Many districts canceled their summer sessions. In others, priorities were given to certain programs, the highest priority assigned, typically, to occupational and transfer courses and the lowest to community services and noncredit courses. Community service activities were cut back dramatically.

California taxpayers may have been reacting to a phenomenal rise in property values (and hence taxes) and a state treasury surplus exceeding $5 billion more than they were censuring the publicly supported agencies. Nonetheless, educators were forced suddenly to look to the state for their funds. Within two years the state's share of community college revenues increased from 42 to nearly 80 percent. Several other states, notably Arizona, Colorado, Hawaii, Illinois, and Washington, passed legislation similar to California's Proposition 13.

A shifting funding base was the most dramatic, but not the only, problem affecting community college finance. During the 1970s sizable salary gains were made by instructors working under negotiated contracts, but staff productivity, by any measure, did not increase. This was no surprise to students of educational structures; in fact, Coombs (1968) had outlined an impending educational crisis worldwide because, since teachers' productivity does not rise along with their salaries, the costs per student must rise. Hence, each year an educational system needs more finances simply to accomplish the same results as the previous year. As he put it, "To assume that costs per student will be held at a standstill by far-reaching, economy-producing innovations still to be introduced is to indulge in fantasy" (p. 51). No innovation can rescue educational systems from serious financial difficulty as costs accelerate in what he called one of the last handicraft industries.

Community college administrators had retarded the rapidly accelerating costs of instruction by employing part-time faculty members. Often paid at an hourly rate or at a fixed fee on a per-course basis, these instructors generated high numbers of credit hours at costs as little as one-third the cost of similar courses taught by the full-time faculty. By the end of the 1970s there were as many part-time as full-time instructors.

The fiscal discomfort felt by the institutions' managers was accentuated by the different types of students. Many observers had applauded the institutions' attempts to reach "new students," but few considered the added costs that came along with them. "New or expanded functions of the colleges such as community services, career education programs, special programs for disadvantaged and minority students, financial aid, health services, and counseling accompany the increases in enrollment. Instructional innovation generates experiments, new teaching methods, and technical devices that often cost more money and usually increase the unit cost of education" (Lombardi, 1973b, p. 13). The extra costs of campus law enforcement, utilities, and theft that resulted from offering night classes for part-timers were rarely calculated. And few colleges could properly fund the small classes and personal attention necessary to teach the less well-prepared students who had so swelled enrollments since the 1960s. Even extramurally funded programs added to costs when additional people had to be employed to administer them.

The new students have occasioned new costs. Every increase in enrollment brings demands for special programs for disadvantaged and minority students and for additional student services. It is foolish to expect to serve new populations properly without increasing the operating costs.

Although transferring costs from the local districts to the states seemed merely to shift the problems, not to solve them, some benefits did accrue. As Breneman (1979) noted, because the proportion of school-age children in the population was declining and the proportion of older people increasing, and because state and local governments traditionally have had responsibility for the support of their younger rather than their older citizens, state and local governments would probably be in a better cash position in coming years. Nonetheless, senior institutions had begun competing for lower-income students who brought financial aid with them and for occupationally directed students who found programs of their choice as the universities expanded their career education efforts. This development seemed to presage continuing change in the composition of the community college student body. And by 1980, enrollment ceilings and other limits to growth had been set in place in several states.

Controlling expenditures has been difficult because education is labor-intensive, but it is not impossible. If it were, expenditures would not differ from college to college as much as they do. The per capita cost, the most common measure, is generally derived by dividing the total cost of operation of a college by the number of full-time equivalent students. Sometimes it is determined by cost per credit hour—that is, total cost divided by the number of credit hours taken by students. This concept of per capita costs nearly always refers to current expense of education and rarely to capital-outlay expenditures. The cost per student varies according to the mix of programs that a college offers; some courses cost more than others. Another element of per capita costs is the price of the instructors. Instructors with long tenure and doctorates cost more than those with shorter tenure and without the doctorate.

Bowen (1981) reported considerably less difference in expenditures per student among types of institutions than among different institutions of the same type. Using data from 268 institutions sampled from among those that had reported in the Higher Education General Information Survey in 1976-77, he showed that the median expenditure per full-time freshman or sophomore student equivalent was $2,020 at public research universities, $2,025 at comprehensive universities and colleges, $1,959 at two-year colleges. But the range for public two-year colleges was from $1,102 to $4,150. Data from each state also revealed wide disparities, although the range within states was not nearly as great. Bowen ascribed these differences among community colleges to variance in the relative emphasis on expensive occupational programs and less costly academic programs. However, Marks (1980) found that the costs for humanities courses were increasing because the humanities faculty was stable but was serving proportionally fewer students; the proportion of full-time humanities instructors was increasing, and hence costs per instructor were higher; and decreasing class size in the humanities courses made them more costly than courses outside the humanities, where class size was increasing by comparison.

Where does the money go? A survey of 184 public community colleges provided comparative figures on expenditures during 1978-79. The median spent 61 percent of their budgets on instruction, including faculty salaries, research, library, and academic support. They spent 36 percent on student services, administration, and plant operation and maintenance; less than 4 percent went to utilities (Dickmeyer, 1980).

Solving the Problems

Crisis or no, financial planning became a watchword, and hiring freezes and selective cuts in personnel, equipment, courses, activities, and services were made. Cuts in personnel were the most difficult to effect because of contracts, tenure, and seniority. Managerial efficiency was sought through employing efficiency experts and training staff members in budget management. Colleges also responded to fiscal exigencies through more effective use of physical facilities, including year-round use of buildings and scheduling patterns that distributed class offerings over more of the day. New college buildings became increasingly difficult to justify and the use of rented space ever more prevalent.

Placing faculty members in contact with more students through larger classes or increased teaching hours has been a favored method of increasing faculty productivity, but that has not been an easily implemented reform because of the tradition equating low teaching load with quality. Similarly, the economies desired by introducing reproducible media for instruction have not been readily seen. Some economy in instruction has been effected where faculty members have begun awarding credit for prior experience; the appeal of assessing what students know rather than the time they have spent in the classroom lies in the savings in instructor salaries and cost of facilities.

Several commentators, including Lombardi (1973b, 1979c), Sussman (1978), and Wattenbarger (1978), have listed ways to control expenditures through better planning and, specifically, by reducing the number of low-enrollment classes, restricting staff leaves and travel, employing more hourly-rate faculty members, offering courses in rented facilities off campus, using reproducible media, encouraging early retirement of staff, reducing student support services, such as tutoring, counseling, athletics, and placement, freezing orders for supplies and equipment, and offering credit for experience. But Lombardi cautioned that contracts achieved through collective bargaining would build in salary increases, and new functions and services occasioned by federal monies would add to the fiscal burden "when financing the service that a grant has started with seed money becomes the full responsibility of the college" (1973b, p. 14).

Justifying the Costs

At the outset of the 1980s, notable shifts in the colleges' mission seemed imminent because efforts to reduce expenditures could go only so far. The colleges' tradition of taking all who applied and keeping them as long as they wanted was under attack, the threat by state legislatures of enrollment ceilings if costs per student were not reduced representing a first salvo. The tightening of standards for academic progress in many colleges was a second. Gradually community college advocates were realizing that their proudly voiced claims of unlimited enrollment growth had become passé. As Richardson and Leslie stated, "The current practice of accepting all who apply regardless of the funding authorized conveys several messages to legislators, all of them undesirable. The first message is that quality is not an important concern of the community college. ... A second ... is that very little relationship exists between the amounts appropriated and the numbers of students served" (1980, p. 37). They recommended instead approval for defined functions and first-come, first-serve enrollment procedures—in short, maintaining the open door only to the extent that resources permit and ensuring that quality be a hallmark.

It did seem that enrollment caps would become widespread. Lower schools had no choice in the number of students they admitted; every child not only had a right but by law was required to attend school. Community colleges were different;

they could restrict their enrollments by cutting the variety of programs offered, by "marketing" less vigorously, and through numerous other stratagems, including dismissing students who were not making satisfactory progress toward completing a program. The only question was whether colleges would do so voluntarily or wait until the legislatures mandated the changes.

Some college leaders have recognized that, as Nelson (1980) recounted, political factors are more important than economic factors in determining community college financing. (Echoes of William Allen White's admonition to the farmers of the 1930s: "Raise less corn and more hell!"?) It does seem that the colleges will have to cooperate with other sectors of higher education in order to maintain a united front in the state capitols. This cooperation means they must remain part of higher education and not try to go it alone, because for the remainder of this century, at least, there will be more graduates of the University of California than of Los Angeles City College in Sacramento, more graduates of the University of Florida than of Miami-Dade Community College in Tallahassee. Unfortunately, as Wattenbarger and Starnes remarked, "It is an anomaly, perhaps, that after struggling for fifty years to become an accepted member of 'higher' rather than 'secondary' education, the community colleges now find themselves accepted as part of the level of education for which the public has the most serious questions" (1976, p. 82).

A more active involvement in the local economy can have economic as well as political benefits. Community colleges will have to help the local economy start generating real growth. But there are problems in demonstrating the effects in terms of efficiency and equity. Efficiency relates to the ratio between the benefits deriving from some good or service and the costs of producing it. Equity relates to the extent to which different members of society attain like benefits from public expenditures. In the case of publicly supported education, the two obviously overlap: A highly efficient institution would spend its dollars only on the people who would use their training to make substantially greater incomes, thus paying back significantly more in taxes than their education cost. But such an institution would be inequitable because the members of certain social groups would not receive any of its educational benefits.

How do the community colleges fit in? Economists often categorize school expenditures as investments in general human capital, in specific human capital, and in consumption benefits with little investment value. The classifications "academic," "occupational," and "community service" fit these respective categories rather well. Compensatory programs help people become productive members of society and thus benefit the public by reducing transfer payments. However, the cost is high because of the high-risk nature of the students.

Career programs benefit society because of the increased productivity of the labor force, the higher probability of students' going to work after graduation, and the aid to industries that will stay in an area where a trained work force is available. Thus, although students benefit individually from occupational training, substantial public benefits are also present.

Community services are most likely to be of the consumer education sort, with benefits accruing only to the individual, not to the public. Accordingly, charges for the full cost of providing these services, such as university extension divisions charge, should be assigned to the users. However, certain types of community service or noncredit courses, such as courses on childcare, family nutrition, or energy efficiency, seem to slide over into the category of public benefits.

Aside from the general issues of efficiency and equity, the schools have always had difficulty in determining how well they do when their actual output is measured against their professed aims. Part of the problem has been their inability, or at least their unwillingness, to set their priorities in operational terms. If they were judged solely by the size of enrollments, the criterion used by many advocates, questions of content and quality would not arise. But the legislator, the economist, and the lay citizen might question what the students have been learning, how much, how well, and how fast. And even then an institution may be at once good and bad: good when judged by internal criteria, such as student performance on examinations; bad when judged by relevance to the needs of its surrounding community.

Some attempts have been made to demonstrate more direct economic effects. Bess and others (1980) studied the economic impact of six Illinois community colleges by tabulating college-related business volume, value of local business property because of college-related business, expansion of local bank credit base resulting from college-related deposits, college-related revenues received by local governments, cost of local government services attributed to college-related influences, and number of local jobs and personal income of local citizens from college-related activities. They found a sizable positive effect on all indicators and estimated the difference between the positive impact and the costs to local government of supporting the college and its staff as at least $850 million, projected statewide for fiscal 1978. The greatest effects were in business volume created by the expenditures of the college and in the expansion of bank deposits. The difference among colleges in impact per dollar expended was attributed to the percentage of staff members living in the district, amount of salaries spent within the district, amount of college funds spent in the district, percentage of student body that was full-time, and amount of funds deposited in banks in the district.

Despite the importance of demonstrating value, documenting it has rarely been done. The reasons are not clear, but it is likely that during periods of rapidly expanding budgets and enrollments, college managers believe that the increases themselves speak for the worth of the enterprise. And during periods of decline they have used marketing techniques and political persuasion in attempts to reverse the trend. Carefully controlled studies of institutional efficiency and outcome seem to fall between the planks of advertising, on the one side, and lobbying, on the other.

The world of politics, public relations, and illusion surrounds all public educators who recognize the importance of maintaining an institutional image of fiscal prudence. But a public agency must spend all the money available to it; therefore, an educational system will be as inefficient in its use of resources as it is allowed to be, because efficiency leads to reduction in funding. College managers who learned their craft in an era when those statements were true find it difficult to shift away from that concept, the bedrock of public-agency maintenance. If cuts become necessary, managers try to keep all programs, services, and functions intact in order to avoid the difficult decisions to drop any of them. If further cuts become necessary, they are made where they will be most visible. And larger units, such as multicampus districts, may give the appearance of fiscal prudence because they have fewer top-line administrators, even though the infrastructure may in fact be more expensive.

Issues

College leaders will be forced to face several issues regarding finance in coming years.

What are the inequities among community college districts where the local taxpayers bear a large share of the financial burden? Should stricter limitations be placed on the amount that wealthier districts spend on their community colleges?

How can costs be managed in a labor-intensive enterprise? Bargaining units will restrict the savings that managers formerly gained by employing part-time faculty members and by increasing class size. Reproducible media demand sizable start-up costs and have yet to yield far-reaching financial benefits.

How can accounting procedures document the additional costs to the institution engendered by categorical aid and demands for special programs stemming from external agencies? More broadly, on what grounds can an institution that has prided itself on offering something for everyone refuse to begin a new service even when the costs of providing it exceed the revenues it brings?

Can sufficient funds be generated locally to maintain community education programs? Can a convincing justification be made for switching the funding of community education to the state level? If so, can equitable formulas be found? More broadly stated, what concepts, standards, and definitions actually differentiate between credit and noncredit education?

Does low or no tuition make sense in light of substantial student aid? At what point does tuition without offsetting financial aid reduce equity? What are the actual, as opposed to the conceptual, relations between levels of tuition and institutional efficiency? In brief, can benefits be run to one group without offsetting losses to another?

Compensatory studies and high school completion courses seem destined to occupy a major portion of the community college effort. A plausible case can be made for reorganizing many of them along the lines of the 6-4-4 plan that was in effect in some districts in the early years. How can colleges obtain funds to teach the basic education that was supposed to have been completed in the lower schools?

Those portions of career education that benefit certain industries are difficult to justify on the grounds of efficiency. How can the colleges expand the targeted portions of their occupational education and defray the costs by effecting greater numbers of contracts without irreparably damaging the integrity of a publicly supported institution?

What measures of institutional productivity can be introduced so that increased costs can be justified? Answers to that question depend on the effects the institution is trying to achieve. Can education be defended in its own right, or must the criterion always be the financial return to the students and the community?

Difficult questions all, but the college administrator who would be an educational leader would see them as a challenge and set to them with vigor.

6

Instruction

Old Methods and New Media

The importance of good teaching has been emphasized since the earliest days of the community colleges. College planners never envisioned these institutions as the homes of research scholars. The community colleges could not reasonably expect to influence total student development, because few of them built residence halls, and commuter institutions have minimal environmental impact on students. Nor did custodial care of the young, a major feature of the lower schools, became significant in the community colleges, because attendance was not required. Classroom teaching was the hallmark.

Observers of the community college have reported unanimously that teaching was its *raison d'être*. Koos pointed to the

147

"superiority of teaching skill" found among two-year college instructors because most of them came from the ranks of high school teachers and had their training in pedagogy, unlike their counterparts at the universities (1924, p. 201). Eells called the junior college "a teaching institution *par excellence*" (1931, p. 389). Thornton proclaimed instruction the prime function, saying that it had to be better in the two-year college than in the university because the students covered a broader range of abilities, and their prior academic records tended to be undistinguished: "It is fair to say that most community college students are able to learn but are relatively unpracticed. Under good instruction they can succeed admirably, whereas pedestrian teaching is more likely to discourage and defeat them than it would the more highly motivated freshmen and sophomores in the universities" (1972, p. 42).

Most writers followed their exhortations regarding good teaching with the observation that it was indeed to be found in the two-year colleges. Although rarely heard since the colleges grew large, the pronouncement that instruction was better because of their small classes was often voiced in an earlier time. Numerous allegations of good teaching centered on the instructors, who were considered to be better than those in the universities because their responsibilities were only to teach, not to conduct research, and because their pedagogical preparation was more evident.

Koos reported that "a conservative interpretation of the data . . . would be that *classroom procedure* in junior colleges is assuredly on at least as high a plane as is instruction of freshmen and sophomores in colleges and universities. . . . There are, of course . . . very good and very poor teachers in both groups, but there is no doubt in the writer's mind that junior college teachers as a group are superior in technique" (1924, p. 219). Blocker (1965-1966) merged the findings of two studies of faculty members of community colleges and universities conducted in the early 1960s and, after comparing the qualifications and roles of the groups, noted that both the master's degree and extensive experience in secondary or higher education indicate potentially successful teachers.

The dean of instruction or vice-president for instruction,

as the chief administrative officer for the formal educational program, typifies community colleges' commitment to teaching. The dean usually chairs a curriculum and instruction committee responsible for all major changes in those areas. The committee comprises program heads, department chairpersons, and representatives of the library and counseling services. This assigning of instructional leadership to the administrators has enabled them to coordinate the work of several faculty members and offer incentives through instructional development grants, sabbaticals, and released time to develop new techniques. The administrators can also allocate instructional aides and media production assistants. By the late 1970s, around two thirds of community college instructors had media production facilities that they could use. Other types of perceived available assistance and the extent to which the instructors used them are shown in Table 17.

Table 17. Perceived Availability of Assistance and Use by Instructors (Percentages)

Forms of Assistance	Humanities Instructors (N = 860)		Science Instructors (N = 1,275)	
	Available to	Used by	Available to	Used by
Clerical help	80	59	82	69
Test-scoring facilities	45	17	53	25
Tutors	40	21	51	36
Readers	13	5	11	5
Paraprofessional aides, instructional assistants	13	6	18	14
Media production facilities	68	41	65	38
Library/bibliographical assistance	82	54	64	34
Laboratory assistants	N.A.	N.A.	25	20
Other	3	3	2	2

Sources: Cohen (1978); Cohen and Hill (1978).

Innovation

As the community college developed, innovation in instruction became one of its hallmarks. Johnson (1969), who surveyed community colleges around the country, tabulated the incidence of cooperative work-study education, programmed instruction, audiotutorial teaching, television, dial-access audio systems, instruction by telephone, multistudent response systems, the use of film and radio, gaming and simulation, computer-assisted instruction, and a host of other techniques ranging from electronic pianos to a classroom in the sky. Hardly an instructional medium could be identified that was not in place at some community college.

Television has been one of the most generally adopted teaching tools. Programs have been presented on closed circuit for students in the classrooms and through open circuit for the benefit of the public. Many of the open-circuit televised courses can be taken for college credit, and some institutions generate a sizable proportion of their course enrollments through the use of that medium. Enrollments in the televised courses presented by the Dallas County Community College District alone rose from their beginnings in 1972 to over 10,000 per academic year in eighteen courses in 1978 (Dallas County Community College District, 1979). The Chicago City Colleges organized a TV College in the 1950s, and several other community colleges also received licenses for the cultural enrichment and entertainment of the public.

The community colleges' interest in television led many of them to develop their own materials. Video production facilities were constructed in most of the larger institutions, and numerous staff members were involved in program generation. A few college districts, most notably Miami-Dade (Florida), Coastline (California), Chicago, and Dallas, have become widely recognized for the sophistication of their programming. (Interestingly, whereas a university's prestige often rests on its faculty's scholarship and research discoveries, the export of high-quality television programs provides one of the few ways that a community college can gain a reputation beyond its own district's boundaries.) Interdistrict cooperation in production and distribution of televised courses became common, and several consortia were developed to share programs and production costs.

The advent of the computer gave the colleges another opportunity for instructional innovation. A Washington State report on the use of computers in instruction (Howard and others, 1978) divided patterns of use into (1) computer-based instruction, the use of specialized computer programs, such as models and simulators, in the teaching of economics, business, and engineering, (2) computer-managed instruction, which supports teaching by maintaining student records, administering tests, generating progress reports, and prescribing the most suitable types of instruction, and (3) computer-assisted instruction, the presentation of linear and branching instructional programs. In addition to use of the computer in teaching programming, computer languages, and numerous other courses directly related to computing, it was being used in ancillary fashion in courses in around half the twenty-seven community colleges in the state.

Computer-assisted and computer-managed instruction was adopted in numerous community colleges, often in combination. Thompson (1977) described the Teaching Information Processing System as an elaborate and flexible computer program designed to amplify classroom instruction at Riverside City College (California). The system maintained information on student characteristics and achievement, prescribed remedial or enrichment work, and generated student progress reports in two macroeconomics classes. A Time-Shared Interactive Computer-Controlled Information by Television System, installed at Northern Virginia Community College in 1974, has been used to present the entire course material for college grammar, basic algebra, English composition, and certain mathematics courses while scoring tests, teaching modules, and maintaining records of grades (Sasscer, 1977). The computer at the Community College of the Air Force has been used to maintain a file of student characteristics, aptitude scores, indexes of reading ability, and educational background; select and present the best course material for each student, record student responses, and administer tests and supplemental training; predict students' completion dates; and evaluate and revise the course materials (Campbell, 1977). The Mathematics Learning Center at Miami-Dade Community College used a computer-assisted program that determined the student's preference for audio, tutorial, programmed, or slide/tape materials or workbooks and then presented the student with a series of learning units and tests (Palow, 1979).

Miami-Dade also combined computer-managed and computer-assisted instruction. Its Open College allowed students to enroll in classes, buy course materials, and go through the course work at their own pace without going to the campus except for examinations. Interaction between instructor and student was handled through the computer; information was transmitted through television. The system evolved to include a Response System with Variable Prescription (RSVP), a sophisticated mode of individualizing instruction and recordkeeping. The RSVP package maintained students' records and their responses to various surveys and exams, printed reports to students informing them of their progress, and provided information to instructors about student performance and collective class data. Used both in the Mathematics Learning Center and in English composition courses, the RSVP also delivered personalized letters to students, prodding them to maintain progress. The program was used to diagnose student writing and to provide corrective prescriptions for various types of errors and explanations of basic writing concepts (Miami-Dade Community College, 1979; Emerson, 1978; Kelly and Anandam, 1977).

Several other instructional innovations have been introduced. Instruction in English composition and in mathematics received much attention because of the numbers of students enrolled in the basic courses and because of the apparent difficulties in teaching them to write and to calculate. Laboratories combined a kaleidoscopic variety of media and aides. The mathematics learning center at Tacoma Community College (Washington) included thirty mathematics courses, from arithmetic to calculus, taught in various combinations of independent and tutorial study (Spangler, 1978). Hunter (1977) described innovative composition programs at six community colleges, including a grammar-oriented approach at Houston Community College (Texas), a classroom tutorial approach at Tarrant County Junior College (Texas), and an "applied alternative" at Meramec Community College (Missouri).

Attempts to define and map students' "cognitive style" have received some attention as devices for determining students' best mode of learning and to place them in courses that fit. An educational cognitive-style map based on the work pioneered by Hill at Oakland Community College (Michigan) was prepared for each new student in the allied health division of Spartanburg Technical College (South Carolina) in 1978, and various plans for counseling and teaching the students accordingly were discussed (Atkins, 1978). Mountain View College (Texas) designed a cognitive-style program in 1972 to determine preferred learning styles for the students and aid them in selecting appropriate courses (Ehrhardt, 1980). Funds from the Elementary and Secondary Education Act and the Vocational Education Act were used to bring information on cognitive styles to community colleges in New York, show instructors how to use it, and arrange programs for cognitive-style mapping for the colleges in that state (Martens, 1975; Rotundo, 1976).

Traditional Instruction

It is reasonable to assume that in an institution dedicated since its inception to "good teaching," new instructional forms will be tried. However, despite the spread of reproducible media, most students still meet traditional methods of instruction. Visitors to a campus might be shown the mathematics laboratories, the media production facilities, and the students working through computer-assisted instructional programs, but on the way to those installations they will pass dozens of classrooms with instructors lecturing and conducting discussions just as they and their predecessors have been doing for decades.

The drive toward innovative instruction is not without its detractors. Many faculty members continue to believe that close personal contact with them is the most valuable, flexible instructional form that can be developed. Purdy's (1973) in-depth study of the faculty at a college widely known for its audiotutorial laboratories, computer-programmed course segments, video cassettes, and other reproducible media (a national magazine dubbed it "Electronic U") revealed a sizable group resistant to all those media. Cohen (1970) found that the instructors in three colleges believed their personality was the most important component of their instruction. And 27 percent of the 2,135 respondents to the CSCC studies of humanities, sciences, social sciences, and technologies in 175 colleges thought "smaller classes" made for better instruction.

Other findings from the CSCC studies showed widespread use of reproducible media, but they were being used as adjuncts to traditional instructional methods. Over half the instructors reported that they had their students view or listen to filmed or taped media at least part of the time, but lecturing was the most prevalent teaching form, and class discussion ranked second. The textbook was, of course, the most frequently used reading material. Student grades were based, for the most part, on examinations and written papers. Quick-score or objective tests accounted for a sizable portion of student grades in around half the classes, and essay exams were a prime determinant of grades in slightly under half. Detailed information on instructional practices is given in Tables 18 through 21. Information for each

Table 18. Use of Class Time for Activities

	Humanities		Science/Social Science	
Activity	Percentage of Instructors Using	Percentage of Class Time by Instructors Using Activity	Percentage of Instructors Using	Percentage of Class Time by Instructors Using Activity
Own lectures	96	46	94	48
Guest lecturers	25	7	12	6
Student presentations	49	17	25	10
Class discussion	91	23	81	18
Viewing or listening to media	68	14	46	9
Simulation/gaming	19	10	10	9
Quizzes/examinations	87	9	88	11
Field trips	14	6	10	7
Lecture/demonstration experiments	N.A.	N.A.	29	11
Student laboratory experiments	N.A.	N.A.	34	33
Laboratory practical exams/quizzes	N.A.	N.A.	19	9
Other	11	29	13	38

Source: Center for the Study of Community Colleges (1978b).

Table 19. Percentage of Classes Using Instructional Media
Frequently or Never

Medium	Humanities		Science/ Social Science	
	Fre- quently	Never	Fre- quently	Never
Films	13	22	9	44
Single-concept film loops	1	65	1	68
Filmstrips	6	40	3	64
Slides	12	34	8	54
Audiotape/slide/film combinations	5	45	3	62
Overhead projected transparencies	11	45	20	39
Audiotapes, cassettes, records	18	26	3	62
Videotapes	4	46	3	63
Television (broadcast/closed circuit)	2	55	1	72
Maps, charts, illustrations, displays	36	13	20	31
Three-dimensional models	2	60	10	47
Scientific instruments	N.A.	N.A.	18	44
Natural preserved or living speci- mens	N.A.	N.A.	9	64
Lecture or demonstration experi- ments involving chemical reagents or physical apparatus	N.A.	N.A.	10	54
Other	5	0	6	1

Sources: Cohen (1978); Cohen and Hill (1978).

academic discipline is presented separately in "Instructional Practices in the Humanities and Sciences" (Cohen and Brawer, 1981).

For several reasons, although many instructors have adopted the new media, more have not. Changing instructional techniques is difficult and time-consuming; the manager of student learning must put in more hours than the instructor who delivers ad hoc lectures. Innovators must prove the positive effects of their techniques, while traditionalists can usually go their way without question. Teaching as a profession has not developed to the point at which proper conduct in the instructional process can be defined and enforced in the face of individual deviation. Hence, whereas lower teaching loads would allow more time for instructional reform, they would not be sufficient to revise instruction; merely giving people more time to do what they are bent to do does not change the perception of their role.

Table 20. Percentages of Classes Using Certain Reading Materials and
Average Number of Pages Students Were Required to Read

	Humanities		Science/ Social Science	
Reading Material	Percentage Using	Average No. Pages	Percentage Using	Average No. Pages
Textbooks and other assigned reading	94	442	95	308
Lab materials and workbooks	23	95	44	101
Collections of readings	34	182	14	126
Reference books	28	130	22	114
Journal and/or magazine articles	32	59	25	23
Newspapers	19	38	11	22
Syllabi and handout material	70	30	62	29
Problem books	N.A.	N.A.	10	90
Other	10	243	8	121

Sources: Cohen (1978); Cohen and Hill (1978).

Table 21. Percentages of Classes in Which Certain Activities
Accounted for 25 Percent or More of Students' Grades

Activity	Humanities	Science/ Social Science
Papers written outside class	28	9
Papers written in class	12	5
Quick-score/objective tests	41	60
Essay tests	47	41
Field reports	3	2
Oral recitations	10	2
Workbook completion	2	4
Regular class attendance	10	3
Participation in class discussions	14	2
Laboratory reports	N.A.	10

Sources: Cohen (1978); Cohen and Hill (1978).

Moreover, not all innovations in instruction have met with success. Some were greeted with apathy by the faculty at large, and when the initiators tired of them, the innovations died. Others were promoted by administrators who wished to give their colleges an image as forward-moving structures but were unable to persuade the faculty to use the hardware. In some institutions the faculty blamed the administrators for everything from a film projector that broke down to a television studio constructed with funds that faculty members felt belonged in their salaries. Other innovations were dropped because of the expenses involved; the preparation and maintenance of instructional programs presented through reproducible media has never been as economical as some of its promoters claimed it would be.

Some innovations, such as allowing students to drop out of class without penalty, had untoward consequences. Nonpunitive grading was adopted widely in the 1970s, but effectually abandoning failing grades and replacing them with "Withdrawn" or "No Credit" fostered grade inflation and distortion in transferring credits between institutions. The practice may also have contributed to the students' taking a casual approach to their studies.

Learning Resource Centers

The community college library has long been recognized as an important instructional service. Johnson (1939) called it the heart of the college and recommended numerous ways it might become central to the instructional process. Although none of the libraries developed collections of research materials, they did provide books and periodicals sufficient for a textbook-oriented institution. Table 22 presents data on the libraries in the seven largest community college states.

Many community college libraries underwent a major transformation during the 1960s and 1970s, when they became learning resource centers (LRCs). In some colleges this meant only that the library remained intact, but with facilities added for individual study through the use of self-instructional programs. But in many, totally new LRCs were built to encompass a library, audiovisual materials, distribution, graphic and photographic reproduction, video production, audio and video learning laboratories, tutorial services, and a learning assistance cen-

Table 22. Public Two-Year College Library Holdings and
Average Holdings per Student in Selected States

State	Number of Colleges	Avg. No. Students per College	Holdings			Avg. Holdings per Student
			High	Low	Average	
California	98	9,643	155,587	505	56,912	5.9
Florida	28	5,331	254,121	11,294	60,595	11.4
Illinois	48	4,861	80,866	8,979	34,739	7.1
Michigan	30	5,514	158,940	10,000	45,428	8.2
New York	44	5,662	119,662	21,552	54,028	9.5
Texas	54	3,580	144,459	2,928	36,119	10.1
Washington	27	4,220	58,316	4,750	31,106	7.4

Sources: National Center for Education Statistics (1975); American Association of Community and Junior Colleges, *Community, Junior, and Technical College Directory* (1976, 1979).

ter. About a third of the LRCs also had career information centers and computer-assisted-instruction terminals. Table 23 shows the services offered.

The expansion of learning resource centers took place

Table 23. Services Offered in New Two-Year College Learning Centers

Service	1971-72 (N = 47)		1973-76 (N = 108)		1976-77 (N = 34)	
	No. of Centers	%	No. of Centers	%	No. of Centers	%
Library	42	89	98	91	34	100
Audiovisual distribution	41	87	102	94	33	97
Audio learning laboratory	36	77	86	80	26	76
Graphic and photographic production	32	68	79	73	28	82
Audio/video production	30	64	86	80	33	97
Tutorial services	20	43	53	49	21	62
Skills/learning assistance center	18	38	56	52	22	65
Video learning lab	18	38	63	58	22	65
Reprography (other than copy machine)	15	32	44	41	16	47
Career information center	N.A.	—	46	43	15	44

Source: Henderson and Schick (1973, 1977, 1978).

predominantly in the larger community colleges. Bock (1978) reported that thirty-one new LRCs or major remodeling projects were constructed in the year ending June 30, 1978. But a nationwide study of community college presidents found the heads of the smaller institutions still placing greater importance on their librarians' knowledge of books and printed materials, whereas the presidents of the larger colleges emphasized audiovisual materials and library automation (Wallace, 1977).

Because most LRCs included nonprint instructional programs, their staffs became heavily engaged in instructional development, and their directors became prominent in instructional management. Jensen (1978) studied the LRCs in fifteen California community colleges and found instructional development a function in three fourths of them. The LRC staff also had to be aware of the problems of providing special materials and access for handicapped students, and an instrument for assessing such services was developed (Association of College and Research Libraries, 1978).

Problems of converting libraries to learning resource centers in order to provide not only materials but also instructional services were exacerbated by the expansion of courses offered off campus and in satellite centers. Coupled with the general move toward the use of reproducible media in community colleges, this extension of the instructional program to numerous localities in the district led to an increase in the percentage of the operating budget devoted to the LRC. Learning resource center expenditures increased from 3.3 percent of the community colleges' operating budgets in 1965 to 4.7 percent in 1975.

To expand their services beyond the confines of the buildings in which they were housed, the LRCs augmented the proportions of their budgets for producing print and nonprint materials. They also organized remote-access information retrieval systems, so that people could dial in or otherwise call up bibliographic and instructional materials through terminals located away from the collection. However, sophisticated systems were in place at few institutions; according to a survey conducted by Stevens (1977), only one in eight California community college LRCs provided special services to off-campus courses. Although centers in some of the other colleges offered delivery service, in most the instructors of off-campus courses who wanted audiovisual equipment or instructional materials had to go to the campus to get them. Most of the directors reported that they did not have sufficient funds to provide special services to off-campus courses, this despite the fact that 82 percent of the colleges offered courses off campus.

During the 1970s, LRC staffs spent less time in building the collections and teaching people how to use the library and more in participating in the broader instructional program. A Michigan study identified these changes between 1971 and 1977 (Platte, 1979, p. 40). Because of their central position in the acquisition of instructional materials in both print and nonprint forms, the learning resource centers in many colleges had a marked effect on the shape of the entire instructional program.

The Technology of Instruction

One of the most persistent ideas in education is that individualization must be the goal in every instructional program. Numerous articles have begun with the statement "Let's assume that the best ratio of teachers to learners is one to one" and then gone on to explain how one or another instructional strategy might be tailored to fit each student. The most extreme version of individualization was realized when colleges began granting credit for experience gained anywhere. Core courses taught in singular fashion and required of everyone were at an opposite extreme. Each had its proponents and both were seen, often in the same institutions.

A technology of instruction in which goals are specified and a variety of learning paths designed so that most students may reach those goals offered a compromise. A variety of learning outcomes and instructional strategies allowed students to decide whether they wanted to be involved in the programs and, at the same time, enhanced the credibility of the institutions as teaching and learning enterprises. By 1980 it was evident that some community colleges were making distinct efforts to restore their legitimacy by tightening their expectations of stu-

dent progress and by effecting a variety of instructional strategies to accommodate different types of learners (McCabe,
1981).

A technology of instruction made some inroads during
the 1970s, but progress was slow. The definitions of *instruction*
in use offer a clue. *Instruction* may be defined simply as "implementing the curriculum." This definition assumes a sequence
of courses that must be brought to the students. Another definition of *instruction* is "a sequence of events organized deliberately so that learning occurs." This definition does not depend on
a curriculum, but it does include the word *learning,* and it implies a process leading to an outcome. But most instructors
seemed still to define *instruction* as an activity, not a process.
Defining it as a set of activities (lecturing, conducting discussions, cajoling, and so on) in which teachers typically engage removes both the courses and the learners from the definition.

Regardless of the medium employed, the basic model of
instructional technology includes clearly specified learning outcomes or objectives, content deployed in relatively small portions, learning tasks arrayed in sequence, a variety of modes of
presenting information, frequent feedback on student performance, and criterion tests at the ends of instructional units. The
instructors are part of the technology of instruction when they
define the objectives, write the tests, select and/or present the
media, and, in general, connect the student to the learning
tasks.

The technology of instruction has been important for
two-year colleges, typically commuter institutions, in which the
environment of a learning community is not available to exercise its subtle, yet powerful, influence on the students. The
tools basic to an instructional technology have been available
ever since words were first put on paper. The expansion in variety and use of other forms of reproducible media made additional sets of tools available. However, the concepts of instructional technology have been less widely adopted. It is as though
new types of hammers, saws, and trowels had been taken up by
artisans unaware of the shape of the houses they were attempting to construct.

The beginnings of a technology of instruction have been realized in the institutions that have adopted competency-based instruction and its companion form, mastery learning. Both demand converting the learning desired of the students into specific abilities or tasks that they can demonstrate at the conclusion of the sequences. A notable effort on behalf of both strategies was made during the 1970s, when the Fund for the Improvement of Post-Secondary Education sponsored a Competency-Based Undergraduate Education Project. It built on decades of efforts to define the competencies to be exhibited by the graduates of academic programs. The occupational programs rarely had difficulty in specifying the accuracy with which a student was expected to caulk a pipe or type a letter.

However, specifying tangible, desired outcomes has often been perceived as a precarious exercise. The span from broadly stated college goals to tasks to be performed by students at the end of a portion of a course is long, and the connections may be difficult to make. The links between "Making people better," "Helping them cope with society," "Training them for jobs," "Preparing them for clerical positions," and "Students will type 70 words per minute" may be too tenuous. A technology of instruction puts responsibility for learning jointly in the hands of instructors and students; both must participate. Perhaps educators despair of being called to account if they fail. Teaching is not like building a wall; the chances are good that a brick will remain in place, whereas the influences on students, the myriad impressions they receive in addition to their instruction, the predispositions they bring to the task—all can change program results.

Yet the search for a technology of instruction applicable to an institution with a heterogeneity of students has continued, and with good reason. As Drucker said, "Teaching is the only major occupation of man for which we have not yet developed tools that make an average person capable of competency and performance" (1969. p. 338). He was concerned about the perennial search for "better teachers," saying that we cannot hope to get them in quantity: "In no area of human endeavor have we ever been able to upgrade the human race. We get better results by giving the same people the right tools and by organizing their work properly" (p. 338). Drucker's plea was for a technology of instruction that would improve teaching by making it depend more on better techniques than on better people.

Mastery Learning. Mastery learning, a technology of instruction in itself, was described and advocated by several educators, especially by Benjamin Bloom of the University of Chicago. The intent of mastery learning is to lead all students to specified competencies (as opposed to programs that have the effect of sorting students along a continuum of individual ability). In a mastery learning plan, competencies are specified in the form of learning objectives. Practice tests, corrective feedback, additional learning time for those who need it, and a variety of instructional techniques are provided to ensure that all, or at least most, of the students attain mastery of the concepts or skills at the prescribed standard.

Proponents of mastery learning have pointed to sizable cognitive and affective gains made by students who have studied under it. Not only students' test scores but also their personal development has been affected. The gains have been attributed to any or all of the following: more-focused teaching; cooperation instead of competitiveness among students; the definition of specific learning objectives; the amount of class time actually spent in learning; practice and feedback before the graded examinations; and teachers' expectations that most students will attain mastery.

Mastery learning procedures have been adopted in some community college courses and programs, but the concept has not swept the field. Many reasons can be advanced for the failure of this technology of instruction to become more prevalent. Faculty members and administrators who have shied away from mastery learning offer several: It costs too much to develop and operate programs with a sufficient variety of instructional forms; it takes too much of teachers' and tutors' time; outcomes for most courses cannot be defined or specified in advance; the effect of allowing students time to complete course objectives runs counter to school calendars; students may not be motivated if they are not in competition with their fellows for grades; the institution that passes all its students through at prescribed levels of competency is at variance with public perception of institutional purpose and employers' expectations; accrediting agencies and other overseers demand differential grades. Froh and Muraki (1980), who interviewed 40 of the 200 instructors who had been introduced to mastery learning strategies at workshops sponsored by the University of Chicago and the Chicago City Colleges, found that around one third of them had modified or abandoned the components, saying that it was too time-consuming to construct program specifications and tests and to give necessary feedback to the students.

Regardless of the validity of the arguments set forth by proponents and by antagonists of mastery learning, the concept would seem to have a firm place in a teaching institution. If mastery learning can bring most students to the criterion levels, as specified in learning objectives, why should it not be installed? The answer may be that many people within the community colleges see themselves as gatekeepers for the universities and the employers, denying certification to many in order to accredit the few who will achieve at the succeeding institution or place of work. This attitude runs deep in an institution that for most of its history has had to defend itself against charges that it was not a true college. "Haven't the best colleges always sorted their students so that only the brightest went on to the most prominent careers? What would happen to our students if we did not prepare them for the competitiveness that exists in universities where mastery learning is not in place? How would our students fare in the competitive world of work?" So run the objections.

Competency-Based Instruction. Another technology, competency-based instruction, has also made inroads in community colleges. Competency-based instruction depends also on the specification of desired competencies to be exhibited by the students, but it does not include all the specific instructional strategies of mastery learning. The Competency-Based Undergraduate Education Project wrestled with defining the outcomes of liberal education. Ewens (1977) found a paradox in attempting to convert liberal education to competencies. It was the seemingly insoluble dilemma of converting higher education from an ideal-referenced standard to criterion-referenced or norm-referenced standards. "Ideal-referenced judgments presuppose some notion of the good, the excellent, the higher, the best," but most education now deals with minimal competencies, functioning in an environment, meeting acceptable standards of behavior (p. 19). There is no room for the ideal when we ask "What is a competent person?" The dilemma appears with force in the tendency of all education to teach job-related skills. One's job is what one *does*; one's work is what one *is*. If education teaches for jobs, ignoring what the person is, it runs the risk of creating a corps of dissatisfied graduates when they find that a job is not enough for a satisfactory life—not to mention the issue of whether they find jobs at a level for which they were trained.

The competency-based movement could assist in reforming general education in community colleges. Defining just what students will be able to do when they have completed a general education program has been done with some success. However, it has occurred in institutions where faculty members can work face to face in groups that are both small enough to facilitate communication and large enough to encompass a critical number of the college's entire staff—that is, small colleges. The large-scale media productions have been undertaken in institutions that have a sufficiently large student body to pay for production, marketing, and presentation of the instructional package or program. Unless the community colleges build smaller campuses and satellite centers and allow the staff members at those centers to define their own curriculum specifications, their efforts in instructional reform seem destined to continue to be centered on media development.

Effecting Instructional Reform. The most successful programs have several elements in common, even when they are not based on a technology of instruction. Many of the career programs include programmatic funding from outside the college; examinations administered by an external licensing bureau; criterion-based achievement examinations designed and administered by the faculty; follow-up surveys of student job entry, success, and attitudes toward the program; special admissions requirements; entrance and diagnostic examinations; sequenced courses required of all matriculants; and staff identification with the program. These components are usually combined in a program administered by a specially designated coordinator or chairperson. The instructors associated with such a program work together as a unit, often in specially designed facilities. And the more successful the program, the more the program head and the instructors are in control of its various components: student recruitment, admissions, and job placement; course content; selection of instructional technologies; relations with licensing and accrediting agencies; and budgetary expenditures.

These program components are more a function of organization than of different forms of instruction. Yet in combination they exert a powerful influence on their staff and students. By contrast, it is difficult to counsel students into a curriculum when it is in fact a set of separate courses, to select or mandate particular instructional forms when the outcomes desired for the curriculum are vaguely stated, or to manage such a program when a request coming from a dean or a chairperson may be considered, accepted, or rejected by the instructor, who is actually the arbiter of the course and hence of the entire curriculum for those students in it. Courses for the baccalaureate-bound students are more often than not discrete, each with its own goals, media, and standards. The collegiate curriculum is more a myriad of miniature curricula than a program. The technology of instruction in community colleges rests more on the form of a program's organization than on the teaching devices it employs.

Is the community college the home of "good teaching?" Information on the effects of instruction is always hard to obtain because of the number of variables that must be controlled in any study: the entering abilities of the students, the criterion tests and instructional procedures used, and the level of the course or learning unit, to name only a few. Comparative studies are especially difficult because of the unfeasibility of matching student groups and instructional presentations (are any two lecture sessions really the same?). Rather than try to compare learning attained, many studies have used student and instructor preferences as the dependent variable. The value of computer-assisted instruction has been measured by asking students whether they preferred it to live lectures, and the reports usually indicated that many students prefer the interpersonal contact with instructors, while many others do quite well with the instructional programs presented through the computer. But pre- and postinstructional assessments of student learning rarely yield significant differences between treatments, and few researchers in community colleges report this type of study. As one reporter noted after reviewing the literature describing the various ways of teaching remedial mathematics, although comparative studies showed no significant results from using alternative methods, benefits in student attitudes toward mathematics seemed a prime outcome (Pearlman, 1977).

The long-term effects of community colleges on the learning patterns of their clients are difficult to discern. How do people respond when they may drop in and out of an institution, a program, or a course at will, making no advance commitment, receiving no penalty for failure to complete anything? Might students not respond with "Well, if it doesn't matter to them when or whether I complete this course, why should it matter to me?" There was certainly evidence of a casual approach to course attendance and course completion on the part of community college students in the 1970s, when the average number of credit hours per student per term dropped annually.

Nonetheless, judging from the spread of learning resource centers, mathematics laboratories, and large-scale media production units, instruction seems still a major concern. The drawbacks of further development of instructional technologies relate to both staff predilections and program organization. The inducements stem from the instructors and administrators alike who appreciate the significance of the felicitous description that Thornton applied to the community college: "Either it teaches excellently, or it fails completely" (1972, p. 42).

Issues

The major issues in instruction center on the extent to which a technology of instruction will progress. Will more instructors adopt instruction as a process instead of an activity? What types of instructional leadership can best effect this change?

How will the spread of low-cost computers affect instruction? To what extent will they be adopted outside science and math labs?

Will administrator-dominated instructional management evolve? How much responsibility should the learning resource center director have for the entire instructional program? Will instructors gain control over more of the essential elements of instruction?

The consequences of a turn away from print as the primary mode of information transmission have not yet been fully realized. What impact on instruction will be made by students who have gained much of their prior knowledge through nonprint sources? Does an instructional program centered on teachers in classrooms best accommodate them?

Mastery learning has been effected in compensatory and career education. Can it spread to the collegiate function?

Although each new instructional medium, from the radio to the computer, has forced educators to examine their teaching practices, none alone has revolutionized teaching. A general acceptance of instruction as a process that must, by definition, lead to learning might do more in actualizing the prime function of the community colleges.

7

Student
Services

*Providing Adequate
Assistance*

In addition to instruction, the colleges engage in numerous other services and functions. Some, such as counseling and extracurricular activities provided for the direct benefit of students, are often linked under the heading "student personnel services." Others, including institutional research and articulation with other schools, are maintained less directly for the students than for the support of the college as a whole. Taken together, all these activities can be categorized as student services.

Student Personnel Services

The rationale for student personnel services stemmed originally from the institution's need to regulate its clients' activities. According to O'Banion, "One of the historical models for the student personnel worker is that of regulator or repressor. The student personnel profession came into being largely because the president needed help in regulating student behavior" (1971, p. 8). In other words, students need to be controlled for the sake of institutional order, a rationale underlying not only the counseling of students into the proper programs but also the registration, student activities, orientation, student government, and recordkeeping functions.

However, the rationale evolved so that the student personnel services were presumed to be more positively supportive of student development. According to Collins, who reported findings of the Committee on Appraisal and Development of Junior College Student Personnel Programs, "The student personnel program should be the pivot, the hub, the core around which the whole enterprise moves. It provides the structure and creates the pervasive atmosphere which prompts the junior college to label itself as student-centered" (1967, p. 13). Surveying the programs in 123 colleges between 1963 and 1965, the committee identified twenty-one "essential student personnel functions" that should be provided if the colleges were to fulfill their mission of teaching and directing their vast array of students. The functions were categorized as *orientation* (precollege information, student induction, group orientation, career information), *appraisal* (personnel records, educational testing, applicant appraisal, health appraisal), *consultation* (student counseling, student advisement, applicant counseling), *participation* (cocurricular activities, student self-government), *regulation* (student registration, academic regulation, social regulation), *service* (financial aid, placement), and *organizational* (program articulation, in-service education, program evaluation).

Several similar listings of student services have been published. Humphreys (1952) offered six major categories; Thornton (1972) divided the services into five categories; and, more recently, a manual for student services issued by the Washington State Board for Community College Education (Heiner and Nelson, 1977) offered ideal philosophies, goals, objectives, functions, and staffing patterns for the administration of student services, dividing them into eight areas.

Counseling and Guidance. Counseling and guidance have been at the core of student personnel services since the earliest years. Eells (1931) gave guidance a status equal to the "popularizing," "preparatory," and "terminal" functions in his list of the junior college's main activities. The contention has been that community college students are different from the traditional college groups, the affective is as important as the cognitive, students need help in moving into the college and out again into careers and other schools, and individualized instruction through counseling and other nonclassroom-based activities is essential.

Riesman (1981) asserted that guidance is essential because people from traditional college-going populations cannot realize the insecurity felt by students who may want to attend further school but who are terrified at the idea of going to "college." These students may not realize they have more choices than simply the closest community college; a branch campus a few miles away may offer programs better suited for them, while they remain unaware of the differences among institutions. It is also important to counsel these students while they are in community colleges about the possibilities of their going on to senior institutions.

Guidance has always been intended to match applicants to the programs best suited to their own goals and abilities. Medsker (1960) emphasized the necessity of placing students in the programs that are best suited for them. Thornton (1972) found the purpose of guidance to be "to help each student to know, to accept, and to respect his own abilities, so that he may match them with realistic educational and occupational goals" (p. 269). The 1966 edition of his book had carried an even stronger statement: "Until effective counseling procedures are developed to enable students to choose a college objective much more intelligently than they do, a large part of the efforts of the community junior colleges will be dissipated on students with unrealistic objectives" (p. 152), but, perhaps as a result of the college disruptions in the late 1960s, this remark was deleted from Thornton's later book.

The belief that students deserve more than cognitive development in a rigid environment has also guided practitioners.

The expressions "treating the student as a whole" and "assuming responsibility for the full intellectual, social, and personal development of students" are frequently seen in the student personnel literature. By definition, these professionals try to effect student development in psychic, moral, and physical, as well as intellectual, realms. To student personnel advocates, students are not minds apart from their bodies and emotions; they are whole people, and the college should treat them as such.

Helfgot's (n.d.) rationale for guidance was based on a broad view of student development. He contended that the educational process must facilitate the total human development of its clientele rather than simply consider the "student part" of the individual. As the key element in student development, counseling must be integrated with other campus activities, must maximize students' chances to reach their potential, must focus on educational, personal, social, and vocational development, and, being student-centered, must take into account students' interests, aptitudes, needs, values, and potential. Comprehensive counseling should include goal setting, personal assessment, development of change strategies, strategy implementation, evaluation, and recycling of the whole process for each student.

Articulated also by numerous others, this therapeutic view affirms the belief that the best way to educate people is to integrate all their objectives and all their ways of functioning—cognitive, affective, and psychomotor. It holds that students are active and responsible participants in their educational growth and process, that with help and support students must make decisions affecting their lives and must deal with the consequences of their decisions, and that all professionals on the campus must work collaboratively toward greater integration of their services and their professions. In this approach counseling is not imposed on students but initiated and determined by them. It works in partnership with classroom instruction and cocurricular activities. In this student development process, goals are set, the individual's current position in relation to these goals is assessed, the best change strategy or a combination of strategies is implemented; the effectiveness of the strategy is evaluated in terms of meeting the individual's goals, new goals are set, and the process begins all over again (Helfgot, p. 22).

Unresolved conflict remains between guiding students into the programs most consonant with their abilities and allowing them to reach for their own preferred goals. Many students have wanted to go in one direction but seemed best qualified to go in another. Guidance counselors have devised procedures for ascertaining student goals and assessing student qualifications, trying all the while to strike the proper balance between goals and abilities. But when students appear without distinct career or study goals, when their goals do not match their abilities, or when the testing instruments do not adequately assess them (and all three often come into play at the same time), the role of the counselor has been blurred. When students have decried discrimination and demanded the right to enter any program, the guidance function has staggered. And when institutional policies allow most students access to all but the programs with limited space or limitations imposed by external accrediting agencies, guidance workers have to adjust.

The guidance function suffered further in the 1970s when the proportion of full-time students declined. It was set up to work best with full-time students seeking direction in program planning and career choice; it operates least well when a part-time student takes only one or two courses at a time. And the easier it is to enter classes, withdraw at will, and reenter other classes, the more the students can act as their own guides. They may suffer a loss in time and money, but there are no institutionally imposed academic penalties for wrong choices.

Some critics have taken guidance counselors to task on broader issues. Gay (1977), for example, argued that "while student personnel workers have professed themselves to be educators and to be interested in the whole student, they have served essentially as housekeepers, guardians of the status quo, and have been seen by many in the postsecondary education arena as petty administrators or 'those people who sit in their office and give warm strokes to students who complain about the system, particularly the teacher.' . . . In their present capacities, student affairs workers are clearly providing services, needed services, which contribute to student mobility; but whether or not some of the mundane tasks necessary to the services now rendered are wise use of the skills and talents of counselors and other specialists of student affairs is another question" (p. 18).

And Brick's (1972) review of O'Banion and Thurston's book on student personnel services stated: "At no point does any author whose work is included in this book question the idea that there should be student personnel programs in the community junior college, nor does any author directly deal with the issue of which social agencies should be responsible for the operation of which social services. For example, it is unfortunate that a question such as 'Is psychological counseling an educational function which should be implemented by an educational institution, or is it a public health function which should be implemented by a public health agency?' is not considered in this volume" (p. 677).

Still, counseling and guidance services have been maintained in nearly all community colleges. Morrison and Ferrante (1973) extrapolated from twenty-five colleges to all colleges with the results shown in Table 24. The services will undoubted-

Table 24. Counseling Services at Public Two-Year Colleges, 1970

Service	Percentage
Personal counseling	98.4
Academic counseling	98.4
Vocational-occupational counseling	98.0
Job placement counseling	93.2
Job placement follow-up counseling	69.2

Source: Morrison and Ferrante (1973).

ly continue, but the question of the proper ratio of counselors to students may never be resolved. Collins (1967) recommended 1 to 500 in the smaller colleges, 1 to 300 in the larger ones—ratios no easier to justify than the proper class size.

Recruitment and Orientation. During the 1970s student personnel workers were heavily engaged in devising programs to recruit and retain students. As examples, Reedley College (California) identified certain students to receive intensive counseling. Students who were accorded these special counseling services were less likely to withdraw from school (Clark, 1979). Moraine Valley Community College (Illinois) opened a special program for recruitment and retention. The recruiting activities involved the staff in visiting high schools, bringing students to the campus, and preparing displays advertising the college in shopping centers, while the staff also worked with associate deans and faculty members in determining how to keep students in school (DeCosmo, 1978). The Florida State Department of Education developed a manual replete with ideas for community colleges wishing to retain their students, emphasizing administrators' commitment to retention, course scheduling, and services that might encourage students to stay in school (Farmer, 1980). Reimal (1976) found counseling, childcare services, and block classes important for retaining women students in thirteen northern California colleges, especially when these activities were coordinated through women's reentry programs.

Student personnel workers also planned and operated student orientation programs. Several patterns were described by O'Banion (1971): sessions offered during the summer preceding the term, in one- or two-day sessions at the beginning of the term, in classes meeting throughout the first term, and in seminars for special groups of students. One college offered a three-day retreat for the first 150 freshmen to sign up with faculty members, who helped in leading the activities. Another maintained a series of lectures on issues of concern to students each week throughout the term. Orientation in many colleges was the responsibility of the counselors, who set up small sessions to inform students of college policies. Some colleges had orientation committees composed of faculty members, students, and student personnel administrators, who planned various events for beginning students.

Frequently, student orientation accompanies a psychology course for which credit is awarded. Counselors and instructors often participate jointly in these courses, teaching study skills, career exploration, and individual goal orientation. They may also use psychological-test batteries designed to apprise the students of their own personality profiles and teach study skills and various strategies for "surviving" in college. There have been fewer mass sessions at which new students are welcomed to the college by the president, board members, and other dignitaries and given directions and a listing of the college rules. Session planners have come to realize that such occasions are more ceremonial than instructive.

Programmed instruction booklets have proved useful in helping students plan their course work; the efficacy of orientation through a self-paced instruction book was demonstrated at Mississippi Gulf Coast Junior College, where students learned more about the college through using those materials than comparable students in orientation lectures (Fisher, 1975). However, no single orientation method has proved uniformly satisfactory, and one college often adopts a procedure just as another is abandoning it.

Extracurricular Activities. Various types of extracurricular activities for students have been in place in community colleges since the earliest institutions organized student clubs and athletic events. Eells (1931) listed numerous student activities in the junior colleges of the 1920s, mentioning in particular Pasadena Junior College (California), in which seventy clubs were active. The most popular were athletic clubs, with literary groups, musical activities, and religious and moral organizations following. Eells found science organizations most common in the public institutions, but he reported camera clubs, pep clubs, honor clubs, and so on operating throughout the colleges of the day.

Although all colleges have had student clubs and extracurricular activities, few of them developed programs in which sizable percentages of the students participated. A survey at Johnson County Community College (Kansas) found students recognizing the importance of student activities but not participating because of lack of time and interest (Tolbert, 1971). Fewer than half the students in the Los Angeles Community College District expressed any interest at all in extracurricular activities (Weiser, 1977). Students enrolled in off-campus centers of Prince George's Community College (Maryland) were even less likely to want to take part in extracurricular events (Larkin, 1977c). Kegel (1977) surveyed community colleges nationwide and found part-time students often barred from participation in extracurricular activities even though two thirds of the colleges charged them student activity fees. Rinck (1969) found that married students who commuted to campus were less likely to participate in extracurricular activities at Gateway Technical Institute (Wisconsin); age, work responsibilities, and full-time student status, however, were not significant in determining differences in participation.

Several reasons explain why student activities programs are difficult to organize in community colleges: Freshmen and sophomores lack the leadership experience of university upperclassmen; many students work part-time; few reside on campus; only two years are available to develop student leaders; and many high school leaders elect to attend universities instead of community colleges. These reasons are obvious; the full effect of a campus environment is not available to students who spend little more than an hour or two a day in class. Such students often spend more time working and commuting than full-time students in residential colleges spend on class preparation. And because commuter students spend most of their time away from the campus, other attractions, especially jobs and noncampus activities, make great claims on their time and interests. It is difficult to entice them to participate in activities or attend events other than those that coincide with the time they would be on campus for classes anyway. Community college student personnel directors often consider their activities program a success if only as many as 10 percent of the students participate.

In spite of these handicaps, there have been some vigorous attempts to build student activities programs: providing student leadership training programs, with workshops on group dynamics and communications skills; involving students as full voting members of faculty committees; assigning greater responsibilities to student government organizations, including their legal incorporation; assigning faculty members to student associations as consultants rather than as advisers; instructing student government representatives in procedures for polling student opinion on pertinent issues; requiring orientation courses with emphasis on student activities; developing a strong college art collection and sponsoring frequent, well-publicized exhibitions; and involving students in encounter-group sessions with faculty members and administrators (O'Banion, 1971).

All these plans have been implemented from time to time by student activities coordinators. As an example, recognizing that the high percentage of students attending college in the evening needed activities programs especially tailored for them, Los Angeles City College created a special student board to handle all business and financial matters for the evening students. The group sponsored its own shows and events, with evening students as performers. It also sponsored student memberships in off-campus civic, cultural, and professional organizations so that student representatives could conveniently attend the meetings.

Some commentators have called for student activities and organizations centering on academic departments. Graham (1962) said that such arrangements would help students make vocational choices by bringing them together in clubs and on field trips. Goldberg (1973), however, deplored the inappropriateness of student activities programs as operated at most colleges, arguing that few students participated in the events that their activity fee supported and concluding that the fee should be erased or at least reduced to a token amount. He proposed that instead of charging the students, each college department should have a proportion of its budget allocated for activities other than classroom instruction. This arrangement would involve instructors in publicizing the speakers, seminars, and concerts and in tying the events in with the course work. Such a plan would seem to have merit; most of the respondents to the Center for the Study of Community Colleges' surveys of the faculty indicated there were too few humanities-related colloquia, seminars, lectures, exhibitions, or concerts and recitals offered outside class; few instructors required attendance at out-of-class activities. Departmentally sponsored events would undoubtedly attract more student and faculty interest.

Studies of student athletic activities have found wide variance in the emphasis given to intercollegiate athletics and, indeed, to physical education in general. Blamer (1967) surveyed physical education programs in community colleges nationwide, dividing them into general physical education services, intramural activities, and intercollegiate programs, and found provisions for instruction and equipment varying greatly. Similarly, differences in the types of services offered were reported by Stier (1971). During the 1970s most institutions continued offering intramural team sports for interested students, but as the colleges increased their efforts to attract older, part-time students, these activities declined. Student activities began centering less on team sports, more on individual pursuits. Clubs and ad hoc groups organized to engage in hiking, cycling, scuba diving, backpacking, and jogging became widespread. Exercise classes open to staff members as well as students also sprang up as the concern for physical fitness grew among people of all ages.

Residence Halls. Although the community college residence hall became rarer as the institutions grew in urban areas, it has persisted, with dormitories found in at least a few colleges in most states. In 1977 all public junior colleges in Mississippi except one had dormitories, and 14 percent of students lived on campus (Moody and Busby, 1978). Richardson and Leslie (1980) recommended a return to residence halls as a way of coping with the growing costs of commuting. They also suggested the importance of bringing students to campuses where technological programs requiring laboratory-based instruction could be offered, saying that that was necessary in sparsely settled areas.

Financial Aid. Financial aid for students became an outstanding feature in the 1970s. Federal and state funds administered through Basic Educational Opportunity Grants, Supplementary Educational Opportunity Grants, National Direct Student Loans, Guaranteed Student Loans, and the College Work Study programs grew throughout the decade. Some observers noted that community college students were discriminated against because of program restrictions. For example, some federal programs required that recipients be enrolled at least half-

time, but over 40 percent of community college students registered for fewer than six credits. Others required that they be enrolled for at least six months, or in some cases one year, in a
program leading to a degree or certificate. Some admitted only
those having the equivalent of a high school diploma. And state
student aid programs generally excluded part-time students even
more than did the federal programs. Both state and federal aid
programs were geared to low-income, younger students, whereas the trend in community college enrollments was toward
part-time adults.

Two-year institutions, both public and private, received
less than 16 percent of the federal funds in the middle 1970s
even though they enrolled over 25 percent of all full-time students and over 53 percent of all full-time first-time freshmen
with family income under $10,000. The U.S. Office of Educa-
tion indicated that community colleges had a higher percentage
of students who were potentially eligible for basic grants than
four-year colleges, but they had a much lower percentage of potentially eligible students who actually participated in the programs. Eligibility not only required full-time attendance, it also
depended on institutional action. Nelson (1976) reported that
many two-year institutions simply did not apply for participation in the campus-based programs, while those that did appeared to be asking for less money than their students actually
needed. One reason was the continuing misperception that community college education was free or nearly free and that, therefore, students did not need financial assistance. However, students still had to spend money to live, still commuted to classes,
and, by attending school, were forgoing income that they could
otherwise have earned.

From their survey of several California colleges, Hunter
and Sheldon (1979) reported that 12 percent of the students indicated that money would be a problem for them while they
were enrolled, this in a state that has no tuition charge. However, only 42 percent of those who indicated that money would
be a problem were receiving financial aid from one or another
of the various sources available through the colleges. And 24
percent of those who said money would be a problem were not

aware that the college they were attending had a financial aid office. An Arkansas study found only 485 community college students, compared with 18,185 senior college students, who received aid in 1973-74 (Glover and Chapman, 1975).

Nelson (1976) designated "the most critical factor in the successful administration of student aid in postsecondary education . . . the skill of the person responsible for the administration of the programs and the confidence placed in him or her by the senior officials of the institution" (p. 6). However, his inquiries into the status of financial aid showed that very few institutions felt that they had adequate staff to cover the responsibilities of student aid; some aid officers deliberately understated their requests for aid funds because they felt that it would add to an impossible work load. This report is at variance with Morrison and Ferrante's finding (1973) that more than 90 percent of academically disadvantaged minority students in public colleges were receiving some form of aid. Although white students also received a high proportion of financial aid, they tended to be overrepresented in the group receiving scholarships, as opposed to grants. A Florida study found that black students constituted 14 percent of the community college enrollment in that state but 36 percent of all aid recipients; white students made up 78 percent of the enrollments and 53 percent of the aid recipients (Florida State Department of Education, 1979).

Richardson and Leslie (1980) suggested that community college students are not treated fairly in comparison with university students because student aid was developed in the late 1960s and early 1970s, when most students were young and single or recently married and were enrolled in programs leading to the bachelor's degree. They presented data showing the differential figures (Table 25).

But Nelson (1979), who argued that overawarding of aid to community college students might, in fact, be occurring, enumerated three potential causes: too generous standards for determining cost of attendance; too generous income exclusions of veterans' benefits in calculating expected family contributions; and excessive aid in states where federal and state aid is

Table 25. Distribution of Full-Time Freshman Students, Student
Financial Aid Recipients, and Average Amount of Student Aid,
1972-73

| | Distribution | | | Average Aid Amounts | |
| | Total Full-Time Students (percent) | From Any Source (percent) | Federal (percent) | From Any Source (dollars) | Federal (dollars) |
Institutional Type					
Public four-year	43.3	42.7	41.6	960	921
Public two-year	27.7	23.1	17.2	636	733
Private four-year	21.7	26.8	33.7	1,703	1,400
Private two-year	2.3	2.2	2.2	1,007	876
Vocational	1.7	1.2	0.7	672	654
Other/proprietary	3.3	3.9	4.5	1,664	1,639
	100.0	100.0	100.0		

Source: National Center for Education Statistics (1975, cited in Richardson and Leslie, 1980, p. 27).

uncoordinated. Thus, "there is no evidence that community college students are at a disadvantage in receiving basic grants compared to their counterparts at other institutions" (p. 28), even though current financial assistance programs met a lower fraction of needs for community college students than for those attending either senior public institutions or private colleges. Richardson and Leslie summed up their contentions by saying, "Perhaps it would be more accurate to state that community colleges are not net gainers under student aid" (p. 49). They reported that adult students, who made up so much of the population in a community college, were estimated to receive only 15 percent of student aid funds and concluded that "less than one fifth of adult postsecondary students receive student aid compared to almost half of traditional full-time students" (p. 49).

Student abuse of the financial aid system has often been hinted at but rarely documented. The charge has been made that many students enroll merely for the funds available to them and that student aid thus represents another form of welfare payment. If this were so, the dropout rate for students re-

ceiving financial aid should be lower than the rate for comparable students not receiving such funds. A study conducted at
Central Florida Community College found no difference in the
withdrawal rates of students receiving financial aid and those
who were not (Sutton, 1975), whereas one at North Greenville
College (South Carolina) found a positive correlation between
receipt of financial aid and students' persistence and graduation
rate (Silver, 1978). The findings have, thus, been inconclusive;
moreover, since such a high proportion of community college
students receive funds, the possibilities of comparing groups of
recipients and nonrecipients are limited.

Articulation

Program articulation refers to the movement of students
and, more precisely, the students' academic credits from one
school to another. Articulation is not a linear sequencing or pro-
gression from one point to another. It covers students going
from high school to college; from two-year colleges to universities and vice versa, variously called stopouts or returning transfer students; the double-reverse transfer students, who go from
the two-year college to the university and then back again; the
intercollege interuniversity transfers; the vocational-technical
education majors; and the people seeking credit for experiential
learning as a basis for college or university credit. The concept
includes admission, exclusion, readmission, advising, counseling,
planning, curriculum, and course and credit evaluation.

Until recently, articulation has been largely a one-way situation, a series of policies and procedures dictated by senior institutions. Before 1960, coordinated efforts to improve the
plight of the transfer student were "almost nonexistent. While
articulation agreements between senior colleges and universities
and high schools were generally well developed, programs centering attention on the two-year college graduate were scarce"
(Kintzer, 1973, p. 5). Three styles of articulation agreements
operate in the fifty states: formal and legal policies; state-system
policies, in which the state tends to be the controlling agency;
and voluntary agreements among institutions, whose main fea-

tures are cooperation and negotiation rather than unilateral declaration or legislative statute.

Because the purposes of articulation are to facilitate the flow of students, coordinate programs among institutions, and minimize course duplication and overlap, nearly everyone in the college community is affected. Most of the problems in articulation have centered on the questions "Who decides?," "What shall be the criteria?," and "Who shall have the ultimate authority?" As community colleges have drawn an increasing proportion of entering freshmen, the problems have grown more complex.

Knoell and Medsker (1965) urged the development of master plans at the state level to define institutional roles and plan coordinated curricula because the proper matching of transfer student and institution was probably more important than the matching of freshman student and institution. Wattenbarger (1972) reported that transfer students usually performed in a manner similar to their past patterns of accomplishment; probation and dismissal policies were sometimes discriminatory against transfer students; problems of inadequate goals and finances and lack of self-confidence, which may have influenced students to select a two-year college near home in the first place, did not change when they transferred; students completing two-year associate degree programs were more successful as transfers than those who transferred before completing the two years; most senior institutions had done little to examine policies that discriminated against the transfer student; academic bookkeeping procedures (computing grade-point averages into a single mean) had little validity in predicting desirable outcomes for a college education; the community college served as a second-chance institution for students who would not have been admitted into the university as freshmen; and counselors in two-year colleges and in institutions granting baccalaureate degrees must be in constant contact to facilitate transfer.

Kintzer (1973) felt that articulation was essential but that community colleges should be encouraged to develop their own programs: "Work in the two institutions need not and should not be parallel or imitative, but equal rigor is certainly advisable if a transfer student is to have a fair opportunity to compete in the upper division. Few community colleges, however, have faced the obligation of providing equal opportunity to succeed" (p. 14). He found the problems in articulation as expressed by community college personnel to be that community colleges were not free to develop their own programs; the universities exerted continuing pressure to conform to their guidelines; universities sometimes failed to recognize that transfer students made comparable grades at the university and, therefore, continued to require higher grades of the next group of transfers; universities impeded smooth articulation by formalizing curricular changes arbitrarily, rather than cooperating with the community colleges and giving them reasonable lead time; universities did not offer orientation periods for transfer students; and universities made the associate degree an absolute requirement in some programs and limited enrollment of transfer students. But the university-based respondents felt that the evaluation of community college credit should be made by the baccalaureate-granting institutions and complained that two-year colleges often mixed subcollege with college material in their courses and classified these as credit courses.

The articulation problem has been the topic of several statewide studies. Robinson (1977) discussed the impact of transfers from community colleges to universities in North Carolina, saying that little had been done to ease the flow of students and recommending a transfer expediter who would move from college to college on a prearranged schedule to work with students planning to transfer. A Kentucky study (Kentucky Council on Public Higher Education, 1977) found three sets of problems: the lack of adequate program articulation between postsecondary institutions of different types, particularly between postsecondary vocational or proprietary institutions and the more traditional institutions; the lack of adequate credit for transferring individual courses and application toward degree programs; and the lack of uniformity among institutions evaluating nonacademic or nontraditional experiences for credit in degree programs. Recommendations included establishing a permanent statewide articulation committee to review and recommend policies and articulation agreements, developing course-equivalency guides similar to those currently in use at many institutions, forming a committee at each college to respond to articulation problems, developing a guidebook to explain both institutional and statewide transfer procedures, and establishing mechanisms for the evaluation of credits. Articulation problems in Pennsylvania were found to center both on moving students from one institution to another and on the sharing of facilities and services between colleges. But most community college presidents reported good communication networks between their institutions and the nearby high schools and vocational schools as well as plans for allowing students to stop out before transferring and for the awarding of credit for life experiences (Senier, 1978).

Formalized articulation agreements have spread, hastened by the trend toward coordination by state boards or councils for community college education or for other types of public higher education. In states where upper-division universities have been built, articulation agreements spelling out rules of transfer have been an obvious necessity. A study of the fourteen Southern states (Southern Regional Education Board, 1979) uncovered more than fifty coordinated programs through which students might move from community colleges to senior institutions in technical and career-oriented fields. Although there was little uniformity in the specifics of the joint arrangements, the states with the most programs were those where the state higher education agencies played an important role in developing such programs. Courses taken at state vocational schools tended not to be accepted by the universities. And agreements on a common core of general education courses have been negotiated between the community colleges and universities in several states, most notably Florida and Oklahoma, where periodic renegotiation has been used to keep them current.

Educators concerned with articulation have also had to consider reverse transfers, a large and growing group of community college students. As an example, 16 percent of students at Northampton County Area Community College (Pennsylvania) in 1979 had taken prior courses at a senior college. Most had been full-time students at the university but were part-timers at the community college (Rooth, 1979). The effectiveness of community colleges in aiding students who had transferred to a senior institution, failed academically, returned to the community college, and then reentered the senior institution was analyzed by Grafton and Roy (1980), who found that the students were more successful the second time around. Drakulich and Karlen (1980) reported that reverse transfers at Essex County College (New Jersey) were more certain of their educational plans and had higher career aspirations, suggesting the importance of allowing students ready access. And Temple (1978) argued that the two-year college's contribution to the achievement of reverse transfer students was greater than the university's and hence that the senior institutions must bend their efforts toward making their curricula compatible.

In brief, community college practitioners in the 1970s became much more sensitive to their being the dominant force in mass education, and they deplored the university's lethargy in program articulation. They felt more like equal partners, less willing to be dictated to by senior-institution-based academic specialists whose failures returned to the two-year colleges for successful experiences. But problems of articulation seemed to arise more quickly than interinstitutional committees and state coordinating boards could resolve them, especially as the performance of community college transfers to universities declined. And most instructors and student personnel specialists at both institutions seemed to shrink from requiring standardized tests at the junior level for natives and transfers alike.

One promising move both to stabilize community college entrance and to smooth the way for ultimate transfer was taken by Miami-Dade Community College, which undertook a comprehensive effort in the late 1970s to screen students into certain courses at entry and monitor their progress throughout their tenure at the college (Harper and others, 1981; Kelly, 1981). Previous institutional practices had allowed students to take any courses and to stay at the institution indefinitely, whether or not they were proceeding toward program completion. In the new plan, students were advised of the requirements both for graduation from the college and for transfer to various programs in Florida's universities. The system was mandatory: everyone who matriculated, except those who already had degrees and were taking courses for personal interest, was included in it.

Some internal resistance to the plan came initially from fear that enrollment would decline. And as soon as the strict probation and suspension rules were adopted, Miami-Dade dropped from its rolls several thousand students who were not making satisfactory progress (McCabe, 1981). It cost the institution about 5 percent of its students, or 700 FTE annually, after the number of students who were advised to drop out and the increased loads taken by students who remained in the system were balanced off. But although some students were dropped, many more were helped.

The system added measurably to the counseling load, but it also tended to get the faculty back into the academic advisement process. It made registration less easy; no longer could a student merely drop in and take a course. It did not discriminate against minority students; indeed, completion rates for those groups were improved measurably. As an example, 17 percent of the students and 14 percent of the graduates were black, suggesting that the black students, who began at a lower level of prior academic achievement, were being pulled up.

Issues

As a whole, the college's services to students have grown faster than the instructional activities, but the various services have shown different patterns. Counseling and guidance declined early in the 1970s in response to students' demands to be admitted to courses of their choice and to the increase in part-time students, but these services showed signs of increasing in the 1980s as tight budgets and competition from other schools forced community colleges into streamlining their procedures for guiding students through the system. Recruitment and retention also became prominent concerns of the student personnel staff, which was gradually adopting concepts other than those set down by theorists whose model was the full-time resident student. Articulation has become more important as coordination of all education in each state has developed.

However, not all student services have expanded. Student activities supporters have not been able to convert their programs to fit commuting students, and much of what they formerly did has been adopted by community service directors, a trend in keeping with the expansion of the colleges from campus to community. Financial aid accelerated dramatically during the 1970s, but the rate of growth seemed destined to slow as fewer unrestricted funds were made available.

The challenge for college leaders has been to maintain a balance among all services and coordinate them with the formal instructional program. But issues of educational philosophy swirl around the questions of student personnel work. How much responsibility does the college have for the lives of its students? How personalized can an institution dedicated to mass education afford to get?

Although between-sector comparisons are precarious because of differences in institutional mission, the question whether community college students receive as much aid as their university counterparts has not been resolved.

Program articulation with the secondary schools will have to be expanded. Can the articulation committee members eventually realize that fitting the college's courses to the senior institution's requirements is not the most important, and certainly not the only, job they must do?

The necessity for student personnel workers to explain the implications of the changed student body to the faculty has long been present. How can they educate the faculty more effectively? As an example, how can they assist the faculty in making the instructional modifications necessary to accommodate the increasing numbers of handicapped students?

University training programs for community college student personnel workers have rarely fit the realities of the institutions in which the trainees will work. How can the programs be modified? To what extent can the community colleges train their own staff?

The concepts underlying student activities stem from an era long past. How can programs be restructured to fit the adult, part-time, nonresident student body that predominates in community colleges?

Answers to these questions will determine the future course of student services in the community colleges. As with all other questions of the types of services that community colleges provide, the answers rest on the energy and political skills of the advocates of one or another service. And that, above all, is why the services vary as much as they do in colleges across the country.

8

Career
Education

*Preparing Students
for Occupations*

A group of prominent citizens called together by the American Association of Junior Colleges (AAJC) in 1964 to serve as a National Advisory Committee on the Junior College concluded that "the two-year college offers unparalleled promise for expanding educational opportunity through the provision of comprehensive programs embracing job training as well as traditional liberal arts and general education" (American Association of Junior Colleges, 1964, p. 14). The committee recommended that "immediate steps be taken to reinforce occupational education efforts" (p. 1), a statement similar to those emanating from many other commissions and advisory groups, including the AAJC's own Commission on Terminal Education a quarter century earlier. Its words were notable only because they came at a time when the floodgates had just opened and a tide of career education programs was beginning to inundate the two-year colleges.

The year 1963 marked the federal Vocational Education Act, which broadened the criteria for federal aid to the schools. Along with the new criteria, Congress appropriated funds generously—$43 million in 1968, $707 million in 1972, and $981 million in 1974—and these funds were augmented with additional monies for occupational programs for the disadvantaged and for handicapped students. On this surge of monies occupational education swept into the colleges in a fashion dreamed of and pleaded for but never before realized by its advocates.

Early Development

Calls for occupational education in the two-year colleges had been made from their earliest days. In 1900 Harper had suggested that "many students who might not have the courage to enter upon a course of four years' study would be willing to do the two years of work before entering business or the professional school" (cited in Brick, 1965, p. 18). The founders of the junior colleges in California had indicated that one purpose of their institutions was to provide terminal programs in agriculture, technical studies, manual training, and the domestic arts. Lange had indicated that the junior colleges would train the technicians occupying the middle ground between manual laborers and professional people. And Koos described and applauded the occupational curricula in the junior colleges of the early 1920s.

Arguments on behalf of occupational education were raised at the earliest gatherings of the American Association of Junior Colleges. At its organizational meeting in 1920 and at nearly every meeting throughout the 1920s and 1930s, occupational education was on the agenda. Brick traced these discussions and noted that "the AAJC was aware that it had to take a leadership role in directing the movement for terminal education" (p. 120). He quoted Colvert, who, in a 1941 address, had admonished junior college educators for not encouraging the national government to fund occupational education for people of junior college age: "Had not we of the junior college been so busy trying to offer courses which would get our graduates into the senior colleges instead of working and offering appropriate and practical courses—terminal courses—for the vast majority of junior college students, we might have thought to ask for, and as a result of having asked, received the privilege of training these young people" (cited in Brick, 1965, p. 121).

The association itself had been diligent. In 1939 it created a Commission on Junior College Terminal Education, which proceeded to study terminal (primarily occupational) education, hold workshops and conferences on its behalf, and issue three books summarizing junior college efforts in its area of interest. Much had been done, but as the commission noted, more remained to do: "At the present time probably about one third of all the curricular offerings in the junior colleges of the country are in the nonacademic or terminal fields. Doubtless this situation is far short of the ideal, but it shows a steady and healthy growth in the right direction" (Eells, 1941a, pp. 22-23).

The commission prepared a Statement of Fundamental Principles: "The junior college . . . essentially a community institution . . . has a special obligation to meet fully the needs of its own constituency . . . [and because] the junior college marks the completion of formal education for a large and increasing proportion of young people . . . it should offer curricula designed to develop economic, social, civic, and personal competence." To meet this responsibility, the commission members dedicated their efforts "to aid junior colleges to formulate suggested curricula which . . . will meet the educational needs of youth who will complete their formal education in the junior college" (Eells, 1941b, p. 1).

In 1940 terminal programs were offered in about 70 percent of the colleges. The most widely offered included business and secretarial studies, music, teaching, general courses, and home economics. About one third of the terminal students were in business studies; enrollments in agriculture and home economics were quite low. Tables 26 and 27 present data on the numbers of colleges and programs.

The terminology of career education has never been exact:

Table 26. Percentage of Total Curricular Offerings Classified as
Terminal or Vocational in Junior Colleges, 1917-1937

	All Junior Colleges		Public Junior Colleges		Private Junior Colleges	
Investigator	Number of Colleges	% of Offerings Terminal	Number of Colleges	% of Offerings Terminal	Number of Colleges	% of Offerings Terminal
McDowell (1917)	47	14	19	18	28	9
Koos (1921)	58	29	23	31	35	25
Hollingsworth-Eells (1930)	279	32	129	33	150	29
Colvert (1937)	–	–	195	35	–	–

Source: Eells (1941a, p. 22).

The words *terminal, vocational, technical, semiprofessional, occupational,* and *career* have all been used interchangeably or in combination, as in *vocational-technical.* To the commission and the colleges of 1940, *terminal* meant all studies not applicable to the baccalaureate, but programs designed to lead to employment dominated the category. Earlier, *vocational* had generally been used for curricula preparing people for work in agriculture, the trades, and sales. But because it usually connoted less-than-college-level studies, most community college educators eschewed the term. *Semiprofessional* typically referred to engineering technicians, general assistants, laboratory technicians, and other people in manufacturing, business, and service occupations. *Technical* implied preparation for work in scientific and industrial fields. *Occupational* seemed to encompass the greatest number of programs and, along with *career,* was used most often by the 1970s for all curricula leading to employment.

Although the college-parallel (collegiate) function was dominant in community colleges until the late 1960s, the structure for career education had been present from the start. The community college authorization acts in most states had tended to recognize both. The California District Law of 1921 allowed junior colleges to provide college preparatory instruction; training for agricultural, industrial, commercial, homemaking, and

Table 27. Number of Students Enrolled in Each Terminal Field, 1938-39

| Group | Number Enrolled in All Terminal Curricula | | | | | | Number Enrolled in | | | | | |
		Gen. Cultural	Agri-culture	Busi-ness	Engi-neering	Fine Arts	Health Services	Home Economics	Jour-nalism	Public Service	Miscel-laneous
All institutions	41,507	6,205	1,673	14,511	4,449	3,406	1,603	1,387	808	6,500	965
Public	30,261	4,724	1,631	11,278	3,915	2,341	1,029	876	673	3,033	761
Private	11,246	1,481	42	3,233	534	1,065	574	511	135	3,467	204

Source: Eells (1941a, p. 239).

other vocations; and civic and liberal education. The 1937 Colorado act defined a junior college as an institution providing studies beyond the twelfth grade along with vocational education. Mississippi required that the junior college curriculum include agriculture, home economics, commerce, and mechanical arts. By 1940 nearly half the state junior college laws enacted specifically set forth the terminal functions along with the college-parallel studies. And the national and regional accrediting associations of the time also wrote that provision into their rules.

However, student enrollments did not reach parity. Well into the 1950s, occupational program enrollments accounted for only one fourth or less of the whole. In 1929, 20 percent of the students in California and 23 percent in Texas were in terminal programs (Eells, 1941a, p. 24), and not all of those were in occupational studies; the figures include high school postgraduate courses for "civic responsibility." Eells (1941a) reported 35 percent in terminal curricula in 1938, but when nonvocational terminal curricula are excluded, the percentage drops to less than 25. As late as 1960, Venn pointed out that only one fourth of community college students were enrolled in occupational programs, half of them in California and New York and another 20 percent in Illinois, Michigan, and Pennsylvania (Monroe, 1972). Table 28 recounts the proportions for later years.

Table 28. Two-Year College Terminal-Occupational Program Enrollments as a Percentage of Total Enrollments, 1963-1975

Year	Total Enrollments	Terminal-Occupational Program Enrollments	Percentage of Total	Percentage Increase
1963	847,572	219,766	26	—
1965	1,176,852	331,608	28	50.9
1969	1,981,150	448,229	23	35.2
1970	2,227,214	593,226	27	32.3
1971	2,491,420	760,590	31	28.2
1972	2,670,934	873,933	33	14.9
1973	3,033,761	1,020,183	34	16.7
1974	3,428,642	1,134,896	33	11.2
1975	4,001,970	1,389,516	35	22.4

Source: U.S. Department of Health, Education and Welfare (1963-1975).

These statistics were disappointing to national leaders. Eells, one of the strongest proponents of terminal education and ordinarily optimistic about its future, admitted that "recognition of the terminal function . . . existed more as aspiration in the minds of administrators than as realization in the experience of students and parents" (1941a, p. 18). He reported that although 75 percent of students entering junior college as freshmen did not continue beyond the sophomore year and hence were terminal students by definition, only about one third of them were enrolled in terminal curricula. "The difference of these two figures shows that *more than 40 percent of all junior college students are enrolled in curricula which are not planned primarily to best meet their needs*" (Eells, 1941a, p. 59). In an earlier book he had quoted numerous state department of education and university officials who indicated that at least 60 percent of the students would benefit most from vocational studies (1931, pp. 288-289).

Limitations

Why did the career programs fail to flourish before the 1960s? First, their terminal nature was emphasized, and that tended to turn potential students away; few wanted to foreclose their option for further studies. For most students, going to college meant striving for the baccalaureate, the "legitimate" degree. That concept of collegiate education had been firmly established.

Another handicap to the growth of career programs was the small size of the colleges. Average enrollment remained below 1,000 until 1946. Colleges with low enrollments could not offer many occupational courses; the costs were too high. Eells (1941a) reported a direct relation between size and occupational enrollments—small colleges (up to 99 students) had 10 percent in terminal curricula; medium colleges (100-499 students), 32 percent; large colleges (500-999), 34 percent; and very large colleges (1,000 and over), 38 percent.

A third reason for limited terminal offerings was the association of many early junior colleges with high schools. In these colleges administrators favored collegiate courses because they were more attractive to high school students than vocational courses, they entailed no new facilities or equipment, they could be combined with fourth-year high school courses in order to bolster enrollments, and they would not require the hiring of new teachers.

The prestige factor was important. Most of the new junior colleges were opened in cities and towns where no college had existed before. Citizens and educators alike wanted theirs to be a "real college." If it could not itself offer the bachelor's degree, it could at least provide the first two years of study leading toward one. In the eyes of the public, a college was not a manual training shop. Well into the 1960s, college presidents reported with pride the percentage of their faculty holding doctoral degrees.

Costs were an important factor. Many career programs used expensive, special facilities: clinics, machine tools, automotive repair shops, welding equipment. By comparison, collegiate studies were cheap. The transfer courses had always been taught in interchangeable classrooms. The same chairs and chalkboards, and often the same teachers, can be used for English, history, or mathematics.

For all these reasons, and despite the efforts of Eells and his commission and subsequent AAJC activities, college leaders did not rally around the calls for terminal occupational studies. In some states—Mississippi, for example, where occupational education was a requisite, and California, where the institutions were large enough to mount comprehensive programs in both occupational and collegiate studies—occupational education did well. But in the smaller institutions in states where the popularizing function, the function of promoting higher education, was dominant, sizable career programs were not developed. The demands for trained personnel occasioned by World War II provided an impetus for occupational education as the colleges of the time participated in pilot training programs and programs to prepare workers for war industries. But the college-parallel courses remained paramount.

Exhortations

Calls for change continued, with the impetus provided by other national commissions. In 1944 the Educational Policies Commission of the National Education Association published a report, *Education for All American Youth,* stressing the desirability of one or two years of occupational education. In 1947 the President's Commission on Higher Education recommended an increase in the number of community colleges so that students who might not benefit from a full four-year course of studies could attain an education enabling them to take their place in the American work force. The commission recommended the expansion of terminal programs for civic and social responsibility and occupational programs that would prepare skilled, semiprofessional, and technical workers.

And the AAJC-affiliated advocates of occupational education pressed unrelentingly for more vocational curricula and courses and for greater efforts to encourage students to enroll in them. For example, in the chapter "Development of the Junior College Movement" in the second edition of *American Junior Colleges,* Ward devoted twelve lines to the college transfer function but more than a page and a half to the status of technical education. She observed that despite the growing interest in and "the overwhelming need for terminal education . . . the development of these courses generally has been very slow" (Ward, 1948, p. 15). In fact, she felt it safe to generalize "that effective terminal courses have never been offered in sufficient numbers to meet the need for them—that is, terminal courses which provide education both for an occupation and for personal adequacy" (p. 14). Jesse Bogue, executive secretary of the AAJC, urged the colleges to "strike out boldly, demonstrate that they are not bound by tradition or the desire to ape senior colleges for the sake of a totally false notion of academic respectability." He warned educators that unless they acted, legislatures would follow Texas's example of setting a minimum of "40 percent of programs . . . in so-called terminal fields [to] qualify for state aid" (1950, p. 313).

Other writers supported occupational studies. Starrak and Hughes (1954) tabulated the hindrances to the introduction of terminal courses (traditional entrance requirements, accrediting agencies, lack of qualified instructors, expense, and social discrimination between the two groups of students) but concluded, "In view of the magnitude and urgency of the need to be served by terminal curricula, these hindrances do not seem to be extremely significant nor impossible to overcome. . . . There has been outstanding success by the few junior colleges which have wholeheartedly attacked the problem of providing vocational-technical instruction of a terminal character, avowedly without sacrificing their regular college preparatory offerings" (pp. 40-41). They quoted Hollinshead, who had noted in 1940 that "if junior colleges instead of trying to imitate the four programs would offer courses close to the interest of the student, and suited to his abilities, they would begin to occupy one of the most important places in American education" (p. 40).

Increase in Occupational Enrollments

The major shift that began in the second half of the 1960s is revealed in the enrollment figures. The Bureau of Labor Statistics reported in 1968 that 40 percent of all full-time and part-time students in two-year colleges were enrolled in career programs (Bushnell, 1973). Since the early 1970s, Parker's annual survey of selected two-year institutions has reported that more than half of the students were enrolled in career programs (Parker, 1974). (Because of varying definitions, these figures diverge widely from those reported on page 196.)

As reported in Lombardi's monograph *Resurgence of Occupational Education* (1978a), data from several states showed that beginning in the mid 1970s, the rise in occupational enrollment more than kept pace with the large increase in total enrollment and in most states outstripped the rise in transfer enrollment (see Table 29). However, Lombardi cautioned that enrollment statistics are not reported uniformly between states: The unit of measurement—head count, unduplicated head count, full-time equivalent—varies; some data indicate opening fall enrollments,

Table 29. Enrollment in Career Programs as a Percentage
of Total Enrollment in Selected States

State	Year	Percentage Career Enrollment
Florida	1970	24
	1975	28
Illinois	1969	26
	1976	33
Iowa	1968	37
	1975	48
Massachusetts	1967	44
	1974	59
Mississippi	1972	30
	1975	33
Washington	1967	27
	1974	47

Source: Lombardi (1978a).

others fiscal-year enrollments; and the states differ in classification of students and in the kind of student enrollment reported.

Sizable increases were found in several states not shown in Table 29 (Lombardi, 1978a). For example, enrollment in occupational programs in California jumped by 38 percent in 1970-71 over 1969-70 and continued growing by 6 to 7 percent annually until 1974-75. In 1968, 47 percent of North Carolina students were enrolled in technical programs, 29 percent in vocational, and 24 percent in college transfer; in 1974 enrollments in technical programs increased to 57 percent, while enrollments in vocational and transfer each fell by 5 percent. In 1975 occupational enrollments in Virginia represented approximately 51 percent of the total.

College reports confirm the shift from transfer to vocational programs. In a five-year study of day class enrollments at Los Angeles City College between 1970 and 1974, Gold (1975) found that enrollments increased in twelve of seventeen career departments but only six of fifteen noncareer departments. In the nine colleges of the Los Angeles Community College District, 65 percent of the 137,000 students enrolled in 1975 were classified as vocational, up from 50 percent in 1969. In Prince George's Community College (Maryland), for the 1969-1973 period, enrollments in career programs grew from 747 to 2,557, a 242 percent gain, in contrast to a 79 percent growth rate for the total enrollment (Larkin, 1974b). Prince George's graduations by program type showed a similar pattern—the 57 graduates of career programs represented 19 percent of the 302 graduates in 1970; the 395 career program graduates represented 49 percent of the 807 graduates in 1974 (Larkin, 1974a). A Macomb County Community College (Michigan) report noted: "The shift to occupational education continues. Over 46 percent of the students, by head count, were in occupational programs during the 1972-73 school year compared to about 44 percent during the 1971-72 school year" (Macomb County Community College, 1973, p. 1).

The enrollment rise was reflected in employment of occupational instructors. Phair's survey of new staff and faculty members hired in the fall of 1976 by California colleges showed that "the academic and liberal arts areas continued to be depressed" while the occupational areas were flourishing. "The paraprofessional, occupational, and vocational-technical training programs, especially in the industrial trades, employed sizable numbers of new staff," approximately 25 percent of the total (Phair, 1977, p. 3). In Illinois in 1967, instructors with less than a bachelor's degree (primarily occupational instructors) made up about 4 percent of the full- and part-time faculty (Anderson and Spencer, 1968); in 1970 they accounted for nearly 10 percent (Illinois Junior College Board, 1971).

The premium on vocational education in terms of higher funding patterns encouraged colleges to classify as vocational many programs that had been classified as general education or liberal arts. And in order to show high enrollment in career programs, educators may have classified as occupational students those who took one occupational course, whether majoring in an occupational or a liberal arts transfer program. Several efforts to refine the data were made in response to criticism of these practices. California, for example, developed a Student

Accountability Model (SAM), a "uniform method for classifying occupational courses and identifying occupational majors" (Gold and Morris, 1977, Preface). Under the SAM guidelines an occupational course is defined as one that is intended to develop skills and related knowledge needed for job performance, is part of the course sequence of an occupational program offered by the college, and is designed primarily for job preparation and/or job upgrading or updating and not for general education purposes. As a result of a similar redefinition of classifications of courses by a Washington committee of deans of instruction working with the staff of the State Board for Community College Education, academic enrollments increased by 4 percent and vocational enrollments decreased by 4 percent (Price, 1977).

Regardless of data reliability, there is little question of the general popularity of career education. The national figures on the percentages of community college students enrolled in and graduating from career programs are reflected in surveys done at individual institutions. Career program enrollees tend to graduate at a rate approximately equivalent to their representation in the student body. As Table 30 shows, the number of occupational program graduates reached parity with the general or

Table 30. Associate Degrees Conferred by Institutions of Higher Education by Type of Curriculum, 1970-71 to 1979-80

Year	All Curriculums	Arts & Sciences or General Programs	Percentage of Total	Occupational Curriculums	Percentage of Total
1970-71	253,635	145,473	57.4	108,162	42.6
1971-72	294,005	158,496	53.9	135,509	46.1
1972-73	318,234	161,291	50.7	156,943	49.3
1973-74	347,173	165,520	47.7	181,653	52.3
1974-75	362,969	167,634	46.2	195,335	53.9
1975-76	395,393	176,612	44.7	218,781	55.3
1976-77	409,942	172,631	42.1	237,311	57.9
1977-78	416,947	168,052	40.3	248,895	59.7
1978-79	407,471	158,738	39.0	248,733	61.0
1979-80	405,378	152,169	37.5	253,209	62.5

Source: National Center for Education Satistics (1978, 1981).

liberal arts graduates by 1973 and by 1978 had reached a 60-to-40 ratio.

This rise in career education is attributable to many causes: the legacy left by early leaders of the junior college movement and the importunities, goadings, and sometimes barbs of later leaders to prod community colleges to develop occupational curricula and courses; the Vocational Education Act of 1963 and the later amendments; the increase in the size of public two-year colleges; changing economic conditions, particularly the high unemployment among four-year college and university graduates; the increase in part-time, women, disadvantaged, handicapped, and older students; and the community colleges' absorption of adult education programs and postsecondary occupational programs formerly operated by the secondary schools.

The Vocational Education Act was not the first to run federal funds to two-year colleges. The 1939 Commission on Junior College Terminal Education noted that at least sixty-two junior colleges in fourteen states were receiving federal funds that had been appropriated under the 1917 Smith-Hughes and 1937 George-Deen acts. The federal monies were earmarked for institutions where the education was less than college grade: "It does not mean that the *institution* must be of less than college grade—only that the particular *work offered*, for which federal aid is received, must be of less than college grade" (Eells, 1941a, p. 29). The U.S. Office of Education called programs of trade and industrial education less than college grade if college entrance requirements were not prerequisites for admission, the objective was to prepare for employment in industry, the program did not lead to a degree, the program was not required to conform to conditions governing a regular college course, and the instructors qualified under state plans.

The 1963 act and the amendments of 1968 and 1972 vastly augmented the federal funds available to community colleges. And for every federal dollar appropriated, state governments and local districts provided more than $3 in 1968, almost $5 in 1972, and more than $6 in 1974 (Davenport and others, 1976). The 1968 amendments added the requirement of an Advisory Council on Vocational Education in every state desirous of receiving federal funds.

These augmented funds came at a time when the colleges were increasing in size, a condition conducive to the growth of occupational programs. Between 1960 and 1965 the number of public two-year institutions increased from 405 to 503, but enrollments doubled. By 1969, there were 794 colleges, with enrollments averaging over 2,000.

As enrollments increased, so did the occupational programs. In Illinois, where many of the new districts were formed on the promise to the electorate of having more than 50 percent of the programs in career education, 1,871 curricula, or 66 percent of all curricula, were occupational (Illinois Community College Board, 1976). In Florida, associate degree and certificate occupational programs exceeded 200. The small Hawaii system offered 80 different programs (Career Information Center, 1974).

Both directly and indirectly, the relatively high unemployment among four-year college and university graduates helped occupational education. It also undermined or at least raised doubts about the long-held assumption that a baccalaureate or higher degree is certain to lead to a high-paying job (Trivett, 1977). According to Freeman, "For the graduates of the mid 1970s, falling salaries, scarce job opportunities, and dwindling career prospects are the new reality" (1976, p. 31). At the same time, blue-collar wages increased at a high rate, in some cases at a higher rate than white-collar and professional salaries.

Both these developments made occupational education more appealing to community college students. They also caused a sizable number of unemployed senior college graduates to turn to the community colleges to learn a skill to tide them over until the professional job situation would improve. This group of "reverse transfers" has consistently grown, and the significance of this economic dislocation, insofar as it affects the acceptability of occupational education, lies in reexamining the thesis that a senior college education assures a greater earning capacity than a two-year occupational education (Lee, 1976; Bethune, 1977).

The growth in part-time, women, disadvantaged, handi-capped, and older students also contributed to the rise in occu-pational enrollments. Bushnell (1973) pointed out that al-though 40 percent of all students enrolled in career programs, only 25 percent of full-time students did so. The proportion of women who chose career programs was 35 percent, while among men it was only 17 percent. Disadvantaged and handi-capped students were encouraged to enroll in occupational pro-grams through special grants. Occupational enrollments in Cali-fornia, Florida, Iowa, North Carolina, and Oregon consisted largely of older, part-time students.

Some of the enrollment increases resulted from the up-grading of institutions and the transfer to the community col-leges of functions formerly performed by other segments of education—secondary and adult schools, technical institutes, and area vocational schools or centers. This trend has been most marked in Florida, where fourteen of the twenty-eight commu-nity colleges had a department designated as an area vocational education school, and others had cooperative agreements with school boards that operate area vocational-technical centers; in Iowa, where all the public community colleges were merged with area schools; in Nebraska, where the state was divided into technical community college areas; and in North Carolina, where the technical institutes were part of the community col-lege system (Lombardi, 1975). In some states (California, for example) community colleges have expanded their occupational offerings with and without formal agreements with other insti-tutions. Nearly all the publicly supported occupational educa-tion in Long Beach, San Diego, and San Francisco was offered by the community college districts. Similarly, in Chicago the adult and vocational education programs were transferred from the city schools to the community college system.

The combination of these forces has counteracted to a considerable degree those open and subtle forces that caused students, their parents, and society to place the baccalaureate over the occupational programs. In its statewide master plan for 1978 to 1987, the Maryland State Board for Community Col-leges reported that the "increasing emphasis on occupational programs reflects changing values and attitudes among students and their families as to the level of education required to qualify for desirable employment opportunities. This shift is reflected in national projections predicting that throughout the next decade, 80 percent of available jobs will require less than the bachelor's degree" (Maryland State Board for Community Colleges, 1977, p. 34).

Success of Occupational Programs

Career programs are established with the intention of serving students by preparing them for employment and serving industries by supplying them with trained workers. Program need is ascertained by perusing employment trends in the local area and by surveying employers there. Program coordinators are appointed and advisory committees composed of trade and employer representatives established. Funds are often secured through priorities set down by state and federal agencies. The entire process suggests rational program planning. Nonetheless, questions have been raised about the appropriateness of certain programs and whether the matriculants are well served, and much research on program effects has been conducted.

Most students in occupational programs seem satisfied with the training they receive. A study of graduates of a Pennsylvania college indicated that the majority of respondents thought the institution had given them good technical skills (Selgas, 1977a), a finding confirmed in studies of students in Maryland (Licata, 1977). And most students eventually obtain employment in areas closely related to the programs in which they were enrolled: 76 percent of the full-time students in a California community college (Queen and Rusting, 1978), 80 percent in an Illinois college (Baratta, 1978), 73 percent in a Pennsylvania college (Selgas, 1977a), 68 percent in a New York college (Queensborough Community College, 1977), 80 percent in a Kansas college (Quanty, 1977), two thirds in a Missouri college (Johnson and others, 1976).

Cooperative work-experience programs, which relate work experience with the content of the curriculum, also gained positive attention from their constituents. Brightman (1973) reported that cooperative education students tended toward positive attitudes about education and both attempted and completed more course units per semester, although their stay at the college was no longer than that of students not enrolled in cooperative education. These cooperative education students rated the income earned and the on-the-job experiences as the most meaningful features of the cooperative education program. Heermann (1973) suggested that cooperative education should be part of the total community college strategy, not just another innovation, and that it should be integrated in all program areas, as at LaGuardia Community College (New York). Further, such programs should be tailored to the individual and based on defined outcomes, specific measures of what the students shall learn.

Students have been less sanguine about the help they received in obtaining jobs. Graduates of a Maryland college listed the weakness of college job placement services as a problem area (Gell and Armstrong, 1977), and similar comments were received in surveys of students in a Pennsylvania community college (Selgas, 1977a). Such assistance seemed to be given through the occupational programs themselves rather than through a collegewide job placement service.

Career students' relative success in finding and maintaining jobs in the areas for which they were trained has always been a controversial topic. Depending on the data obtained and the criteria for defining success, different researchers reach different conclusions. Noeth and Hanson (1976) studied a sample of 4,350 students who had been surveyed at 110 community colleges and technical schools in 1970. The students were enrolled in business and marketing, accounting, science, social science, arts and humanities, electrical engineering technology, auto mechanics, and nursing programs. The jobs they held five years after the testing date showed a continuation of their interests in the fields in which they had been enrolled: Half the graduates and dropouts from the business and marketing programs held business contact jobs, and a large number held business detail jobs. All who had completed the registered-nursing programs were working in nursing, students from accounting programs held business detail jobs and business contact jobs, and so on through the programs, with those from the technology programs holding technology jobs and those from the auto mechanics programs holding trades jobs. Students who had enrolled in arts and humanities programs were spread out across several types of jobs.

People from the business and marketing and the auto mechanics programs had mixed feelings about whether they needed postsecondary training to obtain their jobs, but most of the people from the other programs felt that they did. "Such a finding might suggest that perhaps students are becoming employable before they complete their programs and thus are essentially being overeducated for the jobs they will take" (Noeth and Hanson, p. 29). About three quarters indicated they would enter their training programs again if they had it to do over.

The authors concluded that occupational programs have a positive effect on their students: "A high percentage of those students who complete educational programs are employed in occupations related to their training. Even those students who did not complete the program they entered are frequently employed in program-related occupations. In addition, those individuals who are still in school are generally in educational areas related to the program they began in 1970" (p. 30).

Wilms and Hansell (1980), however, reached a different conclusion when they studied graduates and dropouts from both community college and proprietary school programs in San Francisco, Chicago, Boston, and Miami that were designed to train people for six occupations (accountants, computer programmers, electronics technicians, secretaries, dental assistants, and cosmetologists). They found that few students obtained professional, managerial, technical, or sales jobs; most graduates and dropouts from the accounting, computer, and electronics programs obtained clerical or lower-level jobs. Students from the secretarial, dental assisting, and cosmetology programs did better in obtaining the jobs for which they had been trained.

Pincus (1980) also took the occupational programs to

task, arguing that no one seems to know whether terminal vocational education programs are effective. He deplored the lack of data on unemployment rates and incomes of recent graduates and nongraduates of community college vocational programs, compared with such figures for recent high school graduates, four-year college graduates, and so on, with statistical controls for age, sex, race, and other variables. Although he rejected the inconsistent methodology in the various studies cited, he erected a table and calculated an average showing that "unemployment rates among former vocational students are high" (p. 349) and that "unemployment for vocational dropouts was generally higher than it was for graduates." He noted that vocational graduates are less likely to be unemployed than high school graduates but may be no more employable than college graduates: "The best that can be said is that vocational graduates are no more likely to be unemployed than college graduates" (pp. 349-350). He suggested that the burden of proof was on the advocates of vocational education to show how their graduates do better and concluded, "The economic benefits of vocational education are at best modest. Although most students get jobs in the fields for which they are trained, a substantial minority does not. The employment rate of vocational graduates is no better than that of college graduates and may be much worse. It is impossible to make any clear statements about the relative incomes of vocational graduates and college graduates" (pp. 353-354).

Wilms and Hansell (1980), too, attempted to show that occupational program graduates have few advantages over dropouts in the job market. But their data might well be interpreted in other ways. The upper-level programs they studied—accounting, computer programming, and electronics technology—train people for occupations that are moving toward professional status, and hence employers may be seeking people with baccalaureate-degree-program experience. These three areas are widely found in senior colleges as well as in community colleges and preparatory schools. Senior-college-program graduates or dropouts may have an edge on those from the lower schools in obtaining first-level positions in these fields.

In Wilms and Hansell's study, people trained as secretaries, dental assistants, and cosmetologists were generally successful in getting positions in those fields. And as the authors pointed out, "Most important, graduates of these programs were significantly more successful than dropouts" (p. 17). These are occupational certificate programs, seen by the public, the colleges, and people within the trades as properly belonging to the community colleges and proprietary schools. Few baccalaureate degree-granting institutions have such programs. Wilms and Hansell expressed surprise that "graduates did not earn significantly more than dropouts on their first jobs" (p. 18) but failed to suggest that many students enter such programs in order to find a job and remain only until they find one.

The Broader Issues

Some critics of career education are concerned that the programs do little in equalizing status and salaries among types of jobs. They view with alarm the high dropout rates without realizing that *program completion is an institutional artifact.* To the student who seeks a job in the field, completing the program becomes irrelevant as soon as such a job is available. The categories "graduate" and "dropout" lose much of their force when viewed in this light. This phenomenon is not peculiar to community colleges; generations of young women participated in teacher training programs in universities even though few of them expected to teach more than a few years and fewer than half entered teaching at all. If one merely surveys the career program graduates who are working in that area or places graduates in one category and dropouts in another, the true services rendered by those programs may be lost.

Few critics of career education acknowledge that questions about its value are much more complex than simplistic data on job entry and first salary earned can answer. What is the value of an occupational education program when an enrollee hears about an available job, obtains it, and leaves after two weeks? In that case the program has served as an employment agency of sorts. What is the value of a program in which a person who already has a job spends a few weeks learning some new skills if the person then receives a better job in the same company? There the program has served as a step on a career ladder. What of the person who enrolls to sharpen skills and gain confidence to apply for a job doing essentially the same work but for a different company? And what of the students who enter occupational programs but then transfer from them to other programs in the same or a different college?

A few studies of both graduates and nongraduates of career programs have shown that although most enrolled to obtain job entry skills, many sought advancement within jobs they already held. Around two thirds of the respondents to a survey of career students in a Kansas community college gave "job entry skill" as their reason (Quanty, 1977; Tatham, 1978), but around one third had enrolled primarily for advancement. A somewhat smaller percentage of students enrolled in career programs in California community colleges (34 percent) reported that they sought to prepare for jobs; 11 percent of that group had enrolled to improve skills for their present job (Hunter and Sheldon, 1980). Such data often fall between the planks when program follow-up studies or comparative wage studies are made.

Another important finding in studies of graduates and current enrollees in career programs is the sizable number who plan on transferring to four-year colleges and who do eventually transfer. In a California statewide study, 25 percent of students enrolled in career curricula said they intended to transfer (Hunter and Sheldon, 1980). And even if intentions are not always realized, sizable percentages do eventually transfer. Almost half the graduates of a two-year college in New York eventually entered an upper-division institution (State University of New York, Delhi, 1972), and within ten years, 71 percent of them had received the baccalaureate. Sizable, though not quite as great, numbers have been reported in other institutions: 22 percent of the graduates of a hotel and restaurant program in a Missouri community college had continued through to the baccalaurate (Johnson and others, 1976). Transfers from occupational programs to senior institutions numbered 21 percent in a Maryland college (Larkin, 1977a), 27 percent in a California college (Queen and Rusting, 1978), 30 percent in an Illinois college (Baratta, 1978). Nationwide, since 1975 the transfer rate from career programs has exceeded the rate from so-called transfer or college-parallel programs.

A curriculum is often viewed as a conduit through which people move in order to prepare themselves to do or be something other than when they began. Yet for some people the curriculum has served an essential purpose if it but allows them to matriculate and be put in touch with those who know where jobs may be obtained. At the other extreme are the students who go all the way through the curriculum, learn the skills, but either fail to obtain jobs in the field for which they were trained or, having attained them, find them unsatisfying. For them the institution has been a failure. The critics cannot seem to accommodate the fact that for many dropouts the program has succeeded, while for many of its graduates it has failed.

Career education has other implications: To what degree *should* the schools be in the business of providing trained workers for the nation's industries? None, say the academic purists; totally, say many community college leaders. A lengthy list of commentators and educational philosophers would argue that the preparation of people specifically to work in certain industries is not the school's purpose because the school should have broader social aims and because the industries can do the particular job training much more efficiently. And those who take this approach are not necessarily those who plead for a return to an era when higher education was for providing gentlemen with distinctive sets of manners.

Is career education primarily an individual or a social benefit? The individuals gain skills that make them more employable and at higher rates of pay; society gains skilled workers for the nation's businesses and technologies. Solmon (1976) argues that community colleges can and should work closely with employers to facilitate students' passage through to the labor market. To the extent that they do, everyone benefits: students, their families, the colleges, business, and the general public. Solmon contends that the costs must be maintained by all.

Students forgo earnings while they are in school for the gain of ultimate entry into the labor force with greater skills. Although employers must provide expensive apprenticeships, they can benefit by using cooperative programs to identify students whom they would like to retain. The colleges lose some control over their students when business firms decide whom to involve in cooperative programs and when those programs become more susceptible to external evaluation. However, they gain by doing a better, more direct job for students and by keeping them enrolled longer.

Nevertheless, other writers in education, and certainly the majority of those who comment on the role of the community colleges, suggest that education is an essential expenditure for economic growth and is not merely a nonproductive sector of the economy, a form of consumption. To the extent that the schools are viewed as investments of this type, educators can make a more effective claim on national budgets. To justify this claim, the schools must be brought in line with the goals of society; if they are to foster economic growth, they must provide trained workers, and the more they provide trained workers, the more they will be looked upon to fit those trainees to the jobs that are available. Hence, they can be criticized to the extent that their graduates do not obtain jobs or are not able to function effectively in the jobs they get. And thus the term *overeducated* can be used to describe those who are prepared for nonexistent jobs or who have jobs to which they do not apply the type of education they received.

Eells (1941a) deplored the fact that 66 percent of the students were enrolled in programs designed primarily to prepare them for what 25 percent would do—transfer to the upper division. At the time he was writing, there was no great difference between the public and the private junior colleges: "The problem is essentially the same for both types of institutions" (p. 63). However, Eells also noted that "of all groups, only the private junior colleges of the New England states and the public junior colleges for Negroes report an enrollment in terminal curricula which even approximates the proportion of terminal students" (p. 59). Now, there were colleges that knew what they were doing! The private junior colleges of New England could fit the girls for homemaking, sales, and secretarial work, and the public junior colleges for Negroes in the South could prepare their students for the manual trades.

Recently the urge to completely vocationalize the community colleges has been strong among college managers who are aware of the sizable funds and handsome political support attendant on career education. Their arguments sound plausible: Since many students neither transfer nor get an associate degree, they should stop trying to compete academically and obtain a marketable skill before leaving the educational system. Nevertheless, there are risks, too. Breneman (1979) has pointed out that emphasizing the financial return for undergraduate education proved a disservice to the colleges, not because the analysis was wrong but because educational leaders accepted the economists' determination that people who went to college earned more in their lifetime than those who did not, and they used this argument in their presentations to legislatures and the public.

The earnings differential between people who had been to college and those who had not was severely reduced in the 1970s, at least for entry-level positions. That is, a college graduate entered the labor force at only a slightly greater rate of pay than a nongraduate (a fact that, of course, says little about earnings over a lifetime). If the shortage of young people suited to take entry-level jobs continues, and if the drive toward occupational education fitting people for those jobs continues—both likely eventualities—the curve of greater earnings to be obtained by people who have been to college may again rise.

Trends

Whether or not career education is useful or proper, it has certainly captured the community colleges. Its advocates have increased, and more of them are being appointed to administrative positions, mostly in vocational areas but occasionally in positions involving academic program supervision. Upgrading of instructors, which started in the 1950s, was supported by the enlarged appropriations for staff development programs and encouraged by salary schedules that provided incentives for academic degrees. Many of the instructors who formerly had only trade experience have acquired bachelor's and master's degrees, removing one of the most potent symbols of inferiority in the academic community.

All these factors—enrollment surge, staff upgrading, and financial support from business, industry, and government—have given occupational educators a buoyancy that shows up in new courses, programs, teaching strategies. They have a large reservoir of funds, mostly public but some private and foundation, to undertake studies and sophisticated research on every conceivable aspect of occupational education: preparing model courses and programs, conducting follow-up studies of graduates, assessing employment trends, establishing guidelines for choosing new courses and curricula, and developing criteria for weeding out the obsolescent and the weak courses and programs or for upgrading others to conform to new job specifications.

Career educators' confidence in the future has been most noticeable in their projections of new courses and curricula. As an example, in 1977 the Maryland community colleges proposed 244 new career programs, in contrast to 11 new liberal arts or transfer programs (Maryland State Board for Community Colleges, 1977). Career educators have been flattered that four-year colleges and universities have been showing greater interest in two-year occupational courses and programs but concerned about losing enrollment to the competition. They worry also about losing the programs themselves if the baccalaureate becomes the requisite degree.

Many liberal arts advocates have become understandably apprehensive about the future of their area, fearful that the higher favor enjoyed by career education will mean the further slighting of their disciplines. Instructors have watched their once-popular classes fade, but they have not been able to counter the attrition. In contrast, college leaders who subscribe to the marketplace as the prime determinant of the curriculum accept career education, just as they accepted the transfer function of an earlier day. For them, the enrollments are the measure of all value.

Merging Academic and Occupational Studies

Some eloquent pleas for merging career and liberal studies have been made. Solmon (1977), who has done several studies of the relations between college going and the kinds of jobs that graduates get and the extent to which they are satisfied with those jobs, points to several commonly held misconceptions: Job preparation in college is antithetical to short-term enjoyment of being in college or preparation for citizenship and appreciation of the arts; students tend to get jobs for which they were specifically trained in a major field or in a job-related training program; more education increases the chances of getting a good job. On surveying numerous graduates of all types of programs several years out of college, he found them wishing they had had more preparation in English, psychology, and ways of understanding interpersonal relations. He recommended breadth in studies in all programs.

Sagen (1979) has made an eloquent plea for a merger of career and liberal education, saying that, conceptually, education for work should be merged with liberal arts studies because both are part of the functioning person. Practically, a merger should be effected because graduates of liberal arts programs have difficulty obtaining jobs in the field for which they are prepared. Historically, graduates of these programs have gone into teaching or government positions, but the market for both teachers and nontechnical employees in the federal government has diminished. Sagen made several suggestions for integrating the programs and concluded: "Liberal arts education should continue to be a viable method of career preparation in this market provided liberal arts graduates can demonstrate a high level of relevant generalized competencies and a moderate amount of specialized expertise required for entry-level positions" (p. 21).

Feldman (1967) has said that the schools can best serve their students by supplying them with access to open-ended jobs, jobs that make enhanced responsibility, salary, and advancement available to them: "Merely to offer blind-alley employment and obsolescing trades to youngsters in a dynamic technological society is to exchange one kind of subservience and dependence for another" (p. 2). In an argument for career education he pointed out that the work world is a valid component of educational content. "The most glaring defect in the present piecemeal, ill-coordinated effort to develop manpower at the fringes of society's mainstream is the separation between educational and occupational skill development" (p. 4).

Harris and Grede (1977) discussed career potential for the liberal arts in the context of what they called "the hopeless job prospects of two-year college graduates in liberal arts and general studies" (p. 227). The common purpose of liberal education in all ages is that it must prepare people for the type of life they will lead. At one time only those who were educated were preparing for leisure or for directing people in other classes. More recently liberal education has meant preparing for work. Because all people are free and all people work, a truly liberal education for a free person must include a work component. In that sense all education is vocational education.

These authors pointed out that it is well past time for a merger of liberal education and occupational education. Certain content from most of the liberal arts disciplines is essential for workers in most occupations. And since most liberal arts graduates will have to be employed for most of their lifetime, they should understand the world of work. Harris and Grede predicted a breakdown in the rigid dichotomy between liberal arts and vocational curricula or between transfer and nontransfer curricula in community colleges and foresaw a time when teachers of the liberal arts would recognize the importance of career education, and teachers of vocations the importance of the liberal learning.

Other arguments in favor of merging liberal and career education can be raised. Of itself, occupational training involves a higher risk for the student than liberal arts education. The costs in tuition and forgone earnings may be the same for both, but occupational training is almost entirely wasted if there is no job at the end. The liberal arts at least hold the person's options open, a perception certainly accounting for at least some of the liberal arts' continuing popularity among students. And since it seems impossible to predict with much accuracy the types of jobs that will be available by the time an entering student leaves school, the problem can be accommodated in two ways: Make the educational system open enough so that people may return successively for retraining throughout life; make the initial training sufficiently broad that the skills learned are applicable to a variety of situations. Such a position has been advocated by Cohen and Brawer (1977), who recommend that the humanities be integrated into occupational programs—for example, instruction in ethics for auto mechanics and for students enrolled in the medical technologies.

Occupational education has become the major function in most community colleges, but the high growth rates experienced since 1964 cannot be sustained forever. Unless more community colleges become exclusively vocational-technical postsecondary institutions—as at least 15 percent of them were by 1980—enrollments in the career programs will probably hover around 50 percent of the total credit-course enrollment. But this percentage will depend in large measure on the way programs are classified.

The major change in the latter half of the 1970s most often overlooked by observers was that career programs in community colleges increasingly became feeders to senior institutions, which were undergoing their own form of vocationalization. Students were finding that many of the credits they earned in their two-year occupational programs were acceptable for transfer. Thus the categories "occupational" and "transfer" became inadequate to describe the realities of the community colleges, and "terminal" certainly became obsolete. Sizable percentages of the transfer students sought leisure-time pursuits; sizable percentages of the occupational students desired certification for transfer. A view of the community colleges as terminal institutions and of the universities as institutions for students interested in the liberal arts is woefully inaccurate.

Occupational programs may be the first step toward upward mobility for those who cannot afford the long financially nonproductive time that four- to six-year collegiate programs entail. In the process of obtaining a technical or semiprofessional skill, the person is also exposed to liberal arts or general education offerings. This experience may help achieve upward mobility, especially in the light of research showing that children of college-educated parents are more likely to attend college than children of non-college-educated parents and that there exists a direct relation between the educational attainments of parents and students (Bowen, 1977).

C. P. Snow posed a distinction between the humanities and the sciences. One of his "two cultures" was the scientific, attempting to describe laws of the natural world, optimistic that problems could be solved. The other was the literary world, pessimistic, assured that they were the learned while the others were the barbarians. According to Snow, the literary intellectuals or artists lacked foresight, were unconcerned with their fellow humans, did not understand what science can do. The scientists thought of the artists as lacking precision in thought and action, as speaking in phrases capable of a myriad of interpretations.

However, the two cultures may be presented another way. Perhaps on one side are those who have a vision of the future, who work with discipline, pride, and rigor, who articulate their ideas through language that has consistent meaning, who value the intellect. On the other side are those who demand quick gratification, who refuse to be told what to do or what to study, who are antiliterate, rejecting language, who deal with feeling, not thinking, with emotions, not intellect. If these are the two cultures, the split is not between the liberal arts, on the one hand, and career education, on the other. That argument is passé, even though community colleges are still organized as though the real distinction were between people who were going to work and those who were not. Work in the sense of vocation demands commitment, planning, delay of gratification, application of intelligence, acceptance of responsibility, a sense of present and future time. As such, it differs less from the concepts surrounding the liberal arts than it does from the antiliterate, language-rejecting, stultified group who cannot understand themselves or their environment in terms that have common reference.

As though it anticipated later developments, toward the

end of its statement the AAJC's 1964 National Advisory Committee concluded, "Time must be provided, even in a two-year curriculum, for at least basic courses in languages, arts, and social sciences. The technicians of the future must be inoculated against the malady of overspecialization. . . . They must not be forced to concentrate so narrowly on technology that they cannot be useful citizens or cannot accommodate changes in their own specialties" (American Association of Junior Colleges, 1964, p. 14).

Issues

Can career education maintain the ascendant position it gained in the 1960s and 1970s? By 1980 it seemed to have leveled off at around half the enrollments. Will its position as the dominant curriculum be superseded by a different field—compensatory studies, for example?

Can career education be effectively merged with the collegiate function? Few prior attempts to integrate esthetic appreciation, rationality, ethics, and other elements of the higher learning with programs training people for particular jobs have met with success. Can the staff itself do it? Does the community college leadership want it?

The lines between career and collegiate education have become blurred since more students began transferring to universities from community college career programs than from the so-called transfer programs. Questions of the conceptual differences between occupational and liberal studies have often been raised, but the answers have yielded little to influence program design in the community colleges. What type of staff training, program reorganization, or external incentives might be provided to encourage faculties and administrators to reexamine both programs in light of the practicalities of their own institutions?

Much of the value in career education programs derives from their connecting students with jobs. Can the colleges demonstrate this value? How can they capitalize on it?

Programs designed to prepare students to work in particular industries should be supported, at least in part, by those industries, and many examples of this type of support have been set in place. But how can industry be assigned its proportionate share of all training costs? What channels can be opened to merge public and private funds so that an equitable share is borne by each?

Career education remained a subordinate function throughout the first fifty years of community college development, until federal funding moved it to the fore. Will the separate funding channels be maintained? How will they change if the programs preparing people in the high-level technologies move to the universities?

The full effects of career education as the prime function have yet to be discerned. The public's view of community colleges as agents of upward mobility for individuals seems to be shifting toward a view of the institutions as occupational training centers. This narrowing of the colleges' comprehensiveness could lead to a shift in the pattern of support.

9

Compensatory Education

Enhancing Literacy Through Remedial Studies

Nothing is easier to decry than the ineffectiveness of the schools. One observer of American education noted, "Paradoxical as it may seem, the diffusion of education and intelligence is at present acting against the free development of the highest education and intelligence. Many have hoped and still hope that by giving a partial teaching to great numbers of persons, a stimulus would be applied to the best minds among them, and a thirst for knowledge awakened which would lead to high results; but thus far these results have not equaled the expectation. There has been a vast expenditure . . . for educational purposes . . . but the system of competitive cramming in our schools has not borne fruits on which we have much cause to congratulate ourselves." The sentiments in this passage, written *in 1869* by Francis Parkman (p. 560), have been echoed countless times since.

Numerous critics have taken the position that the schools may teach people to read and write, but they fail to teach them to think. Parkman himself felt that the school "has produced an immense number of readers; but what thinkers are to be found may be said to exist in spite of it" (p. 560). One hundred years later Ciardi complained that "the American school system has dedicated itself to universal subliteracy. It has encouraged the assumption that a clod trained to lip-read a sports page is able to read anything. It has become the whole point of the school system to keep the ignorant from realizing their own ignorance. . . . An illiterate must at least know that he cannot read and that the world of books is closed to him" (1971, p. 48). Simon asked, "What good is reading and writing to people who cannot think?" (1979, pp. 16-17). Mencken asserted that "the great majority of American high school pupils, when they put their thoughts on paper, produce only a mass of confused puerile nonsense. . . . They express themselves so clumsily that it is often quite impossible to understand them at all" (cited in Lyons, 1976, p. 33). And a more contemporary novelist offered this devastating critique: "Our civilization has achieved a distinction of sorts. It will be remembered not for its technology nor even its wars but for its novel ethos. Ours is the only civilization in history which has enshrined mediocrity as its national ideal" (Percy, 1980, p. 177).

More recently the charge has been raised that not only do students fail to become well educated, they do not even learn the rudiments of reading, writing, and arithmetic. The title of Copperman's 1978 book reflects one indictment: *The Literacy Hoax: The Decline of Reading, Writing, and Learning in the Public Schools and What We Can Do About It.* Copperman reports studies showing that over 20 million American adults, one in every five, are functionally illiterate—that is, incapable of understanding basic written and arithmetic communication to a degree that they can maneuver satisfactorily in contemporary society. Many commentators, Copperman among them, do not blame the schools alone. However, although each generation's cohort of criers with alarm has had its favorite target, most of them eventually disparage the public schools.

Decline in Literacy

Broad-scale denunciations are one thing, accurate data quite another. Information on the literacy of the American population over the decades is difficult to compile, even though data on the number of people completing so many years of schooling have been collected by the Bureau of the Census for well over 100 years. One reason that intergenerational comparisons are imprecise is that different percentages of the population have gone to school at different periods in the nation's history. A century ago only the upper socioeconomic classes completed secondary school or enrolled in higher education. Further, the United States does not have a uniform system of educational evaluation. Nonetheless, the available evidence suggests that the academic achievement of students in schools and colleges registered a gradual improvement between 1900 and the mid 1950s, an accelerated improvement between the mid 1950s and the mid 1960s, and a precipitous, widespread decline between then and the late 1970s. The Scholastic Aptitude Test taken by high school seniors showed mathematical ability at 494 in 1952, 502 in 1963, and 470 in 1977; verbal ability went from 476 in 1952 to 478 in 1963 and dropped to 429 in 1977. The scores made by entering community college freshmen who participated in the American College Testing Program also declined notably between the mid 1960s and the later 1970s, as shown in Table 31. And the National Assessment of Educational Progress reported that seventeen-year-olds' command of the mechanics of writing declined between 1970 and 1974 (Educational Testing Service, 1978, pp. 1-2).

Reports emanating from the colleges confirm the slide. Several surveys of instructors have found them deploring their students' lack of preparation (Brawer and Friedlander, 1979; Center for the Study of Community Colleges, 1978a). The Educational Testing Service (ETS) notes: "At the University of Cali-

Table 31. Mean ACT Scores for Two-Year College Freshmen, 1964-1979

Year	English	Math	Soc. Sci.	Nat. Sci.	Composite
1964	17.6	17.4	18.2	18.5	18.0
1965	16.9	17.6	18.8	18.9	18.2
1970	17.2	17.7	18.0	19.0	18.1
1975	15.8	14.9	15.2	18.9	16.3
1977	15.7	14.2	14.7	18.5	15.9
1979	15.8	13.9	14.4	18.4	15.8

Source: American College Testing Program (1966, 1972, 1976-77, 1978-79, 1980-81).

fornia at Berkeley, where students come from the top eighth of California high school graduates, nearly half the freshmen in recent years have been so deficient in writing ability that they needed a remedial course they themselves call bonehead English' " (p. 2). The ETS list of institutions where entering freshmen were found to be seriously deficient in basic communication skills reads like a list of the most prestigious universities in the country: Harvard, Yale, Cornell, Brown, Stanford, and, as they put it, "countless other institutions that have introduced some form of basic writing instruction in the past few years" (p. 3). And although most of the freshmen at the City University of New York had at least an 80 average in high school, one third of them lacked even basic literacy, and 90 percent took some form of remedial writing instruction.

No one can say with assurance which social or educational condition was prime in leading to the decline in student abilities that apparently began in the mid 1960s and accelerated throughout the 1970s. Suffice it to say that numerous events came together: the coming of age of the first generation reared on television; a breakdown in respect for authority and the professions; a pervasive attitude that the written word is not as important as it once was; the imposition of various other-than-academic expectations on the public schools; and a decline in academic requirements and expectations at all levels of schooling. This last is worthy of elaboration because it is the only one that is within the power of the schools to change directly.

Several premises underlie schooling—for example, that

students tend to learn what is taught; that the more time they spend on a task, the more they learn; that they will take the courses required for completion of their programs. Hence, when expectations, time in school, and number of academic requirements are reduced, student achievement, however measured, seems certain to drop as well. ETS reported, "The nub of the matter is that writing is a complex skill mastered only through lengthy, arduous effort. It is a participatory endeavor, not a spectator sport. And most high school students do not get enough practice to become competent writers" (p. 4). Since the 1960s, the schools have put less emphasis on composition, and even in the composition courses, "creative expression" is treated at a higher level than are grammar and the other tools of the writer's trade.

Copperman recounted the depressing statistics regarding the deterioration of the secondary school curriculum, showing that the percentage of ninth- through twelfth-grade students enrolled in academic courses dropped between 1960 and 1972: from 95 to 71 percent in English courses and proportionate drops in social studies, science, and mathematics. In other words, the average high school graduate had taken four years of English in 1960 and only three years in 1972. And the curriculum in English shifted from sequential courses to electives chosen from courses in creative writing, journalism, public speaking, classical literature, science fiction, advanced folklore, composition, mass media, poetry, and a host of other options. In sum, "The weakness in the current elective system is that it enables a student to avoid the kind of rigorous work he needs to develop his primary academic skills" (1978, pp. 96-97).

Not only are students taking less science, math, English, and history, but "in the academic classes students do take, the amount of work assigned and the standard to which it is held have deteriorated badly" (Copperman, p. 76). Further, the readability level of the texts used in secondary schools and two-year colleges has dropped markedly. Copperman cited textbook publishers who said that they "can no longer sell a textbook that has been written with a readability level higher than two years below the grade for which it is intended" (p. 81).

Another shift in the pattern of secondary schools has been reduction in the length of the school day. Between 10 and 15 percent of juniors and seniors in high schools nationwide leave school in the afternoons, most to go to work under various work-experience programs. Budgetary problems have led many school systems to cut the school day from six periods to five, whether or not a work-experience program was in place. In the late 1970s, the Los Angeles public secondary schools were on a five-period schedule, making it nearly impossible for students to complete the courses required for admission to selective universities.

The decline in secondary school performance led to the introduction of competency or high school completion tests. In the 1970s students in New York, Florida, Arizona, California, and several other states were expected to pass a test of achievement before a high school diploma would be awarded. And even that did not suffice: In 1980 at Miami-Dade Community College, 50 percent of the matriculants were below the eleventh-grade level on reading and writing, and 60 percent were below on mathematics. The high school competency test apparently could be passed at a level far below that pattern of literacy that would enable a student to enter college-level studies with any hope of success. One commentator reported, "In New York, the test . . . has—shockingly, albeit unsurprisingly—elicited tremendous opposition. Even though its demands seem to me very far from draconian, it is being denounced as a fiendish tool for depriving countless innocent young people from advancement in life" (Simon, 1979, p. 16).

The criticism of the schools' ability to teach students to read and write extends to higher education. Specialization is a favorite target. Because each academic discipline has its own jargon, the students who study it learn to be literate only within its confines and never learn to read or write in general. Each college department is criticized for desiring primarily to produce majors and graduate students in its own discipline and hence never to be concerned with literacy in general. English departments come in for their share of attack. The professors who are concerned with literary criticism and esoterica, who demean the teaching of composition and those who do it, are familiar figures.

But none of this is really new. Comments on students' lack of preparation for college-level studies may be found as early as the beginnings of the colleges in colonial America. Rudolph (1977) noted, "Because the colonial colleges were founded before there existed any network of grammar schools ... most entering students were prepared privately, often by studying with the local minister" (p. 52). And so many colleges were built in the first three decades of the nineteenth century that they could not find enough students who were prepared for the higher learning. Hence, "college authorities, defining their own course of study, learned to restrain their expectations in deference to the preparation of the students who came their way" (p. 60).

College Admissions

Because each college set its own standards, and because the founding of colleges preceded the development of a widespread secondary school system, the early colleges displayed a wide variety of admission requirements. By the latter part of the nineteenth century most of them were operating their own compensatory education programs. In 1895, 40 percent of entering students were drawn from the preparatory programs operated by the colleges and universities themselves (Rudolph, p. 158).

Numerous attempts to stabilize college admissions have been made. In 1892 the National Education Association organized a Committee on Secondary School Studies, known as the Committee of Ten, which was to recommend and approve the secondary school curriculum for college matriculation. In 1900 the College Entrance Examination Board began offering a common examination for college admission. Nonetheless, the wide variety of types and quality of colleges in America made it impossible to devise uniform admission standards. There has never been a standard of admission to all colleges in the United States. The Educational Testing Service and the American College

Testing Program offer uniform examinations across the country, but each college is free to admit students regardless of where they place on those examinations.

Of all postsecondary educational structures in America, the public community colleges have borne the brunt of the poorly prepared students in the twentieth century. Few maintain admission requirements: Hardly any of them demands a minimum high school grade-point average; less than one in five imposes an entrance test; one third do not even require the high school diploma (see Table 32). Throughout their history most of them have taken pride in their open door.

Table 32. Admission Criteria in Public Two-Year Colleges, 1970

Criterion	Percentage of Colleges
High school diploma or equivalent	86
Minimum age	27
High school grade average	0
Test scores	28
Interview	7
Letter of recommendation	16
Physical examination	41
High school diploma or certificate only	34
Minimum age only	5
High school diploma or minimum age only	55

Source: Morrison and Ferrante (1973, p. 27).

When sizable cohorts of well-prepared students were clamoring for higher education, as in the 1950s and early 1960s, the community colleges received a large share of them. But when the college-age group declined and the universities became more competitive for students, the proportion of academically well-prepared students going to community colleges shrank. Thus, the colleges were dealt a multiple blow: relaxed admission requirements and the availability of financial aid at the more prestigious universities; a severe decline in the scholastic abilities of high school graduates; and a greater percentage of applicants who had taken fewer academic courses.

The community colleges responded by accommodating the different types of students without turning anyone away. They have always tended to let everyone in but have then guided students to programs which fit their aspirations and in which they had some chance to succeed. Students who qualified for transfer programs were never a serious problem; they were given courses similar to those they would find in the lower division of the four-year colleges and universities. Technical and occupational aspirants were not a problem either: Career programs were organized for them. Internal selectivity was the norm; failing certain prerequisites, applicants were barred from the health professions and technology programs. And the students who wanted a course or two for their own personal interest found them both in the departments of continuing education and in the transfer programs.

The residue, the poorly prepared group of high school pass-throughs, has been the concern. What to do with marginally literate people who want to be in college but do not know why? How to deal with someone who aspires to be an attorney but who is reading at the fifth-grade level? Shunting these students to the trades programs was a favored ploy, giving rise to Clark's (1960) cooling-out thesis. Offering a smattering of remedial courses where they would be prepared, more or less successfully, to enter the transfer courses—or entertained until they drifted away—was another. But the decline in achievement exhibited by secondary school graduates—and dropouts—in the 1970s hit the colleges with full force and, by most accounts, was increasing in intensity as the 1980s began. The issue of the marginal student became central to instructional planning.

The guiding and teaching of students unprepared for traditional college-level studies is the thorniest single problem for community colleges. Some institutions seem to have given up, as evidenced by their tendencies to award certificates and degrees for any combination of courses, units, or credits, in effect sending the students away with the illusion of having had a successful college career. Others have mounted massive instructional and counseling services especially for the lower-ability students, stratagems designed to puncture the balloon of prior school failure. But in most programs in most institutions, expectations for student achievement have declined. The weight of the low-ability student hangs like an anchor on the community colleges.

Remedial Studies

Compensatory education is not new to the community colleges. Compensatory programs were formerly composed almost exclusively of disparate courses designed to prepare students to enter the college transfer program, and students were placed in the courses on the basis of entrance tests or prior school achievement. The courses were usually not accepted for credit toward an academic degree. Morrison and Ferrante (1973) estimated that in 1970 most public two-year colleges had developmental, preparatory, or remedial programs. Extrapolating from the sample of schools used in the American Council on Education's Cooperative Institutional Research Program, they concluded that all the colleges had some sort of special services for the academically disadvantaged, either special programs (39 percent), special courses (99 percent), or both.

Remedial, compensatory, and *developmental* are the most widespread terms for courses designed to teach literacy—the basics of reading, writing, and arithmetic. The magnitude of this form of education can be estimated by counting the class sections that the colleges designate as remedial. Using the 1977 catalogues and class schedules from a national sample of public and private colleges, the Center for the Study of Community Colleges tallied the sections in the humanities, sciences, and social sciences. The findings (see Tables 33 and 34) are notable in that about three in eight English classes were presented at below college level and nearly one in three mathematics classes taught arithmetic at a level lower than college algebra. A 1975 survey done by the American Mathematical Association of Two-Year Colleges found remedial math courses in 91 percent of institutions (Baldwin and others, 1975).

Remedial courses in other fields are less widespread, although increased emphasis on the sciences for students in allied

Table 33. Level of English Class Sections Offered in 129 Colleges,
1977-78 (Percentages)

Level	Percentage
Remedial/Developmental	36.9
Composition	17.3
Reading	19.6
College-Level	63.1
Composition	56.9
Reading	6.2
Total	100.0

Source: Center for the Study of Community Colleges (1978b).

health programs has led to an increase in the number and type of remedial science courses. The *Journal of College Science Teaching* and the *Journal of Chemical Education* report examples of remedial courses in biology and chemistry that include instruction in reading because students frequently have trouble understanding the textbooks and laboratory manuals.

The most prominent development in compensatory education in the 1970s was the integrated program combining instruction in the three Rs with special attention to individual students. Most of the programs share several elements. Students

Table 34. Level of Science Courses Offered in 175 Colleges,
1977-78 (Percentages)

Discipline	Remedial/ Developmental	Parallel to Lower- Division College Courses
Agriculture	0.1	71.1
Anthropology	6.5	90.3
Biology	1.9	70.6
Chemistry	13.4	63.4
Earth/Space Sciences	0.1	93.5
Economics	0.1	87.0
Engineering	0.7	46.5
Integrated Sciences	6.9	69.0
Math	32.6	54.5
Physics	2.2	60.0
Psychology	0.7	87.4
Sociology	0.1	92.6

Source: Center for the Study of Community Colleges (1978b).

participate voluntarily or are placed in the programs on the basis of scores made on an entrance test—ACT, SAT, SCAT, or a homemade exam. Special counseling procedures are established, and each student's attendance and progress are monitored. The specially designated students take "How to Study" courses and "Human Potential" seminars together. They are tutored individually, by professionals or peers, and they are led through reproducible programs in learning laboratories. Program operators report a variety of successes for their students, compared with similar students who did not receive special treatment: increased grade-point averages, more regular attendance, greater satisfaction with school, dropout rates up to 80 percent lower, enhanced sense of personal responsibility, and increased test scores.

Hundreds of studies reported in the published literature and in the ERIC files suggest that the compensatory programs are successful. The student placement procedures seem valid: In a study of remedial English classes in fourteen community colleges, the students' writing ability at the end of the courses was found to be, on the average, equivalent to the writing ability of the students who were beginning the regular college English classes (Cohen, 1973). Unfortunately, the data are not always reliable nor the comparisons always valid. However, the programs do seem to lower student dropout. Staff members pay closer attention to the students, integrate teaching with counseling, provide a greater variety of learning materials than ordinary students receive, and seem to cause their enrollees to devote more time to their studies. In short, when special treatment is applied, when students are given supplemental counseling, tutoring, and learning aids, when they are singled out for additional work, they tend to remain in school. Perhaps there is nothing surprising in that; special treatment of any sort yields special results.

Some compensatory education programs have been designed, often in conjunction with other agencies, for people who were not regularly enrolled at the college. These include programs for special populations, such as Navajo Indians (Smith, 1979) and inner-city adults working in construction jobs (Howard, 1976). In cooperation with local public agencies,

New Start, sponsored by Spoon River College (Illinois), was created to provide broad-based education that included both academic and vocational skills and personalized educational placement and counseling for people with minimal incomes, low reading levels, erratic employment patterns, or arrest records. Between 1977 and 1978, the program had 741 participants; of these, 549 were new enrollees, 543 were enrolled in the pre-GED (General Education Development) and GED review courses, 115 acquired their GED certificates, and 337 continued their education at the college (Conti and others, 1978).

Compensatory education thus involves the colleges not only with the students who come to the campus seeking academic programs, degrees, and certificates but also with adult basic education. The adult studies are often funded and organized separately, as in the aforementioned examples. Sometimes, especially where the colleges are responsible for adult education in their district, adult programs lead to entirely separate structures. The Urban Skills Institute operated by the City Colleges of Chicago enrolled 45 percent of the district's students in 1980. The College Centers maintained under the egis of the San Francisco Community College District provide another example. These structures take some of the pressure for compensatory education away from the colleges' regular programs.

Compensatory courses and programs can be built within the colleges, but several questions remain: How does compensatory education affect the college staff? How can it be conducted in the context of an open-admissions institution without jeopardizing the college's standards and its legitimacy in higher education? How can the segregated compensatory education programs respond to the charges of racism and class-based tracking? How many times should the public pay the schools to try to teach the same competencies to the same people?

Effect on the Staff

The first question relates primarily to the college faculty members who face the students daily. How do they feel about the massive compensatory education efforts and the poorly prepared students in their classes? The students' abilities exert the single most powerful influence on the level, quality, type, and standard of curriculum and instruction offered in every program in every school. Other influences—instructors' tendencies, externally administered examinations and licensure requirements, the entry levels imposed by succeeding courses in the same and other institutions—pale in comparison. Nothing that is too distant from the students' comprehension can be taught successfully. All questions of academic standards, college-level and remedial courses, textbook readability and coverage, course pacing and sequence come to that.

The students are part of the instructors' working conditions. Except for faculty members recruited especially to staff the compensatory programs, most feel that their environment would be improved if their students were more able. In response to the question "What would it take to make yours a better course?" over half the respondents to the Center for the Study of Community Colleges' 1977 national survey of two-year college science instructors noted, "Students better prepared to handle course requirements" (Brawer and Friedlander, 1979, p. 32). That choice far outranked all others in a list of sixteen.

If students cannot be more able, at least they might be more alike so that instruction could be more precisely focused. Teaching groups of students whose reading or computational abilities range from the third to the thirteenth grade is demoralizing; everything is more difficult, from writing examinations to showing group progress. Hence the unremitting pressure for ability grouping, remedial courses, learning laboratories that serve to remove the poorer students from the classrooms.

Thus, compensatory education affects the staff in several ways. The traditional faculty members remember their college in the 1950s and early 1960s, when they had well-prepared students. They may feel nostalgic, perhaps even betrayed because the conditions under which they entered the colleges have changed so. At the same time, they may be pleased that the segregated compensatory education programs remove the poorest students from their own classes; over one fourth of instructors teaching the traditional academic courses (humanities, sciences, social sciences, and technologies) would prefer "stricter prerequisites for admission to class" (Center for the Study of Community Colleges, 1978a). Nonetheless, the teachers in the compensatory education programs run the risk of becoming pariahs, similar in that regard to occupational education instructors in the pre-1960s era.

Legitimacy

The question of legitimacy is one of image in the eyes of the public, the potential students, the funding agents, and the other sectors of education. Like any public agency, an educational institution must maintain its legitimacy. The community colleges have strived to maintain their claim to a position in the postsecondary sector through numerous stratagems. One was their behavior in the 1950s and 1960s when they sought people with doctoral degrees to serve as staff members and rewarded current staff members when they obtained the higher degree, even though possession of a doctorate bore little or no relation to a faculty member's professional activities. The doctorate was a way of saying, "We are as good as the senior institutions." One of the reasons for the move toward segregated compensatory programs has been an attempt to regain the legitimacy lost when the colleges accepted adult basic studies and job training programs that could in no measure be considered college-level.

Actually, a school's legitimacy rests on its academic standards and the definition of its guiding principles. Academic standards certify that a student holding a certificate or degree has met the requirement for employment or for further study at another college; they are the basis for the reputation of institutions and the people who work within them. Even though community colleges typically maintain open-admissions policies, they must still attend to these concerns. Their students must be certified; their instructional programs, testing and counseling services, course content, course requirements must all relate to a shared vision of desired competencies and outcomes. Their certificates or degrees must evidence some set of proficiencies achieved at some minimum level.

What are the standards in compensatory education? Here the special programs exhibit several problems in common with the traditional. One of the main problems is the difficulty in setting fixed *exit* criteria (grading standards) for courses and programs that have no set *entry* requirements. If anyone may enroll regardless of ability, a wide range of students will be attracted. Accordingly, either the exit criteria must be fluid, with a different standard for each student, or the time and type of instruction must be greatly varied, or the instructors must maintain exceedingly modest expectations. All three options are at play in practically all programs.

Standardized expectations of accomplishment, or exit criteria, suggest social norms as contrasted with standards for individuals. Social norms suggest that people who would function adequately in particular social settings (the workplace, further schooling) must act to a certain standard. The alternative, relating accomplishment to the desires or entering abilities of individuals, suggests that any accomplishment is satisfactory and that the institution has succeeded if any gain in individual ability can be shown. This conflict between social and individual standards is an issue of the absolute versus the relative, and it strikes at the heart of compensatory education.

Different groups take different positions on the issue. Community college instructors tend to argue in favor of absolute standards. The Academic Senate for California Community Colleges (ASCCC) has studied the problem extensively, surveying its members and sponsoring state conferences on the issue ("Report of the ASCCC Conference on Academic Standards," 1977). The ASCCC deplores some of the pressures to lower standards: students entering the college with inadequate basic skills but with expectation of passing the courses, as they have done throughout their prior school careers; ill-prepared students insisting on enrolling in transfer courses rather than remedial courses; the virtual elimination of D and F grades and concomitant wider use of passing grades; reduction in the number of required subjects; and the cult of growth afflicting community colleges, as evidenced by aggressive student recruiting drives. The ASCCC Academic Standards Committee recommended that standards should be maintained through the use of diagnostic and placement testing, directive counseling, academic prerequisites for courses, and proficiency testing before awarding academic degrees.

Advocates of the concept of lifelong learning often provide an opposing view. To them, any seeker of knowledge should find the institution a resource to be used for an infinite variety of purposes. Cross (1978, pp. 19-20) put that position well, arguing that substantial changes in school forms are needed so that anyone may learn anything at any time: "My concern is that in our exuberance for recruiting adults and certifying that *their* learning projects meet *our* standards, we will corrupt independent, self-directed learners into learners dependent on someone else to determine where, when, and how people should learn. Visions of a learning society with people of all ages enthusiastically pursuing learning that interests them could so easily turn into a joyless learning society with people grimly fulfilling requirements and seeking legitimacy for every conceivable variety of learning." These opposed positions suggest differing views of present and potential students. Some see them as lethargic illiterates; others as humanistic knowledge seekers.

The Dilemma of Tracking

Issues of segregating students in compensatory programs turn on definitions of literacy and course level and intent. Academic standards as absolute or relative measures also come into play. Most of the colleges' practices suggest relativism. The assumptions and definitions on which compensatory education is based suggest relativism. The concept "functional literacy" provides an example. One of its definitions is the level of reading, writing, and calculating ability that people need to succeed in the public realm in which they choose to operate. Under this definition, the level of literacy required to function as a citizen, taxpayer, homemaker, or merely "on the street" serves as a criterion. A second definition is the level of reading, writing, and ability to send and receive messages that it takes to obtain and maintain a job. And, obviously, different levels of literacy are required for performance in different types of jobs. A third definition of functional literacy is that required to perform successfully in a college program. Here again, different types of programs require different levels of competency. All these definitions, then, can be subsumed under the statement "Functional literacy is that ability to communicate in the symbolic language of reading, writing, and speaking that is adequate for people to maintain themselves in the context of particular situations."

So defined, functional literacy is related to the milieu in which people find themselves. It is relative; there are no absolute minimum standards of competence. A functionally literate person in some school settings may be functionally illiterate in certain jobs. And a person who is quite able to communicate within the confines of certain jobs may be functionally illiterate for purposes of a college transfer program.

The college transfer program that most two-year institutions provide may similarly be variously defined. People may be transfer students when they enroll at the college and declare their intention to transfer to baccalaureate institutions. Another way to define *transfer* is to restrict the term to those who successfully complete an Associate in Arts or an Associate in Sciences degree or to those who in fact do transfer to a senior institution. And yet a third way of defining *transfer education* and *transfer student* is to so label certain courses and those enrolled in them.

Depending on the definition used, the numbers of transfer students and the types of experiences they enjoy while at the institution shift around. If students say they are transfer students regardless of the types of courses in which they enroll, they enjoy the self-applied appellation. If they are not transfer students until they have successfully transferred or completed a degree, the definition must be suspended until the person has gone on to another institution or successfully completed program requirements. Most commonly, however, the definition used is the one that is institutionally mandated: A transfer student is one who is enrolled in a transfer course; a transfer course is one that the college so labels, subject to the constraints of accrediting agencies, senior institutions, and state-level agencies.

Hence a dilemma. Institutional legitimacy and faculty predilections rest on standards, defined outcomes, certifiable results. But the definitions guiding staff efforts and the precepts of continuing education or lifelong learning are relative. Each person brings idiosyncratic backgrounds and aspirations to the institution; each finds a separate set of experiences. How can the two be reconciled in an open-admissions institution? The question is not limited to compensatory education, but the influx of low-academic-ability students has brought it to the fore. In addition to providing a more useful learning experience for the poorly prepared students, many of the compensatory education programs have segregated them into separate enclaves, thus protecting, at least temporarily, the legitimacy of the other portions of the college.

Issues of minority student segregation and tracking are not so easily submerged. Compensatory education is designed to do what its name suggests—to compensate for deficiencies. Morrison and Ferrante (1973) suggest that these deficiencies are not merely those occasioned by failures of the lower schools but that they relate to cultural differences. For example, in families from the lower classes, where obtaining food, clothing, and shelter is a matter of daily concern, a tendency toward immediate gratification is built in. Where the necessities of life are not cause for daily concern, aspects of family life will allow for deferred gratification, and the norms guiding childrearing will include using formal education as a means of reaching for rewards to be obtained later. Morrison and Ferrante go on to say that the idea of using the school as an avenue for potential advancement in the culture is alien to people from the lower classes. Instead, if school is to be used as an avenue of advancement in any realm, it is toward higher-status employment. Yet their tendencies toward immediate gratification make it difficult for members of these groups to accept the regimen of years of study needed before one obtains certification. Morrison and Ferrante conclude, *"One perspective of the term 'disadvantaged,' then, is socialization into attitudes, values, and norms which serve to inhibit advancement into the mainstream of society and especially advancement into the occupational positions which would provide the material rewards desired. . . .* We may therefore regard the term 'disadvantaged' as synonymous with 'culturally different' " (pp. 4-5).

The terms *disadvantaged* and *culturally different* are applied most frequently to members of ethnic minorities, particularly blacks, Hispanics, and American Indians. The community colleges not only enroll more than half the minority students in higher education, numbers of them actively recruit more. Morrison and Ferrante estimate that one third of public institutions employ special minority recruitment teams and nearly three fourths of them use community contacts to entice minority students to enroll (1973, p. 23). Cross (1971) surveyed 141 colleges and similarly found a majority of them employing special efforts to this end. As shown in Tables 35, 36, and 37, the col-

Table 35. Nature and Extent of Federally Funded and State-Funded Aid to Academically Disadvantaged Minority Students in Public Two-Year Colleges, 1970 (Percentages)

Type of Aid	Federal	State
Scholarships	39	61
Guaranteed loans	66	29
Work-study	79	42
Co-op	10	2
Other aid	17	3
No aid	5	16

Source: Morrison and Ferrante (1973, p. 32).

leges also channel various types of federal aid to these students and provide special instructional and counseling services for them.

Thus, the establishment and operation of segregated compensatory education programs become freighted with overtones of racism. Because requiring a literacy test for admission to college transfer programs tends to discriminate against members of the ethnic minorities, who may have been less well prepared in the lower schools, the compensatory programs take on the appearance of programs for the culturally different, giving rise to charges that reading tests are culturally biased and that writing

Table 36. Instructional Services for Academically Disadvantaged
Minority Students in Public Two-Year Colleges, 1970

Instructional Service	Percentage
Programmed instruction	72
Reduced course loads	86
Liberalized probationary or readmission practices	58
Attention to development of study skills	100
Stress on communication skills	100
Stress on reading skills	100
Stress on writing skills	91
Stress on speaking skills	77
Stress on listening skills	83
Stress on use of traditional English	58
Stress on understanding of student's own dialect	52
Special courses in ethnic studies	17

Source: Morrison and Ferrante (1973, p. 31).

tests discriminate unfairly against those whose native language is other than English. Olivas (1979) summarizes the issues well, concluding that community colleges provide opportunities for minorities to enroll while perpetuating inequities.

As long as the colleges admit everyone but maintain certain admission requirements for different programs, the controversy will continue. Selective admission to any program is as discriminatory as it is justifiable. Regardless of the yardstick applied, the people who are shut out of the programs in which they wanted to enroll have been discriminated against. And yet,

Table 37. Special Guidance and Counseling for Academically
Disadvantaged Minority Students in Public
Two-Year Colleges, 1970

Service	Percentage
Special guidance and counseling	91
Special tutoring	91
Use of regular faculty in tutoring	92
Use of specially trained faculty in tutoring	52
Use of regular students for tutoring	89
Use of advanced students for tutoring	57

Source: Morrison and Ferrante (1973, p. 24).

with accrediting agencies, state licensing boards, and senior institutions looking in, program directors feel justified in admitting only a select few, particularly if the field of endeavor for which the program prepares people can take only so many graduates or if college facilities allow for only so many matriculants.

Should the colleges restrict admissions to certain programs? If some applicants cannot gain admission to a program because their level of literacy is lower than a cutting score, the issue is resolved for them. But if applicants *are* admitted to the program, then program operators have the responsibility to teach the students the skills required for them to succeed in it. The pattern of allowing all to enter and using the program itself to screen out the unworthy should be discounted—first, because one cannot at the same time teach and judge; second, because it is too expensive, in terms of concern for humans, to allow sizable numbers to enroll with the expectation that many of them will not complete the course of study.

The pressures for selective admission to various programs have grown in recent years. In the 1950s, most colleges screened students into remedial programs if their prior high school grades or entrance-test scores suggested that they might not be able to succeed in the transfer programs. In the 1960s, the pressure to allow anyone to enter a transfer program grew, the reason being that remedial programs were seen as catchalls for the less worthy, as holding tanks for students who must be "cooled out" of higher education. In the 1970s, the pendulum swung back, with many institutions building compensatory programs, screening students into them, moving away from the attitude of letting students try everything and fail if they must. And that seemed the trend as the colleges entered the 1980s.

However, it is quite possible to teach functional literacy in the transfer program. Some notable efforts at mainstreaming —that is, allowing lower-ability students to take the regular college classes even while they are being assisted supplementally— have been made. Many of these efforts involve the use of learning laboratories. As examples, in the Developmental Studies Program at Penn Valley Community College (Missouri), the Learning Skills Laboratory (LSL) was used as an extension of the math and English classroom. Students could complete LSL instructional activities, as prescribed by faculty members, before progressing to the course or concurrently with it (Ford, 1976). And Sacramento City College (California) initiated a Higher Education Learning Package (HELP) to promote the success and retention of students with basic skill deficiencies while mainstreaming them into regular courses. Students who were reading at a sixth-grade level worked with instructors and tutors in small groups and on a one-to-one basis. Using an integrative team-teaching approach, instruction was built on student experience, and progress was measured in terms of established competency criteria (Bohr and Bray, 1979).

Several studies done by the City Colleges of Chicago revealed that tracking students into remedial courses had not produced desirable outcomes: Student achievement in remedial courses did not result in improved performance in regular college courses, student retention was very low, and enrollment in remedial courses had a highly adverse effect on students' self-concept (Chausow, 1979). The college planners attempted instead to introduce concepts of mastery learning into the regular college courses. Results indicate that in classes using the mastery learning concept, student achievement and retention not only are superior to those attained in remedial program efforts but are generally higher than achievement and retention of students in the regular programs and courses taught in nonmastery fashion; well-planned supportive materials and services can compensate for poor college preparation; and cooperative staff and faculty efforts in improving the learning process can result in more successful college learning experiences for more college students. Thus, remediation does not have to come in the form of segregated remedial courses.

It is likely that most students can succeed in the transfer and occupational programs if they are required to supplement their courses with tutorials, learning labs, special counseling, peer-group assistance, and/or a variety of other aids. But it takes more than willingness to provide these services; it takes money. The question is how much effort the colleges are willing to put into the extra treatment required by students who enter programs they are not capable of coping with. Given a choice between an admissions screen to keep students out of the programs and the allocation of sizable funds to assure students' success if they are admitted, many institutional managers faced with static budgets opt to keep the less well-prepared students out of the transfer courses by placing them in remedial courses or segregated compensatory education programs.

But denying students admission to programs of their choice is difficult to justify. The open-door philosophy of the community college implies that these students should not be denied. The fact that some can succeed suggests that they should not be denied. And the fact that students who are denied access to the collegiate programs are typically denied exposure to the humanistic and scientific thought on which these areas are based mandates that they must not be denied. Community colleges have succeeded in opening access to all; if that access is limited to a compensatory program that offers primarily the same type of basic education that failed the students in the lower schools, then students have been cruelly denied access to the higher learning. The colleges cannot afford to operate separate programs for the less qualified.

The question of the public's willingness to pay repeatedly for the schools to teach literacy in all their courses is one of public policy; it cannot be answered by school practitioners alone. It rests on the state of the economy, the power groups in state legislatures, the types of federal funding available, the agency heads in state capitals and federal bureaus—in short, it is beyond practitioners' control. And no one can predict with assurance how these forces will affect compensatory education in community colleges.

Teaching the basic skills to people who failed to learn them in the lower schools is difficult and expensive. Questions of impact on college staff and image pale before the issue of cost. No form of teaching is easier, and hence cheaper, than a course for self-directed learners; the teacher-student ratio is limited only by the size of the lecture hall. None, not even education in the higher technologies, is more expensive than the varied media and close monitoring demanded by slow learners.

Many college leaders fear publicizing the extent of their compensatory education programs lest their funding be threatened by legislators and members of the public who raise embarrassing questions about paying several times over for education that was supposed to be provided in the lower schools.

Those who would impose standards for programs at any level face difficulties stemming from lack of consensus on institutional purpose, antagonism to the idea of group norms, and, in the case of secondary schools and community colleges, the inability to impose entrance requirements. Selective screening into the collegiate programs could not be maintained in an earlier era because students demanded and got the right to fail, and that contributed to the unconscionable attrition figures of the 1970s. Selective admission into the collegiate programs has been tried again because it is easier to screen students out *en bloc* than to establish criteria for functional literacy course by course. And yet, unless those criteria are defined, selective admissions will again be unsuccessful. Even though it is impossible to bring all students to the point at which they can succeed in the courses and programs of their choice, the community colleges must continue trying.

Reconciling the Dilemma

Three options are available to colleges that would reconcile the conflict between maintaining standards and allowing all students to enter the programs of their choice. The first involves defining exactly the competencies required to enter and succeed in each course. "College-level," "program proficiency," and "academic standards" are not sufficiently precise. There is too much variation among courses in the same program—indeed, among sections of the same course—for these criteria to hold. Standards are too often relative instead of absolute. Screening tests can be used at the point of entry to each class. And precise exit criteria, also known as specific, measurable objectives, can be set.

The second option is to allow all students to enroll in any course but to limit the number of courses that poorly prepared students can take in any term and require that those students take advantage of the available support services. Thus, students might take only one course at a time and participate in tutorial and learning-laboratory sessions on the basis of three hours for each credit hour attempted.

The third option is for the colleges to abandon the pretext that they offer freshman- and sophomore-level studies. They could enroll high school dropouts, adult basic education students, job seekers, and job upgraders, offering them the services they need outside the "credit hour" structure.

All three options are now in play to some extent. The colleges that are involved in mastery learning and other techniques that rely on precisely specified measures of student progress have built their programs on absolute standards. Those that monitor student progress and insist that students participate in the auxiliary instructional efforts have moved well toward building the kinds of collegewide instructional effort that teaching poorly prepared students demands. And those that have erected separate institutes that concentrate exclusively on adult basic education and career-related studies have abandoned collegiate studies de facto. The Urban Skills Institute operated by the City Colleges of Chicago since 1974 makes no pretense of mixing collegiate studies with its basic literacy and career education objectives. There, the idea of "credit hour" is not applied to the time students spend in their studies, nor is it used as a measure of faculty work load; getting the students' skill level to the point at which they can find an entry-level job is the institute's mission. As Richardson and Leslie (1980) noted, "Colleges will have to face squarely the issue of whether this type of institute will be tolerated" within the framework of the traditional community college. If not, "the alternative is to develop special institutes outside the community college structure, an occurrence which may not be all bad" (p. 39).

As community colleges become involved more heavily in compensatory education, they will have to reconcile their relations with the secondary schools, from which they broke away. Education at any level depends on prior preparation of the students. The decline in the secondary schools during the 1970s was one of the most notable events of the decade in education. Why it happened is not relevant to this discussion; reduced school budgets, the coming of age of a generation reared on television, the assigning of noneducative tasks to the schools, and numerous other causes have been cited. But much of the blame can be placed at the colleges' doors. The dearth of communication between college and secondary school staff members, the lack of articulation in curriculum, the failure to share teaching materials except on the basis of a random encounter—all must be mentioned. Concerns for social equity replaced a prior concern for admission standards. And in their haste to expand access, the colleges neglected to assist the secondary schools in preparing the people who would be coming to them and even, in many cases, to recommend the secondary school courses that the students should take. Reconciling the dilemma will force them to rectify this omission. The Carnegie Council on Policy Studies in Higher Education summarized years of studies of its own with similar recommendations and suggested that the community colleges place themselves in a position to ease the transition from schooling to work for people aged sixteen to twenty.

Issues

Whether or not the community colleges pick up the seventeen-year-olds who have left high school early, and whether or not they serve as a bridge between schooling and work for their older students, compensatory education fits within their mission of connecting people with opportunities. They will be involved in compensatory education in one form or another, and their career education efforts have already enrolled half their students. Linking the two may be a natural next step. Can the colleges do it?

The colleges need more information about the effects of the compensatory education in which they are so heavily engaged. Do segregated compensatory programs lead to higher standards in other courses? Do the faculty members outside the programs add content to the courses from which the lesser-ability students have been removed? Do they pass students through the courses more rapidly when they are relieved from having to wait for the slower students? If so, all these results should be tabulated as benefits of the separate programs. If not, the better students have not gained from the absence of the poorer ones.

Several attempts to engage instructors in defining the outcomes of their courses in specific, measurable terms have failed. What forms of staff development would be successful? What incentives could be used? Would allowing them to test the students who sought entry to their classes and bar those who did not pass the test suffice to encourage them to become accountable for passing a specified percentage?

Required support services would increase instructional costs. Can the colleges find sufficient funds for the necessary tutors, counselors, learning-laboratory technicians, and paraprofessional instructional aides? Can the faculty be encouraged to work with these aides so that classroom and auxiliary instruction lead to parallel objectives?

What patterns of learning are demanded of students in the courses currently in place? Finding answers to that question demands analyses of classroom tests and teaching techniques, a form of research rarely seen in the contemporary college. Will the faculty and administrators demand it?

The overriding issue is whether community colleges can maintain their credibility as institutions of higher education even while they enroll the increasingly less well-prepared students. If they can, they will fulfill the promises of their earliest proponents.

10

Community Education

Reaching Out with Extended Services

Community education, the broadest of all community college functions, usually embraces adult education, adult basic education, continuing education, community services, and community-based education. Found in the earliest community colleges, these activities were carried along for decades on the periphery of the career and collegiate functions. From the mid 1970s on, however, they began expanding at a far greater rate.

Community education covers a wide range. It may take the form of classes for credit or not for credit, varying in duration from one hour to a weekend, several days, or an entire school term. Community education may be sponsored by the college, by some other agency using college facilities, or jointly by the college and some outside group. It may be provided on campus, off campus, or through television, the newspapers, or radio. It may center on education or recreation, on programs for personal interest or for the good of the entire community.

The main link among the numerous forms of community education is that its participants tend to have short-term goals rather than degree or certificate objectives. They are usually older than college-age students, and their range of prior school achievement is more varied: Many of them already hold baccalaureate or graduate degrees; many more never completed high school. They usually attend the course or activities intermittently or part-time. Table 38 shows the variety of goals among community service participants in ten Florida colleges and the extent to which their expectations were met.

Rationale

Beginning with Jesse Bogue, who popularized the term *community college,* the leaders of the AACJC have been vigorous in their support for community education. Roger Yarrington, the association's vice-president, said, "One of the basic objectives of the American Association of Community and Junior Colleges is to help its member institutions become increasingly community-based" (1976, p. 20). Edmund J. Gleazer, Jr., president of the association from 1958 until 1981, wrote extensively in favor of education for direct community development, the expansion of the colleges beyond their role in postsecondary education, and continuing education as the main purpose. He emphasized the "community," rather than the "college," in the institution's title. To him, the institution was a resource to be used by individuals throughout their lifetime and by the general public as an agency assisting with community issues.

One of Gleazer's prime contentions was that "the community college is uniquely qualified to become the *nexus* of a community learning system, relating organizations with educational functions into a complex sufficient to respond to the population's learning needs" (1980, p. 10). He thought the institution capable of serving as a connector by virtue of its stu-

Table 38. Students' Reasons for Enrolling in Community Service Courses and Extent to Which Their Expectations Were Met in Ten Florida Community Colleges (N = 4,631)

Reason for Taking Community Service Courses	Percentage of Enrollment	Percentage Expectation Met
To learn skills for a sport or game	14.1	86.8
To improve my citizenship skills	12.8	83.3
To prepare for my retirement	16.4	83.6
To improve my reading skills	5.5	60.7
To help me understand alternate life-styles and how to cope with them	20.5	85.5
To help with an alcohol- or drug-related problem	1.9	40.0
To improve my financial planning abilities	28.7	87.6
To improve my consumer skills	21.0	85.8
To learn about family planning	3.4	55.6
To learn how I might adjust to a major change in the family (birth, death, marriage, divorce, loss of job, promotion, and so on)	14.8	81.0
To learn a certain hobby	33.5	90.2
To further my cultural or social development	38.7	92.6
To learn skills for effective membership and participation in clubs and organizations	12.7	80.7
To learn health maintenance skills	17.3	85.1
To learn homemaking skills	10.5	76.8
Because it was aimed at improving communication and understanding between the different ethnic groups in the community	9.6	83.1
To learn more about my cultural heritage	4.5	64.7
To improve my chances of employment	42.1	90.0
To learn job-getting skills like résumé writing and interview technique	6.7	59.3
To improve my teaching skills and/or learn how to deal with a particular teaching problem	8.7	73.5
As a part of an in-service training program organized by my employers and the college	11.9	75.9
Other	27.4	89.6

Source: Nickens (1977, pp. 16-17).

dents and staff members, who frequently work at other jobs in the community. The college would be a link among all community organizations that provide any sort of learning activities. "Among these are radio and television stations, newspapers, libraries, museums, schools, colleges, theaters, parks, orchestras, dance groups, unions, and clubs" (p. 10). As for the money to pay for all this, Gleazer made repeated calls for fiscal formulas that would recognize the diverse programs presented by community colleges. However, by the late 1970s, he recognized that "a kind of riptide exists between the interest in lifelong education and the apparently limited financial resources available for conventional education for traditional students" (1976, p. 6).

Numerous other commentators have favored community education as a dominant function for community colleges. In an issue of *New Directions for Community Colleges,* Myran traced the community education concept through university extension services and the adult and continuing education that has been offered by the public schools for the past century. He noted that since the 1940s, "community services, based on the idea of providing educational services to individuals and groups without being wed to traditional academic forms such as credits, semesters or quarters, and grades, found a responsive new clientele. Adults seeking job upgrading or wanting to expand their vocational interests found these new programs of the community college well suited to the natural grain of their lives" (1978, p. 3). He saw the community-based college as "characterized by its efforts to coordinate planning with other community agencies, its interest in participatory learning experiences as well as cognitive ones, the wide range of ages and life goals represented in its student body, and the alternative instructional approaches it arranges to make learning accessible to various community groups" (p. 5). Thus, the mandate of the college to provide degree and certificate programs would not change, but the college would expand into a "diversity of programming, planning, organization, and delivery systems" for adults who would "move in and out of educational experiences as a natural part of their daily lives," achieving "educational objectives that are personally rewarding, but not always marked by a credential or diploma" (p. 5).

Other authors in that issue of *New Directions* further promoted the concept. Keim (p. 17) recommended a cadre of full-time program managers to select the instructors for community education activities. Smith (p. 19) suggested separating curriculum development and instruction, with the full-time faculty doing development and part-timers doing the instruction. Mills (p. 40) foresaw the colleges as brokers steering students to other institutions, with that function becoming more prominent if funds are run directly to students as vouchers and entitlements.

Harlacher and Gollattscheck recommended a college that would be a "vital participant in the total renewal process of the community . . . dedicated to the continual growth and development of its citizens and its social institutions" (1978, p. 7). They saw such a college offering the kinds of education community members want, not the kind that pedagogues think is good for them, at locations where the learners are, not where the college says they should be. They recommended that community colleges cooperate with all sorts of social, governmental, professional, educational, and neighborhood agencies in mutually supportive advisory relationships and in joint ventures. They saw the barriers to the development of such far-flung institutions to be budgetary and governance structures, accreditation, articulation with other educational institutions, faculty traditionalism, and inertia.

What stimulated these calls for completely revised structures? What made these advocates so concerned with community building and noncampus forms? One clue is provided by the nature of community colleges' political and fiscal support. The colleges draw minuscule funds from private donors and have few foundation-supported research contracts. Instead, they depend almost entirely on public monies awarded in a political arena. And here they have difficulty competing with the more prestigious universities for support in legislatures dominated by state university alumni. They seem to be turning to their local constituents, seeking links with taxpayers at the grass roots. It may also be that they are attempting to head off competition from proprietary schools, staking out a ground for themselves in anticipation of a time when sizable public funds run directly to students through vouchers and entitlements.

Community education proponents foster activities different from the traditional courses taught by regular faculty members, saying that these are archaic, restrictive, discriminatory, and narrowly focused. They seem to feel that doing away with the traditional forms in which education has been conducted will necessarily lead to a higher quality of service. In their desire to eschew elitism, they articulate populist, egalitarian goals. The more diverse the population served, the less traditionally based the program, the better.

The overarching concept of community education is certainly justifiable; few would quibble with the intent of an institution to upgrade its entire community rather than merely to provide a limited array of courses for people aged eighteen to twenty-one. However, the total seems less than the sum of its parts. The components of community education must be addressed separately in order to understand its scope and effect. Are all segments of equal value? Who decides what shall be presented and who shall pay for it?

Categories

Brawer (1980a) reviewed the most commonly found definitions of community education and found *adult education* most usefully defined as instruction designed for people who are beyond the age of compulsory school attendance and who have either completed or interrupted their formal education. *Continuing education* was the learning effort undertaken by people whose principal occupations were no longer as students, those who saw learning as a means of developing their potential or resolving their problems. There is an obvious overlap between adult and continuing education, and the term *lifelong learning* further compounds the two. Brawer saw lifelong learning as intermittent education, whether or not undertaken in school settings. *Community services* was the broadest term: whatever services an institution provides that are acceptable to the people in its service area. The term *community-based education,* of recent coinage, was used for programs designed by the people served and developed for the good of the community.

A few other attempts to categorize community education are worthy of note. Respondents to a nationwide survey of directors of continuing education defined it as "courses and activities for credit or noncredit, formal classroom or nontraditional programs, cultural, recreational offerings specifically designed to meet the needs of the surrounding community and using school, college, and other facilities" (Fletcher and others, 1977, p. 12) "Community-based" education was more related to community problem-solving activities.

Nickens (1976) developed a taxonomy including instructional services (cultural and occupational), noninstructional services (coordination, consultation, and research and development), and facility services (use of property and equipment). And Leo (1976) saw the college fulfilling five roles in its relationship to the community: "The Deliverer," providing postsecondary courses for those who want them; "The Convener," offering the use of its facilities; "The Planner," building comprehensive plans to serve community health or training needs; "The Coordinator," linking other agencies; and "The Collaborator," taking an active role on behalf of community issues.

Conceptually, community education includes elements of career, compensatory, and collegiate education. Career education is organized around programs that prepare people for the job market, whereas community education includes short courses offered for occupational upgrading or relicensure. Collegiate education is directed toward preparing people for academic degrees, whereas community education may include regular college courses taken by adults, the awarding of college credit for experience, and noncredit courses actually taught at the college level—for example, conversational foreign languages. Compensatory education is designed to remedy the defects in student learning occasioned by prior school failure, whereas community education may include adult basic studies that focus on literacy, high school completion, and general education development. Some elements of community education—programs for the handicapped and for prison inmates, for example—may cut across all three of the other functions. However, other elements in community education relate more to providing noneducative services to the community than they do to the educational dimension itself. In this category would fall the opening of college facilities for public functions and a variety of recreational services.

Practically, the source of funds tends to divide community education from the other functions. Community education activities are more likely to be self-supporting, funded through tuition or with money provided by an outside agency on the basis of a contract for services rendered. In some cases local tax monies and categorical grants are used for community education, whereas career and collegiate education are funded by the states through various formulas, usually based on student enrollment or credit hours generated.

Enrollments

The variations in definition make it difficult to estimate the magnitude of community education. Enrollment figures, especially, are unreliable; they are usually understated except when being pronounced by advocates intent on showing that the colleges serve nearly everyone in their district. Because degree-credit courses are funded at a higher, more consistent level than most of community education, the tendency is to classify as much as possible as degree credit, thus inflating those numbers at the expense of community education enrollment figures. Actually, the total would far exceed the combined enrollment in the career certificate and collegiate degree programs if people enrolled in college credit classes but without degree aspirations were classified instead as adult basic education students, enrollees in short courses offered in continuing education programs, and participants in community service activities.

The enrollment figures that are available are worth recounting. Community education enrollments (in service, recreational, and life enrichment programs that are not part of for-credit, academic programs) have been reported in the AACJC *Directory* beginning with the 1975-76 academic year (see Table 39).

However, the introduction to the *Directory* states that

Table 39. Community Education Enrollments, 1975-1980

Control	1975-76	1976-77	1977-78	1978-79	1979-80
Public	3,203,604	2,801,778	3,045,730	3,386,295	3,951,187
Private	56,368	50,895	32,349	35,763	25,863
Total	3,259,972	2,852,673	3,078,079	3,422,058	3,977,050

Source: American Association of Community and Junior Colleges (1976-1980).

"because these programs vary in length, with no clearly defined registration periods, it is difficult to get a clear picture. . . . Some institutions do not routinely collect enrollment figures from community education students" (1980, p. 3). By way of comparison, the *Directory* reported enrollments in regular degree-credit programs as 4,825,931 for October 1980.

Other data corroborate the magnitude of community education enrollments. The 1955 *Directory* showed enrollments in the "Others" category at 59 percent of total community college enrollments in 1953-54, up from 15 percent in 1936-37. The *Digest of Education Statistics* reported nondegree-credit enrollments in 1975-76 as 35 percent of the total.

As Lombardi (1978b) has emphasized, community education enrollment figures cannot be compared between states because some include adult basic education and/or participation in recreational activities and others do not. Further, head-count enrollments in community education usually include duplicate enrollments occasioned when the same person participates in more than one noncredit course or activity during the year. Nonetheless, state enrollments are useful as an estimate of the magnitude and type of functions included in the community education definition.

The AACJC *Directory* reports 153,086 participants in community education in 1979 in California, compared with a total enrollment of 1,101,648 students in degree-credit programs. This relatively low ratio reflects the predominance of the California secondary schools in adult education in most of the districts, because in the three community college districts that had jurisdiction over adult education, more than half the students were classified as adults. However, a large proportion of the California students who were enrolled in credit classes were part-time and older, and a sizable proportion of the students in college credit courses were actually in remedial classes that were not included in the community education data. Obviously using a different definition, Brossman (1976) had found more than 357,000 in community development and outreach projects, 1.25 million served by nonclass activities, and millions more touched through such additional services as public information activities, community recreation programs, and open-circuit radio and television programs. Welch reported that instances of participation in community service activities in the district served by his college exceeded the district's population (1976, p. 38). As some observers of the California system have pointed out, "Continuing education for part-time, adult students has become the dominant function of the community colleges" (Knoell and others, 1976, p. i). But all definitions and enrollment figures careened wildly after the passage of Proposition 13 cut off the local funding base for community services.

Toward the end of the 1970s, the Florida community colleges had major responsibility for offering courses to adults sixteen and older who had legally left the lower schools. They also provided courses in English as a second language and courses for people preparing for the General Education Development tests, which enabled them to receive a high school equivalency diploma. The enrollment of those students plus people in continuing education, compensatory education, and supplemental and apprenticeship programs designed for students who wanted to upgrade skills in areas in which they were already employed totaled 504,000 in 1977. This figure is triple that of the college credit enrollment, and it does not include students enrolled in occupational programs and regular credit classes who did not intend to obtain certificates or degrees.

In 1977 Illinois reported a total of 269,000 students in various categories of community education, compared with 230,000 in collegiate and career credit courses. The community education enrollments included general studies (adult basic education and remedial courses), community service activities (forums, workshops), and noncredit adult continuing education classes (Illinois Community College Board, 1978). In addition, 71 percent of the degree-credit students were part-timers, at least a sizable percentage of whom were adults pursuing continuing education goals.

Other states, too, report high participation in community education. The 1976 Iowa enrollment data showed a total community college head count of 418,400, of whom 360,867 were in adult education. Community education in Oregon includes supplementary vocational education, self-improvement and hobby courses, and courses paid under contract from outside agencies. For 1975-76, enrollments in these categories exceeded those in the degree and certificate programs by 121,500 to 80,200.

In all states where data are available, head-count enrollments in community education exceed enrollments in degree-oriented programs. However, the full-time equivalent enrollments in degree programs are larger; students typically take between four and ten courses a year, whereas the community education numbers reflect people who may only have attended a weekend workshop. In Iowa, for example, community education provided 28 percent of the full-time equivalent student enrollments; collegiate, 24 percent; and career, 48 percent. However counted, community education represents a sizable proportion of the community college effort.

Scope

The scope of community education is reflected in documents emanating from colleges around the country. Continuing education alone covers a broad area.

- A report of the activities of the Division of Continuing Education and Extension Services at New York City Community College described their various programs for the continuing education of such diverse groups as parents of handicapped children, apartment-house owners, and elderly citizens who would work as teacher aides in public schools (Eisenstein, 1979).

- The extension division of Essex County College (New Jersey) reported noncredit offerings in the arts, personal finance, and test preparation, along with counseling for both academic and personal needs (Karlen, 1980).
- A survey of California community colleges revealed that 43 percent of the institutions offered special classes or programs for retired persons. The most popular courses were estate planning, tax preparation, budget management, physical fitness, and health and nutrition (Charles, 1979).
- Several hundred community colleges have participated in the Servicemen's Opportunity College network, which provides tuition reimbursement and other support services for military personnel who enroll (American Association of Community and Junior Colleges, 1974). Navy enlisted personnel receive full tuition reimbursement through the Associate Degree Completion Program for course work that need not be related to their service duties.

The awarding of college credit for experience is a growing component of community education.

- A survey of Texas community colleges revealed that 76 percent awarded credits applicable to an associate degree. Continuing education units were granted by 8 percent, vocational credit hours by 65 percent, and technical credit hours by 37 percent. The learning was validated by examination (53 percent), a verified experience record (35 percent), personal interview (6 percent), or combinations of these and other methods (Golemon, 1979).
- Sinclair Community College's (Ohio) Credit for Lifelong Learning Program involved 1,000 people who took "Portfolio Development" as a credit course in 1979. The program awarded an average of eighteen hours of credit to each student, nearly all of which was applicable to a degree (Heermann, personal communication, 1981).

Several types of cooperative endeavors between community colleges and other community agencies may be found. The

AACJC's Policies for Lifelong Education project surveyed cooperative relationships between colleges and community groups in
1978 and reported an average of fifty-nine cooperative arrangements serving 8,781 people at each of 173 colleges. The total
came to around 10,000 cooperative arrangements serving 1.5
million students. Dominant among these arrangements were local and state clubs and organizations as well as other educational institutions. Cooperative arrangements were also found
between the community colleges and community groups,
county and municipal government agencies, and private enterprise, including industrial concerns. Cooperative arrangements
with local clubs and organizations tended to involve shared
facilities only, whereas agreements with other educational institutions, private enterprise, and government agencies centered on
jointly sponsored courses. The majority of funds came from tuition and fees charged participants, but many of the programs
were supported by college community service funds, often generated by local taxes (Gilder and Rocha, 1980).

Cooperative arrangements have been reported by individual colleges.

- The Communities Alive for Living and Learning project at
  Kishwaukee College (Illinois) involved more than 4,000 participants annually in drama productions, athletics, and arts
  and crafts in three rural communities (Gober and Wiseman,
  1979).
- South Oklahoma City Junior College and the Metropolitan
  Library System of Oklahoma County joined together in offering both credit and noncredit courses and special programs and workshops (South Oklahoma City Junior College,
  1979).
- Clackamas Community College (Oregon) has been involved
  in cooperative arrangements with those community schools
  that it helped establish in its service area (Warford, 1978).
- John Wood Community College (Illinois) uses the concept of
  educational service contracts, whereby students are admitted,
  counseled, and given financial aid through the institution but
  actually attend an established postsecondary institution in

the area. The college also contracts for cooperative programs with local industry (Heath and Peterson, 1980).

Contract education involves the community colleges with other publicly funded institutions and with private industry.

• Several programs operated by community colleges for prison inmates were described by Cohen and Associates (1975). Hagerstown Junior College entered the field of prison education in 1969 at the Maryland Correctional Training Center. Guidelines were prepared by both institutions; it was necessary that qualified inmates be selected, that they succeed, and that the education program contribute to their return to a free society. One feature of this program was a college-initiated campus release program designed as a goal to which inmates might aspire. By 1976, fifty-eight inmates had participated in college release, with nine failures (Galley and Parsons, 1976).
• In 1967 thirty-one state correctional systems were providing inmate education in cooperation with postsecondary education in their correctional institutions, and in 1976 forty-five states had such a program. Community colleges in Canada, too, have been urged to contract with prisons in their areas to provide academic and vocational assessment, diagnostic and remedial programs, and languages and life-skills training for the inmates (Dennison, 1979).

Community colleges have played a notable role as contractors for programs funded under the Comprehensive Employment and Training Act of 1973 (CETA), as shown in Table 40. The AACJC prepared a document summarizing this legislation, listing possible services, and describing the contracting process (American Association of Community and Junior Colleges, 1979b). The California Community and Junior College Association (1978a) did the same for California colleges, showing how programs were developed with the participation of advisory boards. And the Illinois Community College Board

Table 40. AACJC Member Institutions' Level of Participation
in CETA Programs, 1976 (N = 919)

Amount Received	Number of Institutions
$500,000+	28
$100,000-499,999	150
$1-99,999	241
None	44
Undeterminable	400

Source: Olson (1977, p. 2).

(1977) showed how the colleges of that state could act as prime
sponsors of CETA activities. An individual college's involvement
with CETA was described in several documents prepared at
Cuyahoga Community College (Ohio). Eppley outlined the
CETA program and Cuyahoga's role in it (Employment and
Training Administration, 1978) and described its proposed Manpower Training Institute (Eppley and Mackie, 1979). Cuyahoga
also conducted staff development for county government employees and established a clearinghouse for information on area
employment problems (Mackie and Eppley, 1978).

The CETA program was only one of many efforts developed in cooperation with employers. Numerous others had been
formed with funds provided by the Manpower Development
Training Act of 1962 (MDTA). The intent of both acts was to
help the colleges design their occupational programs in accordance with local job needs and in cooperation with employers in
the area. Korim (1974) reviewed the skills centers and other
programs effected with MDTA funds and found useful activities
in most areas.

Several colleges have facilitated community education-
work councils to assist people in making the transition from
schooling to work. Coordinated by the AACJC with funds provided by the U.S. Department of Labor, these councils developed partnerships between the local schools and businesses
(American Association of Community and Junior Colleges,
1979a).

Community forums have been a popular form of community education. Black Hawk College (Illinois) has developed com-

munity-based discussion forums in which activities centered on courses by newspaper. In addition, the college has joined with other community organizations in sponsoring town meetings and film discussions (Stevens, 1978). Elsewhere, the community forum procedure has been used to bring the humanities to participants through lectures, panels, debates, dramatizations, films, and radio broadcasts. These forums have involved college humanities instructors working together with citizen groups in planning and presenting the programs (Eisenberg, 1979).

Much of the success of community education has rested on broadcast media. Several community colleges have been actively involved in the preparation and presentation of television programs; some of the more successful programs have presented courses in the liberal arts. Notable among these institutions are the Coast Community College District (California), which operates its own television station, Miami-Dade Community College (Florida), which prepares programs for export and for broadcast over the local educational channel, and Chicago City College, which was a pioneer in presenting televised courses in the 1950s. The Dallas County Community College District (Texas) operates complete televised-course production facilities and has prepared several complete college credit telecourses, which it presents and also markets for presentation by other institutions. Enrollments in those courses in the district rose to more than 10,000 per academic year by 1977-78 (Dallas County Community College District, 1979).

Because the concept of community education describes an area of service that knows no limits on client age, prior educational attainment, interest, or intent, the scope of offerings is limited only by staff energies and imagination and by the funds available. According to Coastline Community College (California) administrators, "The community is its campus, both physically and philosophically. The college nurtures the community and is, in turn, sustained by it. . . . Virtually any course may be offered if it is approved by the state, can attract sufficient enrollees to make it cost-effective, and if suitable instruction is available. Considerable latitude in programming decisions devolves upon the college, which, as a result, is encouraged to adopt a fairly aggressive marketing posture" (Luskin and Small, 1980-81, pp. 25-27).

The organization of Coastline and similar institutions stimulated the development of a new form of professional community college educator. The managers of these institutions not only must be curriculum and instructional designers, the role played by practitioners in all colleges, but must also interact with community advisory committees, find agencies to bear the cost of their programs, advertise for students, employ part-time staff members continually, produce varieties of new instructional media, and resolve jurisdictional disputes with other agencies. Even though such roles are not as well defined in the more conventional community colleges, those with sizable community education efforts have, of necessity, a number of people acting in those capacities.

Separate administrative entities have also been organized within several individual community colleges. Valencia Community College (Florida) began an Open Campus in 1974 to coordinate all continuing education, community services, and functions that the college was providing away from the campus. Headed by a provost reporting directly to the president, the Open Campus was organized as a unit equal in autonomy to the other branch campuses of the college. Facilities in local schools, churches, theaters, libraries, and other available spaces were used for noncredit courses and workshops. The Open Campus also provided counselors to assist people who were considering completing high school or receiving college credit for prior experience (St. John, 1977). The off-campus learning center operated by Lansing Community College (Michigan) included a director of continuing education, a formal contract between the college and the local school districts, a broad selection of courses, and the same basic support services that were provided at the central campus (Herder and Standridge, 1980).

Organization and Funding

Myran (1969) identified five organizational patterns for community service programs operating within traditional college structures. In the *departmental extension* pattern, community service programs are located in and generated through the departmental structure. The other four patterns consist of differentiated administrative structures. The *college centralized* pattern involves professional community service staff members who divide their time between community needs assessments and coordinating programs. They are located in a separate department or division. Staff members in the *community specialist* model are located in the community rather than on the campus. In addition to semipermanent advisory committees that may be coordinated by a college staff member, the *community advisory group* arrangement includes ad hoc committees dealing with critical issues. Administrators in the *college affiliate* pattern have direct responsibility to organizations in the community and an affiliate relationship with the college.

The ways that community education has been funded reflect its growth and variety. Some community education activities receive no direct aid; all expenses are borne by the participants themselves or by an agency with which the institution has a contract. Others are funded by enrollment formulas that tend to be lower than the formulas used for the career and collegiate courses. Funding for the recreational and avocational activities within the community education definition is the most difficult to obtain because those activities seem least justifiable for support at taxpayer expense. The Open Campus at Valencia has relied extensively on grants and contracts from philanthropic foundations and federal agencies. As of 1977 about three fourths of the staff were being paid under grant funds. The recreational activities coordinated through the Open Campus were self-supporting, but certain community service activities qualified for state funding.

Evans (1973) surveyed funding patterns in the seven states with the most widely developed community college systems and concluded that community service advocates needed to continually justify their programs and to be ever more resourceful in obtaining funds. He found that in Washington community services were self-supporting, while in other states the support from fees charged to participants ranged from 74 percent in Texas to around 5 percent in California, before Proposition 13 (see Table 41). Roed's (1977) survey revealed that no

Table 41. Sources of Funding for Community Services
in Seven Pacesetter States

State		Fees Charged Partici- pant	Public Funds			Private Funds		
			Local	State	Federal	Business and Labor	Founda- tions	Other
California	No.	13	31	5	4	0	0	1
	%	5.4	92.6	1.5	.3	0	0	.3
Florida	No.	7	0	10	2	1	0	2
	%	23.5	0	71.0	1.0	1	0	3.5
Illinois	No.	11	11	12	4	2	0	2
	%	23.1	28.8	39.3	5.4	1.7	0	1.7
Michigan	No.	9	7	8	5	1	2	0
	%	43.3	16.7	21.4	14.4	.7	3.5	0
New York	No.	10	6	8	2	1	0	0
	%	52.5	16.6	27.8	2.5	.5	0	0
Texas	No.	7	4	4	2	0	0	1
	%	73.6	10.7	12.1	2.9	0	0	.7
Washington	No.	9	0	1	1	1	0	0
	%	91.2	0	5.0	3.7	.1	0	0
Pacesetter states average	%	44.7	23.6	25.4	4.3	.6	.5	.9

Source: Evans (1973, p. 22).

state funding was provided for community services in ten states, and in eight others, only partial funding was forthcoming; support by participants' fees and local taxes was typical.

The activities other than community services conducted within the community education definition have fared better. Some states fund adult basic education at the same rate as career and collegiate programs. Others fund them well but use different formulas. In Florida in 1975-76, developmental and community instructional services received nearly as much state money per full-time equivalent student as the career and collegiate functions. However, Illinois provided only about one-third as much per credit hour for remedial courses as for degree-credit programs. Continuing education courses in Iowa were not eligible for state aid. Oregon reimbursed colleges for remedial and continuing education courses at approximately the same level as for collegiate and career programs. Maryland funded continuing education courses that met certain criteria, especially if they focused on occupational, developmental, and consumer education; recreational courses were not eligible for reimbursement (Maryland State Board for Community Colleges, 1980). Once again, it is important to note that between-state comparisons cannot accurately be made because the definitions of the courses and programs included in the different categories vary widely.

There is no best plan for financing community colleges in every state, and disputes over financing often disguise disagreements over the community college mission. In this context, Breneman and Nelson (1981) point out that community college leaders who try to convert their institutions into life-long-learning centers are gambling that political and financial support for such programs will grow. However, state officials seem less likely to accord high priority to financial support of these programs, compared with the traditional academic and occupational functions. Historically, community services have been funded more by local sources, and as community college finance shifts toward the state level, funding becomes more precarious. Martorana (1978) also alluded to the problems in funding the community-based mission with state funds, saying that the concept had not been sufficiently well defined, interpreted to the public, or accepted by the educators to warrant its being seen as a major shift in institutional direction. And Young and others (1978) found that the more successful community education programs were supported locally.

The precarious base of funding for community education was revealed during the 1978-1981 period, when tax-limitation legislation was passed in several states and a national administration pledged to reduce taxes was elected. Soon after the 1978 passage of Proposition 13 in California, the average community services budget was cut by at least 50 percent. These cuts resulted in a 76 percent increase in courses for which fees were charged and a 24 percent decrease in courses funded through college budgets (Ireland, 1979). Kintzer (1980b) detailed the cuts, showing that 20 percent of the 4,600 noncredit courses were eliminated and 10 percent were placed on a fee basis. Recreational noncredit classes were reduced by 60 percent, and senior citizen programs were halved statewide as twenty-one colleges deleted their community service budgets. Overall, since Proposition 13 "eliminated the five-cent permissive property tax that had protected community services activities, including programs, personnel, and some capital construction, for nearly fifteen years, the fiscal basis for this function was destroyed" (p. 7). Moreover, on the national level, CETA was one of the first programs to be cut drastically as soon as the Reagan administration took office in 1981.

Although state aid formulas vary, one generalization can be made with certainty: The priorities for state funding are, in descending order, career and collegiate studies leading toward certificates and degrees; adult basic education; adult and continuing education; and community services. These legislators' priorities are usually consistent with public perceptions of institutional purposes. As an example, the Field Poll showed Californians favoring basic skills education along with career and collegiate studies; continuing education was rated as less important, and cultural/recreational activities were lowest in priority (Field Research Corporation, 1979). But a 1979 survey of a representative sample of people in the Santa Ana College (California) area found them rating vocational, transfer, and personal-interest education most important, with basic skills education not very important (Slark and Bateman, 1980).

Much of community education transfers the cost of certain programs from one public agency to another. The training programs conducted by community colleges on behalf of police and fire departments that are too small to operate their own academies offer an example. Where the departments pay the college to do the training, little changes except that the college coordinates the training. But in some instances, law enforcement programs are converted to degree or certificate credit programs, thus qualifying them for support through the state's educational funds. This then moves the cost of the programs from the local to the state government budget. Similarly, some industries contract with community colleges to train their workers, paying for the services. But there are numerous examples of such specifically targeted training programs being given for credit, thus shifting the cost from the industrial concern to the state budget.

College managers tread carefully when developing training programs for the employees of local industries. The programs are often presented at the plant site, using the company's equipment. There is no problem if the company pays all expenses, including the instructors' salaries, on a flat rate or cost per head. But if the programs are offered for college credit and the usual state reimbursement procedures are in effect, they must be open to all applicants, thus potentially compromising the company's work rules. In many cases existing courses offered at the college have been modified to fit a major employer's requirements, thereby maintaining intact the faculty contracts and preexisting course accreditation. The company may provide new equipment, paying in kind for the special service. Program development costs may also be charged to the company, but the accounting procedures occasioned by the charge-back can be difficult to effect.

Contracts to train military personnel are particularly intricate. They specify the site, the curriculum, and the tuition that may be charged. They are overseen not only by the college accrediting agency but also by the military officials, the Veterans Administration, and other federal agencies. Difficulties arise when, for example, the college faculty is covered by a union contract, but the military does not recognize union membership for its employees. Such involvements also add greatly to the college's administrative costs because of the complexities of arranging the contracts and maintaining elaborate files for the auditors.

In sum, the variety of activities within the scope of community education provides an opportunity not only for serving new clients but also for manipulating the funding to the institution's advantage. If a course can be designated as degree-credit and thus become eligible for state aid, it may be moved to that category. If a program can be offered on a contractual basis with a different government agency or a private industrial concern paying for it, it may be so arranged and thus not drain the college's operating funds. And although administrative costs may be high, community education offers the opportunity for creativity in program planning and staff deployment to college managers who find their efforts in the traditional programs hamstrung by external licensing bureaus and negotiated contracts with the faculty.

Program Validity

What is the prognosis for community education? It expanded dramatically during the 1970s and by the end of the decade was considerably larger than the traditional programs. Nonetheless, several questions remained. Despite the pronouncements of community education advocates, questions of intent and quality control had not been answered. Nor was it certain how community education affects institutional credibility. And with the shift in funding patterns occasioned by these new programs, the question of who should pay for what forms of community education was also still open.

Advocates answer questions of intent by saying that through community education they can serve the entire populace rather than just the relatively few people of traditional college age. To them, community education is a natural extension of the open-door policy and the egalitarian impulses that gave rise to community colleges in the first place. Instead of serving only the children of the middle classes, they now include among their clients the minorities, the physically and mentally disadvantaged, adults of all ages, institutionalized people, and job seekers, along with the children of the poor.

The idea of community uplift has also been presented as a main purpose for community education. To those subscribing to that idea, the development of a sense of community is the goal. The college serves as the focal point for community pride. The events that it sponsors enhance a sense of community in the district; the act of planning, teaching, and participating in recreational programs and personal-help workshops fosters community spirit. By this line of reasoning, any activity that brings people together will suffice—health fair, senior citizens' day, hobby course offered in a convalescent home, or college-sponsored trip to a foreign country.

Less noble, but nonetheless prevalent, is the intent to aggrandize the institutions or at least to maintain their current size. Decline is painful. College leaders who peruse the demography charts, consider the competing institutions in their area, and study the potential market for their own programs may wonder about sources of students. Much of community education acts as a marketing device not only for the activities offered within it but also for the traditional college programs. The awarding of credit for experience offers a prime example; as many as 80 percent of the people who receive such credit go on to take additional courses at the college. The term *changing markets* is frequently used by those who exhort the institutions to move into new service areas lest they suffer the fate of once-prosperous industries that failed to adapt to changing conditions.

Community education seems also a way of blunting charges of failure in other areas. Less seen recently, but widespread in the 1950s and 1960s, were contentions that community colleges would enable the disadvantaged to move upward on the socioeconomic ladder and would teach skills of citizenship and literacy to people whom the lower schools had failed. College spokespersons also promised to provide an avenue to the baccalaureate for students of lesser ability and lower income. All these goals prove more elusive than their proponents expected. It is easier to propose new roles for the colleges than to explain away their inability to fulfill old ones.

The issue of institutional credibility must also be addressed. Is the community college a true college? Most community education advocates and most of those who make fervent calls for a "new mission" make light of that question, but it has been posed both by members of the public and by professional educators. Faculty members trying to maintain collegiate standards in their courses certainly take a dim view of most community education activities. Correspondingly, most community education proponents find little place for the regular faculty members in their programs, preferring instead to staff them with part-timers working ad hoc with little or no commitment to the institution itself. Community education has thus fostered internal dissension: Administrators may perceive the traditional faculty members as anchors dragging at an institution that would propel itself into a new era; the faculty tends to cast a jaundiced eye on the efforts to attract masses of ill-prepared students to the institution as well as on the recreational activities and the contract programs that use instructors as interchangeable parts to be dismissed when the particular programs for which they were employed have ended.

To those whose memories of college center on courses in the liberal arts taught on a campus, community education threatens to debase the institution. Their perception of college is as a place of mobility for individuals who, through exposure to the higher learning, take their place as productive members of society. To them, community uplift is an alien dimension; its aspects seem to be frills or peripheral functions at best, anti-intellectual at worst. They question the standards in the noncredit, open-circuit, and continuing education programs, wonder about quality control in an institution lacking a corps of full-time professional scholars. They reject contentions that an institution serving up a pastiche of uncoordinated functions to the masses bears any relation to an institution of higher learning. Community education advocates may try to dismiss these critics as anachronisms nostalgic for the ivy-covered college for an elite group, but the ranks of the critics include sizable percentages of the public who want their community college to serve as an avenue of mobility for their children, not as a purveyor of circuses and illusions.

The dilemma of reconciling the less-than-college-level activities and the community service dimensions of community education with the idea of the college as an institution of higher education may be resolved by continued attempts to broaden the generally apprehended definition of higher education, by a de-emphasis of the collegiate character of the community college, or by both. The definition of collegiate-level instruction in all colleges has undergone a continual change since the days when colleges were small academies teaching the classics, philosophy, and rudimentary science to the sons of the monied classes. Higher education had to adapt to several revolutionary changes: the opening of its doors to women and to the children of the poor; a curriculum broadened to include professional schools and studies for those who would embark on business careers; a professional ethos revised to center on research and scholarship. To the community education proponents, one more redefinition is not out of order.

The less-than-college-level aspects of community education may be resolved by creating separate institutions, such as Valencia's Open Campus and the Community College Centers operated by the San Francisco District. Certainly the large districts have the option of placing community education in a separate entity, just as the universities placed their other-than-college-level-functions in extension divisions. The other alternative, transforming the entire college into a new type of non-collegiate institution, is more remote; the overwhelming sentiment among the college staff, concerned legislators, and members of the public seems to militate against it.

Future Development

A most promising area for community education might be toward assuming those functions that the secondary schools have dropped. The education of youth aged sixteen to twenty bodes to be a significant social problem as well as a fruitful area for expanding educational services. In the late 1970s, the Carnegie Council on Policy Studies in Higher Education conducted several studies pointing to the importance of revised educational forms encompassing both schooling and work for sizable percentages of youth. Special funds from state and federal governments and philanthropic foundations will be run to this area in increasing volume. Expansion of community colleges' activities to include special services for youth would be consistent with their tradition. Throughout their history they have been the recipients of technical and vocational functions that previously had been assigned to trade schools affiliated with the public school districts. The flowering of career education in the community colleges was merely the most recent development in that trend.

Adult basic education also presents an area for expansion in community education. In almost every state, special funds have been made available for literacy training for adults, and in many states, this responsibility has been shifted from the lower-school districts to the community colleges.

It seems, then, that the areas of community education most promising for further development during the 1980s are those that have taken the community colleges away from their higher education affiliation. But this redefinition in the direction of career and literacy training differs markedly from the idea of the community college as an agency of direct community uplift. It is the community college as latter-day secondary school, not as social welfare bureau. It is the community college as educational structure rather than as purveyor of recreational activities and quasi-educative services.

The prognosis for other forms of continuing education is less clear. It is certain to vary in different institutions, depending mainly on the directors' vigor in attracting funds and publicizing offerings. The large market frequently noted by proponents of lifelong learning is composed, in the main, of people teaching themselves to play tennis, make furniture, cope with their families, understand their own physiology, and deal with cyclical changes in their lives. Those who need the discipline afforded by structured, institutionally sanctioned activities may be enticed away from their self-help books and informal study groups. But it is doubtful that they will greet eagerly the intervention of an agency that would coordinate all their learning efforts.

The issue of social versus individual benefits looms large in connection with community education. Most economic theorists would contend that funds collected from the taxpayers at large should be used to benefit society; hence, if a program is more beneficial to the individual than to the broader community, the person receiving that benefit should bear the cost. This is the basis for the legislative antagonism toward supporting courses in macramé and ceramics. And, indeed, many community education advocates were caught with their premises down when those human "needs" for activities that were provided by the college during the period of liberal funding dried up as the recreational programs were put on a pay-as-you-go basis, and enrollments declined to the extent that tuition advanced.

However, much of community education cannot be neatly categorized into services that benefit individuals rather than the broader society. When people complete a program in nursing at public expense and go on to work as trained nurses in the community, who benefits more, society or the individuals? Society gains trained nurses; the individuals gain access to a profession in which they can earn many more dollars than they could without the training. At the farther extreme are those forms of community education that assist society most clearly. One example is provided by community forums that explore patterns of energy use, quality of life, the effects of zoning, and the environment in the local community. Citizens are provided with information important to their making decisions within the social unit.

Those who would expand community education might do well to articulate and adhere to certain principles underlying its structure. The programs most defensively supported by public funds are, first, those that are more toward the socially useful, as opposed to the individually beneficial, end of the continuum —for example, the forums instead of the self-help programs. Second, they are the verifiably educative programs, as opposed to those which are predominantly recreational, which provide credentials offering the illusion of learning, or which are thinly disguised contributors to transfer payments. The third criterion might be those services that are not readily available elsewhere for members of the population served by them. Thus, the better-integrated businesses would manage their own employee training programs while the colleges concentrated on assisting workers in less well-organized industries, such as restaurant workers in their area, who might benefit from periodic refresher courses in health care and sanitation. Heretofore, members of these latter groups have been the least likely to participate in education of their own volition, but the true community service institution would bend all effort to serve.

The advocates might also reduce their claims that community education has the potential for solving community problems. As Talbott observed, the college is confusing its ability to take on the whole community as its province with taking on all of the community's problems and expecting to solve them: "To take on the role of an omniscient social welfare agency strains the credibility as well as the resources of the college. It is not set up to revamp the courts, to change the traffic pattern, to purify the water, to clean the air of smog" (1976, p. 89).

Gottschalk also noted the dissimilarities between serving individuals and society by differentiating between problems and issues. Problems are individual; issues are broad enough to affect the community. Individuals who are unemployed have problems that the community college can mitigate by training them sufficiently so that each may obtain paid employment. But thousands of unemployed people are a community issue over which the college has little control. High-risk issues also put the college in a position of conflict with other community agencies or with community power structures, too high a cost for involvement. Gottschalk pointed out that despite the rhetoric, "community college interest in dealing with community problems is largely illusionary. By selecting . . . low-risk community problems, a community college projects the image of involvement; however, concern for dealing with the major issues which are at the core of community development or change is nonexistent" (1978, p. 6).

Community colleges are on safer ground when they attack what Gottschalk called "educational components of solutions" than when they try to deal with "educational solutions of community problems." Any community problem has an educational component, but education itself does not solve the problem. That takes political action and other forms of social engagement. Yet even there, as Gottschalk observed, community college personnel are reluctant to get involved with highly charged community issues. A forum on energy conservation is safe; a forum on the history of a local labor dispute is risky.

Regardless of the philosophical bases, funding will continue to be the most difficult problem to resolve. The use of formulas that pay the institutions on the basis of full-time equivalent student attendance at a time when the number of credit hours generated by each student is declining penalizes the institution with a high proportion of part-time students. Community education advocates grope for ways of financing all the services that fall outside the traditional programs, and they deplore the advantage that funding agencies give to the career and collegiate functions. Gleazer reviewed the funding issues and concluded, "A mechanism to continually adjust the fabric of the community college—by integrating need, priority, social politics, money, governance, and accountability into one framework—presents our most immediate challenge and potential as organizations for lifelong education" (1980, p. 151). But a formula that would fund all programs equitably has not yet been found.

Lombardi (1979c) has predicted that the financial problem will be partially solved by imposition of tuition and fees. For some services—hobby courses, for example—the total cost will be borne by the students. Costs of some courses will be borne by firms or public institutions through contractual arrangements. Other services, such as adult basic education for illiterates and non-English-speaking people and special education for the handicapped and for senior citizens, will receive state support, with no or low fees. In between will be credit courses, supported by formula and by tuition and fees.

The time may be ripe for a new classification of all the community education components. The units of analysis typically have been programs and functions. That view might be shifted to the participant or client. Courses and activities alike would be classified on the basis of the intent of their participants. The classification might be along the lines outlined by Brawer (1980a):

1. *Credit-Free Programs.* Participants seeking high school diploma or adult basic education; recreation; social interaction; cultural enrichment; personal development; skills development.
2. *Credit Programs.* Participants seeking associate degree; certificate of completion; university transfer; general education; career upgrading.
3. *Community-Based Programs.* Participants seeking problem-solving techniques; coordination with other community agencies; access to college expertise; use of college facilities; specialized training.

This classification scheme anticipates a form of voucher or entitlement plan wherein people receive a number of fiscal credits to be used in the educational program of their choice. It is likely that in refined versions of a voucher plan, credits available to those who would upgrade themselves occupationally will differ in amount from those awarded to people who would use them for general-interest courses. Hence, the class in woodworking might well have students paying with different sums, depending on whether they are carpenters or hobbyists.

In the 1970s community education became the third major phase of community college activities. The first, the collegiate function, dominated from the beginnings of the institutions until the 1960s, when career education accelerated with the influx of federal funds. Then the percentage of part-time students, participants in short courses, and spectators in a variety of activities expanded dramatically. It was at this time that the community colleges began reaching out in earnest, spreading beyond the confines of their campuses to offer short courses and events in cooperation with other community agencies, open-circuit broadcasts, and innumerable educative, quasi-educative, and recreational activities.

Several prominent spokespersons for community colleges have urged institutional leaders to direct their efforts beyond the campus-based career and collegiate education activities, despite the dim view of this expansion of services taken by most local community college staff members. In the intervening years, community education has not reached parity with degree and certificate credit programs either in funding or in internal and external perceptions of the college's main mission. For the foreseeable future, the community college as nexus for all the area's educational forms is an even less likely eventuality.

Issues

Funding is a major issue in all college programs, but the fiscal aspects of community education are particularly tenuous. How can an institution funded predominantly by the state respond appropriately to local needs?

How can noncredit courses that may be every bit as valuable as credit courses be funded equitably?

Cultural and recreational activities conducted as part of community service programs have declined in the face of limited budgets and concomitant conversion of these functions to a self-sustaining basis. Should colleges try to maintain their recreational functions? Can cultural presentations be offered as part of the regular humanities programs and thus absorbed into their funding packages?

Should colleges expand their efforts at educational brokering? Who benefits? Who should pay?

Should colleges seek additional contracts to provide educational services to industries and government agencies? How can the costs of these services be distributed equitably?

How can quality be controlled in community education programs that do not come under the scrutiny of any outside agency or under internal curriculum review?

Any public agency ultimately can be supported only as long as the public perceives its value. Each noneducative function may have a debilitating long-term effect, as it diffuses the college mission. The educative aspects of community education —its short courses, courses for institutionalized populations, and courses offered on job sites—are its strengths. Each time the colleges act as social welfare agencies or modern Chautauquas, they run the risk of reducing the support they must have if they are to pursue their main purpose.

11

Collegiate Function

New Directions for the Liberal Arts

The collegiate function incorporates that portion of the curriculum which is centered on the higher learning. It is the part of the college that seeks to make people reflective and responsible; to relate art, music, and literature to their lives; to increase their understanding of the past, present, and future of the society of which they are members; to bring them into the culture. Its roots are in the Greek ideal of liberal education, of educating people for participation in the polity.

Liberal Arts

Originally the liberal arts embodied the collegiate function. They were the main and, in some cases, the only curriculum in the early American colleges. Codified in the medieval European universities, they were brought into the colleges as reflecting the best in human thought. From the ancient grammar, rhetoric, logic, music, astronomy, geometry, and arithmetic considered essential for the learned person, they gradually came to include the classical languages, philosophy, and natural science. By the end of the nineteenth century, the physical and social sciences had also shouldered their way into this curriculum.

The later nineteenth century was the time when the universities gained dominance over the liberal arts colleges and, together with them, assumed responsibility for defining the educated person. Before that time, people studying the liberal arts were as likely to do so in their own home, in a society of amateurs, in a church or monastic setting, or in an independent laboratory as within a school. But the universities institutionalized the teaching of science and of those aspects of the humanities that had not theretofore been part of the curriculum—modern foreign languages, literary criticism, art, and history—and made the study of them tantamount to being educated.

This institutionally based definition of education was fostered by an intramural revolution: the ascendancy of scholarship. The universities were grounded on the assumption that they would sustain the work of contemplative scholars advancing the frontiers of knowledge. For their part, the scholars felt they could best pursue their work by organizing themselves into academic disciplines. Thus, along with all other areas of intellectual endeavor considered worthy of inclusion in the higher learning, the liberal arts took disciplinary form. And one who would be ennobled by them studied them from the viewpoint of the disciplines as defined by the scholars. The organization of the curriculum became ineluctably associated with the form of the discipline.

This conversion of the liberal arts predated the advent of the community colleges. By the time these new institutions came on the scene, the collegiate function had already been so codified in terms of the academic disciplines that no college, no legislature, no educator's call for a "student-centered curriculum," no student's cry for "relevance" could shake it. All attempts to tailor the students' studies to their own interests produced little more than rearranging the number or sequence of courses required for graduation, wide varieties of course distribution requirements, or laissez faire elective systems. The liberal arts were captives of the disciplines; the disciplines dictated the structure of the courses; the courses encompassed the collegiate function.

Ideally, the liberal arts provide contexts for understanding, rather than the knowledge that some bit of esoterica is true or false. They are to assist people in evaluating their society and the contentions of experts, to foster the images and principles governing a person's sense of what is right and what is important. This sense is not inborn; it is nourished through studies in which the relations among forms and ideas are explicated, the "general education" ideal. The conversion of the liberal arts from these precepts to the academic disciplines reflected a major shift away from the individual to the organization as the arbiter of learning.

Transfer Courses

Thus structured, the collegiate function was adopted *in toto* by the community colleges. In their drive for acceptance as full partners in the higher learning, with their faculty trained in university departments, they arranged their curricula in the university image. The terms *college parallel, college transfer,* and *college equivalent* were (and are) used to describe their academic programs. Their collegiate function, their part in the acculturation of the young, was embodied in the transfer courses. The more closely those courses resembled university courses, the higher their status.

The most pervasive and long-lived issue in community colleges is the extent to which their courses are accepted by the universities. Articulation agreements (sometimes written into state education codes), interinstitutional standing committees, and policy statements that date from the earliest years of the community colleges to the most recent all attest to the importance of transferability. For all the rhetoric emanating from community colleges about their autonomous curriculum for special students and purposes, the universities have dominated the collegiate function by specifying what they accept for transfer credit, what they require for the baccalaureate degree. Major or sudden changes in certain courses can often be traced to a nearby university's changing its graduation requirements and/or its specifications for the courses that must be on the transcripts of incoming transfer students.

The community colleges rarely considered the secondary schools, where courses in the various disciplines developed inconsistently. United States history, American government, literature, biology, and modern foreign languages were included in the secondary school curriculum, but philosophy, anthropology, art history, Western civilization, religious studies, and interdisciplinary sciences and humanities were rarely seen. Community college practitioners of those disciplines, as well as all the other disciplines within the liberal arts, have looked to the universities for guidance in forming their courses. There has been no tradition of articulation or flow-through from the lower schools and a minimum of give and take of ideas, course patterning, or texts.

The collegiate function as transfer courses in the liberal arts was prominent in the earliest community colleges. Koos (1924) studied the curriculum in fifty-eight public and private junior colleges during 1921 and 1922 and found the liberal arts totaling three fourths of the offerings. Ancient and modern languages alone accounted for one fourth of the curriculum. English composition was taught, but literature courses accounted for more than half the courses in English. Agriculture, commerce, education, engineering, and home economics, along with all other occupational studies taken together, came to less than one fourth of the whole (see Table 42).

With some variation in the proportion of courses within the transfer offerings, this emphasis on the liberal arts continued well into the 1960s. All observers of the community colleges were aware of it. Medsker in 1960 discussed the prestige value of "regular college work." Six years later Thornton wrote

Table 42. Average Number of Semester Hours and Percentage of
Total Curricular Offerings in Junior Colleges by Subject, 1921-22

Subject or Subject Group	Number of Semester Hours	Percentage of Total Offering
English	17.1	7.9
Public speaking	2.9	1.4
Ancient languages	16.9	7.9
Modern foreign languages	40.0	18.6
Mathematics	15.9	7.4
Science	29.9	13.9
Social subjects	22.3	10.4
Bible and religion	2.3	1.1
Philosophy	2.1	1.0
Psychology	3.0	1.4
Music	6.2	2.9
Art	4.2	2.0
Physical education	2.5	1.2
Agriculture	3.0	1.4
Commerce	10.9	5.1
Education	7.9	3.7
Engineering and industrial	13.1	6.1
Home economics	12.5	5.8
Other occupational	1.9	0.9

Source: Koos (1924, p. 29).

that transfer "is still the function on which the junior colleges
expend most effort and in which most of their students express interest" (1966, p. 234). And even after the flowering of
career education, Cosand reported, "Community colleges were,
are, and will be evaluated to a major degree upon the success of
their transfer students to the four-year colleges and universities"
(1979, p. 6).

However, the 1970s saw an extreme narrowing of the collegiate curriculum. Except for political science, history, and literature, many two-year associate-degree-granting institutions
abandoned the humanities entirely. Cultural geography, religious studies, and ethnic studies were found in less than one
third of the colleges. Cultural anthropology, art history and appreciation, interdisciplinary humanities, theater history, and
philosophy were offered in between one third and two thirds.
The greatest number of humanities courses was seen in the older

institutions, a legacy of the days when the colleges fed from one fourth to one third of their students into senior colleges. The trend has been decidedly toward introductory courses for the transfer students. Enrollments in specialized courses were dominated by adults taking them for their own interest, not for degree credit.

Table 43 presents total enrollments and average class size in all courses offered in each discipline in the humanities, sciences, and social sciences in 1977-78. Total enrollments are not presented, because the figures represent head counts and the same student may have taken two or more courses. Figures are extrapolated from the 175 colleges sampled by CSCC to the universe of 1,215 colleges. Laboratory sections in the sciences were not included. Detailed information about the curriculum and instructional practices in each discipline may be found in "Instructional Practices in the Humanities and Sciences" (Cohen and Brawer, 1981).

Beneath the stultifying sameness of a curriculum shrunken to introductory courses, a notable variety can be perceived. Specialized courses flourished where instructors with a bent toward designing and marketing those courses were found. Nearly every college in the CSCC sample had one or a few instructors concerned with presenting something of particular interest, determined to do something different for the different students with whom they were confronted. The oft-heard contention that the curriculum cannot be centered on the collegiate function because the pragmatic students would not attend the courses and because the transferring institutions do not force them to attend did not hold. Exciting, active, lively engagements with ideas, tastes, and values did attract audiences, just as in the broader society the cinema and the stage have survived commercial television. Faculty members who have determined to break away from their transfer-credit, lecture/textbook course offerings have been able to do imaginative college-level work with their students. Unfortunately, their ideas typically were uncoordinated and unexported and had to be reinvented afresh by their counterparts in other colleges.

The collegiate function has tended to center on courses

Table 43. Total Enrollments and Average Class Size in Community College Humanities and Sciences, 1977-78

Humanities	Total Enrollment	Average Class Size	Sciences	Total Enrollment	Average Class Size
History	335,000	33	Math/computer science	449,000	28
Political science/government/law	255,000	31	Psychology	225,000	39
Foreign languages	162,000	19	Biology	208,000	39
Literature	132,000	23	Sociology	204,000	35
Interdisciplinary humanities	90,000	37	Engineering/engr. tech.	128,000	24
Philosophy	89,000	27	Economics	103,000	35
Art history and appreciation	60,000	31	Chemistry	73,000	30
Music history and appreciation	46,000	30	Earth and space sciences	66,000	34
Cultural anthropology	36,000	31	Physical anthropology and inter-disciplinary social sciences	44,000	30
Religious studies	under 20,000	28	Agriculture	38,000	26
Ethnic studies	under 20,000	22	Physics	35,000	24
Total		28	Total		31

Source: Center for the Study of Community Colleges (1978b).

based on reading and writing, textbooks and examinations. In the 1970s, that function suffered a dual assault from students oriented toward careers and from students who were ill prepared in the lower schools. However, it tended to thrive in the continuing education component of community education, just as it did in university extension programs within the senior institutions that themselves faced the same types of shifts in student desires and capabilities. A true picture of the collegiate function is obscured by perceiving it only through the filter of the transfer-credit courses.

Some of the changes in pattern can be discerned. In the 1970s, community colleges tended to offer fewer courses in the history of any world region other than the United States, comparative or specialized political science, literature of a single author, languages other than Spanish and English as a second language (ESL), ethnic and women's studies, and cultural geography. However, more colleges offered social history, career-related Spanish, and courses in film appreciation and the history of art in certain cultures. Most of these changes attracted students to areas in which enrollments had been diminishing. Introductory classes in music appreciation declined, but enrollments in courses in jazz and other specialized music forms increased. The notable increases in career-related Spanish and ESL brought students to the study of languages; it is unlikely that those same students would have enrolled in German, Russian, or Italian. And many of the interdisciplinary courses in the humanities and sciences were able to enroll students who might otherwise have shunned specialized courses in those fields.

These changes may be traced through most of the disciplines. Art history instructors capitalized on student interest in certain cultures by presenting the art of Mexico or Asia to students who might not have studied the art of Europe. New courses in folklore, magic, and mythology attracted some students who would not have enrolled in anthropology courses dealing with kinship systems. Students who would not take classes in climatology signed up for "The Living Desert" or "The Tidepools of California." Specialized courses in problems of the city replaced introductory sociology, just as courses in family life took students from introductory psychology. An interest in ecology drew students who were not interested in or qualified for courses in physics or chemistry to "The Oceanic Environment." Although precise figures cannot be obtained, taking all categories of students together, these specialized, current-interest courses accounted for around 20-25 percent of enrollments in the liberal arts.

Although student interest in careers took enrollments away from the traditional transfer programs, the collegiate function was maintained in different form. Courses in political science and jurisprudence were found in every program for law enforcement officers. Students in social welfare programs took specially modified courses in sociology. The allied health programs in numerous institutions included medical ethics and Spanish. And the faculty in some institutions built such courses as "The Humanities in a Technological Society" for career education students so that they might meet general education requirements without taking the traditional history and literature courses.

The collegiate function also survived elsewhere than in course formats. According to CSCC data, about half the colleges presented between two and five art exhibitions a year, and just under half offered between two and five concerts or recitals. Theatrical productions and lectures open to the public were also presented at slightly less than half the colleges; about one in five institutions offered ten or more lectures a year. Around one fourth of the students attended one or more of these public events.

The popularity of special events may be attributed, in part, to their not requiring reading or writing. The decline in student literacy levels coincided with a drop in enrollments in the courses that required the most reading and writing. Literature and religious studies classes required the most reading, with anthropology, history, and political science also falling above the norm. But where students could participate in interdisciplinary humanities courses through viewing and discussing films, in conversational language classes, in science courses that did not require a background in mathematics, and in all types of courses that did not require written papers or essay examinations, they continued to enroll. The requiring of regular class attendance as an important determinant of the student's grades was seen in music appreciation, art history, and foreign language classes, all of which maintained enrollments when they focused particularly on students' current interests.

Articulation

The tendency of many community colleges to develop a pattern of courses and events tailored particularly for their own students was reflected in the types of articulation agreements maintained between community colleges and the senior institutions in their area. Community college representatives almost invariably tried to encourage the senior institutions to accept for transfer credit the special-interest and interdisciplinary courses designed apart from adherence to traditional concepts of the academic disciplines. Although the changes in university requirements affected enrollments in individual courses in community colleges, their effect on overall enrollments was less clear. Frequently, a community college would respond to a change in, say, history requirements by no longer requiring its own students to take a survey of American history but maintaining a three-hour history requirement for the associate degree and allowing students to choose a course in local history or the history of a particular culture. Private two-year colleges, especially, reported little or no influence on their curriculum from the senior institutions.

Articulation agreements often specified the courses the two-year colleges might *not* offer, rather than those they must offer; junior- and senior-level courses offered by the senior institutions, particularly, were out of bounds. In some states, articulation boards reviewed noncredit offerings as well as credit courses and acted, for example, to discourage conversational language offerings in two-year college community education programs because those courses were considered the province of the senior institutions.

Paradoxically, the decline in students' literacy and in

their interest in the liberal arts did not stimulate articulation between community colleges and secondary schools. Community college humanities instructors rarely spoke to their counterparts in high schools. They tended not to accompany counselors on their annual visits to the high schools to advertise their offerings, and they made little attempt to recruit promising students of the liberal arts from secondary schools. Counselors seemed more inclined to emphasize the job-related features of the community colleges than to advertise the collegiate function as such.

And so the collegiate function weakened. Based on the liberal arts, which themselves were reformed by academic disciplinarians in the universities, it has been maintained predominantly through the traditional transfer courses. Why has it been so attenuated? Can it survive? What forms might it take?

Reasons for Decline

The first question relates to both intramural and extramural forces. Taking the extramural first, part of the decline in collegiate studies must be placed alongside the decline in confidence in contemporary social institutions. Not only has faith in the schools wavered, but also faith in government, in business corporations, and indeed in the authority of adults. The students' cry of the 1960s "You have no authority to tell me what to study!" was accepted as valid by educators, who themselves were members of a community that had lost faith in its institutions. They had come to expect, even to welcome, corruption in government and business because governments were by definition oppressive and businesses rapacious. The evidence was all around. Nixon's derelictions, the congressional peccadilloes revealed in Abscam, corporations bribing government officials were normal. The crime was in getting caught.

McClintock traced the decline to a decline in the purpose of education as preparing people to become members of a free society: "Where people no longer possess the kind of freedom they were presumed to possess in the design of liberal education, that form of education will have no real purpose to serve"

(1979, p. 637). In different eras, different forms of education would properly be liberal. The free citizen in one society needs different sets of understandings than the free citizen in another. Thus, liberal education might change without declining. "A real decline of liberal education can result only as the purpose that one or another variant of it was designed to serve falls into disuse. A decline of liberal education results from a decline in the freedom and autonomy enjoyed by the persons who receive the education, not from a change in the mode of the education they receive" (p. 637). Unless people perceive themselves "as autonomous participants in a common enterprise, there will be no purpose for liberal education, whatever its program" (p. 638).

McClintock related the decline also to the specialization demanded of the individual in contemporary society: "Insofar as a person accepts an abstractly defined function, agreeing to judge and act according to the specified rights and duties, powers and responsibilities, regardless of personal abilities, aspirations, or convictions, that person can be at best but partly involved, a limited participant, one no longer fully autonomous in thought or action" (pp. 639-640). Contemporary society demands this division: "Neither the market nor the state, in contemporary form, could function at all without thorough reliance on the abstract division of activity that they so powerfully enforce" (p. 640). Given the specialization of function in a corporate society, the best that liberal education can offer is a path to freedom for the individual within the structure. The liberally educated person lives by the maxim "You may bind my actions but not my spirit." This is more than education for leisure-time pursuits; it is education for the life that nearly everyone leads.

But because liberal education as taught in the schools did not make the conversion from education for the polity to education as freedom for people in a society of specialists, many of its recipients now show up as dropouts from the businesses and professional specializations. The manual laborer, tradesman, or assembly-line worker who writes or reads extensively, purchases or creates original art, performs classical music and attends concerts—the truck driver with a library card—may be a liberally educated person. Such people are relatively free from corporate and governmental restraints, but it is unlikely that they have incorporated their education into their work.

In the 1970s, the collegiate function was assailed as being irrelevant to the students. The study of history came under particular attack because many American social institutions and traditions were similarly under attack. The belief in social progress and in a nation that allowed opportunity for all its citizens was weakened. Allegations about racism, sexism, and unjust wars came together as criticisms of American society. Hence, requiring students to study a bland history that emphasized the social justice and democracy of America was condemned. Similar accusations were leveled at literature, fine art, and the other cornerstones of the liberal arts. Even language symbolized oppression because it denied the person's individuality, and "black English" and bilingual studies received intramural support accordingly.

Because numerous educators agreed that their curriculum was unworthy, the terms *relevance* and *individualism* replaced the calls for teaching values and a common heritage. Accordingly, the supporters of the liberal arts had little defense against the demands for occupational education. Consumerism became the hallmark of education in the 1970s, a consumerism whereby the client-consumers dictated the terms under which they would study, what they would study, and what they expected to obtain from their efforts. Under these conditions, an education that demanded commitment, adherence to traditions, the intensity of scholarly inquiry, examination of alternative value systems—the bases of the liberal arts—could not sustain itself. It had few adherents within or outside the academy.

The cult of relevance, of meeting student needs, of allowing every student to define a particularized curriculum came to be considered the highest form of schooling. An institution that could adjust most suitably to an infinite variety of student desires was the ultimate in responsiveness. Relevance was interpreted as providing job skills to the young, who, save the intervention of the schools, might be unemployed. As Hurn summarized, "Lacking any consensus as to the content of liberal education, and lacking confidence in their prescriptive authority

—as the catchphrase puts it, 'to impose their values upon others'
—educators were in a weak position to mount a defense of anything other than an educational supermarket, where customer
preferences, in the middle and late 1970s at least, were clearly
for the more immediately utilitarian and basic items on the
shelf" (1979, p. 632).

By the end of the 1970s, attempts were being made to
sweep the collegiate function out of community colleges. Numerous legislators and institutional trustees were lauding the
colleges as places designed to prepare workers, whose training
had no space for liberal arts courses. And liberal arts devotees,
who remained convinced that the traditional academic transfer
courses were the sole vehicle for transmitting the liberal arts, inadvertently fed these contentions. The more successful the colleges became in their mission of providing trained workers for
the community, the more precarious became the idea of liberal
education within them.

The Faculty

Accordingly, both extramural and intramural forces con-
spired to feed the decline in collegiate studies. Can these studies
survive? Any assessment of the future of the collegiate function
must consider the faculty. When the liberal arts were brought
from the universities into the community colleges, the ethos of
academic scholarship did not accompany them. The colleges are
not supportive of scholarship, and the university training that
instructors received was not, in itself, adequate to foster teachers who would attend to the reflections and meanings of their
disciplines. Further, too few instructors have remained current
in their disciplines. The result is a curriculum frozen in time as
it was when the instructors themselves received their grounding
in the disciplines. The few imaginative interdisciplinary courses
in the sciences, social sciences, and humanities stand out like
beacons. The argument that the universities would not accept
new types of courses for transfer credit is spurious; practitioners
within two-year colleges have not pursued them with sufficient
diligence.

The idea that the faculty, as independently functioning practitioners, should have the power to define the curriculum stems from the turn-of-the-century university model. The concept of academic freedom, of instructors teaching what they want within the confines of their own classrooms, was not accepted by the secondary schools. But the community colleges adopted it even though few of their instructors had become sufficiently professionalized to develop courses that fit the institution's broader social purposes. Within the liberal arts especially (but not exclusively), the departmentally designed and administered examination is resisted. Common textbooks for courses taught in multiple sections by different instructors are more the exception than the rule. Although community college instructors ostensibly all work from common syllabi on file in the dean's office for display to visiting accreditation teams, those documents rarely give direction to the courses. Any request for uniformity—any request for explanation—is as likely as not to be refused.

If the liberal arts exist within an anarchy, if scientists and humanists work within different frameworks of ideas, the curricula that they articulate will be diverse. In universities, however, the expectation is that instructors will be affiliated with the academic disciplines and that the curriculum will reflect the tenets of those disciplines. In community colleges, where disciplinary affiliation is much weaker, the unseen hand of the academic discipline is much less strong as an influence on the form of courses or on instructors' activities. Accordingly, the innovation and flexibility so prized by community college spokespersons derive less from educational philosophy than from the fact that the curriculum is without a rudder. One instructor's whim will change the pattern, emphasis, and direction of a course and hence a curriculum. Whereas the university organizes the intellectual world in a division of *intellectual* labor and necessarily accommodates a plurality of diverse intellectual stances, the community college organizes its world in a division of *faculty* labor and necessarily accommodates a plurality of diverse instructor stances. The amorphous, sporadic monitoring of instructors by department chairpersons, deans of instruction, accredi-

tation teams, and peers is of little consequence. Instructors'
work is influenced by the writers of textbooks they use, the
speakers at conferences they attend, the new information they
learn in in-service programs or on their own. But the enterprise
is chaotic, directionless.

An example is provided by contrasting the modes of
teaching the liberal arts and the occupational courses. Traditionally, the liberal arts have been taught by a teacher in a room
equipped with chairs and a chalkboard. Instructors have acted
as though contact between themselves and the students were
the key element, as though all that is necessary for a person to
learn were to engage in dialogue and to read and reflect in a soli-
tary fashion. Career educators, in contrast, have taken the position that they need laboratories, shops, equipment, and links
with the business and industry community in order to teach
people a trade. They say their students must practice the craft,
not merely talk about it.

What if the faculty in the liberal arts took similar views?
Music appreciation instructors might allege that for students to
properly learn to appreciate music, the college should provide
each student with a stereo set and a couple of hundred classical
records. Instructors teaching art appreciation would say that
students could not learn unless they were provided with slide
viewers, sets of slides showing all the principal art in the Western world, and funds to travel to museums. Anthropology instructors might insist that students be paid to work at archeo-
logical digs for them to properly learn the ways of thinking in
earlier cultures. Political science instructors would have students serving as apprentices to politicians and bureaucrats in all
types of government agencies so that they could learn how decisions are really made. And certainly the best way to learn a language is to live in a country where that language is spoken, with
the colleges sponsoring such trips. But liberal arts faculty members rarely advocate such views, whereas nursing educators insist
that they must have laboratories, equipment, on-the-job training. It would not occur to them to try to teach nursing in a
room equipped with nothing more than chairs and a chalkboard. They get the clinics and the funds they need to maintain

their small student-teacher ratios. The liberal arts instructors get chalk dust on their clothing.

These variant attitudes stem from the different ways that the career and collegiate functions were taught before they came into the colleges. Career preparation evolved from a history of apprenticeships in work settings, the traditional mode of learning a trade. The liberal arts were the province of a group inclined toward contemplation. Thus, it costs more to teach the occupations because the workplaces are duplicated or at least simulated on site. Liberal arts educators in community colleges do not even have the benefit of sizable library collections. And they do not act in concert to modify the conditions.

The collegiate function in community colleges has been characterized by a reduction in emphasis on the academic disciplines. Community college instructors tend not to conduct scholarly inquiry, not to belong to disciplinary associations, not to be excessively concerned with disciplinary purity. All to the good for faculty members who are instructed to teach in areas of current student interest and who must often cross disciplinary fields; the instructor whose work load comprises one course in anthropology, another in sociology, and two in American history does not have the luxury of maintaining currency in all fields.

However, the turn away from disciplinarianism has had some untoward effects. Many courses are characterized by an appeal to immediate relevance and by an excessive focus on the person. They confront the students with art, music, literature, or current events and ask for personal reactions. "How did you like it?" is the key question, not "What are you seeing? Why is it there? What is the meaning of this? How does this relate to other phenomena?" One test of the level of a course is the degree to which it makes intellectual demands of its students. Many courses within the liberal arts have strayed far from the collegiate ideal. Under the guise of presenting a student-centered curriculum, courses that reflect the popular literature of self-help books on coping, gaining singular advantage, and other personal concerns are often built within the liberal arts framework.

All curriculum must, in the end, be based on knowledge.

No matter what the ultimate intent of a student-centered course, for that course to maintain its collegiate character, something must be taught. That something is the subject; that subject stems from the discipline. As Anderson (1970) noted, "This applies to vocational, technical, experience-emphasizing institutions as well as to those with a strong liberal-general-education emphasis, conservative or classical in educational orientations" (pp. 52-53).

The demise of the academic disciplines as the organizing principle of collegiate courses has both reflected and served to limit faculty members' awareness of recent trends in their academic fields, an awareness important even for such a seemingly simple task as evaluating the new textbooks that appear. But it is important for more than that; the academic disciplines need reconceptualizing to fit compensatory, career, and community education, the institution's dominant functions. This reconceptualization cannot be made outside the colleges themselves. For the sake of the collegiate function, community college instructors must reify their own disciplines. It is difficult for a group that has severed connection with its disciplinary roots to accomplish that.

Transfer Students

A first requisite for modifying the collegiate function is the recognition that it is not embodied exclusively in the transfer courses. The collegiate function, the higher learning, teaches reflection, use of the intellect. It broadens choices and connects people to their culture and to past and contemporary society. The coincidence of this function with the transfer courses in the liberal arts has made the two seem immutably associated. But the percentage of students transferring to senior institutions has been declining since the early 1970s, and those who do transfer often take routes other than through the liberal arts.

Data on the number of transfers are not readily obtainable because follow-up studies are far from uniform. They may concentrate on first-time transfers, transfers attending senior institutions at a given time, transfers who completed a minimum number of units or terms, transfers to state public institutions. For comparative purposes they use head-count enrollment, full-time equivalent enrollment, graduates, four-year undergraduate enrollment. Table 44 shows the transfer rate in three states. However, Cohen (1979) criticized those figures, showing that data from the same state in successive years may not even be comparable. The best available data, though, suggest that less than 5 percent of the total enrollment moves on to senior institutions in any given year.

Even more pertinent are shifts in the community college programs taken by students who eventually transfer. In 1970-71, the first year for which separate figures are available, associate in arts and sciences degrees accounted for 144,883, or 57 percent, of the 252,610 two-year degrees awarded. By 1977-78 those degrees, while increasing in number to 167,036, had declined as a percentage of the total to 41 percent of the 412,246 associate degrees awarded; the others were in various occupational fields. Table 30 details this trend.

These shifts reflect changes in curricular choice. Since the mid 1970s, more students have transferred to universities from career education programs than from college-parallel programs. The transfer function has changed. The students with distinct objectives move through the programs in engineering, forestry, and business and transfer to senior institutions. Those who are less certain of their directions, along with the few who adhere to the ancient view of college as a place for developing self and learning to control one's environment, take the liberal arts classes. Some of them transfer; most do not. Thus the link between the collegiate and transfer functions has been weakened.

By equating the collegiate function with transfer courses, its proponents do it a disservice. Few community college matriculants adhere to graduation requirements; few obtain associate in arts degrees; few transfer to the universities at all; most are part-time students taking a course or two for personal interest or career education for whom transfer to the university is irrelevant. Many students who do intend to transfer find that they can study the liberal arts in greater breadth as well as depth at the senior institutions. The transfer function, then,

Table 44. Selected Data on Transfers from California, Florida, and Washington Community Colleges
to Universities and Four-Year Colleges, 1973-1978

Year	California			Florida			Washington		
	No. of Transfers	Head-Count Enrollment	%	No. of Transfers	Head-Count Enrollment	%	No. of Transfers	Head-Count Enrollment	%
1973	41,282	856,400	4.8	13,344	134,223	9.9	4,568	137,663	3.3
1974	40,459	997,235	4.1	14,040	148,804	9.4	4,764	146,784	3.2
1975	43,539	1,119,300	3.9	15,585	169,788	9.2	4,584	159,386	2.9
1976	39,776	1,092,800	3.6	14,642	172,748	8.5	4,545	154,564	2.9
1977	40,393	1,134,899	3.6	14,901	183,363	8.1	4,236	171,068	2.5
1978	37,802	1,073,396	3.5	14,059	190,726	7.4	3,852	180,922	2.1

Source: Lombardi (1979b, p. 12).

serves as a will-o'-the-wisp, leading liberal arts proponents to rely on it to fill their classes although at the same time it has changed its character.

The collegiate function cannot be sustained *in its traditional form*. Brann's analysis of collegiate education inadvertently revealed why. Brann equated *education* and *literacy,* calling them "convertible terms." She confined *education* to reflection on the books and ideas that make up the tradition of the civilization. She rejected an education centered on social problems as though the individual could solve them, as though human affairs were amenable to easy treatment, saying, "It is a faith encouraged by certain academics who . . . want to invest their subject with irresible urgency" (1979, p. 30). Students need a much better intellectual foundation and some critical independence before they can apply solutions to social ills. This type of education is as portable as books, but it cannot be attained without them. According to Brann, the Western tradition is set down in books, and hence it must be apprehended by the study of texts. Therefore it is not available to the person who cannot or who does not read. It is appropriated by applying the intellect, in distinction from the world's business: "As instrumental learning by its very nature neglects ends, so learning done for its own sake pursues them—the good is the implicit object of wonder" (p. 62).

To the purist, then, the collegiate function demands students who want an education for the good life. They must be willing to delay career-related studies, to read and reflect, to learn as though "the good" were the implicit object of wonder. In community colleges, a minuscule proportion of students, many of them adults who already have degrees, fit that category. The collegiate function could be maintained, even expanded, for them. But as the colleges are currently organized, the only other way to provide it would be to effect selective admissions into the liberal arts, degree-credit classes. There is precedent for such selectivity—it was widespread before 1960— but imposing it in the 1980s would prove difficult; the demands for open access are powerful. Further, instructors themselves, a majority of whom want students better qualified to handle course requirements, shy away from seeking more stringent pre-requisites for their classes, even though one without the other is wishful thinking.

Effecting a Merger

If any semblance of the collegiate function is to remain, it will have to be fit to the career, compensatory, and community education programs as well as being maintained within those degree-credit liberal arts classes that demand literacy. The first issue, though, for those who would pursue the collegiate function in community colleges, is whether those institutions are, or properly ought to be, educational structures. If the colleges are only to provide access, a stepping stone to a job or some other school, along with the illusory benefits of credits and degrees, then their status as schools is marginal. The second issue is whether they are properly part of higher education. How much of their efforts are devoted to developing rationality? To leading students to form habits of reflection? Many institutional leaders have seized on the term *postsecondary education* to characterize their colleges' place. To them, the collegiate function is irrelevant.

For the sake of their students and communities, the community colleges should maintain a place in higher education, but a reorientation is required. One area of possible integration of the liberal arts with career education is in a merger of principles stemming from both the humanities and the sciences. Technology is ubiquitous; students would have little difficulty understanding generally how the history, politics, ethics, sociology, and philosophy of science and technology affect their world. Those who would be more than mechanics would attend to the fundamental assumptions undergirding what scientists and technologists do. Where the colleges have built courses around such productions as Bronowski's *Ascent of Man,* they have succeeded in emphasizing these principles. In general, literature and art in the community colleges have not dealt sufficiently with technology, but a fully integrated course could be required in all career programs. A second point of integration for career and collegiate education is in the portions of the liberal arts designed especially for key courses in the career programs, a pattern described more fully in the next chapter.

The context for the reading and writing courses that make up compensatory education can be the literature that addresses basic human concerns. The courses themselves can be made competency-based, a part of the general curriculum. The students can be awarded credit for attending art exhibitions, recitals, forums, and lectures in the same way that credit is given for noncollege experience. Spectator events can be used to encourage reflection.

And it is certainly feasible to maintain the collegiate function in courses for adults who seek an environment and a stimulus for reading, reflecting, and discussing great works and issues. To them, education is not the literate activity of a leisured interlude between childhood and professional training; it is that which takes place when the other requisites of their life have been accommodated. It is utilitarian, not for a living but for living the good life. For students to participate in liberal education, they must suspend their immediate anxieties about the jobs they will obtain as a result of attending college, must shift from the short-term goals of education to its longer rewards. The young seem unable to do that, but many adults can.

Can It Happen?

The waves of fashion, trends in funding, interests of students, imaginativeness of the faculty all affect the prognosis for collegiate studies in community colleges. Several trends favor the expansion of this function. Aspects of finance favor collegiate studies because they are less expensive than the career and compensatory programs. Tradition is on their side; they have been present since the first days of the institutions, and tradition (or inertia) plays an important role in education. And those who would abandon collegiate studies must answer to charges of denying opportunity to the great numbers of students who still see the community college as a stepping stone to the higher learning.

Collegiate studies also remain the favorite of many people

who already have jobs but who want to attend college for the personal benefits it brings. These students may increase in number. There will be less competition for entry-level jobs as the younger age group decreases as a percentage of the population. Hence, students may be free to study the liberal arts without fear of being closed out of employment. And when the current wave of distrust of social institutions passes, the authority of the school as an arbiter of the curriculum may be reinstated. A sizable percentage of the population seems still to believe that the school has a responsibility to define what its students should study.

But trends suggesting that the collegiate function will weaken even further can also be identified. Students who demand that the institution provide them with a skill they can sell in the employment marketplace still account for a sizable majority of all entrants. They may take the collegiate courses but only if they can be shown the value attendant on such studies. Less easily traced, but certainly influential, is the continuing move away from print as a medium of communication. Students reared on a diet of instant information presented through electronic media may find the reflectiveness and self-discipline basic to the collegiate function difficult to master. Although some imaginative efforts at integrative courses presented through television have been made, the long-term effects of a turn away from print have not yet been fully appreciated. Not least is the idea that the college has no reason for existence other than to serve its students and the business community, no right to a life of its own as an intellectual community. Accordingly, it is easy to reduce the institution's value to the increase in its graduates' income.

The community college faculty's tendency to be translators of ideas rather than seminal thinkers ill serves the collegiate function at a time when it must be reformed for the clients. The disciplinary streams through which the collegiate function has been codified, advanced, studied, and taught are rarely seen in the community colleges. Not only are instructors' disciplinary affiliations weak, but also the purposes and operations of community colleges tend toward areas other than the academic disciplines. The disciplines are useful for training scholars; the community college does not train scholars. The disciplines are useful for learning about a subject in depth; the community colleges tend toward providing knowledge in breadth. Any reformation must be undertaken outside the academic-discipline stream and thus in uncharted waters.

Nonetheless, if such a reformation is to occur, it must be based in the community colleges themselves. There is no external agency organized for the purpose of revising collegiate studies in a manner that would better fit. The best examples of integrated course presentations in the humanities and the sciences have come from those practitioners who have understood the problems of translating the liberal arts for their students and have merged elements from several disciplines into imaginative instructional programs. And they have usually come from the large institutions that have the resources to commit to faculty members working in concert and to the reproducible media that frequently form the core of such programs.

For the students who come to an institution asking, "What kind of job can I get as a result of my attendance?" the community colleges have many programs. The students rarely ask themselves, "What sort of self am I in the process of making?" The institution has the responsibility of creating that question in the minds of its matriculants, eschewing the facile rejoinder that for community college students, individual freedom begins with economic security. The greater service to students may well be to insist on their studying the liberal arts.

The term *overeducated* may prove to be among the most pernicious perversions of the idea of schooling ever set forth. It suggests that one who has broader understandings is ill fitted for work. It glorifies as the finest product of our schools the drone who exists on the assembly line without any familial or civic responsibility. It suggests that no learning is of value except that which is of immediate and obvious utility. It denies the essence of humanity and of civilization.

It is perhaps arrogant to believe that thought and intelligence must undergird all human activities; the notion runs counter to the tendency of many within and outside the acaddemy who extol irrationality, emotion, and hedonism. Practitioners of higher education have been justly accused of overemphasizing the intellect to the exclusion of other dimensions of human life. But because people think, thought being that which differentiates them from the animals, they think that reflection on purposes is itself the purpose of human life.

Two-year colleges are not of themselves going to produce reflective human beings; no single institution can claim a monopoly on that strategy. What the colleges can do is to provide some portions of the education for the masses that tends toward encouraging exercise of the intellect. There is no surplus of agencies encouraging that form of reflection in America, certainly not for the community colleges' clients.

Liberal education is for the informed citizen. It gave rise to the ideal of preparing the individual to be a homemaker and a participant in civic affairs, the rationale for the terminal general education articulated by those early-century community college proponents who saw the institution providing a capstone education for those who would not go on to the specializations of the baccalaureate. That same rationalization will have to be used as the base for the necessary redefinition of the collegiate function.

The argument that community colleges should concentrate on career and compensatory education because they do it better than senior institutions has been articulated by numerous observers, including Breneman and Nelson (1981), who suggest that the collegiate function is best maintained in senior residential colleges, where students have a better chance of progressing through to the bachelor's degree. Here they are in accord with Astin (1977), who set forth the benefits for the residential experience in terms of the holistic development of students and particularly in maintaining their attendance through to the level of the bachelor's. However, these arguments hold to a simplistic view of the college experience, differentiating unnecessarily between the typical undergraduate experience and the best principles of a college education.

The universities have never done well in preparing students for the broad range of public and private life experiences;

they have been too discipline-bound, too ruled by the academic departments. Nor were they prepared for the influx of students poorly prepared in a secondary school system that since the 1960s has been eroding rapidly. The typical lower-division curriculum at the senior institutions has been built for students coming out of high school with certain sets of skills and academic pretensions, the types of students who entered the universities between 1910 and 1960. When the full impact of the deterioration in American secondary schools is felt during the 1980s, the universities' advantage in propelling students through to the bachelor's will be diminished as higher percentages of students fail the courses, drop out, or take more than four years to complete the degree.

The community colleges may be better equipped to offer the best form of lower-division studies. Their experiences with compensatory education will help. They certainly have had more experience with it, since from their inception they have been populated by less well-prepared students. The community colleges have an opportunity to reconceptualize their collegiate functions, not by maintaining arbitrary and artificial standards of the senior university type but by building truly integrated general education. Their compensatory education programs should not be limited to adult basic education but should be broadened to include study of science, technology, the humanities, and the broader concepts of the culture that students formerly obtained through a secondary school curriculum that is no longer functioning properly. There is room for the collegiate function but in revised form.

Issues

The overriding issue is whether the community colleges should maintain their position in higher education. If they should not, no deliberate steps are necessary. A continuation of the recent deterioration in the transfer courses will suffice. But if they should, what can they do?

Can the collegiate function be expanded beyond the college-parallel courses? Can it be made part of the career programs?

What can the liberal arts say to the student who wants nothing more than job upgrading or new skills?

Must the collegiate function decline along with the decline in students' tendency to read and write? Can the liberal arts be offered in a manner that fits less well-prepared students' ways of knowing?

Which elements of the liberal arts are most usefully presented in community education? Will community education directors build components of the higher learning into their programs?

What would stimulate the liberal arts faculty as a group to translate the concepts of their disciplines so that they fit the community colleges' dominant programs?

Advisory committees comprising concerned citizens, labor leaders, and employers have been influential in connecting the career programs to the world of work. Can lay advisory committees for the liberal arts similarly help connect those programs to the broader society?

The collegiate function has many advocates within and outside the colleges. The future of the community college as a comprehensive institution depends on how they articulate its concerns.

12

General Education

Developing an
Integrated
Curriculum

Confronted on the one side by universities wanting better-prepared students and on the other by secondary schools passing through the marginally literate, captives of their own rhetoric to provide programs to fit anyone's desires, the community colleges erected a curriculum resembling more a smorgasbord than a coherent educational plan. What else could they do? Their policies favored part-time students dropping in and out at will, whose choice of courses was often made more on the basis of convenience in time and place than on content. Their funding agents rewarded career, transfer, and continuing education differentially.

Most colleges responded by abandoning any semblance of

311

curricular integration, taking pride instead in their variety of presentations for all purposes. Except in career programs monitored by external licensing agencies and accreditation societies, the idea of courses to be taken by every student pursuing a degree diminished. The ultimate in rejection of sequence, of the belief that knowledge builds predictably on other knowledge, was reached when the colleges began awarding individualized-studies degrees for any set of courses or experiences that the students offered in evidence.

The disintegration of the sequential curriculum was not confined to community colleges. The universities have been plagued with course proliferation since the turn of the century, and a similar, if less pronounced, phenomenon affected the secondary schools in the 1970s when the number of electives that might be taken to fulfill graduation requirements increased. Yet the belief that some studies are important for all students dies hard. Pleas for core curricula have been sounded from innumerable platforms where secondary schools and universities alike are chided for allowing students to pass through them without enjoying any experiences in common.

The calls for an integrated curriculum frequently use the term *general education*. General education is the process of developing a framework on which to place knowledge stemming from various sources, of learning to think critically, develop values, understand traditions, respect diverse cultures and opinions, and, most important, put that knowledge to use. It is holistic, not specialized; integrative, not fractioned; suitable more for action than for contemplation. It thus differs from the ideal of the collegiate function: The liberal arts are education *as*; general education is education *for*.

General education received widespread publicity in 1977 when the Carnegie Foundation for the Advancement of Teaching published a book indicating the imminence of the first curriculum reforms in higher education in thirty years. The Carnegie Foundation said the time was right because the test scores of students entering college were down, and it was obvious that much was wrong in precollegiate education. Further, students seemed to be learning less in college, and even though remedial education had been tried by all types of colleges, it was difficult to show the efficacy of these efforts. The foundation proposed a reform toward integration in a curriculum that had become fractionated, toward education in values in a curriculum that had purported to be value-free. It sought a return to general education.

So it is one more time around for general education. What happened to it the first time it flourished, in the early nineteenth century? And the second time, between 1920 and 1950?

Background

General education can be traced to the moral philosophy courses found in American colleges during their first 200 years. These integrative experiences were taught usually by the college president and presented to all students. Remnants of the integrated courses pulling together knowledge from several areas may still be seen in the capstone courses required of all students in a few contemporary institutions. However, that type of general education broke apart in most colleges in the second half of the nineteenth century, to be replaced by the free-elective system. No longer were there to be courses that all students would take; no longer would the colleges attempt to bring together threads of all knowledge in a unified theme. Blame the rise of the academic disciplines, the professionalization of the faculty, the broadening of knowledge in all areas, the increased numbers of students, each with his or her own agenda—all these accusations have been made. But, for whatever reason, the elective system took over. The old classical curriculum died out, taking with it the idea of the curriculum as a unified whole to be presented to all students. By the turn of the twentieth century, most American colleges had come down to an irreducible minimum in curriculum: faculty members with academic degrees teaching courses of their choice to those students who elected to study with them.

All curriculum is, at bottom, a statement a college makes about what it thinks is important. The free-elective system is a philosophical statement quite as much as is a curriculum based on the Great Books or one concerned solely with occupational education. Free election—any student, any course—is an admission that the college no longer has the moral authority to insist on any combination of courses, that it no longer recognizes the validity of sequence or organized principles of curriculum integration. The system was not without its critics. The early-century Carnegie plan—assigning units of credit for hours of study—was introduced in an attempt to bring order out of the free-elective curricular chaos. It had the opposite effect: By ascribing units of credit of apparently equal merit, it snipped to pieces whatever unity was left in the academic subjects themselves. Three credits of algebra had the same meaning as three credits of calculus; a three-credit introductory course in a discipline was of equal value to an advanced seminar in the same field. When a student may accumulate any 120 credit hours and obtain a baccalaureate degree, when all credits are the same, all unity of knowledge falls apart.

The initial reaction against the free-elective system gave rise to distribution requirements—curriculum defined by bureaucratic organization. Groups of courses were specified in a process of political accommodation among academic departments. In order that the history department would vote a six-unit English requirement, the English department was expected to reciprocate by voting a six-unit history requirement. Protecting departmental territory became the curriculum organizer. Placing a disintegrated mass of free-elective courses into a set of distribution requirements gives the appearance of providing the curriculum with a rationale. Thus, the noble truths of general studies arose post hoc to justify the politics of distribution— whence the popular statements that colleges provide a breadth of studies, ensuring that their students leave as well-rounded individuals. In the 1970s, the Carnegie Council found that students spend about one third of their time in college taking distribution requirements, the other thirds going to the major and to electives. The political accommodations among departments were in equilibrium.

The success of distribution requirements as an organizing

principle for curriculum did not stop those who advocated curriculum integration. Their early attempts to return order were founded in survey courses. Columbia University's "Contemporary Civilization" course, first offered in 1919, is usually seen as the prototype. These courses give the overview, the broad sweep, in history, the arts, the sciences, and the social sciences. The academic discipline is the organizing principle of the course, but the course is supposed to show the unity of knowledge, to integrate disparate elements from many disciplines. Survey courses became quite popular during the 1920s and 1930s. Surveys of social sciences, for example, were built into the "Individual in Society" courses. The humanities surveys became "Modern Culture and the Arts." Separate surveys of natural, physical, and biological sciences were also attempted but with less success.

Advocates of survey courses had constantly to struggle to maintain the integrity of their offerings against the faculty tendency to convert each course into the introduction to a discipline, to teach concepts and terminology in a particular academic specialization as though all students were majors in that field. The faculty objection to the survey courses was that they were superficial, trying to encompass too many different portions of human knowledge. As each course slid away from a true interdisciplinary orientation to become the first course in an academic discipline. it tended to lose its general education characteristics.

Nonetheless, many interdisciplinary courses survived. Much seemed to depend on the level of specialization within the discipline. Social science instructors had little trouble putting together political science, sociology, economics, and anthropology into a general social science survey. Science instructors, however, may have felt they were teaching a general survey if they integrated molecular and organismic biology into one course. It was difficult for them to include the physical and earth and space sciences. In 1935, Cowley found social science courses first in number of colleges offering surveys, followed by natural science, physical science, biological science, and only a few humanities surveys (Johnson, 1937). However, the humanities courses have fared better recently; in fact, enrollments in integrated humanities courses in community colleges increased in the 1970s in the face of a decline in the specific disciplines within the humanities.

General education suffered originally from the free-elective system and the broadening of knowledge properly a part of the college curriculum. Rudolph's history of the undergraduate curriculum traced the concept into the 1970s and concluded, "Where highly publicized general education requirements reshaped the course of study in the 1940s and 1950s, less publicized erosion of those requirements took place in the 1960s and 1970s" (1977, p. 253). What happened to it this time? Rudolph said that general education fell victim to faculty power, lack of student interest, increased demands on faculty time, difficulty in integrating the disciplines, and most of all from its lack of demonstrated value and the superficiality of the presentations. General education has remained a noble idea but a practical backwater in most of American higher education.

Definitions

A good part of the difficulty with general education rests with its definition. The term has been in use for more than sixty years and has been defined innumerable times. It has been seen as narrowly as the trivium and quadrivium, the discipline of the medieval scholars, and as broadly as that education which integrates and unifies all knowledge. It has been confounded with the liberal arts, and it has been connected to the human developmental cycle. It has been defined as what it is not. Following are some of the definitions.

On the side of breadth, the 1939 Yearbook of the National Society for the Study of Education saw general education as concerned with the "widest possible range of basic human activities." It was to guide the student "to the discovery of the best that is currently known in thought." It was "dynamic," "democratic," "systematic." The student was to gain "a real grasp of the most widely ramifying generalized insights—intellectual, ethical, and esthetic" (p. 12). The Harvard "Red Book," *General Education in a Free Society* (Committee on the Objectives of a General Education in a Free Society, 1945) also announced that general education was to bring all knowledge together. And in an argument for general education in the high school, Henry (1956) called for an education that would achieve a "qualitative synthesis."

General education has also been defined as that which everyone should know. The Executive Committee of the Cooperative Study in General Education said it should provide "the basic understandings and skills which everyone should possess" (*Cooperation in General Education,* 1947, p. 17). Mayhew said it should establish "a common universe of discourse—a common heritage" (1960, p. 16). In the proceedings of a 1959 Florida junior college conference on general education (Florida State Department of Education, 1959), the idea of commonality, those learnings that should be possessed by all persons, was articulated repeatedly. Boyer and Kaplan argued for a common core that should be taught to all students. They spoke of a need for "comprehensive literacy" and "an awareness of symbol systems" that everyone in contemporary society must have (1977, p. 67).

General education has also been defined by what it is not: It is nonspecialized, nonvocational; it is not occupational education; it is not learning to use the tools of a discipline or learning a specialized language. A report of a conference held at a community college in Florida in 1976 offers a wondrous example of definition by exclusion: "At the operational level, general education . . . is not special; that is, it is not designed for specific groups of people or special activities. . . . It is *not* an introduction to disciplines as the first step in specialization. It is *not* content for its own sake. It is *not* the development of skills or the acquisition of knowledge precisely for their applicability to a job, a career, or another specialization. It is *not* a collection of courses. It is *not* simply a rearrangement of content, like an interdisciplinary program or course for the sake of being interdisciplinary. It is *not* so abstract and future-oriented that it can only be hoped for, wished for, or assumed to happen somewhere, sometime. It is *not* merely being able to read, to write, and to do arithmetic" (Tighe, 1977, pp. 13-14).

Another way of defining general education has been to

compare it with liberal education. Educators have always agreed that education should be useful for something (all curricula are justified for their practical value). Apologists for liberal education have held that it frees people from such external tyrannies as caste biases, societal constraints, and professional experts as well as from the internal tyrannies of ignorance, prejudice, superstition, guilt, and what the Thomists might call "the appetites." Having to do with the virtues, it has been rationalized as affording knowledge for its own sake.

In general education, in contrast, knowledge is power—the power of coping, understanding, mastering the self and social interaction. It must lead to the ability to do, to act; gaining rationality alone is not enough. People who have had a general education are supposed to act intelligently. This view grounds the construct in the everyday affairs of a person: dealing with supervisors and coworkers, choosing associates, coping with family problems, and spending leisure time in socially desirable and personally satisfying ways. To be successful, a general education program not only makes explicit the skills and understandings to be attained but also relates those competencies to external referents, to what people are doing when they have gained them. As Schlesinger noted, "The crucial question involves what the student *does* with the bits of information he/she picks up in a course or text or from personal experience. If all we ask is that the student remember it, we do a disservice" (1977, p. 42).

Accordingly, general education is often defined in terms of the competencies to be gained by those whom it touches. A group studying general education in California community colleges in the early 1950s (Johnson, 1952) offered a list of twelve competencies to be exercised by those who were generally educated:

- Exercising the privileges and responsibilities of democratic citizenship.
- Developing a set of sound moral and spiritual values by which the person guides his life.
- Expressing his thoughts clearly in speaking and writing and in reading and listening with understanding.

- Using the basic mathematical and mechanical skills necessary in everyday life.
- Using methods of critical thinking for the solution of problems and for the discrimination among values.
- Understanding his cultural heritage so that he may gain a perspective of his time and place in the world.
- Understanding his interaction with his biological and physical environment so that he may adjust to and improve that environment.
- Maintaining good mental and physical health for himself, his family, and his community.
- Developing a balanced personal and social adjustment.
- Sharing in the development of a satisfactory home and family life.
- Taking part in some form of satisfying creative activity and in appreciating the creative activities of others.

That list, or portions thereof, still appears verbatim in many community college catalogues because it gives the appearance of being competency-based even though it is sufficiently broad to justify any course or program.

Instability

Given the plethora of definitions, the failure to maintain general education consistently is easily understood. General education is prey to any group with a strict view of curriculum. Throughout this century, the same forces that splintered knowledge into academic disciplines have continued their antagonism to a general or unifying education. The academic profession had become departmentalized in its specializations, thus posing a contradiction for the integration of learning. The academic departments insisted that students pick a major—the earlier the better. Courses were built as introductions to disciplines with their own logic, terminology, goals, organizing principles, modes of inquiry; adding distribution requirements while leaving the internal organization of the course intact did not enhance knowledge integration, common learnings, or competencies. In short, the academic discipline, with its hold on the faculty and the organization of the college, was the first and most pervasive deterrent to general education.

The definition itself has been part of the problem. If general education is defined by what it is not, instead of what it is, it is open to any type of course or experience. Constantly denying the restrictive organization of occupational and discipline-based education has propelled general education into the areas of unstructured events, counseling activities, courses without content, programs with broad goals impossible of attainment—the anticurriculum.

The breadth of the positive side of the definition hurt too. The most specialized course in Elizabethan literature might lead students to "understand their cultural heritage." The most trivial course in personal habits and grooming might assist students to "maintain good mental and physical health." Guidance and orientation programs could assist students to "develop a balanced personal and social adjustment," and so on throughout the list of competencies and throughout the range of activities and services provided by colleges. Where anything can be related to general education, it falls victim to the whims of students, faculty members, and administrators alike.

General education was tainted early on. The phrase *terminal general education* was in use in the 1930s, suggesting that it was an education for the student who would never go on to the higher learning. In some senior institutions, separate colleges were devised as holding tanks for students deemed unqualified to enter the regular programs. Here they would get the last of their formal education, nondisciplinary, nonspecialized, and—according to many professors—of dubious merit. If general education was seen as a curriculum for students unable to do real college work, it was doomed to suffer. Perhaps it was an extension of high school general education, but then what was it doing in a real college? And how could a self-respecting faculty member have anything to do with it? Credit the idea of terminal general education as one of the factors leading to the failure of general education to hold the attention of the academy.

Another clue to the unstable history of general education can be found in its emphasis on individual life adjustment. Early proponents of general education fostered guidance activities. B. Lamar Johnson, a spokesperson for general education during much of his half century in higher education, said in 1937, "Uniformly colleges committed to general education stress guidance. This is reasonable, for if general education aims to help the individual adjust to life, it is essential to recognize that this adjustment is an individual matter—dependent upon individual abilities, interests, and needs. Upon these bases the colleges assist the student to determine his individual objectives and mould a program to attain them" (p. 12). But if the individual is to mould a program based on his own "abilities, interests, and needs," then anything may be seen as general education for that individual. The person may take the most specialized courses or no courses at all. Such a definition dooms the idea of integrated courses—indeed, of all common courses. Thus, general education in the 1930s was so fractionated that it included everything from the Great Books curriculum to life-adjustment courses and student guidance.

The idea that the student should be led to a "satisfactory vocational adjustment" was also common in definitions of general education at midcentury. Occupational education has achieved great success in American colleges and universities but for different reasons: It was built on an alliance of educators seeking support, students seeking jobs, and business people seeking workers trained at public expense; it has capitalized on legislators who are pleased to assign schools the task of mitigating unemployment; it has been enhanced by parents who want the schools to teach their children to do something productive. It has done well, and if it is a part of general education, then general education has done well, too. But when general education is defined as leading students to understand relationships between themselves and society, gain a sense of values and an appreciation for cultural diversity, and fulfill the other broader aims of the program, occupational education is left out. Credit its inclusion with blurring the image of what general education is or could be.

The expansion of higher education to include more than three thousand colleges has also added to the difficulties with general education. Free from the imposition of state-level requirements throughout much of their history, the colleges were able to develop an indigenous curriculum. When institutions could define their own patterns of study, it was possible for a strong president to leave a mark, for an institution to develop its own philosophical set. Some colleges were reorganized around specific curriculum plans when their prior offerings proved inadequate to attract a sufficient number of students to keep the college going. But in nearly all cases, it was the strong central figure who articulated the philosophy and used it to install a specialized curriculum and particular course requirements. Rarely did a group of local-campus faculty members and second-line administrators put together a viable curriculum. Rarely did a state legislature or a federal agency design integrated general education programs. At best, the states mandated distribution requirements, thus ensuring some form of curriculum balance; at worst, through their reimbursement schedules, they encouraged the expansion of occupational programs and courses to fit special student groups, thus stultifying indigenous curriculum development.

Last in this list of inputs to the instability of general education is the decline in literacy that forced compensatory education into the colleges. When faculty members are concerned with teaching basic reading, composition, and computational skills, they often think they must abandon instruction in critical thinking, values, and cultural perspectives. The influx of what were euphemistically called "nontraditional students" led to a failure of will even among some of the proponents of general education, who proposed warmth, love, and counseling, instead of curriculum, for that group. General education was shunted aside by those who failed to understand that it could be taught to everyone.

Except for an excessive concern with the academic disciplines, all these problems were more pronounced in community colleges than in universities. The lack of strong educational leadership, a failure to define general education consistently, the rise of occupational education, and adult literacy training affected the community colleges markedly. The colleges were so busy recruiting "new students," that they forgot why they wanted them; the idea that they were to be generally educated was lost. Student and community demands for relevant or instant education, for something pragmatic or useful, were interpreted as a need for occupational training. And the colleges' place in statewide networks of postsecondary education allowed them to excuse their curricular shortcomings by saying that true general education would not be accredited or would not articulate well with the senior institutions' curriculum.

Still, general education survives. Is it relevant? Pragmatic? Pertinent to community needs? Legitimate in the eyes of the public? General education in community colleges will rise or fall in answer to those questions. It will depend also on the definitions accorded to it and to the terms *education* and *curriculum*.

We define *education* as "the process of learning," of change in attitude or capability. It may take place in school or outside; it may be guided, monitored, or haphazard; but it is something that happens to the individual. *Curriculum* is "any set of courses." This definition excludes those aspects of schooling that take place outside a structured course format. It should not be difficult for community college staff members to accept; as participants in a commuter institution, they have always been uneasy about ascribing value to student activities, clubs, dormitories, and other appurtenances of the residential college. The terms have to do with organized sequences—hourlong, weeklong, yearlong—designed to lead individuals from one set of abilities or tendencies to another; in short, to teach.

Why in Community Colleges?

Why general education in community colleges? Statements on its behalf have been advanced not only by educators as far back as the earliest writers on community colleges—Lange, Koos, and Eells—but also by groups outside the academy. In 1947, the President's Commission on Higher Education noted the importance of semiprofessional training but contended that it should be "acquired in an environment that also cultivates general education, thus offering the student 'a combination of social understanding and technical competence' " (Park, 1977, p. 57). Ten years later President Eisenhower's committee also articulated that combination, viewing it as the particular responsibility of the community colleges. Subsequently, an American Council on Education task force recommended that any institution offering an associate degree should attest that its students have become familiar with general areas of knowledge and have gained "competency in analytical, communication, quantitative, and synthesizing skills" ("Flexibility Sought . . . ," 1978). The degree should state not only that the students gained their training in a college but also that the training included a general education component.

These groups see the community colleges as the place where general education should be offered, not only because general education is necessary but also because other types of schools have tended to neglect it. The secondary schools once were repositories of general education, but that function weakened during the 1960s. Boyer (1980) reported on what was left of general education in the secondary schools in 1973 by noting the courses offered by 50 percent or more of the nation's schools:

English I and II	Biology I	Chorus
Public Speaking I	Chemistry I	Art I
General Math	Spanish I	Home Economics I
U.S. History	Driver Education	Typewriting I
Algebra I and II	Band	

"This list—these fourteen courses—represents the closest thing we have to a core curriculum—a list based not on what the students *study* but what most frequently is *offered*" (p. 10).

The community colleges have been caught with some of the same problems. They have taken over much of the basic literacy training for adults as well as remedial education in all areas for high school graduates who failed to learn the first time around. But the organizing principles for these programs are little better developed, and the breakdown in standards of competency that occurred in high schools a generation ago is also endemic. Faced with students of a type they never anticipated and demands for a variety of nontraditional studies to accommodate them, many community college educators have allowed their focus on achievement to be clouded. Further, in the past twenty years, the move to career education has led to severe curriculum imbalance. Students graduate from the programs with no core of basic knowledge; the alumni of nursing programs have learned nothing in common with the people who have studied computer data processing. Students learn job entry skills, but they may not learn how to continue to advance within the job. Career educators have also run the risk of frustrating trainees who cannot find the jobs for which they were specifically trained. And they seem contemptuous of their students to the extent that they deny them the joys of learning for the sake of their lives off the job. The career programs are not automatically relevant or valuable; they can be as meretricious as the most esoteric discipline-based course.

Numerous forces prevent excess in any curriculum for too long. Accrediting agencies, student enrollments, institutional funding sources, and the professional intelligence of the staff all act to maintain curriculum balance. The trend in community college curriculum was decidedly toward career and compensatory education in the 1970s; succeeding decades may see it swing back toward preparing the generally educated person. Career education can be too specialized; without the breadth that accompanies general education, the colleges would be occupational schools undifferentiated from industrial training enterprises. Compensatory education is limited in scope because it does not accommodate the human needs for self-expression, social interaction, and understanding of the world. The slogans "salable skills" and "back to basics" are not sufficient for mounting a program in higher education.

Curiously, the idea of lifelong learning, the same phenomenon that excused the abandonment of general education, may be the best argument for maintaining it in community colleges. Hutchins took issue with the idea of lifelong learning that would train and retrain people for occupations, saying that anything to be taught to young people should be useful to them throughout their lives, that successive, ad hoc retraining in specific skills would not lead them to understand anything of importance about their own life or the world around them. But it is precisely the older students who perceive the need for general education, even while they seek upgrading within their own careers. They know that employment depends less on skill training than on the ability to communicate and get along with employers and coworkers. They know that a satisfying life demands more than production and consumption. They know that they must understand the ways institutions and individuals interact, that for the sake of themselves and their progeny, they must understand and act on social issues. They know that they must maintain control over their lives, that what they learn assists them in maintaining individual freedom and dignity against a society that increasingly seeks to "deliver" health care, information, and the presumed benefits of living. And that is why they come to the colleges with interest in the arts, general concepts in science, understanding the environment, relations with their fellows, questions of personal life crises and developmental stages—all topics in a true general education curriculum.

Inherently, the community colleges are neither more nor less able to offer a distribution of courses that would satisfy a general education requirement than are the universities or secondary schools; it is a matter of labeling and packaging. However, their students are less likely to accept distribution requirements, because the associate degree has little value in the marketplace and the universities will allow students to transfer without it. Integrated general education courses, however, could find a home in community colleges if faculty members and administrators believed in their value. Instructors are not closely tied to the academic disciplines, nor do they typically engage in research and specialized writing. Many of the colleges have formed divisional instead of departmental structures. The colleges have some advantage, too, in developing problem-centered courses in general education through their ties to the local community.

For which of the many types of students coming to community colleges shall general education be provided? The answer is that the college should provide general education for all its enrollees. The college must guarantee the availability of general education throughout a person's life. Lifelong learning is more than the opportunity for successive retraining as one's job becomes obsolete; it is access to the form of general studies that leads to understanding of self and society. And general education must not be optional, lest the gulf between social classes in America be accentuated as members of the elite group learn to control their environment, while the lower classes are given career education and training in basic skills. The colleges must provide general education for the young students, whether or not they intend to transfer to senior institutions, and for the adults, who see the world changing and want to understand more about their environment.

A key question in general education is "How?" The question must be resolved in the context of the open-access institution. "Open access" means "open exit" as well. If a student may enter and drop at will, the ideal of the curriculum as a set of courses is severely limited. There can be no continuity of curriculum when a student takes one course, goes away for a number of years, and comes back to take one more. This casual approach is unprecedented in higher education and requires special planning if general education is to be effective. At the very least, each course must be considered as a self-contained unity rather than as part of a set.

Those who would plan general education must take care that they not repeat the cosmic rationalizations offered by early-day apologists for general education, who saw the students becoming imaginative, creative, perceptive, and sensitive to beauty; knowing about nature, humanity, and culture; acting with maturity, balance, and perspective; and so on. The colleges are simply not that influential. However, general education must not be debased by tying the concept exclusively to reading, writing, calculating, operating an automobile, using appliances, consuming products, practicing health, preparing income tax forms, borrowing money, and so on. Important as these tasks are, they can be learned elsewhere.

The rationale for general education in the community

college is the freedom enjoyed by the informed citizen. Only when people are able to weigh the arguments of the experts are they truly free. These experts may be discussing issues of the environment, whether to put power plants or oil docks in or near cities. They may be advising on governmental questions. Or they may be telling people who may be born, who has a right to live, what it means to be healthy, and how, where, and when one should die. People need to understand how things work—social systems and persuaders, artists and computers. General education is for the creation of a free citizenry.

Freedoms gained through a general education extend from the person to the society. The ability to think critically, to place one's own problems in broad perspective, to make informed choices about the conduct of one's own life is the cornerstone of freedom for the individual. The idea of freedom is different now than it was in an earlier era. To be free economically does not mean setting up one's own farm; it means having alternative ways of working within the modern corporate system. To be free politically does not mean going to town meetings and deciding on local issues; it means understanding the consequences of actions taken by bureaucrats and the ways of influencing or countering those actions. Being free morally and personally does not mean abiding by community mores; it means having the ability to understand and predict the consequences of one's actions for self and fellows in the context of a higher order of morality. According to Broudy, the form of freedom gained through general education means "that the individual citizen could make up his *own* mind in political affairs, carve his *own* economic career with a minimum of interference, and could shape his *own* decisions by the dictates of his *own* conscience. . . . It is freedom for self-mastery as much as freedom from restraint by others. . . . Knowledge and insight into the principles of the good life are necessary conditions for genuine freedom. . . . That is why throughout the ages, general studies in one form or another have been regarded as the content of liberal education, education for those who would be free" (1974, pp. 27-28).

The cross-currents that affect community colleges generally affect their involvement with general education. It is possible to be optimistic about the future of general education because there is an irreducible minimum in curriculum and instruction below which the college ceases to be. The curriculum must be educative; staff members must act like educators; students must learn. A publicly supported college cannot operate indefinitely with the curriculum perceived as a set of haphazard events, a corps of part-time instructors with no commitment to the institution in general, let alone to the planning of curriculum in particular, and students who drop in casually if they have nothing better to do that week. Such an institution may continue functioning, but it has lost its guiding ethos. A general education that leads to the ways of knowing and the common beliefs and language that bind the society together is offered in every culture through rituals, schools, apprenticeships. The community colleges are responsible for furthering it in the United States.

Examples

The community colleges have attempted to devise general education patterns. The integrated course has its own history. Medsker (1960) reported the number of these courses offered in seventy-eight colleges in 1956 (see Table 45).

Several other descriptions of interdisciplinary survey courses in community colleges have been reported. Course outlines have been reprinted, ways of organizing the courses have been detailed, and problems in maintaining course integrity have been discussed. As an example, interdisciplinary humanities courses have been described by Brown (1976), Dehnert and others (1977), Nash (1975), and Zigerell and others (1977). Courses for general education have also been centered on contemporary problems: race relations, drug use and alcoholism, ecology and the environment, evaluating social controversies, world peace. In the 1930s, such courses were often built on political problems—at that time, fascism versus democracy; in the 1950s it was communism versus democracy. In the 1960s, political problems gave way to issues surrounding the individual, and courses

Table 45. Fields in Which Courses Especially Designed for General
Education Were Offered in Two-Year Colleges, 1956 (N = 78)

Subject	Number of Colleges	Number of States	Percentage of Colleges
Natural science: general courses in physical and biological science and special courses in specific natural science fields	67	11	86
Social science: general course and special courses in specific fields	62	11	79
Psychology and personal development: applied psychology, orientation to college, family life education, and personal development	52	8	67
Language arts: communication, English, speech, and others	46	10	59
Humanities: general course, Western civilization, philosophy, world literature, Great Books classes, and others	40	10	51
Fine arts: music and art appreciation, special art courses	19	4	24
Mathematics: special courses	16	5	21
Health education	15	3	19
Homemaking: home economics, consumer economics, personal finance, and others	11	3	14
Preprofessional orientation: introduction to business, engineering orientation, and others	10	5	13
Miscellaneous: courses with "general education" or "general curricula" labels	9	8	12
Occupational orientation: vocational planning, work experience, industrial relations	4	2	5
Agriculture and conservation	4	2	5

Source: Medsker (1960, p. 60).

on "The Individual and Society," "Understanding Human Values," and "Intergroup Relations" became more prevalent.

Many colleges that tried such courses subsequently returned to distribution requirements based on a variety of courses. As examples, Santa Fe Community College (Florida) opened in 1966 with common courses in science, social science, and humanities. In 1972 the integrated courses were dropped and distribution requirements installed. When Miami-Dade opened in 1960, instructors were hired especially to develop and teach an integrated humanities course. Over the years, however, the course became eight weeks each of art, philosophy, music, literature—a mosaic pattern. The social science course remained integrated but evolved into popular psychology, human relations, and the quest for the self. The college did not build an integrated science course, and by 1977 the general education requirement in science could have been satisfied by choosing two courses from a given list, the communications requirement by one course in English composition plus a literature elective (Lukenbill and McCabe, 1978). However, the pendulum swung again, and by 1978 Miami-Dade had developed a core of five multidisciplinary courses: "Communications," "The Social Environment," "The Natural Environment," "Humanities," and "The Individual." Table 46 shows Miami-Dade's general education requirements in 1978.

Some other community colleges have installed integrated courses successfully. Los Medanos College (California) provides one example. In preparing a general education plan for the college in the mid 1970s, the organizers rejected many patterns of general education then existing. They had found that most California colleges were giving general education credit for virtually all academic transfer courses, and some were giving credit for certain vocational or technical courses. Any course that had even a tenuous connection with science, social science, or humanities was being used to satisfy a general education requirement. The organizers rejected those patterns in favor of a core of six generic courses in behavioral, social, biological, and physical sciences and in language arts and humanistic studies. Students were expected to enroll in one or, preferably, two of these courses each semester. To receive an associate degree, the student had to complete all six. And students were encouraged, though not required, to take a capstone course called "The Interdisciplinary Colloquy." The courses emphasized problem areas: The generic course in behavioral sciences was entitled

Table 46. General Education Requirements for the Associate in Arts Degree at Miami-Dade, 1978

Basic Skills

Math Competency (Required for Graduation)	Reading and Writing Competency (Required for the Core Communications Course)

General Education Core

Communications	Humanities	The Social Environment	The Natural Environment	The Individual

Required single, multidisciplinary courses—*15 credits.*

Distribution Groups

Communications	Humanities	Social Sciences	Natural Sciences	Physical Education
English Composition Creative Writing* Introduction to Literature* Speech*	Art Drama Foreign Language Literature Music Philosophy Interdisciplinary Humanities	Anthropology Economics Geography History Political Science Psychology Sociology Interdisciplinary Social Sciences	Biology Chemistry Earth Sciences Mathematics Physics Interdisciplinary Natural Sciences	Physical Activities Health Maintenance
3 credits *Can be selected only if English Composition competencies have been met.	Four courses, including at least one from each of these three groups, are required—*12 credits.* Each campus will designate a short list of courses for each group; the discipline areas listed here are only illustrative.			*2 credits* (These credits are not included in the 36-credit general education requirement.)

Electives

6 credits—selected from a collegewide list.

Source: Lukenbill and McCabe (1978, p. 57).

"The Nature of People in Society" and dealt with such topics as variant life-styles, rationalism, and mysticism. The course in humanistic studies, entitled "The Creative Process," considered themes in current literature. Every instructor was involved with the planning of the generic course that was introductory to the specialized courses he or she taught (Collins and Drexel, 1976).

The Los Medanos College general education plan is notable less for its content than for the way it was organized. The college had four divisions, each headed by a dean; hence the first principle: There was administrative coordination of the curriculum. Second, each course was required for all students. Third, the college employed a full-time staff development officer to work closely with the faculty in preparing the common course outlines. The result was that about one third of the college's total enrollments were in the general education basic courses. The courses were undergirded with special laboratories to teach computational and compositional skills and with the tutorials. All this occurred in a college drawing its student population predominantly from a low-socioeconomic-status community with a high proportion of ethnic minorities.

Spokespersons for most other community colleges would say they pursue general education, but an examination of their catalogues reveals they are defining the term as distribution requirements. In the typical institution these requirements may be met by taking courses from a list arranged by department or division. The programs in liberal arts, business administration, general science, pre-engineering, accounting, architectural technology, and so on state various numbers of minimum semester hours to be taken outside the main field. The social science electives may be selected from courses in anthropology, economics, political science, psychology, sociology; the science electives from courses in physics, chemistry, biology, astronomy; the humanities electives from courses in music appreciation, art history, literature, philosophy; and the courses in communication from composition, speech, journalism, or writing. That is the most prevalent pattern. It satisfies the accrediting agencies, comfortable with it because of its familiarity, and the universities because it fits their own curricular mode. Few within the colleges question it. Their rationale is based on freedom of choice for the students. But the result is curricular chaos.

A Model

A general education pattern for all community college students can be devised if the staff adheres to certain premises. Curriculum is not put together in a vacuum; it is not the responsibility of each professional person acting independently. A general education curriculum needs a faculty working together, a group coordinated by a dean or division head or program manager. This leads to the first premise: *Faculty role definition is essential.* General education cannot be considered only—or even primarily—classroom-centered. The faculty member who wants to hide behind the classroom door and develop courses and instructional strategies independently cannot beneficially participate in a general education program. The part-time instructor with only a casual commitment is of limited value as well. The general education program demands a corps of professional staff members who know how to differentiate their responsibilities.

The leadership for a general education program must come from a staff person whose sole responsibility is to further it. The president can set the tone for general education but is limited in influence on curriculum. Deans of instruction formerly dealt with general education, but in most colleges they have become senior-grade personnel managers. Assigning responsibility to the faculty in general is not sufficient; someone must be in charge. *A general education program must have a program head*; chair, dean, or director—the title is not important.

Third, the general education program should be *vertically integrated*: a program head and faculty members with designated responsibilities. Several technological programs have adopted this model. Wherever there is a program in nursing, for example, there is a director of nursing with a staff that attends to curriculum, student recruiting and admissions, student placement, and the instructional aspects of the program. General education must be similarly organized.

Next, the general education program should be *managed*

at the campus level. Strasser (1977) suggested the importance of each campus in his multicampus district having its own philosophy and operational definition to guide the general education requirements and saw the need for various patterns of general education at the college. He was on target because, apart from the managerial problems in trying to coordinate instructional programs on many campuses from a general office, the same type of program does not fit all campuses within a district. Although powerful forces are leading toward more homogeneity among campuses—and, indeed, among all colleges within a state—this trend can be turned around. But campus instructors and administrators must understand the importance of taking the leadership in curriculum development if they would avert centralized curriculum decision making.

A utopian model for effecting general education is offered here. The faculty would be organized into four divisions: Culture, Communications, Institutions, and Environment. Faculty members in these divisions would separate themselves from their academic departments or the other divisions into which the rest of the faculty was placed. The general education program would have its own budget. The faculty would prepare and operate the integrated courses, course modules, course-exemption examinations, student follow-up studies, and relationships with high schools and senior institutions. Funding such divisions would not be a problem; they would generate enough FTE to pay for all their efforts. They would do their own staff development as well.

Although each campus or each college would develop its own programs, it is possible to trace an outline of how the programs would operate. Begin with general education in the career education programs. First, a delegate from each of the four divisions would examine those programs to determine whether intervention might be made. Course modules—portions of courses to be inserted into the occupational programs—would be sought. As an example, in a fashion design program, the faculty from Institutions might prepare a short unit on the role of fashions in society; the Communications staff might do one on advertising copy and another on distribution, ordering, and inventory control; the Culture group would do one on fashion as folk art and another on traditional symbolism in fashion. For the allied health programs, general education modules in the process of grieving around the world and dealing with the terminal patient might be done by the Culture faculty; the faculty from Institutions would do a unit on medical ethics. The program in automotive maintenance and transport would be offered modules on energy utilization by the Environment staff, the laws governing highway construction and use by the Institutions group, the automobile in American culture by the Culture faculty.

These types of course sections, or modules, would be arranged in consultation with the career program faculty. They might start with one lecture only, tying the occupation to the broader theme, and eventually work into entire courses, depending on the success of the module and the apparent desirability of continuing it. They can attend to the meaning of work, to concepts surrounding the occupation at hand, to the values undergirding particular vocations. They can suggest options for that portion of the students' life not involved with work. And they can expand students' capabilities within the occupation itself by examining the derivation of that function and how it is maintained in other cultures. Some instructors in the health fields have welcomed a unit of a course taught by an anthropologist that considers the puberty rites in various cultures around the world or a unit on the ethics of euthanasia presented by a philosophy teacher. Course modules on the Greek and Latin roots of medical terminology taught by instructors of classical languages have been successfully introduced. Some occupational programs have accepted entire courses in medical ethics or the rise of technology, courses that encompass the dynamics of the occupation and the themes and problems associated with it. Such courses could be pursued vigorously, and the career programs should pay the costs for such courses and course modules.

The four general education divisions would build their own courses for the students enrolled in the collegiate and compensatory programs. Each would do one course only, to be required for every student intending to obtain a certificate or a degree. The courses would be organized around themes, not around academic disciplines. The intent of each would be to point up how contemporary and past, local and distant peoples have dealt with the problems common to all: communications, energy use, social institutions, the search for truth, beauty, and order. The courses would be prepared by the general education staff, specialists in that curriculum form. Their goal: a free people in a free society, thinking critically, appreciating their cultural tradition, understanding their environment and their place within it.

The general education faculty on each campus would build its own four required courses, and depending on local conditions, there would be great variation among them. The Communications staff might do a course called "How We Communicate," dealing with propaganda, advertising, interpersonal communications, and literary criticism—not criticism of Joyce, Steinbeck, and Salinger but of such contemporary literary forms as the administrative memo, the protest statement, the news release. Students would learn to read the language behind the words.

The Institutions staff might build a course around "People and Their Institutions." This would not be a "Survey of Social Science" or a "History of Western Civilization" course; it would emphasize how people have had to grapple with social institutions throughout the history of civilized society. How did the English kings impinge on the lives of their people? How were the Pharoahs able to organize the populace into tremendous labor gangs? What is the grip that modern China has on the minds of its people? How must we deal with our own bureaus and commissions? Here, too, knowledge of the terminology in academic disciplines, the jargon of the specialists, would not be the proper goal.

The Culture staff might do a course on "People and Culture." The theme would be how people have attempted to come to grips with the ultimate questions of all mankind: Who are we? Where did we come from? What mark can we leave? The content would be the types of self-expression through art, music, literature, and dance. Comparative religion would be part of this course only if it were based on the question "Why religion at all?" The way novelists have tried to speak to the human condition would be explored.

The course on "The Environment" could incorporate elements of astronomy, biology, physics—all the earth, life, and physical sciences. It would be concerned with the effects of technology, patterns of energy consumption, shifting concepts in earth and space sciences, how agricultural engineering can be used to solve the problem of famine, what can be known through empirical science and what can be known only through intuition, introspection, or revelation.

The pattern of each faculty group doing one large theme-centered course would allow general education to have its own organizing principles. The course would not offer a few weeks of instruction in each academic discipline lest it fracture along disciplinary lines. And if provision were made for a student to exempt or test out of the course, the general education program staff would develop and administer its own examination or other measure of knowledge sufficiency.

Nothing in this type of reorganization would do away with the specialized courses; the college would still teach "Spanish for Correctional Officers," "General Chemistry," "Introduction to Music," and the hundreds of other discipline-based courses that make up a full curriculum. However, the four theme-centered courses might supplant most of the general or introductory courses now offered.

The general education staff would build modules and specifically designed courses for the occupational students, theme-centered courses for the transfer students, and yet another type of course for the large and growing number of continuing education students. These students, attending the institution part-time, picking up courses that strike their fancy because of current interest or because of the social interaction that the college offers, deserve something different. Naturally, they would be invited to enroll in the major theme-centered courses; however, they need special problems courses, an extension of the problems touched on in the broader themes courses.

A model for this group is afforded through current practice in community college adult divisions and university extension divisions, in which around one fourth of the courses are for general enlightenment. Here is where the specialized course of local interest comes into play. If sufficient interest in the history of a local labor dispute or the latest theories about astronomical black holes can be found, the general education faculty would take part either by offering such a course itself or by enlisting the ad hoc assistance of other staff members. The important point is that these courses be offered and their availability advertised. It would be incumbent on the general education faculty to tap community interest in, set up, and promote these courses. The common characteristic of the courses is that they be educative; they must not be presentations of unknown effect.

The instructional forms used in these courses can be as varied as necessary. Members of a general education faculty of the type described may find that they need to write their own extensive syllabi and text materials. They would probably find it expedient to divide responsibilities, some of them lecturing, others building reproducible media, others writing and administering examinations. But they must stay together as a group organized to provide integrated general education. They will find little difficulty in attaining accreditation of such courses and approval by transferring institutions. Coming into the 1980s, the community colleges were in a better position than ever in their history to articulate and defend their general education offerings; the senior institutions cannot be excessively stringent in their interpretation of what shall be qualified for credit at a time when nearly half the college freshmen begin in two-year institutions.

To conclude, this form of general education can and should be constructed. The greatest impediment to it is within the institution itself. A sufficient number of college leaders— trustees, administrators, and the instructors themselves—must see the urgency of this pattern of curriculum development. The conflict is between pluralism as a goal—every person studying when, how, and where he or she wants—and the use of curriculum as an aid to social integration. If individualism is raised to such heights that the common themes underlying the free person in the free society cannot be perceived, it will be impossible to devise a core curriculum.

Issues

Building a general education program in the community colleges will be no easier in the future than it was in the past. The same centrifugal forces operate to fractionate the curriculum.

How can people trained in a discipline become broad enough to develop interdisciplinary courses? What are the implications for staff development? How are general education leaders trained?

How can the notion of individualism, of every student's right to define his or her own curriculum, be reconciled with requiring certain courses?

Will career education faculty and advisory groups feel that general education requirements have usurped their prerogatives? If so, how can they be convinced that general education benefits their clients?

Can general education courses be credible for university transfer if they enroll all students entering community colleges? Would the universities reject transfers from courses that enrolled the poorly prepared students?

Can the staff in all higher education accept the definition of general education as providing basic understandings for people to act as citizens, rather than as practitioners in narrowly based professions or academic disciplines?

In some states the community colleges have been relegated to a role as career and compensatory education centers. Will this preclude their offering an appropriate form of general education?

In the 1970s, the entire academic content of community college education fell into jeopardy. The threat did not come from career education—the technical programs often made rigorous demands on their students. It came from the colleges that offered a few presentations on television, a sizable number of community service programs, and credit courses in hundreds of locations with noncredit options—all with no attempt to ensure that the presentations were educative. The threat came also from the colleges' proudly stated policies that encouraged all to drop in when they want, take what they want, and drop out when they want—the ultimate in curriculum disintegration. A curriculum centered on general education could restore institutional integrity while promoting the form of social cohesion that derives from shared beliefs and people making informed decisions.

13

The Social
Role

*A Response to the
Critics and a
Look to the Future*

Few serious scholars have been concerned with the community
colleges, even though they enroll more than one third of all students in higher education. The scholarly community has tended
to allow institutional spokespersons free rein. McLuhan is said
to have observed, "If you want to learn about water, don't ask
the fish." Yet people who have wanted to understand the community colleges of American have had little choice; few other
than those within them spoke up.

When the community college is examined by outsiders,
the commentary usually takes the form of criticizing the institution in its social role or the institution as a school. In the
first of these criticisms, the college is often seen in a negative

light: It is an agent of capitalism, training workers to fit business and industry; it is a tool of the upper classes, designed to keep the poor in their place by denying them access to the baccalaureate and, concomitantly, to higher-status positions in society. When it is criticized as a school, questions are raised about its success in teaching: Do these colleges really teach the basic skills that the lower schools failed to impart? Can they provide a foundation for the higher learning? Here too the answers are usually negative; since the community colleges pass few of their students through to the senior institutions, they are said to have failed the test.

Criticizing the Role

Several distressingly similar papers have taken community colleges to task for their failure to assist in leveling the social-class structure of America. Karabel (1972) asserted that the community college is an element both in educational inflation and in the American system of class-based tracking. The massive community college expansion of the 1950s and 1960s, he said, was due to an increase in the proportion of technical and professional workers in the labor force. This increase caused people who wanted any job other than the lowest-paying to seek post-secondary training, thus contributing to a heightened pressure for admission to higher education in general. Hence educational inflation: an increased percentage of people attending school and staying longer. But this has not changed the system of social stratification: "Apparently, the extension of educational opportunity, however much it may have contributed to other spheres such as economic productivity and the general cultural level of the society, has resulted in little or no change in the overall extent of social mobility and economic equality" (pp. 525-526). Students yes, equality no.

Karabel cited data showing that community college students were less likely to be from the higher socioeconomic classes than were students at four-year colleges or universities. They were more likely to be from families whose breadwinner was a skilled or semiskilled worker, had not completed grammar school or had not completed high school, and was not a college graduate. (Not incidentally, these facts had been noted by Koos, the first analyst of junior colleges, fifty years earlier.) Karabel added that most community college students aspired to higher degrees but rarely attained them, and that students of lower social-class origins were more likely than others to drop out.

Karabel accepted the notion that lower-class students were tracked into occupational programs as a way of deflecting their aspirations for higher degrees and higher-status employment, noting that the local businesspeople supported this tracking because of their desire for docile workers. Other supporters of community college occupational programs included the federal government through its vocational education funds, the American Association of Junior Colleges, which, "almost since its founding in 1920, has exerted its influence to encourage the growth of vocational education" (p. 546), and the university, which, "paradoxically, . . . finds itself in a peculiar alliance with industry, foundations, government, and established higher education associations to vocationalize the community college" (p. 547).

Zwerling followed with the thesis that the community college plays an essential role in maintaining the pyramid of American social and economic structure: "It has become just one more barrier put between the poor and the disenfranchised and a decent and respectable stake in the social system which they seek" (1976, p. xvii). The chief function of the community college is to "assist in channeling young people to essentially the same relative positions in the social structure that their parents already occupy" (p. 33). The institution controls mobility between classes, keeping higher-class people from dropping down and people in the lower classes from moving up. Zwerling insisted that the community college is remarkably effective at doing this because its students come primarily from the lowest socioeconomic classes of college attenders, its dropout rate is the highest of any college population, and dropouts and graduates alike enter lower-level occupations than the equivalent students who attend higher-status colleges. This

dropout rate is "related to a rather deliberate process of channeling students to positions in the social order that are deemed
appropriate for them" (p. 35).

Zwerling was consistent. He contended that the expansion of occupational education in the community college was
"an ingenious way of providing large numbers of students with
access to schooling without disturbing the shape of the social
structure" (p. 61). He showed that in states where the community colleges were at the bottom tier of the postsecondary education hierarchy, they received less money per student than the
senior institutions. Hence the lowest-income-level students had
the least spent on them.

Pincus, another writer in the same genre, also discussed
the community colleges in terms of class conflict, with a particular emphasis on their role as occupational education centers.
He traced the development of the occupational function, showing how it fit everyone's needs exactly: "Corporations get the
kind of workers they need; four-year colleges do not waste resources on students who will drop out; students get decent jobs;
and the political dangers of an excess of college graduates are
avoided" (1980, p. 333). And he alleged that "business and government leaders—those at the top of the heap—regard postsecondary vocational education as a means of solving the political
and economic problems created by the rising expectations of
the working class" (p. 356).

Pincus deplored the unemployment rates for college graduates, saying that "between one fourth and one half of those
graduates who found jobs were 'underemployed'; that is, they
held jobs that did not require a college degree" (p. 332). And he
cited Clark's (1960) cooling-out thesis: "These two-year colleges screen out students who did not have the skills to complete a bachelor's degree and, instead, channel them toward an
appropriate vocational program" (p. 333). He showed that nonwhite and low-SES students were more likely to attend community colleges than senior institutions and were more likely to be
enrolled in the occupational programs than in the transfer programs. In justice to Pincus, he did conclude that "capitalism in
the United States cannot always deliver what it promises. There

are a limited number of decent, well-paid jobs, and most working-class and nonwhite young people are not destined to get them. Vocational education does not and cannot change this" (pp. 355-356). His argument, then, was less with the schools than with the system itself.

Data to support the arguments regarding class-based tracking are easy to find. After examining patterns of college-going in Illinois, Tinto (1973) concluded that low-SES students who go to community colleges are more likely to drop out than their counterparts who attend senior institutions. Katz (1967) studied a California community college and determined that it did not equalize opportunity because it did not provide equal educational outcomes. His conclusion was that the college helped maintain the social-class structure because the lower-class students tended to drop out earlier; the dropout was occasioned because of the economic sacrifice of attending school and because of the middle-class character of the school itself. Using national data, Astin (1977) showed that even when students were equated for entering ability, parental income, and aspirations, those entering community colleges were more likely to drop out. He concluded, "For the eighteen-year-old pursuing a bachelor's degree, the typical community college offers . . . decreased chances of completing the degree" (p. 255).

These arguments that schools tend to perpetuate the social-class structure in America are new only in that they name the community college as the villain. Schools at all levels have long been criticized for failing to overturn the social-class system. In 1944 Warner and others asserted that Americans were not sufficiently conscious of the class structure and the place of the schools in it. They felt that lack of understanding of the class system would lead eventually to a loss of social solidarity. Their concern was for equality of opportunity, for curricular differentiation, and for teaching people to accept the idea of social status.

More recently the belief in the inevitability of the class structure has become less pronounced, confounded now with social justice, equality of opportunity, cultural deprivation, and a determination to correct the abuses historically heaped onto certain peoples. The fact that blacks, Hispanics, and other identifiable ethnic groups tend to be overrepresented in the lower socioeconomic classes has contributed to this confusion. Americans historically have had as a common belief a distinct distrust of anyone who preached class consciousness. Now, that distrust has become abhorrence of anyone who suggests the idea of class, because the suggestion is tantamount to racism. And so those who say that the number of people with qualifications for top jobs is quite small, that by definition not enough high-status jobs are available for everyone, and that people are not born equal but that they have diverse potentialities are termed racists endeavoring to maintain their privileged positions by keeping the lower classes in their place. By extension, an institution that predominantly serves the lower classes becomes a racist institution, a tool of the capitalists. The heated arguments engendered by critics who discover anew what they perceive to be the community colleges' pernicious role typically overlook the occasional commentator who says, as Ravitch (1978) did, that class analysis must be handled with care because the assumption that the United States is composed of distinct, rigid classes is tentative.

Criticizing the School

A second set of criticisms pertains to the community colleges as schools. Can they really teach the basic skills that the lower schools failed to impart? Do they provide a foundation for the higher learning? Do their students learn the proper skills and attitudes that will enable them to succeed on jobs or in senior institutions? Stripping away the rhetoric and social implications reduces these questions to the following: How many occupational education students obtain jobs in the field for which they were trained? How many students transfer to the senior colleges? How well have they been prepared for upper-division studies?

Although reliable nationwide data are not readily available on the degrees of success achieved by students in career programs, some statewide studies have been reported. A study in Texas found that 71 percent of graduates from occupational programs in fifty-four colleges were full-time employees in their field of training or in a related field (Texas Education Agency, 1977). A study of Oregon community college students showed that 90 percent of health occupation graduates were working in related fields, but only 38 percent of graduates of technical programs were in jobs related to their training (Oregon State Department of Education, 1977). Nearly 75 percent of the respondents to a survey of both graduates and nongraduates of occupational programs in Virginia community colleges between 1966 and 1969 were working in full-time jobs related to their training (Carter, 1976). Around 70 percent of the graduates of Hawaii community colleges from 1976 through 1978 were working full-time (University of Hawaii, 1977, 1978, 1979). Approximately 83 percent of the graduates of occupational programs in Illinois community colleges in the mid 1970s had obtained jobs (Illinois Community College Board, 1979a).

Data on the numbers of students who transfer from community colleges to four-year colleges and universities are similarly scattered because the ways of counting transfers vary greatly from system to system and from state to state. Patterns of student flow have never been linear; they swirl, with students dropping in and out of both community colleges and universities, taking courses in both types of institutions concurrently, transferring from one to another frequently. Among the students in junior standing at a university may be included some who took their lower-division work in a community college and in the university concurrently, some who started as freshmen in the university but who dropped out to attend a community college and subsequently returned, some who took summer courses at community colleges, some who attended a community college and failed to enroll in the university until several years later, and some who transferred from the community college to the university in midyear. In some reports, *none* of these students would be considered community college transfers; in others, *all* of them would. A single college or a single state may have more or less reliable information, but it is impossible to tabulate in association with corresponding data from other colleges or other states because of the various definitions and reporting procedures used.

Even allowing for the vagaries of the data, it seems that fewer than 5 percent of students enrolled in all types of community college programs complete two years at those institutions and transfer to a university. The critics might say that the community college is doing a poor job as a feeder institution to the universities, that it serves as grades 13 and 14 for only a small percentage of its matriculants and "cools out" the others. A more accurate interpretation is that community college enrollments in adult education and occupational certificate programs have grown so that they have driven the percentage of transfers down to a minuscule level.

What happens to the small percentage of transferring students after they get to the universities? Some figures are available. In 1979, 1.1 million students were enrolled for credit in California community colleges; fewer than 60,000 transferred to a senior public institution within the state, and of those, fewer than 6,000 transferred to the University of California. As a University of California report noted, "The decline in the number of community college transfers has been so dramatic that we are now sending more students to the community colleges than they send to us" (Kissler, 1980a, p. 8). The report went on to point out that there has been a severe decline in the academic performance of students who transfer: "Compared to our own freshmen who eventually become juniors, community college transfers get lower grades, are more likely to be on probation, and are less likely to graduate" (p. 9). The decline in the performance of students transferring to the University of California has increased sharply in recent years; 30 percent of the transfers in 1978 dropped out before the end of their junior year, up from 25 percent five years earlier.

This finding of "transfer shock" is certainly not new; the phenomenon has been traced for decades. The first publication of the ERIC Clearinghouse for Junior Colleges, "Follow-Ups of the Junior College Transfer Student" (Roueche, 1967), summarized twenty-four research reports on transfer students' success. The consensus was that the transfers' grades were lower than those earned by upper-division students who had entered the university as freshmen, the transfers were less likely to graduate, and those who did obtain baccalaureate degrees took

longer to get them. Menke (1980) reviewed around 100 studies
and found that most of them corroborated the drop in grades
suffered by transfers and the increase in time taken to complete
a degree.

These types of reports fuel the argument that the community colleges are a major element in the class-based tracking
system of American education. Karabel suggested that the community colleges were becoming more distinct from the rest of
higher education both in class composition and in curriculum,
that they were becoming more terminal than transfer, more vocational than general education. Numerous other commentators
have also written off community colleges as pass-through institutions, saying that they have made their biggest contribution
by extending some limited higher education to those segments
of the population that had never expected any, by providing a
little vocational training, and by providing adult education as
one way of helping people cope with leisure.

Responding to the Critics

What can we make of these criticisms? The critics are on
firm ground when they present data showing that relatively
small percentages of community college students transfer, that
the community colleges enroll sizable percentages of minority
students and students from low-SES backgrounds, and that of
those students who do transfer, the smallest percentage is
among students from the minorities and lower-income groups.
But their conclusions are not always warranted. Several of the
commentators suggest elevating the class consciousness of community college students so that they become aware of the social
trap into which they have been led. Zwerling's prescription for
change takes the form of "an acknowledged political application." He suggests pointing out to the students the social-class
structure of America and how they are being channeled within
it, saying that students should know how the school is an instrument of power so that they can act to resist it. Pincus similarly
seeks to elevate class consciousness: "If community college educators want to help working-class and minority students, they

should provide them with a historical and political context from which to understand the dismal choices they face. Vocational education students might then begin to raise some fundamental questions about the legitimacy of educational, political, and economic institutions in the United States" (1980, p. 356).

Other critics reach different conclusions. Some want to make the community colleges equal to the universities somehow so that the low-SES students who attend them will have an equal chance at obtaining baccalaureate degrees and higher-status positions. Zwerling suggests converting all two-year colleges into four-year institutions. Astin suggests equating funding so that the community colleges and universities each get the same number of dollars per student. He goes further and suggests that "states or municipalities that wish to expand opportunities for such students should consider alternatives to building additional community colleges or expanding existing ones. Although community colleges are generally less expensive to construct and operate than four-year colleges, their 'economy' may be somewhat illusory, particularly when measured in terms of the cost of producing each baccalaureate recipient" (1977, p. 55). Reid has demanded a form of guaranteed educational attainment as a corollary to equality of opportunity for admission: "Educational equity means nothing if it does not mean equality of educational attainment" (Winkler, 1977, p. 8). Karabel at least acknowledges that increasing the proportion of funds going to community colleges or transforming those institutions into baccalaureate degree-granting structures would not seriously affect the larger pattern of class-based tracking. He admits that the colleges are caught in a dilemma: If they increase their occupational offerings, they increase the likelihood that they will track the lower-class students into lower-class occupations, and if they try to maintain comprehensiveness, they increase the likelihood that their students will drop out without attaining any degree or certificate.

And so the critics skirt the notion of the community college as an agency enhancing equal opportunity. Faced with the unreconcilable problem of social equalization, they present draconian solutions. Suppose all two-year colleges were converted into four-year institutions: Would all colleges and their students then miraculously become equal? There is a pecking order among institutions that even now are ostensibly the same. Harvard and Northeastern University, the University of California and Pepperdine University, the University of Chicago and Northern Illinois University all offer the doctorate. But in the eyes of the public, they are not equivalent. Authorizing the community colleges to offer the bachelor's would not change public perceptions of their relative merit; it would merely establish a bottom stratum of former two-year colleges among the senior institutions.

Suppose funding were equalized: Would the colleges then contribute less to the maintenance of a class structure? Perhaps two-year colleges would teach better if sizable funds were diverted from the universities and run to them. Perhaps they would not. But one thing is certain: The major research universities would be crippled. That eventuality might well satisfy those critics who are obsessed with the idea of social class. They would argue that the power of the schools to maintain the social-class structure could be reduced quite as effectively by chopping down the top-rank institutions as by uplifting those serving the lower groups.

One response to the critics might be that the community colleges are no more able to overturn the class structure of the nation than the lower schools have been, that all schools are relatively low-influence environments when compared with other social institutions. But the critics' fundamental flaw is that *they have attempted to shift the meaning of educational equality from individual to group mobility*. If equal opportunity means allowing people from any social, ethnic, or religious group to have the same chance to enter higher education as people from any other group, the goal is both worthy and attainable. And few would question the community colleges' contribution to the breaking down of social, ethnic, financial, and geographical barriers to college attendance. But when that concept is converted to *group* mobility, its meaning changes, and it is put beyond the reach of the schools. Ben-David put it well: "Higher education can make a real contribution to social justice only by effectively educating properly prepared, able, and motivated individuals from all classes and groups. . . . Higher education appears to have been primarily a channel of individual mobility. . . . It can provide equal opportunities to all, and it may be able to help the disadvantaged to overcome inherited educational disabilities. But it cannot ensure the equal distribution of educational success among classes or other politically active groups" (1977, pp. 158-159). In sum, neither the community colleges nor any other form of school can break down class distinctions. They cannot move entire ethnic groups from one social stratum to another. They cannot ensure the equal distribution of educational results.

Suppose the figures on the percentage of students who transfer to universities are incorrect. Certainly the data are not reliable. Suppose the number of students who transfer short of completing a community college program or who take only a few courses in the community college prior to or concurrent with their university matriculation were added in. What if the 4 or 5 percent were doubled to 8 or 10, or even swelled to 15 percent, as in Florida, where several upper-division universities were built especially to accommodate the transfers? Would it matter to the critics? The colleges still would not be doing their part in the critics' fanciful dream of class leveling. Warner and others said: "The decision to be made by those who disapprove of our present inequality and who wish to change it is not between a system of inequality and equality; the choice is among various systems of rank. Efforts to achieve democratic living by abolishing the social system are utopian and not realistic" (1944, p. 145).

Ordinarily it serves neither education nor society well when the schools are accused of misleading their clients by making promises on which they cannot collect. Such charges can have the effect of generating public disaffection, on the one hand, and on the other, intemperate reactions by educators. Many commentators, past and present, have been guilty of exaggerated claims that the community college would democratize American society if only all geographic, racial, academic, financial, motivational, and institutional barriers to attendance were removed (witness the title of Medsker and Tillery's 1971 book on the community colleges, *Breaking the Access Barriers*). But criticizing the rhetoric is one thing; criticizing the institution itself is quite another. Although there has been no public outcry against the community colleges, should one arise, it will be difficult to tell whether the reaction is directed against the institution itself or toward the image that its advocates have fostered and the claims they have made.

Options

Granted that the community colleges are part of an educational system within a larger social system in which numerous institutions sort, certify, ticket, and route people to various stations, what are the options? We could say that society should not be structured along class lines, that it should not support institutions that tend to allocate people to status positions. Those who hold to that view would do well to seek to change the social structure by modifying some considerably more powerful influences—the tax structure, for example. But as long as there are hierarchies of social class (and all societies have them), some social institutions will operate as allocative agencies.

Clark analyzed the allocative function in community colleges and in 1960 applied the term *cooling out* to describe it. He showed that the process began with preentrance testing, shunting the lower-ability students to remedial classes and eventually nudging them out of the transfer track into a terminal curriculum. The crucial components of the process were that alternatives to the person's original aspirations were provided, the aspiration was reduced in a consoling way, encouraging gradual disengagement, and the students were not sent away as failures but were shown the relative values of career and academic choices short of the baccalaureate degree.

Twenty years later, Clark (1980) reexamined his thesis, asking whether the cooling-out function might be replaced by some other process and whether the roles of community colleges could be altered so that the process would be unnecessary. He named six options: preselection of students, to take place in the secondary schools or at the door of the community college; transfer-track selection, which would bar the students from enrolling in courses offering transfer credit; open failure, whereby students who did not pass the courses would be required to leave the institution; guaranteed graduation, which would have the effect of passing everyone through and depositing the problem at the doorstep of the next institution in line; reduction of the distinction between transfer and terminal programs, which could be done if the community colleges had no concern about the percentages of their students who succeed in universities; and making the structural changes that would eliminate the two-year college transfer function, convert all two-year institutions into four-year ones, or do away with community colleges entirely.

Clark rejected all those alternatives, saying that preselection "runs against the grain of American populist interpretations of educational justice which equate equity with open doors" (p. 19); limiting the number of people who can take courses for transfer credit would shatter the transfer program at a time when students are in short supply; open failure is too public and is becoming less a feature in four-year colleges as well as in community colleges because it seems inhumane; the dangers of guaranteed graduation have already been realized in the secondary schools ("Everyone is equally entitled to credentials that have lost their value," p. 21); reducing the distinction between transfer and terminal courses "has limits beyond which lies a loss of legitimacy of the community college *qua* college ... (auto repairing is not on a par with history or calculus as a college course)" (p. 22); and doing away with the community colleges is unlikely because of the reluctance of senior college faculties to esteem two-year programs and because of the continued and growing need for short-cycle or university-extension-type courses.

Clark concluded: "The problem that causes colleges to respond with the cooling-out effort is not going to go away by moving it inside of other types of colleges. *Somebody* has to make that effort, or pursue its alternatives" (pp. 23-24). He pointed to examples in other countries where the longer the higher education system held out against short-cycle institutions and programs, the greater the problem when educators tried to open the system to wide varieties of students coming for numerous purposes. The trend there is toward greater differentiation of types of institutions and degrees, but "the dilemma is still there: Either you keep some aspirants out by selection or you admit everyone and then take your choice between seeing them all through, or flunking out some, or cooling out some" (p. 28). As he put it, "Any system of higher education that has to reconcile such conflicting values as equity, competence, and individual choice—and the advanced democracies are so committed—has to effect compromise procedures that allow for some of each. The cooling-out process is one of the possible compromises, perhaps even a necessary one" (p. 30). In sum, even if the college only matches people with jobs, providing connections, awarding credentials, providing short-term, ad hoc learning experiences—even if it is not the gateway to the higher learning for everyone that some commentators wish it were—these functions must be performed by some social agency.

Benefits

The real benefit of the community college cannot be measured by the extent to which it contributes to the overthrow of the social-class system in America. Nor can it be measured by the extent to which the college changes the mores of its community. It is a system for individuals, and it does what the best educational forms have always done: It helps individuals learn what they need to know to be effective, responsible members of their society. The colleges can and do make it easier for people to move between social classes. And even though they cannot make learned scholars of television-ridden troglodytes, they can and should show their constituents what it means to be involved in a community where learning is the *raison d'être*. As long as the community college maintains its place in the mainstream of graded education, it provides a channel of upward mobility for individuals of any age. Those who deplore its failure to overturn inequities between classes do a disservice to its main function and tend to confuse the people who have looked on it as the main point of access to, exit from, and reentry to higher education—the lungs of the system.

There is a difference between social equalization and equal access, between overturning the social-class structure and allowing people to move from one stratum to another. The college that teaches best uplifts its community most. People must learn in college, or what is it for? More learning equals a better college; less learning, a poorer college; no learning, no college. The fact that the community colleges serve minority group students, marginally capable students, and other groups never before served by the higher education establishment does not mean they have abandoned their commitment to teach.

A person who receives a degree or certificate and who does not work in the field in which that certificate was earned does not represent an institutional indictment unless no other programs were available to the person. If the community college were a participant in an educational system that said to potential matriculants, "You may enter but only if you are particularly qualified and only in *this* program," subsequent failure to obtain employment in that field might be cause for dismay. But the community college does not operate that way; most of its programs are open to all who present themselves. When programs do have selective admissions, as in dental hygiene, nursing, and some of the higher-level technologies, most entrants graduate and obtain positions in the fields for which they were trained. When programs are open to everyone, as in most of the less professionalized trades, the chances that a matriculant will complete the curriculum and begin working in that field are markedly reduced. "Dropout" is a reflection of the structure of a program. An institution, or a program within that institution, that places few barriers to student matriculation cannot expect a high rate of program completion.

For better or worse, the cooling-out function has worked less well in recent years. All the structural components of the cooling-out process are still in place—English placement examinations, career-planning guidance seminars, and so on—but the community college's allocative function is less effective. For one thing, there are fewer students to whom the structure or intent of cooling out can be applied: More than half the students seek training for careers that may not require the baccalaureate. For another, the stigma of obtaining a job that requires less than a college degree has been markedly reduced as the wage differential between college graduates and nongraduates has shrunk. The community college now seems more to be enhancing lateral career shifts, teaching current employees skills useful in different jobs within the same industry, than to be promoting vertical mobility.

Even if the exigencies of funding, accrediting, or public support were to demand that the community colleges be more effective in their allocative or sorting and certifying function, it would be difficult to effect this form of tightening in an open-access institution. Where might the screens be placed? The number of programs that have selective admissions might be enlarged, thus barring the less qualified at the gate, but accusations of discrimination would still be made. Students could be tested at the beginning of each course, but that suggests behavioral objectives for the classes so that appropriate tests might be devised; it also might tend to drive the less qualified students to the courses with easier standards.

Alternatives

It is possible to sketch the outlines of alternative institutions that would perform the tasks that community colleges now perform. Yet there is no point in taking an ahistorical approach to postsecondary education. Tempting as it is, a view of higher education, of what students need, of what would be good for society, without a corresponding view of the institutions in their social context is not very useful. To start with the questions of what individuals need or what society needs is nice, but regardless of the answers, the current institutions will not disappear. Institutional needs are as real as individual and social needs; in fact, they may be more valid as beginning points for analysis because they offer somewhat unified positions that have developed over time, whereas "individual" and "social" needs are as diverse as a spokesperson cares to make them. And it is thoroughly out of line to pose a view of society with no educational institutions but with everyone learning through the mass media and the home computer. The desire for social interaction is too strong; the demand for certification that must be awarded by some institution is too great.

Any imagined institution must be postulated totally; that is, what changes will be made in funding patterns, institutional organization, role of the professionals within the institution, people's use of their time? The institution's goals must be stated realistically; we have for too long suffered the open-ended goals of those who would break all access barriers, would see all citizens enrolled successively throughout their lifetime, would see the community college taking on functions previously performed not only by the higher and the lower schools but also by welfare agencies, unemployment bureaus, parks and recreation departments, and community-help organizations.

Can we develop a learning community? Some evidence suggests we can. People enrolled in university extension and in the community service divisions of community colleges now exhibit much voluntary educational activity. Add to those the people taking advantage of the opportunities offered through the lower schools, and a sizable cohort who will attend school without being compelled is apparent. In addition, the number of ways that individuals gain information and that society stores and transmits it has grown enormously.

But on the negative side are the individual needs for structured learning situations, the discipline of learning, the sequence that learning demands. Many forms of learning simply do not lend themselves to instant apprehension and immediate applicability; they build one on the other, and a disciplined situation is necessary to hold the learner in the proper mode until the structure is complete. It would also be difficult to fund the infinite variety of learning situations that would be required. Most of the voluntary learning situations now are funded either by the individuals partaking of them or as adjuncts to more structured institutions.

It is possible to pose alternatives to the community college and stay within the context of existing social institutions. In 1968 Devall offered five such alternatives: proprietary trade schools; on-the-job training; universal national service; university extension divisions; and off-campus courses under expanding divisions of continuing education operated by the universities. Certainly if the community colleges were to lose their funding, most of the services they currently provide could be maintained through expansion of these other agencies. But it is not clear that other agencies could do a better job. Proprietary trade schools do not enjoy a history unmarred by excessive claims, inflated costs, fraudulent advertising, and marginally useful instruction. Only to those who feel that the "for profit" sector invariably does a better job than the nonprofit institutions do the proprietary trade schools appear as shining lights.

The other alternatives would also lead to unintended consequences. On-the-job training would narrow educational opportunity by focusing the learner's attention solely on the tasks to be performed, and it would shift the burden of payment to business corporations that might not benefit therefrom if the trained workers chose to take positions with competitors. Universal national service suggests compulsion; it would extend the grip that public agencies have on individuals and, in effect, prolong the period of mandatory school attendance.

Expansion of university extension divisions would have the effect of turning program monitoring back to the universities. But it would also place the programs on a self-supporting basis and would thus deny participation to people with limited discretionary funds. And expanding the university divisions of continuing education would place adult basic education, literacy training, and similar lower-school functions under the egis of an institution that throughout history has attempted to divest itself of them.

Community colleges no longer send a sizable percentage of their matriculants through to baccalaureate degree-granting institutions. Each year the percentage drops. They do offer occupational training and university-extension-type education. For the majority of their students, they provide access to an institution which can connect them with a university but which is more likely to connect them with a job and, more important, to some ideas other than those ordinarily found in the students' environment. They offer access to credentials, the form of certification that people need in a society that penalizes the uncertificated. They offer the chance to maintain progress for individuals who would be penalized without having some form of collegiate training. For when few people have attended college, the one who has stands out, but when many people have been to college, the one who has not is the deviant.

Nonetheless, for several perfectly credible reasons the community colleges refuse to surrender the university-parallel portion of their curriculum. If they did, they would be denying access to higher education to those of their students who do go on, particularly to the minorities and other students from families in which collegegoing is not the norm. They would betray their own staff members who entered the institution with the intent of teaching college courses. They would no longer serve as the safety valve for the universities, which can shunt the poorly prepared petitioners for admission to these alternative colleges and which would otherwise be forced to mount massive remedial programs of their own or face the outrage of people denied access.

Some states have multiple college systems and so separate the collegiate from other functions. The Wisconsin Vocational, Technical, and Adult Education Centers perform all community college functions except for the university lower-division courses; Wisconsin has a university-center system with numerous branch campuses of the state university doing the collegiate work. In South Carolina, state technical colleges coexist with branch campuses of the university. The North Carolina system operates both technical institutes and community colleges.

These and other alternative structures may also be found in large community college districts. Coast Community College District (California) has two full-service, comprehensive community colleges along with one institution devoted exclusively to short-cycle education, open-circuit broadcasting, and community services. A similar pattern prevails in at least six other districts around the country. In addition to the comprehensive community colleges in Chicago, the city system operates an Urban Skills Institute devoted primarily to adult basic education, remedial studies, and occupational skill training. In sum, the institutional forms adapt, but all functions are maintained.

We do not necessarily need new structures. Many forms of reorganization within our existing community colleges can be made to accommodate the changing clientele. Some of the more successful adaptations have been made in occupational programs in which the liaison occasioned by the use of trades advisory councils and other connections between the program and the community have fostered continual modifications in curriculum and instruction. The community service divisions engage in their own forms of modification by slanting their offerings toward areas in which sizable audiences can be found. On-campus media forms are introduced to accommodate the different modes of information gathering exhibited by new groups of students. The list could be extended; the point is that adaptations within existing forms are continually occurring.

But the list of potential changes can also be extended by pointing to accommodations that are rarely made. Long overdue is a reconception of the liberal arts to fit the occupational programs: What portions of traditional liberal arts studies are most useful for students in occupational programs, and how might they best be inserted into those areas? Modular courses have been tried in several institutions, but much more work needs to be done there to build a bridge between the necessary discipline of sequential instruction and the short interest span exhibited by many students. Imaginative ways of funding community colleges to adopt certain functions abandoned by secondary schools should be explored. Ways of monitoring contract relationships between community colleges and other educational and noneducational institutions could be enhanced. And the entire area of assessing the worth of the community college as a social structure needs to be developed.

Assessing Value

How might the social value of community colleges be assessed? The traditional method of measuring the worth of a school has been to gauge the value it adds to its students. Measures of what the students know when they enter and of what they know when they leave are the classic assessment strategies. Single courses, entire programs, entire institutions are measured in this fashion. But many community college people are convinced that their institution should no longer be assessed in that way. They feel they have moved into another sphere, one in which the institution is less concerned with traditional teaching and learning than with providing access, credentials, and connections. Accordingly, when Astin suggested that the two-year colleges were detrimental to students' passage through the system toward the baccalaureate degree, the college spokespersons reacted uproariously. And for similar reasons, the idea of defined outcomes or behavioral objectives has made little headway because the threat of being held accountable for student learning is too much for most staff members to endure. Although there is a small group of community college staff members working toward competency-based measures, the majority seem disinclined to take a value-added or student-learning approach to assessment.

The way people use the community college tends to support this view. For those students who enroll in a photography course so that they can have access to the darkroom, in an art course so that they can have their work criticized, in a literature course so that they can find like-minded students with whom to interact, the institution has become a way of gaining "access to tools" (to use Illich's term for characterizing a useful social institution). The fact that the college classifies those courses in photography, art, and literature as "transfer courses" does not change the reality of the way they are perceived by students. The students who attend the career courses for a short time, learn where the jobs are, and then drop out to go to work have, similarly, gained something of great value.

If it is inappropriate to assess the community college as a school that brings its learners from one measured point of knowledge to another, what alternative modes of assessment might be used? Most current attempts at demonstrating institutional value are crude: here a methodologically suspect accounting of the fiscal contribution a college makes to its region, there a report of the number of people showing up for a class or tuning in to the college's television channel. Assessing the community college as a certification agency has some appeal. Proponents of external degrees are concerned with certifying the learning that people have achieved elsewhere. The students themselves use the institution to gain certification for employment. Therefore, the institution as a social agency that certifies people's competencies gives it one measure of legitimacy. How much are the certificates worth?

Even more far-reaching measures might be used.

A church deals in human hopes, gratification, and superordinate goals. Human satisfaction and assistance with intangible patterns of coping are its stock in trade. To what extent does the community college enhance hope?

Nearly everyone has access to the telephone system. It is a passive, instantly responsive tool that allows people to interact with one another at will. What is the value of the human contact fostered by community colleges?

A television network is another form of passive tool. One turns the television on or off at will, seeking entertainment or diversion. How much is the entertainment provided by the colleges worth?

Museums offer both entertainment and education. A museum may be compared with another museum according to the strength of its collection, the appeal of its exhibitions, and the number of people who participate in its programs. Can community colleges be compared? They never are: There are no quality ratings or institutional rankings.

Government agencies are social institutions designed to provide services. They are successful to the extent that they enhance the quality of life in a community by maintaining order and providing public places where people may conduct their own affairs. Can the colleges be so assessed?

If the colleges were funded as the museums and the parks department are funded, they would be on a programmatic basis, receiving money to provide a service. But what could the measures be? The numbers of people who appear? A comparison of the services the colleges provide against those provided by other agencies of the type?

All institutions, all agencies must be perceived as valuable for something. It is easier to assess them when their functions are clearly articulated, when people know what they are supposed to be doing. Currently the community colleges are suffering from a gap in perception. To many they are still schools and should be assessed as such. Hence, when people use the institutions to gain access to tools or to gain certification, when college personnel speak of the numbers who attend or the numbers who obtain jobs, those who see the colleges as places where value must be added take the approach that inappropriate measures are being used. And funding patterns are at variance if the community college is something other than a school. The institutions receive money for students attending programs that are purported to be moving them in the direction of higher degrees, the higher learning, job skills.

Because so few scholars are concerned with community colleges, there is no true forum. The colleges' own spokespersons do not help much. Either they do not know how to examine their own institutions critically, or they are disinclined to do so. They say the colleges strive to meet everyone's educational needs, but they rarely acknowledge the patent illogic of that premise. They say the colleges provide access to higher education for all, but they fail to examine the obvious corollary question: Access to what? The true supporters of the community college, those who believe in its ideals, would consider the institution's role on both educational and philosophical grounds. Democracy's College deserves no less.

Annotated
Bibliography

The following is a selected bibliography of predominant works in the community college literature and of the major periodicals and monograph series that cover community college education. Entries are arranged under five headings: Institutions, People, Functions, Journals, and Monograph Series.

Institutions

Cohen, A. M. *Dateline '79: Heretical Concepts for the Community College.* Beverly Hills, Calif.: Glencoe Press, 1969.

This work discusses criteria for establishing institutions that effect the educational outcomes to which community colleges are supposedly committed. A hypothetical community college designed purposely to bring about these outcomes is first described, followed by an examination of the discrepancies between community college rhetoric and actual practices, a discussion of the steps required to convert contemporary colleges into institutions that approximate the hypothetical model institution, and a plea for the use of measurable objectives.

Cross, K. P. *Beyond the Open Door: New Students to Higher Education.* San Francisco: Jossey-Bass, 1971.

Cross examines the inability of traditional institutions of higher education to serve the growing numbers of nontraditional students who are attending college under open-door policies. Specific topics covered include the various philosophies concerning who should attend college, the different experiences of traditional and nontraditional students in the American school system, the differences in aspirations, backgrounds, and attitudes between traditional and nontraditional students, and the reforms needed in higher education to better serve the nontraditional student.

Evans, N. D., and Neagley, R. L. *Planning and Developing Innovative Community Colleges.* Englewood Cliffs, N.J.: Prentice-Hall, 1973.

A how-to-do-it plan is presented for starting a new community college. The book includes a discussion of state regulations and methods of securing local support, guidelines for appointing and organizing a board of trustees, an examination of the president's role in organizing college offices and recruiting staff, checklists to be used by curriculum development committees, and a review of factors to consider in organizing administrative services and planning facilities. Organization charts and survey instruments are appended.

Gleazer, E. J., Jr. *Project Focus: A Forecast Study of Community Colleges.* New York: McGraw-Hill, 1973.

The author relates the impressions he gained in conversations with students, faculty members, and administrators at thirty community colleges. These observations relate to, among other items, the unique role of community colleges in American higher education and the special needs of community college students, the concerns and in-service training needs of the faculty, the breadth of the community college curriculum, and problems in organization and governance.

Gleazer, E. J., Jr. *The Community College: Values, Vision, & Vitality.* Washington, D.C.: American Association of Community and Junior Colleges, 1980.

Based on visits to numerous institutions and on the author's many conversations with trustees, students, state officials, and college staff, this monograph presents general impressions, anecdotes, and commentaries on topics related to the contemporary community college. Among other items, the author discusses recent changes in the community college, the role of the college as an agency for community development, problems of state funding, and the maintenance of local college control.

Gollattscheck, J. F., and others. *College Leadership for Community Renewal: Beyond Community-Based Education.* San Francisco: Jossey-Bass, 1976.

A rationale is presented for the development of "community renewal colleges," which provide the kinds of education citizens want and offer instruction at locations convenient for students. The authors suggest that the creation of such institutions would follow the Morrill Act, the Servicemen's Readjustment Act, and the evolution of comprehensive community colleges as a fourth step in the progressive development of American higher education. Examples of community renewal activities at seven colleges are included.

Harper, W. A. *Community, Junior, and Technical Colleges: A Public Relations Sourcebook.* Washington, D.C.: Hemisphere, 1977.

Arguing that public relations is a vital management function, this monograph provides guidelines for establishing and operating a college public relations office. Topics discussed include the organization and staffing of a community relations office; the functions of a community relations office; appropriate public relations techniques for different audiences; methods of handling special situations, such as negative criticism from the outside; and the importance of a national community college public relations effort.

Knoell, D., and McIntyre, C. *Planning Colleges for the Community*. San Francisco: Jossey-Bass, 1974.

Community college planning is discussed in light of six basic themes: switching the planning emphasis from facilities to methods of increasing access; planning a community-based, rather than campus-oriented, instructional delivery system; providing education for multiple adult roles; allowing for more time and options in instruction; making access easier; and integrating academic, fiscal, and facilities considerations into an integrated planning process that involves local, state, and federal authorities. These themes are interwoven throughout the book, which discusses, among other items, planning concepts, policy proposal and review, and methods of ranking alternatives.

Lombardi, J. *Managing Finances in Community Colleges*. San Francisco: Jossey-Bass, 1973.

This work examines problems and practices in community college fiscal management. Part I expresses concern over future funding in light of mounting costs and the public's growing disaffection with the education establishment. Part II discusses community college revenues, with chapters on state support, property taxes, tuition and fees, and federal aid. Part III examines methods of expenditure control.

Monroe, C. R. *Profile of the Community College: A Handbook*. San Francisco: Jossey-Bass, 1972.

Designed as an introductory text or as a work for general readers, this book reviews the history and characteristics of the community college. Chapters examine the historical evolution of community colleges; discuss their commitment to open admissions, the comprehensive curriculum, and community education; examine the general, transfer, and occupational education components of the community college curriculum; and detail student and faculty characteristics. Personal observations based on the author's long career in community college education are offered throughout the book. A bibliography is included.

Palinchak, R. *The Evolution of the Community College.* Metuchen, N.J.: Scarecrow Press, 1973.

Drawing on a bibliography of over 750 works, Palinchak traces the historical roots of the community college movement from the nineteenth century; examines the terminology used in the literature to describe community colleges; and discusses their faculty, students, and curricula. While omitting an examination of administrative issues, the author critically discusses the struggle of the community college to attain a recognized identity within higher education, notes the difficulty of reconciling occupational and academic programs, and outlines sixty-one conclusions regarding the colleges.

Potter, G. E. *Trusteeship: Handbook for Community College and Technical Institute Trustees.* (2nd ed.) Washington, D.C.: Association of Community College Trustees, 1979.

The author outlines eleven major responsibilities of trustees and discusses their role in relation to other board members, the board chairperson, and the college president. In addition, separate chapters are devoted to legal, political, and collective bargaining issues with which trustees should be familiar. Various addenda throughout the handbook provide, among other items, trustee job descriptions and performance evaluation forms, guidelines for selecting the college attorney, and trustee codes of ethics.

Richardson, R. C., Jr., Blocker, C. E., and Bender, L. W. *Governance for the Two-Year College.* Englewood Cliffs, N.J.: Prentice-Hall, 1972.

Designed for current or aspiring community college presidents, this book urges the application of participatory management techniques as a means of reconciling the internal and external forces that impinge on community college administration. The authors review the national, regional, and local forces that influence college governance; describe a participatory theory of community college governance; and examine the organization and responsibilities of college personnel. The book also includes an analysis of the types of human interaction required for the success of a participatory governance model.

Wattenbarger, J. L., and Cage, B. N. *More Money for More Opportunity: Financial Support of Community College Systems.* San Francisco: Jossey-Bass, 1974.

The authors identify trends in community college administration and funding that have emerged during the 1960s and 1970s. These trends include increased state-level planning and coordination, a decreased reliance on local financial support, the use of management techniques in administration, and a growing recognition of the differential costs of various educational programs. The book also categorizes various state funding procedures and examines methods used to calculate program costs.

Zwerling, L. S. *Second Best: The Crisis of the Community College.* New York: McGraw-Hill, 1976.

Drawing from a bibliography of over 400 titles, the author argues that community colleges play an essential role in preserving American economic and social class structure. In developing this thesis, the author cites the large proportion of lower-class students at community colleges, argues that the expansion of vocational programming was a means of providing access to schooling without disturbing the class structure, examines the "cooling-out" function of the community college, and notes the low level of state aid received by the colleges. Reforms designed to eliminate this hidden function of the community college are discussed.

People

Bushnell, D. S., and Zagaris, I. *A Report from Project Focus: Strategies for Change.* Washington, D.C.: American Association of Junior Colleges, 1972.

Methodology and findings are reported for a study conducted to compare student, faculty, and administrator perceptions of the goals pursued by community colleges and of the goals they should pursue in the future. Areas of consensus and divergence among the three groups are noted, and prescient observations on the role of the colleges during the 1970s are presented.

Cohen, A. M., and Brawer, F. B. *Confronting Identity: The Community College Instructor.* Englewood Cliffs, N.J.: Prentice-Hall, 1972.

Written for faculty members who seek a better understanding of themselves and their profession, this work presents a composite profile of community college instructors. The six sections of the book review the role of community colleges, classify the personality types found among community college instructors, categorize the various roles played by these instructors within the college, examine the impact of students on instructors, discuss the process of becoming a teacher, and consider faculty evaluation practices. A 280-item bibliography is included.

Cohen, A. M., and Brawer, F. B. *The Two-Year College Instructor Today.* New York: Praeger, 1977.

Based on a review of the literature and a survey of 1,778 humanities instructors, this monograph examines the attitudes and concerns of faculty members at two-year colleges. Chapters review faculty attitudes and values as measured by the Rokeach Terminal Values Scale, the satisfaction of faculty members with their jobs, faculty concerns for students, the research orientation of instructors, and issues related to faculty development. Additional chapters draw on study findings to discuss the future of humanities instruction, the future role of instructors, and the future of the colleges themselves.

Koos, L. V. *The Community College Student*. Gainesville: University of Florida Press, 1970.

This three-part monograph synthesizes the findings of hundreds of research studies conducted since the 1920s. Part I considers the development, behavior, and interests of later adolescents. Part II examines study findings on college students' aptitudes, social status, academic competence, personal characteristics, attitudes, and personal problems. Part III reviews observations concerning community college curricula and student personnel programs. The author strives throughout the book to show how community colleges can enhance their students' personal development.

London, H. B. *The Culture of a Community College*. New York: Praeger, 1978.

Based on the author's doctoral thesis, this work reviews a study conducted to determine sociological profiles of students and instructors observed at a community college in New England during one academic year. Among other items, findings are discussed in relation to the dissociation from family and peers that students feel while attending college; the tendency of students to view low academic achievement as a personal failing; and the behaviors and attitudes of community college faculty members as they work on the bottom of the higher education prestige ladder. Study methodology and limitations are delineated.

Medsker, L. L., and Tillery, D. *Breaking the Access Barriers: A Profile of Two-Year Colleges*. New York: McGraw-Hill, 1971.

The authors present a statistical profile of junior colleges in the United States and discuss special problems related to clientele, functions, programs, control, staffing, financing, and planning. A separate chapter is devoted to private junior colleges, and a summary conclusion outlines recommendations designed to help two-year colleges reach their potential for increasing educational access.

O'Banion, T. *Teachers for Tomorrow: Staff Development in the Community-Junior College.* Tucson: University of Arizona Press, 1972.

Noting that few instructors are formally prepared to teach the heterogeneous student populations that attend community colleges, the author discusses the special educational and training needs of community college faculty members. This discussion includes an examination of the topics to be covered in preservice education programs and a review of approaches to in-service faculty development. The book's appendices delineate the degrees held by community college faculty members, the sources of community college instructors, the institutions offering graduate degree programs for these instructors, and the various preservice and in-service programs recommended in recent years.

Olivas, M. A. *The Dilemma of Access: Minorities in Two-Year Colleges.* Washington, D.C.: Howard University Press, 1979.

Data on minority participation in community college are presented in support of the thesis that efforts to increase access have resulted in a disproportionate concentration of minorities at two-year institutions. The author critiques the sources of data on minority students, discusses community colleges that are predominantly for minorities, examines the distribution of minorities among faculty and staff, traces minority enrollment in community college programs, delineates undergraduate minority degree patterns, and discusses support services for minority students. Reforms needed to help minority students persist in higher education beyond the initial two years are also examined.

Thornton, J. W., Jr. *The Community Junior College.* (3rd ed.) New York: Wiley, 1972.

Designed as an introductory text for new instructors who are about to join community college faculties, this book reviews the history, organization, curriculum, and functions of the community college. The author discusses the role of the community college within higher education; examines the history of its comprehensive curriculum; and describes patterns of college organization, control, financial support, and administration. In addition, the book includes sample program descriptions for various occupational fields, discusses problems of articulation with four-year institutions, outlines continuing education activities, and proposes a model general education program.

Functions

Barbee, D. *A Systems Approach to Community College Education.* Princeton, N.J.: Auerbach, 1972.

This work describes how the systems approach can be applied to community college education. The author traces the roots of instructional systems to the theories of Skinner, Pavlov, and other behaviorists; examines instructional systems models; and details their common characteristics. Guidelines for using a systems approach are presented, along with flow charts and a glossary.

Cohen, A. M., and Associates. *A Constant Variable: New Perspectives on the Community College.* San Francisco: Jossey-Bass, 1971.

The authors, who are affiliated with the ERIC Clearinghouse for Junior Colleges, synthesize the main theses of the hundreds of documents about community colleges that flow into the ERIC system each year. Part I discusses the concept of an institutional personality and examines the state of institutional research at community colleges. Part II analyzes literature dealing with community college faculty and students. Part III discusses curriculum and instruction, with chapters devoted to teaching styles, the unique nature of the curriculum at community colleges, vocational education, black studies, and the unstated social functions of the community college. A 350-item bibliography is included.

Harlacher, E. L. *The Community Dimension of the Community College*. Englewood Cliffs, N.J.: Prentice-Hall, 1969.

Arguing that community services are an essential college function, the author defines community services, traces their growth within the community college, and discusses the types of services often provided. Problems in community service planning and administration are also examined.

Healy, C. *Career Counseling in the Community College*. Springfield, Ill.: Thomas, 1974.

Based in part on a survey of 200 community college counseling centers, this work describes thirteen replicable career counseling procedures, including procedures to help the student choose a career and methods to help clients with vocational problems stemming from developmental deficiencies. The similarities, differences, and limitations of these procedures are reviewed.

Heermann, B. *Cooperative Education in Community Colleges: A Sourcebook for Occupational and General Educators*. San Francisco: Jossey-Bass, 1973.

Designed as a resource for occupational and general educators, this four-part work examines the administration of cooperative education programs. Part I provides a rationale for cooperative education, details a model program, and discusses potential benefits and problems. Part II reviews administrative considerations in planning and organizing cooperative education programs as well as detailing the roles of the instructor, employer, and program coordinator. Part III examines operational considerations and methods of defining program outcomes. Part IV presents sample forms used in a program-reporting and recordkeeping system.

Johnson, B. L. *Islands of Innovation Expanding: Changes in the Community College*. Beverly Hills, Calif.: Glencoe Press, 1969.

This four-part monograph examines the state of instructional innovation at the community college. Part I discusses the response of American education to the rapid change experienced during this century. Chapters in Part II describe various instructional innovations adopted at community colleges, including cooperative work-study programs, programmed instruction, audiotutorial teaching, educational television, games and simulations, developmental instruction, students as teachers, and group and independent study. Finally, Part III discusses aids and obstacles to innovation, and Part IV examines trends and projections.

Moore, W., Jr. *Against the Odds: The High-Risk Student in the Community College.* San Francisco: Jossey-Bass, 1970.

The author argues that low-achieving students receive an inadequate education at community colleges. He examines the inconsistency of maintaining open-door policies while disregarding the special needs of high-risk students; discusses the inadequate responses of instructors, counselors, and administrators to these needs; and details the ineffectiveness of traditional remedial instruction in aiding the low achiever. A general education curriculum combining basic skills instruction with courses in sociology, science, and the humanities is proposed as a means of better serving the high-risk student.

O'Banion, T., and Thurston, A. (Eds.). *Student Development Programs in the Community Junior College.* Englewood Cliffs, N.J.: Prentice-Hall, 1972.

The nineteen essays in this collection examine the functions and administration of student development programs. Topics include program organization, administration, and evaluation; the importance of student development activities in light of heterogeneous student backgrounds; internal and external forces affecting student development programs; the role of the student personnel worker; and future trends.

Reynolds, J. W. *The Comprehensive Junior College Curriculum.* Berkeley, Calif.: McCutchan, 1969.

Based on a survey of college administrators and on the information gained by the author's long career in junior college education, this monograph presents an overview of the comprehensive curriculum. Separate chapters discuss the number of junior colleges and their characteristics, the major divisions within their curricula, course offerings in applied and academic subjects, student activities, curriculum development, the junior college library, theoretical curricular issues, and the future of the junior college curriculum.

Roueche, J. E., and Kirk, R. W. *Catching Up: Remedial Education.* San Francisco: Jossey-Bass, 1973.

This work describes five successful community college remedial programs and suggests a prescription for the development of remedial programs. Among other items, this prescription calls for total institutional commitment, volunteer instructors, separately organized developmental studies divisions, and the reward of credit for developmental courses.

Roueche, J. E., and Pitman, J. C. *A Modest Proposal: Students Can Learn.* San Francisco: Jossey-Bass, 1972.

Arguing that community college instructional programs too often emphasize grades rather than learning, the authors advocate the adoption of instructional techniques that promote the mastery of identified behavioral objectives. Suggestions are also provided for changing faculty attitudes and behaviors that are detrimental to the learning process.

Journals

College Canada. Scarsborough, Ontario: Association of Canadian Community Colleges.

This journal is the official newsmagazine of the Association of Canadian Community Colleges (ACCC). Articles in the journal discuss programs and trends at Canadian community colleges, provide newsbriefs on community college educators, and chronicle events within the ACCC. Many articles appear in French. Subscription information: 211 Consumer Road, Suite 203, Willowdale, Ontario M2J 4G8, Canada.

Community and Junior College Journal. Washington, D.C.: American Association of Community and Junior Colleges.

Articles in this journal discuss trends, innovations, and research in community college administration and education. In addition, regular features provide newsbriefs on community college programs and personnel. Subscription information: One Dupont Circle NW, Washington, D.C., 20036.

Community College Review. Raleigh: North Carolina State University.

This journal includes commentaries, literature reviews, and research reports on a variety of educational and administrative topics. Subscription information: 310 Poe Hall, North Carolina State University, Raleigh, N.C. 27650.

Community/Junior College Research Quarterly. Washington, D.C.: Hemisphere Publishing Corporation.

Articles in this publication report the methodology, findings, and implications of research projects involving a variety of educational and administrative topics. Each article provides an abstract, data tables (where applicable), and references. Book reviews are included in each issue. Subscription information: 1025 Vermont Avenue NW, Washington, D.C. 20005.

Community Services Catalyst. Blacksburg, Va.: National Council on Community Services and Continuing Education.

The articles in this journal are written primarily by community college practitioners and discuss issues of the content, administration, and outcomes of community services programs.

Subscription information: College of Education, Virginia Polytechnic Institute and State University, Blacksburg, Va. 24061.

Monograph Series

Horizons Issue Monograph Series. Washington, D.C.: American Association of Community and Junior Colleges; Council of Universities and Colleges; Los Angeles: ERIC Clearinghouse for Junior Colleges.

The monographs in this series present in-depth analyses of a variety of educational and administrative topics. Recent editions have examined student development programs, fiscal problems, and the development of constituency programs at community colleges. The monographs are available from the American Association of Community and Junior Colleges and from the ERIC Document Reproduction Service. Ordering information: One Dupont Circle NW, Washington, D.C. 20036.

Junior College Resource Review. Los Angeles: ERIC Clearinghouse for Junior Colleges.

Each of these papers presents an essay of current interest to community college practitioners. Recent titles have included "Appraising Managerial Performance," by Robert G. Lahti; "Responding to Community Needs Through Community Follow-Up," by Mantha Vlahos Mehallis; and "Why Students Drop Courses," by Jack Friedlander. Each paper concludes with a bibliography of ERIC documents and other resources. Ordering information: 96 Powell Library, University of California, Los Angeles, Calif. 90024.

New Directions for Community Colleges. San Francisco: Jossey-Bass.

Each of the sourcebooks in this quarterly series presents a compilation of essays that address a single topic related to community college education or administration. Recent editions have investigated occupational programming, science instruction, and the effective utilization of part-time faculty. The essays in each sourcebook present an overview of current knowledge on the topic in question, theoretical and research-based discussions, examples of new programs and approaches, practical suggestions for action, summary conclusions, and references. Ordering information: Jossey-Bass Inc., Publishers, 433 California St., San Francisco, Calif. 94104.

Humanities in Two-Year Colleges Series.

The six monographs in this series document the status of humanities education at two-year colleges in terms of curricular and enrollment trends, faculty and student characteristics, instructional methods, and the internal and external forces that affect humanities programming. Each monograph draws on the findings of a three-year study that involved an intensive review of the literature, nationwide surveys of two-year college faculty members, and an examination of college class schedules. Bibliographies and data tables are included. Ordering information: 96 Powell Library, University of California, Los Angeles, Calif. 90024.

The Humanities in Two-Year Colleges: A Review of the Students. Los Angeles: Center for the Study of Community Colleges and ERIC Clearinghouse for Junior Colleges, 1975. (ED 108 727).

The Humanities in Two-Year Colleges: Faculty Characteristics. Los Angeles: Center for the Study of Community Colleges and ERIC Clearinghouse for Junior Colleges, 1976. (ED 130 721)

The Humanities in Two-Year Colleges: Reviewing Curriculum and Instruction. Los Angeles: Center for the Study of Community Colleges and ERIC Clearinghouse for Junior Colleges, 1975. (ED 110 119)

The Humanities in Two-Year Colleges: The Faculty in Review. Los Angeles: Center for the Study of Community Colleges and ERIC Clearinghouse for Junior Colleges, 1975. (ED 162 686)

The Humanities in Two-Year Colleges: Trends in Curriculum. Los Angeles: Center for the Study of Community Colleges and ERIC Clearinghouse for Junior Colleges, 1978. (ED 156 285)

The Humanities in Two-Year Colleges: What Affects the Program? Los Angeles: Center for the Study of Community Colleges and ERIC Clearinghouse for Junior Colleges, 1978. (ED 162 686)

Science in Two-Year Colleges Series.

Each monograph in this series documents the status of community college education in one of twelve scientific areas: mathematics, chemistry, biology, engineering, agriculture and natural resources, environmental sciences, interdisciplinary social science, physics, sociology, psychology, earth and space science, and economics. Drawing on a study that involved a literature review, an analysis of college catalogues and schedules, and a nationwide survey of community college science instructors, each monograph details curricular offerings, instructional practices, and faculty characteristics. Bibliographies and data tables are included. Ordering information: 96 Powell Library, University of California, Los Angeles, Calif. 90024.

Beckwith, M. M. *Science Education in Two-Year Colleges: Agriculture and Natural Resources.* Los Angeles: Center for the Study of Community Colleges and ERIC Clearinghouse for Junior Colleges, 1980. (ED 180 567)

Beckwith, M. M. *Science Education in Two-Year Colleges: Interdisciplinary Social Sciences.* Los Angeles: Center for the Study of Community Colleges and ERIC Clearinghouse for Junior Colleges, 1980. (ED 181 955)

Beckwith, M. M. *Science Education in Two-Year Colleges: Mathematics.* Los Angeles: Center for the Study of Community Colleges and ERIC Clearinghouse for Junior Colleges, 1980. (ED 187 386)

Edwards, S. J. *Science Education in Two-Year Colleges: Biology.* Los Angeles: Center for the Study of Community Colleges and ERIC Clearinghouse for Junior Colleges, 1980. (ED 188 709)

Edwards, S. J. *Science Education in Two-Year Colleges: Earth*

and Space. Los Angeles: Center for the Study of Community
Colleges and ERIC Clearinghouse for Junior Colleges, 1980.
(ED 180 535)

Edwards, S. J. *Science Education in Two-Year Colleges: Environmental Sciences.* Los Angeles: Center for the Study of
Community Colleges and ERIC Clearinghouse for Junior Colleges, 1980. (ED 180 558)

Friedlander, J. *Science Education in Two-Year Colleges: Eco-
nomics.* Los Angeles: Center for the Study of Community
Colleges and ERIC Clearinghouse for Junior Colleges, 1980.
(ED 188 719)

Friedlander, J., and Edwards, S. J. *Science Education in Two-
Year Colleges: Engineering.* Los Angeles: Center for the
Study of Community Colleges and ERIC Clearinghouse for
Junior Colleges, 1980. (ED 191 538)

Hill, A. *Science Education in Two-Year Colleges: Psychology.*
Los Angeles: Center for the Study of Community Colleges
and ERIC Clearinghouse for Junior Colleges, 1980. (ED 181
972)

Hill, A. *Science Education in Two-Year Colleges: Sociology.*
Los Angeles: Center for the Study of Community Colleges
and ERIC Clearinghouse for Junior Colleges, 1980. (ED 180
572)

Mooney, W. T. *Science Education in Two-Year Colleges: Chemistry.* Los Angeles: Center for the Study of Community Colleges and ERIC Clearinghouse for Junior Colleges, 1980. (ED
187 397)

Mooney, W. T. *Science Education in Two-Year Colleges: Physics.* Los Angeles: Center for the Study of Community Colleges and ERIC Clearinghouse for Junior Colleges, 1980. (ED
191 534)

Topical Paper Series.

Each of the papers in this semiannual series provides an in-
depth analysis of a topic related to community college education. Recent issues have examined the decline of the transfer
function, methods of classifying community education pro-

grams, and the role of the community college in serving minorities. Most of the papers include extensive bibliographies. Ordering information: 96 Powell Library, University of California, Los Angeles, Calif. 90024.

References

Adams, J. J., and Roesler, E. D. *A Profile of First-Time Students at Virginia Community Colleges, 1975-76.* Richmond: Virginia State Department of Community Colleges, 1977. 58 pp. (ED 153 694)

American Association of Community and Junior Colleges. *Community, Junior, and Technical College Directory.* (Annual.) Washington, D.C.: American Association of Community and Junior Colleges, 1955-1980.

American Association of Community and Junior Colleges. *Community Education-Work Councils: The AACJC Project Sec-*

Note: The Educational Resources Information Center (ERIC) documents listed here (including those that are identified as "unpublished papers") are available from the ERIC Document Reproduction Service (EDRS), P.O. Box 190, Arlington, Va. 22210. Contact EDRS for complete ordering information. Abstracts of these and other documents in the ERIC collection are available from the ERIC Clearinghouse for Junior Colleges, 96 Powell Library Building, University of California, Los Angeles, Calif. 90024.

ond Year Report. Washington, D.C.: American Association of Community and Junior Colleges, 1979a. 253 pp. (ED 168 665)

American Association of Community and Junior Colleges. *The 1978 CETA Act: How AACJC Can Participate.* Washington, D.C.: Office of Governmental Affairs, American Association of Community and Junior Colleges, 1979b. 34 pp. (ED 165 822)

American Association of Community and Junior Colleges/ American Association of State Colleges and Universities. *The Servicemen's Opportunity College: A Network of Colleges and Universities. 1974-75 Catalog.* Washington, D.C.: American Association of Community and Junior Colleges; American Association of State Colleges and Universities, 1974. 83 pp. (ED 093 429)

American Association of Junior Colleges. *A National Resource for Occupational Education.* Washington, D.C.: American Association of Junior Colleges, 1964.

American College Testing Program. *College Student Profiles, Norms for the ACT Assessment.* (Annual.) Iowa City: Research and Development Division, American College Testing Program, 1966-1981.

American College Testing Program. *The Two-Year College and Its Students: An Empirical Report.* Iowa City: American College Testing Program, 1969.

Anderson, E. F. *Three Year Comparison of Transfer and Native Student Progress at the University of Illinois at Urbana-Champaign, Fall 1973 Group.* Research Memorandum No. 77-9. Urbana: Office of School and College Relations, University of Illinois, 1977. 63 pp. (ED 149 820)

Anderson, E. F., and Spencer, J. S. *Report of Selected Data and Characteristics, Illinois Public Junior Colleges, 1967-68.* Springfield: Illinois Junior College Board, 1968. 94 pp. (ED 019 946)

Anderson, G. L. "The Changing Curriculum." *Journal of General Education,* 1970, *22* (1), 51-60.

Anthony, J. "Reflections on the Cluster College." In B. Heermann (Ed.), *New Directions for Community Colleges: Chang-*

ing Managerial Perspectives, no. 13. San Francisco: Jossey-Bass, 1976.

Armstrong, C. L. "The Impact of Collective Bargaining at the Rancho Santiago Community College District (Santa Ana College)." Unpublished paper, Pepperdine University (Malibu, Calif.), 1978. 42 pp. (ED 164 043)

Association of College and Research Libraries. *Needs Assessment Package for Learning Resource Services to Handicapped and Other Disadvantaged Students.* Chicago: Junior College Libraries Section, Association of College and Research Libraries, 1978. 44 pp. (ED 164 035)

Astin, A. W. *Four Critical Years: Effects of College on Beliefs, Attitudes, and Knowledge.* San Francisco: Jossey-Bass, 1977.

Astin, A. W., and others. *The American Freshman: National Norms for Fall 1973–Fall 1980.* (Annual.) Washington, D.C.: American Council on Education; Los Angeles: Graduate School of Education, University of California at Los Angeles, 1973-1980.

Atkins, K. B. "The Utilization of Cognitive Style Mapping of Students to Determine and Implement Alternative Instructional Strategies." Ed.D. Practicum, Nova University, 1978. 63 pp. (ED 174 299)

Augenblick, J. *Issues in Financing Community Colleges.* Denver: Education Finance Center, Education Commission of the States, 1978. 70 pp. (ED 164 020)

Baldridge, J. V. *Power and Conflict in the University.* New York: Wiley, 1971.

Baldwin, J., and others. *Survey of Developmental Mathematics Courses at Colleges in the United States.* Garden City, N.Y.: American Mathematical Association of Two-Year Colleges, 1975. 64 pp. (ED 125 688)

Baratta, M. K. "Follow-Up of 1977 Occupational Graduates." Unpublished paper, Moraine Valley Community College (Palos Hills, Ill.), 1978. 113 pp. (ED 157 578)

Bayer, A. E. "Teaching Faculty in Academe: 1972-73." *ACE Research Reports,* 1973, *8* (2), 1-68.

Belford, M. L. "An Investigation and Analysis of the Public Junior College Music Curriculum with Emphasis on the Problems of the Transfer Music Major." Unpublished doctoral dissertation, School of Education, University of Iowa, 1967.

Ben-David, J. *Centers of Learning: Britain, France, Germany, United States.* New York: McGraw-Hill, 1977.

Berchin, A. *Toward Increased Efficiency in Community Junior College Courses: An Exploratory Study.* Los Angeles: League for Innovation in the Community College, 1972. 236 pp. (ED 063 915)

Bernd, C. M. "The Community Junior College Trustee: Some Questions About Representation." Unpublished paper, Gainesville, Fla., 1973. 13 pp. (ED 086 279)

Bess, R., and others. *A Study of the Economic Impact of Six Community Colleges in Illinois.* Springfield: Illinois Community College Board, 1980. 31 pp. (ED 191 516)

Bethune, S. "Retooling the College Graduate." *Community College Review,* 1977, *4* (4), 36-40.

Blamer, W. C. "A Study of Physical Education in the Public Junior and Community Colleges of the Continental United States." Unpublished doctoral dissertation, School of Education, Michigan State University, 1967. (Available from University Microfilms)

Blocker, C. E. "Are Our Faculties Competent?" *Junior College Journal,* 1965-1966, *36,* 12-17.

Blocker, C. E., Plummer, W., and Richardson, R. C., Jr. *The Two-Year College: A Social Synthesis.* Englewood Cliffs, N.J.: Prentice-Hall, 1965.

Bock, D. J. "Two-Year College LRC Buildings." *Library Journal,* 1978, *103* (21), 2391-2393.

Bogue, J. P. *The Community College.* (1st ed.) New York: McGraw-Hill, 1950.

Bohr, D. H., and Bray, D. "HELP: A Pilot Program for Community College High-Risk Students." Unpublished paper, Sacramento, Calif., 1979. 12 pp. (ED 168 635)

Bowen, H. R. "The Effects of Going to College." *Chronicle of Higher Education,* October 31, 1977, pp. 3-4.

Bowen, H. R. "Cost Differences: The Amazing Disparity Among Institutions of Higher Education in Educational Costs per Student." *Change,* 1981, *13* (1), 21-27.

Boyer, E. L. "Quality and the Campus: The High School/College Connection." *Current Issues in Higher Education,* 1980, *2* (4).

Boyer, E. L., and Kaplan, M. *Educating for Survival.* New Rochelle, N.Y.: Change Magazine Press, 1977.

Brann, E. T. H. *Paradoxes of Education in a Republic.* Chicago: University of Chicago Press, 1979.

Brawer, F. B. *New Perspectives on Personality Development in College Students.* San Francisco: Jossey-Bass, 1973.

Brawer, F. B. *Familiar Functions in New Containers: Classifying Community Education.* Topical Paper No. 71. Los Angeles: ERIC Clearinghouse for Junior Colleges, 1980a. 30 pp. (ED 187 412)

Brawer, F. B. (Ed.). *The Humanities and Sciences in Two-Year Colleges.* Los Angeles: Center for the Study of Community Colleges; ERIC Clearinghouse for Junior Colleges, 1980b.

Brawer, F. B., and Friedlander, J. *Science and Social Science in the Two-Year College.* Topical Paper No. 69. Los Angeles: ERIC Clearinghouse for Junior Colleges, 1979. 37 pp. (ED 172 854)

Breneman, D. W. "Planning as if People Mattered: The Economy." Presentation to the Society for College and University Planning, Kansas City, Mo., July 1979.

Breneman, D. W., and Nelson, S. C. *Financing Community Colleges: An Economic Perspective.* Washington, D.C.: Brookings Institution, 1981.

Brick, M. *Forum and Focus for the Junior College Movement.* New York: Teachers College Press, 1965.

Brick, M. "Review of O'Banion and Thurston Book." *Journal of Higher Education,* 1972, *43* (8), 675-677.

Brightman, R. W. "Effect of Cooperative Work Experience Program on Attitudes of Community College Students." Unpublished doctoral dissertation, Graduate School of Education, University of California at Los Angeles, 1973.

Brossman, S. W. "California Perspective 1975." In H. M. Holcomb (Ed.), *New Directions for Community Colleges: Reaching Out Through Community Service,* no. 14. San Francisco: Jossey-Bass, 1976.

Broudy, H. S. *General Education: The Search for a Rationale.*

Bloomington, Ind.: Phi Delta Kappa Educational Foundation, 1974.

Brown, D. K. "Integrated Humanities in Florida Community Colleges." Unpublished paper, Winter Haven, Fla., 1976. 22 pp. (ED 140 908)

Bushnell, D. S. *Organizing for Change: New Priorities for Community Colleges.* New York: McGraw-Hill, 1973.

Butcher, L. J. *Free and Reduced Tuition Policies for Older Adult Students at Two-Year Community, Junior, and Technical Colleges.* Washington, D.C.: American Association of Community and Junior Colleges, 1980. 36 pp. (ED 184 645)

California Community and Junior College Association. *CETA Comes to College.* Sacramento: California Community and Junior College Association, 1978a. 41 pp. (ED 168 628)

California Community and Junior College Association. *Community College Instructors' Out-of-Class Professional Functions: Report of a Survey of Full-Time and Part-Time Faculty in California Community Colleges.* Sacramento: California Community and Junior College Association, 1978b. 61 pp. (ED 154 873)

California State Department of Education. "Summary of Source and Education Background of New Teachers in California Junior Colleges, 1963-64." Unpublished report, California State Department of Education, 1963-1964.

California State Postsecondary Education Commission. "College Going Rates in California." Unpublished report, California State Postsecondary Education Commission, 1978.

Campbell, D. F. "New Roles for Occupational Instructors." Unpublished paper, Community College of the Air Force (Lackland Air Force Base, Texas), 1977. 12 pp. (ED 146 967)

Career Information Center. "Post-High School Occupational Training Opportunities in Hawaii Public Institutions, 1974-1975." Unpublished paper, Career Information Center, Honolulu, 1974.

Carnegie Commission on Higher Education. *The Open-Door College.* New York: McGraw-Hill, 1970.

Carnegie Foundation for the Advancement of Teaching. *Missions of the College Curriculum: A Contemporary Review with Suggestions.* San Francisco: Jossey-Bass, 1977.

Carter, E. H. "A Follow-Up Study of Former Occupational-

Technical Students at Virginia Community Colleges." Unpublished paper, 1976. 10 pp. (ED 136 899)

Center for the Study of Community Colleges. "Report of Instructor Surveys, 1977-1978." Unpublished report, 1978a.

Center for the Study of Community Colleges. "Science and Humanities Instruction in Two-Year Colleges." Unpublished report, 1978b.

Chang, N. *Organizational Structure in Multi-Campus Community Junior Colleges/Districts.* Denver: Community College of Denver, 1978. 137 pp. (ED 158 795)

Charles, R. F. *Survey Results for Participating Colleges: Classes and Programs for the Aged in California Community Colleges, 1978.* Cupertino: California Community College Continuing Education Association; DeAnza College, 1979. 39 pp. (ED 174 277)

Chausow, H. M. "Remedial Education: A Position Paper." Unpublished paper, Chicago, 1979. 16 pp. (ED 170 013)

Cherdack, A. N. "The Changing Nature of Institutional Research in the Community College." Los Angeles, unpublished paper, 1979. 10 pp. (ED 186 058)

Ciardi, J. "Give Us This Day Our Daily Surrealism." *Saturday Review,* 1971, *54* (24), 48.

Clark, B. R. "The 'Cooling-Out' Function in Higher Education." *American Journal of Sociology,* 1960, *65* (6), 569-576.

Clark, B. R. "The 'Cooling Out' Function Revisited." In G. B. Vaughan (Ed.), *New Directions for Community Colleges: Questioning the Community College Role,* no. 32. San Francisco: Jossey-Bass, 1980.

Clark, R. M. "Reedley College Enrollment/Withdrawal Survey, 1974-1975." Unpublished paper, Reedley College (Reedley, Calif.), 1975. 9 pp. (ED 128 055)

Clark, R. M. "Special Counseling Study, Fall 1978, Entering Class." Unpublished paper, Reedley College (Reedley, Calif.), 1979. 18 pp. (ED 175 498)

Cohen, A. M. *Focus on Learning: Preparing Teachers for the Two-Year College.* Occasional Report No. 11. Los Angeles: UCLA Junior College Leadership Program, 1968.

Cohen, A. M. "Technology: Thee or Me? Behavioral Objectives and the College Teacher." *Educational Technology,* 1970, *10,* 57-60.

Cohen, A. M. "Assessing College Students' Ability to Write Compositions." *Research in the Teaching of English,* 1973, *7* (3), 356-371.

Cohen, A. M. "Work Satisfaction Among Junior College Faculty Members." Los Angeles: University of California and ERIC Clearinghouse for Junior Colleges, 1973. 8 pp. (ED 081 426)

Cohen, A. M. "Instructional Practices in the Humanities, Fall 1977." Unpublished paper, Center for the Study of Community Colleges, 1978. 18 pp. (ED 160 145)

Cohen, A. M. "Counting the Transfer Students." *Junior College Resource Review.* Los Angeles: ERIC Clearinghouse for Junior Colleges, 1979. 6 pp. (ED 172 864)

Cohen, A. M., and Brawer, F. B. *The Two-Year College Instructor Today.* New York: Praeger, 1977.

Cohen, A. M., and Brawer, F. B. "Instructional Practices in the Humanities and Sciences." Unpublished report, Center for the Study of Community Colleges, 1981.

Cohen, A. M., and Hill, A. "Instructional Practices in the Sciences, Spring 1978." Center for the Study of Community Colleges, 1978. 18 pp. (ED 160 144)

Cohen, A. M., and Associates. *College Responses to Community Demands: The Community College in Challenging Times.* San Francisco: Jossey-Bass, 1975.

Cohen, M. D., and March, J. G. *Leadership and Ambiguity: The American College President.* New York: McGraw-Hill, 1974.

Cohen, M. J. "Junior College Growth." *Change,* 1972, *4* (9), 32a-32d.

Collins, C. C. *Junior College Student Personnel Programs: What They Are and What They Should Be.* Washington, D.C.: American Association of Junior Colleges, 1967. 57 pp. (ED 011 459)

Collins, C. C., and Drexel, K. O. *General Education: A Community College Model.* Pittsburg, Calif.: Community College Press, 1976.

Combs, B. E. "A Study of Student Attitudes at Maricopa Technical Community College, Spring 1978." Unpublished paper, Maricopa Technical Community College (Phoenix, Ariz.), 1978. 71 pp. (ED 175 487)

Committee on the Objectives of a General Education in a Free Society. *General Education in a Free Society: Report of the*

Harvard Committee. Cambridge, Mass.: Harvard University Press, 1945.

Conti, G. J., and others. *New Start. General Education (G.E.D.), Job Skills, & Job Placement: A Summary, July 1, 1977–June 30, 1978.* Canton, Ill.: Spoon River College, 1978. 26 pp. (ED 169 983)

Coombs, P. H. *The World Educational Crisis: A Systems Analysis.* New York: University Press, 1968.

Cooperation in General Education: A Final Report of the Executive Committee of the Cooperative Study in General Education. Washington, D.C.: American Council on Education, 1947.

Copperman, P. *The Literacy Hoax: The Decline of Reading, Writing, and Learning in the Public Schools and What We Can Do About It.* New York: Morrow, 1978.

Corson, J. J. *The Governance of Colleges and Universities.* New York: McGraw-Hill, 1960.

Cosand, J. P. *Perspective: Community Colleges in the 1980s.* Horizons Issue Monograph Series. Washington, D.C.: Council of Universities and Colleges, American Association of Community and Junior Colleges; Los Angeles: ERIC Clearinghouse for Junior Colleges, 1979.

Cremin, L. A. *The Genius of American Education.* New York: Vintage Books, 1965.

Cross, K. P. "College Women: A Research Description." *Journal of the National Association of Women Deans and Counselors,* 1968, *32* (1), 12-21.

Cross, K. P. "Access and Accommodation in Higher Education." Paper presented to White House Conference on Youth. *Research Reporter* (Berkeley, Calif.: Center for Research and Development in Higher Education), 1971, *6* (2), 6-8.

Cross, K. P. "Toward the Future in Community College Education." Paper presented at the Conference on Education in the Community College for the Non-Traditional Student, Philadelphia, March 31, 1978. 24 pp. (ED 168 626)

Dallas County Community College District. *ITV Close-Up: The First Six Years.* Dallas: Dallas County Community College District, 1979. 60 pp. (ED 171 361)

Darnowski, V. S. "The Maze in Connecticut." In S. F. Charles

(Ed.), *New Directions for Community Colleges: Balancing State and Local Control,* no. 23. San Francisco: Jossey-Bass, 1978.

Davenport, L. F., and others. "Vocational Education in the 1980's." Papers presented at annual meeting of the American Association of Community and Junior Colleges, Washington, D.C., March 17-19, 1976. 41 pp. (ED 124 249)

DeCosmo, R. "1978-79 Recruitment & Retention Program." Unpublished paper, Moraine Valley Community College (Palos Hills, Ill.), 1978. 23 pp. (ED 172 892)

Dehnert, E., and others. *A Contemporary Course in the Humanities for Community College Students (Optional Sequences).* Chicago: Chicago City Colleges; Costa Mesa, Calif.: Coast Community College District; Miami, Fla.: Miami-Dade Community College, 1977. 208 pp. (ED 140 893)

Dennison, J. D. "Penitentiary Education in Canada: The Role for Community Colleges." Unpublished paper, 1979. 11 pp. (ED 175 522)

Devall, W. B. "Community Colleges: A Dissenting View." *Educational Record,* 1968, *49* (2), 168-172.

A Developmental Program for Metropolitan Junior College, Kansas City. Vol. 2: *Guidelines for Development.* San Francisco: Arthur D. Little, 1968. 85 pp. (ED number not yet assigned)

Dib, E. L. "An Investigation of Selected Community College Programs for Older Adults." Unpublished paper, Los Angeles, 1978. 54 pp. (ED 165 831)

Dickmeyer, N. *Comparative Financial Statistics for Community and Junior Colleges, 1978-79: An Experimental Study of 184 Institutions.* Washington, D.C.: National Center for Education Statistics, U.S. Department of Health, Education and Welfare, 1980. 80 pp. (ED 194 141)

Digest of Education Statistics. (Annual.) Washington, D.C.: National Center for Education Statistics, U.S. Department of Health, Education and Welfare, 1970-1980.

Drakulich, J. S., and Karlen, J. M. *Reverse Transfer Student Characteristics—Fall 1979.* Research Report No. 80-3. Newark, N.J.: Office of Institutional Research, Essex County College, 1980. 32 pp. (ED 184 647)

Dressel, P. L., and Thompson, M. M. *A Degree for College Teachers: The Doctor of Arts.* Technical Report. Berkeley, Calif.: Carnegie Council on Policy Studies in Higher Education, 1977. 71 pp. (ED 150 939)

Drucker, P. F. *The Practice of Management.* New York: Harper & Row, 1954.

Drucker, P. F. *The Age of Discontinuity: Guidelines to Our Changing Society.* New York: Harper & Row, 1969.

Educational Policies Commission. *Education for All American Youth.* Washington, D.C.: Educational Policies Commission, National Education Association of the United States and the American Association of School Administrators, 1944.

Educational Testing Service. *Community College Research: Methods, Trends, and Prospects.* Proceedings of the National Conference on Institutional Research in Community Colleges. Princeton, N.J.: Educational Testing Service, 1976. 205 pp. (ED 187 363)

Educational Testing Service. *The Concern for Writing.* Focus 5. Princeton, N.J.: Educational Testing Service, 1978. 18 pp. (ED 159 674—Available in microfiche only)

Eells, W. C. *The Junior College.* Boston: Houghton Mifflin, 1931.

Eells, W. C. *Present Status of Junior College Terminal Education.* Washington, D.C.: American Association of Junior Colleges, 1941a.

Eells, W. C. *Why Junior College Terminal Education?* Washington, D.C.: American Association of Junior Colleges, 1941b.

Ehrhardt, H. B. "Mountain View College's Cognitive Style Program: A Description." Unpublished paper, Mountain View College (Dallas), 1980. 18 pp. (ED 190 183)

Eisenberg, D. U. *Community Forums: A Boost for the Humanities.* Washington, D.C.: American Association of Community and Junior Colleges, 1979. 13 pp. (ED 178 119)

Eisenstein, F. "Annual Report, 1978-79." Unpublished report, Division of Continuing Education and Extension Services, New York City Community College (Brooklyn), 1979. 70 pp. (ED 179 270)

Emerson, S. "RSVP Basic Math Lab: MAT 1992." Unpublished paper, Miami-Dade Community College, 1978. 27 pp. (ED 188 649)

Employment and Training Administration. *Conference Report on Youth Unemployment: Its Measurements and Meaning.* Washington, D.C.: Employment and Training Administration, Department of Labor, 1978. 397 pp. (ED 176 115)

Eppley, G., and Mackie, L. "Proposal for Manpower Training Certificate Program." Unpublished paper, Cuyahoga Community College (Cleveland, Ohio), 1979. 27 pp. (ED 175 521)

Evans, A. J., Jr. "The Funding of Community Services." *Community Services Catalyst,* 1973, *3* (3), 17-22.

Evans, N. D., and Neagley, R. L. *Planning and Developing Innovative Community Colleges.* Englewood Cliffs, N.J.: Prentice-Hall, 1973.

Ewens, T. "Think Piece on CBE and Liberal Education." CUE Project Occasional Paper Series No. 1. Bowling Green State University (Bowling Green, Ohio), 1977.

Farmer, J. E. *A Practitioner's Guide to Student Retention: A College-Wide Responsibility.* Tallahassee: Florida State Department of Education, 1980. 28 pp. (ED 188 721)

Feldman, M. J. *Public Education and Manpower Development.* New York: Ford Foundation, 1967.

Field Research Corporation. *A Survey of California Public Attitudes Toward the California Community Colleges.* San Francisco: Field Research Corporation, 1979. 125 pp. (ED 194 152)

Fisher, B. W. "A Comparative Study of Two Methods of Freshman Orientation." Unpublished paper, Mississippi Gulf Coast Junior College (Gautier, Miss.), 1975. 16 pp. (ED 105 916)

Fletcher, S. M., and others. "Community Education in Community Colleges: Today and Tomorrow." *Community Services Catalyst,* 1977, *7* (1), 10-15.

"Flexibility Sought in Award of Educational Credit." *Chronicle of Higher Education,* February 6, 1978, p. 9.

Florida State Department of Education. "General Education in Community Junior Colleges." Proceedings, Florida Annual Junior College Conference, 1959.

Florida State Department of Education. *Articulation.* Tallahassee: Division of Community Junior Colleges, Florida State Department of Education, 1976. 32 pp. (ED 125 693)

Florida State Department of Education. *Report of the Distribu-*

tion of Financial Assistance to Students in Florida's Community Colleges 1977-78. Tallahassee: Division of Community Colleges, Florida State Department of Education, 1979. 23 pp. (ED 168 642)

Ford, M. L. "Penn Valley Community College Learning Skills Laboratory: A Resource Center for Developmental Education." In J. R. Clarke and others, *Developmental Education in Higher Education. Advanced Institutional Developmental Program (AIDP) Two-Year College Consortium.* Vol. 2, No. 5. Washington, D.C.: McManis Associates, 1976. 44 pp. (ED 134 272)

Freeman, R. B. *The Overeducated American.* New York: Academic Press, 1976.

Freligh, E. A. "Can Instructional Leadership Survive?" In B. Heermann (Ed.), *New Directions for Community Colleges: Changing Managerial Perspectives,* no. 13. San Francisco: Jossey-Bass, 1976.

Friedenberg, E. Z. *The Dignity of Youth and Other Atavisms.* Boston: Beacon Press, 1965.

Friedlander, J. "Instructional Practices of Part-Time Faculty in Community Colleges." Paper presented at forum of the Association for Institutional Research, San Diego, Calif., May 1979. 23 pp. (ED 169 971)

Froh, R., and Muraki, E. "Modification and Discontinuance of Mastery Learning Strategies." Paper presented at conference of the Mid-Western Educational Research Association, Toledo, Ohio, October 1980. 50 pp. (ED 194 178—Available in microfiche only)

Galley, J. P., and Parsons, M. H. "College Behind the Walls: Factors Influencing a Post-Secondary Inmate Education Program." Paper presented at national convention of the Community College Social Science Association, Kansas City, Mo., October 1976. 13 pp. (ED 130 696)

Garber, R. "West Los Angeles College Student Follow-Up Study Project Report." Unpublished report, West Los Angeles College (Culver City, Calif.), 1979. 78 pp. (ED 175 489)

Garrison, R. H. *Junior College Faculty: Issues and Problems. A Preliminary National Appraisal.* Washington, D.C.: American Association of Junior Colleges, 1967. 99 pp. (ED 012 177)

Gay, E. J. "Student Affairs—Alternative Roles." In H. F. Robinson and others, *Expanding Student Mobility: A Challenge for Community Colleges.* Workshop Proceedings. Atlanta: Southern Regional Education Board, 1977. 71 pp. (ED 164 036)

Gell, R. L., and Armstrong, D. F. *The Graduates 1976.* Rockville, Md.: Office of Institutional Research, Montgomery College, 1977. 54 pp. (ED 142 252)

Gilbert, F. (Ed.). *Minorities and Community Colleges: Data and Discourse.* Washington, D.C.: American Association of Community and Junior Colleges, 1979. 31 pp. (ED 171 345)

Gilder, J., and Rocha, J. "10,000 Cooperative Arrangements Serve 1.5 Million." *Community and Junior College Journal,* 1980, *51* (3), 11-17.

Gleazer, E. J., Jr. *Responding to the New Spirit of Learning.* Washington, D.C.: American Association of Community and Junior Colleges, 1976. 20 pp. (ED 129 381)

Gleazer, E. J., Jr. *The Community College: Values, Vision, & Vitality.* Washington, D.C.: American Association of Community and Junior Colleges, 1980.

Glover, R. E., and Chapman, B. *A Report on Student Aid Needs Within the Postsecondary Education Community in Arkansas.* Little Rock: Arkansas Postsecondary Education Commission, 1975. 99 pp. (ED 119 774)

Gober, L. A., and Wiseman, T. J. (Comps.). *Outcomes, Output, and Outlooks: A Report and Evaluation of Project CALL, a Project in Rural Community Education.* Malta, Ill.: Kishwaukee College, 1979. 53 pp. (ED 175 501)

Gold, B. K. "Trends in Los Angeles City College Day Course Enrollments, 1970-1974." Unpublished paper, Los Angeles City College, 1975. 40 pp. (ED 100 419)

Gold, B. K. "LACC Student Survey—Fall 1978." Unpublished paper, Los Angeles City College, 1979. 18 pp. (ED 165 853)

Gold, B. K., and Morris, W. *Student Accountability Model (SAM): Operations Manual.* Sacramento: Office of the Chancellor, California Community Colleges; Los Angeles: Los Angeles Community College District, 1977. 99 pp. (ED 135 443)

Goldberg, A. "Reflections of a Two Year College Dean." *NASPA Journal,* 1973, *11* (1), 39-42.

Golemon, R. B. *A Survey of Non-Traditional Credit in Texas.*

Austin: Texas Association of Junior and Community College Instructional Administrators, 1979. 9 pp. (ED 170 008)

Goodwin, G., and Young, J. C. *Increasing Productivity in the Community Colleges.* Topical Paper No. 67. Los Angeles: ERIC Clearinghouse for Junior Colleges, 1978. 49 pp. (ED 156 239)

Gottschalk, K. "Can Colleges Deal with High-Risk Community Problems?" *Community College Frontiers,* 1978, *6* (4), 4-11.

Grafton, C. L., and Roy, D. D. "The 'Second-Time Around' Community College Student: Assessment of Reverse Transfer Student Performance in a University Setting." Paper presented at annual meeting of the American Educational Research Association, Boston, April 1980. 33 pp. (ED 184 620)

Graham, R. W. "A Look at Student Activities in the Junior Colleges." *Junior College Journal,* 1962, *33* (1), 43-45.

Hankin, J. N. "Who Bargains with Whom: What's Past Is Prologue." Unpublished paper, Westchester Community Colleges (Valhalla, N.Y.), 1975. 37 pp. (ED 100 476)

Harlacher, E. L., and Gollattscheck, J. F. "Editors' Notes." In E. L. Harlacher and J. F. Gollattscheck (Eds.), *New Directions for Community Colleges: Implementing Community-Based Education,* no. 21. San Francisco: Jossey-Bass, 1978.

Harper, H., and others. *Advisement and Graduation Information System.* Miami, Fla.: Miami-Dade Community College, 1981. 34 pp. (ED 197 776)

Harris, N. C., and Grede, J. F. *Career Education in Colleges: A Guide for Planning Two- and Four-Year Occupational Programs for Successful Employment.* San Francisco: Jossey-Bass, 1977.

Head, C. V., Jr. "Academic Achievement in English in Junior College Transfer Students and Native Students at the University of Mississippi." Unpublished doctoral dissertation, School of Education, University of Mississippi, 1971.

Heath, P. R., and Peterson, S. L. *The Common Market Concept: Contracting for Community-Based Educational Services.* Monograph No. 2. Stockton, Calif.: Cooperative for the Advancement of Community-Based and Performance-Oriented Postsecondary Education, 1980. 12 pp. (ED 190 186)

Heermann, B. *Cooperative Education in Community Colleges: A Sourcebook for Occupational and General Educators.* San Francisco: Jossey-Bass, 1973.

Heermann, B. (Ed.). *New Directions for Community Colleges: Changing Managerial Perspectives,* no. 13. San Francisco: Jossey-Bass, 1976.

Heermann, B. Personal communication, August 11, 1981.

Heiner, H., and Nelson, J. M. (Eds.). *A Manual for Student Services.* Olympia: Washington State Board for Community College Education; Washington State Services Commission, 1977. 47 pp. (ED 145 867)

Heist, P., and Yonge, D. G. *Omnibus Personality Inventory, Form F Manual.* New York: Psychological Corporation, 1962.

Helfgot, S. R. "A Philosophical Statement on Student Development and the Role of Counseling in Illinois Community Colleges." Unpublished paper, Illinois Council of Community Colleges, n.d. 35 pp. (ED 139 461)

Henderson, J. J., and Schick, F. L. (Eds.). *The Bowker Annual of Library and Book Trade Information.* New York: Bowker, 1973, 1977, 1978.

Henry, G. H. "Foundation of General Education in the High School." In *What Shall the High Schools Teach? 1956 Yearbook of the NEA Association for Supervision and Curriculum Development.* Washington, D.C.: Association for Supervision and Curriculum Development, National Education Association, 1956.

Herder, D. M., and Standridge, L. A. "Continuing Education: Blueprint for Excellence." Unpublished paper, Lansing Community College (Lansing, Mich.), 1980. 14 pp. (ED 187 391)

Herzberg, F., Mausner, B., and Snyderman, B. D. *The Motivation to Work.* New York: Wiley, 1959.

Hollinshead, B. S. "The Community College Program." *Junior College Journal,* 1936, 7, 111-116.

Howard, A., and others. *Instructional Computing in the Community Colleges of Washington State.* Olympia: Washington State Board for Community College Education, 1978. 148 pp. (ED 172 891)

Howard, J. H. *Adult Basic Education Career Development Center in the Newark Model Cities Area, for the Period Ending December 31, 1974.* Final Report. Newark, N.J.: Essex County College, 1976. 72 pp. (ED 133 027)

Huff, R., and others. *Training English Teachers for Texas Community Colleges.* Austin: Department of English, University of Texas, 1974. 20 pp. (ED 092 209)

Humphreys, J. A. "Toward Improved Programs of Student Personnel Services." *Junior College Journal,* 1952, *22* (7), 382-392.

Hunter, P. L. "Composition in the Open-Door College." Unpublished paper, Gainesville, Fla., 1977. 107 pp. (ED 140 088)

Hunter, R., and Sheldon, M. S. *Statewide Longitudinal Study: Report on Academic Year 1978-79.* Part I: *Fall Results.* Woodland Hills, Calif: Los Angeles Pierce College, 1979. 86 pp. (ED 180 530)

Hunter, R., and Sheldon, M. S. *Statewide Longitudinal Study: Report on Academic Year 1979-80.* Part III: *Fall Results.* Woodland Hills, Calif.: Los Angeles Pierce College, 1980. 95 pp. (ED 188 714)

Hurn, C. J. "The Prospects for Liberal Education: A Sociological Perspective." *Phi Delta Kappan,* 1979, *60* (9), 630-633.

Illich, I. *Lima Discourse.* Cuernavaca, Mexico: Centro Intercultural de Documentación, 1971.

Illinois Community College Board. "Curriculum Enrollment Summary in the Public Community Colleges of Illinois: 1975-76." Unpublished paper, Illinois Community College Board, 1976.

Illinois Community College Board. *Handbook for Illinois Public Community Colleges and Illinois Prime Sponsors Under the Comprehensive Employment and Training Act (CETA).* Springfield: Illinois Community College Board, 1977. 93 pp. (ED 144 646)

Illinois Community College Board. *Illinois Public Community College Statewide Occupational Student Follow-Up Study: Second Progress Report.* Springfield: Illinois Community College Board, 1978. 85 pp. (ED 148 427)

Illinois Community College Board. *Illinois Public Community Colleges Statewide Occupational Student Follow-Up Study: Final Report of a Three-Year Longitudinal Study of Fall 1974 New Students Enrolled in Occupational Programs.* Springfield: Illinois Community College Board, 1979a. 72 pp. (ED 169 958)

Illinois Community College Board. *Report on Counseling Evaluation Guidelines Developed by Ad Hoc Counseling Task Force and Endorsed by the Illinois Community College Board, January 26, 1979.* Springfield: Illinois Community College Board, 1979b. 21 pp. (ED 167 229)

Illinois Junior College Board. *Report of Selected Data and Characteristics of Illinois Public Junior Colleges, 1970-71.* Springfield: Illinois Junior College Board, 1971. 109 pp. (ED 101 794)

Ireland, J. "Community Services: A Position Paper." Office of Community Services, Rio Hondo College (Whittier, Calif.), 1979. 35 pp. (ED 180 562)

Jencks, C., and Riesman, D. *The Academic Revolution.* Garden City, N.Y.: Doubleday, 1968.

Jenkins, J. A., and Rossmeier, J. G. *Relationships Between Centralization/Decentralization and Organizational Effectiveness in Urban Multi-Unit Community College Systems: A Summary Report.* Ann Arbor: Center for the Study of Higher Education, University of Michigan, 1974. 33 pp. (ED 110 103)

Jensen, M. E. "Structures, Services, and Staffing in Learning Resource Centers in Selected California Community Colleges." Unpublished paper, West Valley College (Saratoga, Calif.), 1978. 17 pp. (ED 154 874)

Johnson, B. L. "The Extent of the Present General Education Program in the Colleges and Universities of America." Paper presented at the University of Florida, July 1937.

Johnson, B. L. *Vitalizing a College Library.* Chicago: American Library Association, 1939.

Johnson, B. L. *General Education in Action.* Washington, D.C.: American Council on Education, 1952.

Johnson, B. L. *Islands of Innovation Expanding: Changes in the Community College.* Beverly Hills, Calif.: Glencoe Press, 1969.

Johnson, D., and others (Comps.). *Evaluation of Hotel, Restaurant, and Institutional Management Graduates: A Ten-Year Review.* St. Louis, Mo.: St. Louis Community College at Forest Park, 1976. 34 pp. (ED 138 327)

Johnson, D. C. "Managing Non-Profit Marketing." In R. E. Lahti (Ed.), *New Directions for Community Colleges: Managing in a New Era,* no. 28. San Francisco: Jossey-Bass, 1979.

Karabel, J. "Community Colleges and Social Stratification." *Harvard Educational Review,* 1972, *42* (4), 521-562.

Karlen, J. M. *Progress Report on the West Essex Extension Center.* Office of Institutional Research, Report No. 80-2. Newark, N.J.: Essex County College, 1980. 11 pp. (ED 181 959)

Katz, J. M. "The Educational Shibboleth: Equality of Opportunity in a Democratic Institution, the Public Junior College." Unpublished doctoral dissertation, Department of Sociology, University of California at Los Angeles, 1967.

Kegel, P. L. "Community and Junior College Concern for and Services Provided to Part-Time Students." Unpublished paper, Marshalltown, Iowa, 1977. 62 pp. (ED 138 324)

Keim, W. A. "Staffing: Where and How." In E. L. Harlacher and J. F. Gollattscheck (Eds.), *New Directions for Community Colleges: Implementing Community-Based Education,* no. 21. San Francisco: Jossey-Bass, 1978.

Kelly, J. T. *Restructuring the Academic Program: A Systems Approach to Educational Reform at Miami-Dade Community College.* Miami, Fla.: Miami-Dade Community College, 1981. (ED number not yet assigned)

Kelly, J. T., and Anandam, K. "Instruction for Distant Learners Through Technology." Paper presented at 3rd International Conference on Improving University Teaching, Newcastle-upon-Tyne, England, June 1977. 16 pp. (ED 139 455)

Kemerer, F. R., and Baldridge, J. V. *Unions on Campus: A National Study of the Consequences of Faculty Bargaining.* San Francisco: Jossey-Bass, 1975.

Kent, T. H. "A Study of the English Instructors in the Junior and Community Colleges." Unpublished doctoral dissertation, School of Education, Indiana University, 1971.

Kentucky Council on Public Higher Education. *Student Transferability Study Group Report.* Frankfort: Kentucky Council on Public Higher Education, 1977. 57 pp. (ED 165 868)

Kessman, M. "Survey of Former Loop College Students; How

1,081 Former Students View Loop College. Student Follow-Up Research Project." Unpublished paper, Loop College (Chicago), 1975. 91 pp. (ED 118 180)

Kintzer, F. C. *Middleman in Higher Education: Improving Articulation Among High School, Community College, and Senior Institutions.* San Francisco: Jossey-Bass, 1973.

Kintzer, F. C. *Organization and Leadership of Two-Year Colleges: Preparing for the Eighties.* Gainesville: Institute of Higher Education, University of Florida, 1980a.

Kintzer, F. C. *Proposition 13: Implications for Community Colleges.* Topical Paper No. 72. Los Angeles: ERIC Clearinghouse for Junior Colleges, 1980b. 39 pp. (ED 188 711)

Kintzer, F. C., Jensen, A., and Hansen, J. *The Multi-Institution Junior College District.* Horizons Issue Monograph Series. Los Angeles: ERIC Clearinghouse for Junior Colleges; Washington, D.C.: American Association of Junior Colleges, 1969. 64 pp. (ED 030 415)

Kissler, G. R. "Report of the Task Group on Retention and Transfer." Unpublished report, University of California at Berkeley, 1980a.

Kissler, G. R. "Trends Affecting Undergraduate Education in the University of California." Paper presented to the University of California Board of Regents, October 16, 1980b. 22 pp. (ED 194 138)

Knapp, M. S. "Factors Contributing to the Development of Institutional Research and Planning Units in Community Colleges: A Review of the Empirical Evidence." Paper presented at annual meeting of the American Educational Research Association, Special Interest Group on Community and Junior College Research, San Francisco, April 1979. 18 pp. (ED 168 663)

Knoell, D. M., and Medsker, L. L. *From Junior to Senior Colleges: A National Study of the Transfer Student.* Washington, D.C.: American Council on Education, 1965.

Knoell, D., and others. *Through the Open Door: A Study of Patterns of Enrollment and Performance in California's Community Colleges.* Report No. 76-1. Sacramento: California Postsecondary Education Commission, 1976. 82 pp. (ED 119 752)

Koehnline, W. A. "A Public Community College in a System of Systems." In S. F. Charles (Ed.), *New Directions for Community Colleges: Balancing State and Local Control,* no. 23. San Francisco: Jossey-Bass, 1978.

Koltai, L. "The Agony of Change." *Junior College Resource Review.* Los Angeles: ERIC Clearinghouse for Junior Colleges, 1980. 6 pp. (ED 187 382)

Koos, L. V. *The Junior College.* Vols. 1 and 2. Minneapolis: University of Minnesota Press, 1924.

Koos, L. V. *The Junior College Movement.* Boston: Ginn, 1925.

Koos, L. V. "Preparation for Community College Teaching." *Journal of Higher Education,* 1950, *21,* 309-317.

Korim, A. S. *Manpower Training in Community Colleges.* Washington, D.C.: American Association of Community and Junior Colleges, 1974.

Kurth, E. L., and Mills, E. R. *Analysis of Degree of Faculty Satisfaction in Florida Community Colleges.* Final Report. Gainesville: Institute of Higher Education, University of Florida, 1968. 135 pp. (ED 027 902)

Lach, I. J., and others. *Abstract of the American College Testing Class Profile for Fall 1978 Freshmen Enrolled in Illinois Public Community Colleges.* Springfield: Illinois Community College Board, 1979. 33 pp. (ED 176 821)

Lahti, R. E. "Concluding Comments." In R. E. Lahti (Ed.), *New Directions for Community Colleges: Managing in a New Era,* no. 28. San Francisco: Jossey-Bass, 1979.

Lander, V. L. "The Significance of Structure in Arizona Community College Districts: A Limited Study." Unpublished paper, Tucson, Ariz., 1977. 83 pp. (ED 139 481)

Larkin, P. G. *Five-Year Trends in Career Program Graduations, 1970-1974.* Report No. 76. Largo, Md.: Office of Institutional Research, Prince George's Community College, 1974a. 8 pp. (ED 099 973)

Larkin, P. G. *Five Years of Career Program Growth: 1969-1973.* Report No. 75. Largo, Md.: Office of Institutional Research, Prince George's Community College, 1974b. 7 pp. (ED 099 072)

Larkin, P. G. *How Students Are Using the Community College to Get Jobs: A Follow-Up of Career Program Graduates.* Report No. 77-17. Largo, Md.: Office of Institutional Research, Prince George's Community College, 1977a. 11 pp. (ED 142 261)

Larkin, P. G. *Increases in Career Program Graduations and Decreases in Transfer Program Graduations in the Mid-Seventies.* Report No. 77-31. Largo, Md.: Office of Institutional Research, Prince George's Community College, 1977b. 14 pp. (ED 142 258)

Larkin, P. G. *Who Wants a Degree? Educational Goals and Related Preferences of Off-Campus Students at Five Extension and Degree Centers.* Report No. 77-5. Largo, Md.: Office of Institutional Research, Prince George's Community College, 1977c. 61 pp. (ED 143 383—Available in microfiche only)

Lee, R. "Reverse Transfer Students." *Community College Review,* 1976, *4* (2), 64-70.

Lee, R. "Age-Related Adult Developmental Stages Among Two-Year College Faculty." Unpublished doctoral dissertation, Graduate School of Education, University of California at Los Angeles, 1977.

Leo, R. J. "The Colleges' Roles for Service." In H. M. Holcomb (Ed.), *New Directions for Community Colleges: Reaching Out Through Community Service,* no. 14. San Francisco: Jossey-Bass, 1976.

Licata, C. M. "Program Evaluation Report: Medical Assistant Program, Takoma Park Campus, Fourth Year, 1976-1977." Unpublished report, Montgomery College (Rockville, Md.), 1977. 49 pp. (ED 143 387)

Lombardi, J. *The Department/Division Structure in the Community College.* Topical Paper No. 38. Los Angeles: ERIC Clearinghouse for Junior Colleges, 1973a. 25 pp. (ED 085 051)

Lombardi, J. *Managing Finances in Community Colleges.* San Francisco: Jossey-Bass, 1973b.

Lombardi, J. (Ed.). *New Directions for Community Colleges: Meeting the Financial Crisis,* no. 2. San Francisco: Jossey-Bass, 1973c.

Lombardi, J. *The Duties and Responsibilities of the Department/Division Chairman in Community Colleges.* Topical Paper No. 39. Los Angeles: ERIC Clearinghouse for Junior Colleges, 1974. 21 pp. (ED 089 811)

Lombardi, J. *Riding the Wave of New Enrollments.* Topical Paper No. 50. Los Angeles: ERIC Clearinghouse for Junior Colleges, 1975. 58 pp. (ED 107 326)

Lombardi, J. *No or Low Tuition: A Lost Cause.* Topical Paper No. 58. Los Angeles: ERIC Clearinghouse for Junior Colleges, 1976. 46 pp. (ED 129 353)

Lombardi, J. *Resurgence of Occupational Education.* Topical Paper No. 65. Los Angeles: ERIC Clearinghouse for Junior Colleges, 1978a. 41 pp. (ED 148 418)

Lombardi, J. *Community Education: Threat to College Status?* Topical Paper No. 68. Los Angeles: ERIC Clearinghouse for Junior Colleges, 1978b. 45 pp. (ED 156 296)

Lombardi, J. "Changing Administrative Relations Under Collective Bargaining." *Junior College Resource Review.* Los Angeles: ERIC Clearinghouse for Junior Colleges, 1979a. 8 pp. (ED 170 015)

Lombardi, J. *The Decline of Transfer Education.* Topical Paper No. 70. Los Angeles: ERIC Clearinghouse for Junior Colleges, 1979b. 37 pp. (ED 179 273)

Lombardi, J. "Proposition 13: Is the Worst Over for Community Colleges?" *Community College Review,* 1979c, *6* (4), 7-14.

London, H. B. *The Culture of a Community College.* New York: Praeger, 1978.

Lucas, J. A. *Student Characteristics as Compared to the Community Profile—1977-1978.* Vol. 9, No. 17. Palatine, Ill.: William Rainey Harper College, 1978. 37 pp. (ED 169 978)

Lukenbill, J. D., and McCabe, R. H. *General Education in a Changing Society: General Education Program, Basic Skills Requirements, Standards of Academic Progress at Miami-Dade Community College.* Miami, Fla.: Office of Institutional Research, Miami-Dade Community College, 1978. 98 pp. (ED 158 812)

Luskin, B. J., and Small, J. "The Need to Change and the Need to Stay the Same." *Community and Junior College Journal,* 1980-81, *51* (4), 24-28.

Lyons, G. "The Higher Illiteracy." *Harper's,* 1976, *253* (1516), 33-40.

McCabe, R. H. "Now Is the Time to Reform the American Community College." *Community and Junior College Journal,* 1981, *51* (8), 6-10.

McClintock, R. "The Dynamics of Decline: Why Education Can No Longer Be Liberal." *Phi Delta Kappan,* 1979, *60* (9), 636-640.

Mackie, L. G., and Eppley, G. *CETA and the Community College.* Cleveland, Ohio: Cuyahoga Community College, 1978. 14 pp. (ED 187 348)

Macomb County Community College. "Information Report: Enrollment, 1972-73." Prepared for a meeting of the board of trustees, Warren, Mich., March 20, 1973.

Marks, J. L. "Forces Shaping the Humanities in Public Two-Year Colleges." Unpublished doctoral dissertation, College of Education, University of Arizona, 1980.

Marsh, J. P., and Lamb, T. (Eds.). "An Introduction to the Part-Time Teaching Situation with Particular Emphasis on Its Impact at Napa Community College." Unpublished paper, Napa Community College (Napa, Calif.), 1975. 46 pp. (ED 125 683)

Martens, K. J. *Project Priority, 1974-1975: An ESEA Funded Project.* Final Report. Albany: Two Year College Student Development Center, State University of New York, 1975. 30 pp. (ED 139 475)

Martorana, S. V. "Shifting Patterns of Financial Support." In R. L. Alfred (Ed.), *New Directions for Community Colleges: Coping with Reduced Resources,* no. 22. San Francisco: Jossey-Bass, 1978.

Maryland State Board for Community Colleges. *Statewide Master Plan for Community Colleges in Maryland, Fiscal Years 1978-1987.* Annapolis: Maryland State Board for Community Colleges, 1977. 227 pp. (ED 139 454)

Maryland State Board for Community Colleges. *Maryland Community Colleges Continuing Education Manual.* Annapolis: Maryland State Board for Community Colleges, 1980. 56 pp. (ED 188 730)

Mayhew, L. B. (Ed.). *General Education: An Account and Appraisal.* New York: Harper & Row, 1960.

Medsker, L. L. *The Junior College: Progress and Prospect.* New York: McGraw-Hill, 1960.

Medsker, L. L., and Tillery, D. *Breaking the Access Barriers: A Profile of Two-Year Colleges.* New York: McGraw-Hill, 1971.

Meier, T. *Washington Community College Factbook Addendum A: Student Enrollments, Academic Year 1978-79.* Olympia: Washington State Board for Community College Education, 1980. 123 pp. (ED 184 616)

Menke, D. H. "A Comparison of Transfer and Native Bachelors' Degree Recipients at UCLA, 1976-1978." Unpublished doctoral dissertation, Graduate School of Education, University of California at Los Angeles, 1980.

Miami-Dade Community College. *RSVP: Feedback Program for Individualized Analysis of Writing, Manual for Faculty Users.* Part I: *Analyzing Students' Writing.* Miami, Fla.: Miami-Dade Community College, 1979. 77 pp. (ED 190 167)

Middleton, L. "Emphasis on Standards at Miami-Dade Leads to 8,000 Dismissals and Suspensions in Three Years." *Chronicle of Higher Education,* February 3, 1981, pp. 3-4.

Monroe, C. R. *Profile of the Community College: A Handbook.* San Francisco: Jossey-Bass, 1972.

Montgomery College. *Unmet Educational Needs.* Rockville, Md.: Montgomery College, 1974. 336 pp. (ED 087 517)

Moody, G. V., and Busby, M. R. *Mississippi Public Junior Colleges Statistical Data, 1977-78.* Jackson: Division of Junior Colleges, Mississippi State Department of Education, 1978. 52 pp. (ED 167 214)

Morrison, J. L., and Ferrante, R. "The Public Two-Year College and the Culturally Different." Paper presented at annual meeting of the American Educational Research Association, New Orleans, February 1973. 35 pp. (ED 073 765)

Moughamian, H. "A Five-Year Longitudinal Study of City Colleges of Chicago Transfer Students, September 1967–June 1972." Unpublished paper, City Colleges of Chicago, 1972. 30 pp. (ED 072 780)

Mundt, J. C. "State vs. Local Control: Reality and Myth over

Concern for Local Autonomy." In S. F. Charles (Ed.), *New Directions for Community Colleges: Balancing State and Local Control,* no. 23. San Francisco: Jossey-Bass, 1978.

Myran, G. A. *Community Services in the Community College.* Washington, D.C.: American Association of Junior Colleges, 1969. 60 pp. (ED 037 202)

Myran, G. A. "Antecedents: Evolution of the Community-Based College." In E. L. Harlacher and J. F. Gollattscheck (Eds.), *New Directions for Community Colleges: Implementing Community-Based Education,* no. 21. San Francisco: Jossey-Bass, 1978.

Nash, P. "Gentrain: An Instructional Delivery System." In L. Koltai (Ed.), *New Directions for Community Colleges: Merging the Humanities,* no. 12. San Francisco: Jossey-Bass, 1975.

National Center for Education Statistics. *Library Statistics for Colleges and Universities.* Washington, D.C.: U.S. Office of Education, Department of Health, Education and Welfare, 1975.

National Center for Education Statistics. *Associate Degrees and Other Formal Awards Below the Baccalaureate: Analysis of 6-Year Trends.* Washington, D.C.: U.S. Government Printing Office, 1978.

National Center for Education Statistics. "Associate Degrees Conferred and Percent Change, by Curriculum Category and Division: Aggregate United States 1970-71—1979-80." *National Center for Education Statistics Bulletin,* 1981, *81-358,* 4.

National Education Association. *Universal Opportunity for Education Beyond the High School.* Washington, D.C.: Educational Policies Commission, National Education Association, 1964.

National Society for the Study of Education. *General Education in the American College.* Part 2. 38th Yearbook. Bloomington, Ind.: National Society for the Study of Education, 1939.

Nelson, J. E. "Student Aid at the Two-Year College: Who Gets the Money?" Paper presented at annual convention of the American Association of Community and Junior Colleges, Washington, D.C., March 1976. 12 pp. (ED 124 223)

Nelson, S. C. *Community Colleges and Their Share of Student Financial Assistance.* Washington, D.C.: Brookings Institution, 1979.

Nelson, S. C. "Future Financing and Economic Trends." *Community and Junior College Journal,* 1980, *51* (1), 41-44.

Nickens, J. M. "A Taxonomy for Community Services." In H. M. Holcomb (Ed.), *New Directions for Community Colleges: Reaching Out Through Community Service,* no. 14. San Francisco: Jossey-Bass, 1976.

Nickens, J. M. "Who Takes Community Service Courses and Why." *Community/Junior College Research Quarterly,* 1977, *2* (1), 11-19.

Noeth, R. J., and Hanson, G. "Research Report: Occupational Programs Do the Job." *Community and Junior College Journal,* 1976, *47* (3), 28-30.

O'Banion, T. *New Directions in Community College Student Personnel Programs.* Student Personnel Series, No. 15. Washington, D.C.: American College Personnel Association, 1971.

O'Banion, T., and Thurston, A. (Eds.). *Student Development Programs in the Community Junior College.* Englewood Cliffs, N.J.: Prentice-Hall, 1972.

Olivas, M. A. *A Statistical Portrait of Honors Programs in Two-Year Colleges.* Washington, D.C.:American Association of Community and Junior Colleges; National Collegiate Honors Council, 1975. 16 pp. (ED 136 890)

Olivas, M. A. *The Dilemma of Access: Minorities in Two-Year Colleges.* Washington, D.C.: Howard University Press, 1979.

Olson, C. *Community and Junior Colleges and the Comprehensive Employment and Training Act: Participation and Recommendations for Improvement.* Washington, D.C.: Office of Governmental Affairs, American Association of Community and Junior Colleges, 1977. 31 pp. (ED 148 405)

Oregon State Department of Education. *1976 Community College Follow-Up Survey Summary of Findings.* Salem: Career and Vocational Education Section, Oregon State Department of Education, 1977. 24 pp. (ED 151 064)

Owen, H. J., Jr. "Balancing State and Local Control in Florida's Community Colleges." In S. F. Charles (Ed.), *New Directions for Community Colleges: Balancing State and Local Control,* no. 23. San Francisco: Jossey-Bass, 1978.

Palow, W. P. "Technology in Teaching Mathematics: A Computer Managed, Multimedia Mathematics Learning Center."

Paper presented at 57th annual meeting of the National Council of Teachers of Mathematics, Boston, April 1979. 8 pp. (ED 184 609)

Park, R. "Proffered Advice: Three Presidential Reports." *UCLA Educator,* 1977, *19* (3), 53-59.

Parker, G. G. *Career Education and Transfer Program Enrollments in 2-Year Colleges, 1973-74.* ACT Special Report No. 11. Iowa City: American College Testing Program, 1974. 44 pp. (ED 103 031)

Parkman, F. "The Tale of the Ripe Scholar." *Nation,* 1869, *9,* 559-560.

Pearlman, D. J. "Alternative Programs in Mathematics in the Community College." Unpublished paper, Tucson, Ariz., 1977. 12 pp. (ED 142 253)

Percy, W. *The Moviegoer.* New York: Avon Books, 1980.

Phair, T. S. *Staffing Patterns in Public California Community Colleges: A 1976-77 Overview.* Sacramento: California Community and Junior College Association, 1977. 22 pp. (ED 135 433)

Pincus, F. L. "The False Promises of Community Colleges: Class Conflict and Vocational Education." *Harvard Educational Review,* 1980, *50* (3), 332-361.

Platte, J. P. (Ed.). *The Status and Prospects of Library/Learning Resource Centers at Michigan Community Colleges.* Lansing: Michigan Community and Junior College Library Administrators; Michigan Community College Community Services Association, 1979. 96 pp. (ED 181 954)

Potter, G. E. "The Law and the Board." In V. Dziuba and W. Meardy (Eds.), *New Directions for Community Colleges: Enhancing Trustee Effectiveness,* no. 15. San Francisco: Jossey-Bass, 1976.

Potter, G. E. *Trusteeship: Handbook for Community College and Technical Institute Trustees.* Washington, D.C.: Association of Community College Trustees, 1977.

Price, E. F. Personal communication, November 3, 1977. Office of the Associate Director, Washington State Board for Community College Education, Olympia.

Purdy, L. M. "A Case Study of Acceptance and Rejection of Innovation by Faculty in a Community College." Unpublished doctoral dissertation, Graduate School of Education, University of California at Los Angeles, 1973.

Quanty, M. *Initial Job Placement for JCCC Career Students, Classes of 1973-1976.* Overland Park, Kans.: Office of Institutional Research, Johnson County Community College, 1977. 61 pp. (ED 144 666)

Queen, J. E., and Rusting, J. *A Survey of Non-Returning Vocational Students: SAM Follow-Up 1976-1977.* Norwalk, Calif.: Office of Institutional Research, Cerritos College, 1978. 31 pp. (ED 156 243)

Queensborough Community College. "A Survey of Queensborough Community College Alumni: 1962-1974." Queensborough Community College (Bayside, N.Y.), 1977, 110 pp. (ED 144 649)

Ravitch, D. *The Revisionists Revised: A Critique of the Radical Attack on the Schools.* New York: Basic Books, 1978.

Reimal, M. W. "A Study of Factors Affecting Attrition Among Women Re-entering Formal Education." Unpublished doctoral dissertation, School of Education, University of Northern Colorado, 1976. (Available from University Microfilms)

"Report of the ASCCC Conference on Academic Standards." Unpublished report, December 2, 1977.

Richardson, R. C., Jr. "Dealing with the Enrollment Depression." *Change,* 1972-1973, *4* (10), 40a-40d.

Richardson, R. C., Jr. (Ed.). *New Directions for Community Colleges: Reforming College Governance,* no. 10. San Francisco: Jossey-Bass, 1975.

Richardson, R. C., Jr., and Doucette, D. S. *Persistence, Performance and Degree Achievement of Arizona's Community College Transfers in Arizona's Public Universities.* Tempe: Department of Higher and Adult Education, Arizona State University, 1980. 140 pp. (ED 197 785)

Richardson, R. C., Jr., and Leslie, L. L. *The Impossible Dream? Financing Community College's Evolving Mission.* Horizons Issue Monograph Series. Washington, D.C.: American Association of Community and Junior Colleges; Los Angeles: ERIC Clearinghouse for Junior Colleges, 1980. 58 pp. (ED 197 783)

Richardson, R. C., Jr., Blocker, C. E., and Bender, L. W. *Governance for the Two-Year College.* Englewood Cliffs, N.J.: Prentice-Hall, 1972.

Richman, B. M., and Farmer, R. N. *Leadership, Goals, and Power in Higher Education: A Contingency and Open-Systems Approach to Effective Management.* San Francisco: Jossey-Bass, 1974.

Riesman, D. *On Higher Education: The Academic Enterprise in an Era of Rising Student Consumerism.* San Francisco: Jossey-Bass, 1981.

Rinck, L. L. "A Comparative Study of Students Active and Inactive in Extracurricular Activities While Enrolled in Second Year Associate Degree Programs on the Kenosha and Racine Campuses of Gateway Technical Institute, Kenosha, Wisconsin." Unpublished paper, University of Wisconsin (Stout), 1969. 133 pp. (ED 171 335)

Robinson, H. F. "The Role of the University in Student Mobility." In H. F. Robinson and others, *Expanding Student Mobility: A Challenge for Community Colleges.* Workshop proceedings, November 7-9, 1977. Atlanta: Southern Regional Education Board, 1977. 71 pp. (ED 164 036)

Roed, W. "State Funding of Community College Community Services Noncredit Offerings: Current Patterns and Problems." Unpublished paper, University of Arizona (Tucson), 1977. 13 pp. (ED 133 008)

Rooth, S. R. "The Reverse Transfer Student at Northampton County Area Community College." Unpublished paper, Tempe, Ariz., 1979. 53 pp. (ED 178 122)

Rotundo, B. *Project Priority: Occupational Emphasis, 1975-1976—A VEA Funded Project.* Final Report. Albany: Two Year College Student Development Center, State University of New York, 1976. 20 pp. (ED 139 476)

Roueche, J. E. "Follow-Ups of the Junior College Transfer Student." *Junior College Resource Review.* Los Angeles: ERIC Clearinghouse for Junior Colleges, 1967. 4 pp. (ED 013 067)

Roueche, J. E., and Boggs, J. R. *Junior College Institutional Research: The State of the Art.* Horizons Issue Monograph Series. Los Angeles: ERIC Clearinghouse for Junior Colleges;

Washington, D.C.: American Association of Junior Colleges, 1968. 77 pp. (ED 019 077)

Rudolph, F. *Curriculum: A History of the American Undergraduate Course of Study Since 1636.* San Francisco: Jossey-Bass, 1977.

Russell, A. A., and Perez, P. L. "Stopping the Attrition of Transfer Students." In F. B. Brawer (Ed.), *New Directions for Community Colleges: Teaching the Sciences,* no. 31. San Francisco: Jossey-Bass, 1980.

Sagen, H. B. "Careers, Competencies, and Liberal Education." Paper presented at annual meeting of the Association of American Colleges, Washington, D.C., February 1979.

St. John, E. *A Study of Selected Developing Colleges and Universities.* Case Study V: *Valencia Community College, Orlando, Florida.* Cambridge, Mass.: Graduate School of Education, Harvard University, 1977. 52 pp. (ED 153 674)

Sanford, N., and others. "New Directions in Higher Education. Iowa City: ACT Program." Paper presented at the Northern California Educational Conference, Sacramento, March 25, 1971. 44 pp. (ED 064 630)

Sasscer, M. F. *1976-77 TICCIT Project.* Final Report. Annandale: Northern Virginia Community College, 1977. 150 pp. (ED 148 430—Available in microfiche only)

Schlesinger, M. A. "Reconstructing General Education: An Examination of Assumptions, Practices, and Prospects." Occasional Paper No. 2. CUE Project, Bowling Green State University (Bowling Green, Ohio), 1977.

Schultz, R. E. "A Follow-Up on Honor Students." *Community and Junior College Journal,* 1967-1968, *38* (4), 9-15.

Selgas, J. W. "1975 Graduates: Spring '77 Follow-Up." Unpublished paper, Harrisburg Area Community College (Harrisburg, Pa.), 1977a. 276 pp. (ED 145 869)

Selgas, J. W. *Student Services: An Evaluation over Time, 1972-1976.* Research Report No. 16. Harrisburg, Pa.: Harrisburg Area Community College, 1977b. 127 pp. (ED 148 408)

Senier, J. *Coordinating Educational Services in Pennsylvania: The Community College Perspective.* Harrisburg: Bureau of Information Systems, Pennsylvania State Department of Education, 1978. 32 pp. (ED 164 071)

Sewell, D. H., and others. *Report on a Statewide Survey About Part-Time Faculty in California Community Colleges.* Sacramento: California Community and Junior College Association, 1976. 40 pp. (ED 118 195)

Shugrue, M. F. *English in a Decade of Change.* New York: Pegasus, 1968.

Silver, J. H. "The Effect of State and Federal Aid Awards on Persistence, Academic Success, and Chances for Graduation Among Freshmen Enrolling at North Greenville College in Fall 1975." Unpublished paper, Tigerville, S.C., 1978. 50 pp. (ED 158 791—Available in microfiche only)

Simon, J. "The Language: Certified Inferiority—A High School Dud by Any Other Name Is Still a Dud." *Esquire,* March 27, 1979, pp. 16-17.

Sinclair, U. B. *Goose Step: A Study of American Education.* New York: AMS Publisher. Reprint of 1923 edition.

Slark, J., and Bateman, H. H. "Community Needs Assessment Survey for Santa Ana College and the Rancho Santiago Community College District." Unpublished paper, Rancho Santiago Community College District (Santa Ana, Calif.), 1980. 75 pp. (ED 186 057)

Slutsky, B. "What Is a College For?" In M. A. Marty (Ed.), *New Directions for Community Colleges: Responding to New Missions,* no. 24. San Francisco: Jossey-Bass, 1978.

Smith, M. F. "Communications Workshops for Navajos in a Community Setting: A Course Plan." Graduate seminar paper, University of Arizona (Tucson), 1979. 31 pp. (ED 174 297)

Solmon, L. C. "The Problem of Incentives." In H. F. Silberman and M. B. Ginsburg (Eds.), *New Directions for Community Colleges: Easing the Transition from Schooling to Work,* no. 16. San Francisco: Jossey-Bass, 1976.

Solmon, L. C. "Rethinking the Relationship Between Education and Work." *UCLA Educator,* 1977, *19* (3), 18-31.

South Oklahoma City Junior College. *Open Access, Satellite Education Service (OASES): Final Annual Report.* Oklahoma City: South Oklahoma City Junior College, 1979. 187 pp. (ED 170 001)

Southern Regional Education Board. *2 + 2 = Expanded Oppor-*

tunity. Cooperative Curricular Planning Between Community Colleges and Senior Institutions in Technical and Career-Oriented Instruction: A Staff Report. Atlanta: Southern Regional Education Board, 1979. 13 pp. (ED 178 139)

Spangler, R. "Mathematics, K–14: A Learning Center Approach at Tacoma Community College." Paper presented at annual meeting of the American Mathematical Association in Two-Year Colleges, Houston, Texas, October 1978. 29 pp. (ED 161 509)

Stankovich, M. J. "Spring 1977 Survey of the Goals and Achievements of Students Enrolled in Spring 1973." Unpublished paper, Macomb County Community College (Warren, Mich.), 1978. 61 pp. (ED 174 274)

Starrak, J. A., and Hughes, R. M. *The Community College in the United States.* Ames: Iowa State College Press, 1954.

State University of New York, Delhi. "Evaluating Educational Outcomes at Delhi—1964-1970. Report 1: Evaluation of Questionnaires Mailed to 1966-1970 Graduates." Agricultural and Technical College, State University of New York (Delhi), 1972. 253 pp. (ED 135 413)

Stevens, C. L. "Models of Learning Resource Services to Community College Off-Campus Classes and Satellite Centers." Unpublished doctoral dissertation, Graduate School of Education, University of California at Los Angeles, 1977.

Stevens, M. A. "CbN Community Forums: The Black Hawk College Model." Unpublished paper, Black Hawk College (Moline, Ill.), 1978. 22 pp. (ED 158 828)

Stier, W. F., Jr. "An Investigation into Nine General Areas and Forty-Four Specific Sub-Areas of Physical Education Currently in Existence Within the Two-Year Institutions of Higher Learning Within the Continental United States, 1970-1971." Unpublished paper, Briar Cliff College (Sioux City, Iowa), 1971. 19 pp. (ED 058 875)

Stine, V. D. "Academic Performance of L.A.C.C. Transfers Entering the University of California During the Academic Year 1974-75 [and] California State University at Los Angeles, 1975-76. Research Study 76-7 [and] 76-9." Unpublished paper, Los Angeles City College, 1976. 39 pp. (ED 133 019)

Strasser, W. C. *Across New Thresholds: Changing Dimension of the Presidency of Montgomery College.* Rockville, Md.: Montgomery College, 1977. 114 pp. (ED 146 982)

Sussman, H. M. "Institutional Responses to Reduced Resources." In R. L. Alfred (Ed.), *New Directions for Community Colleges: Coping with Reduced Resources,* no. 22. San Francisco: Jossey-Bass, 1978.

Sutton, L. S. "Analysis of Withdrawal Rates of Students Receiving Financial Aid at Central Florida Community College." Unpublished paper, Ocala, Fla., 1975. 34 pp. (ED 130 700)

Swenson, N. G. "Statutory Tenure: A Response to Erosion of the Tenure System." *Community College Frontiers,* 1980, *8* (4), 28-31.

Swift, K. D. "A Study of the Effects of the Master Contract on the Eighteen Community Colleges in the State of Minnesota." Unpublished doctoral dissertation, Nova University, 1979. 39 pp. (ED 188 651—Available in microfiche only)

Talbott, L. H. "Community Problem-Solving." In H. M. Holcomb (Ed.), *New Directions for Community Colleges: Reaching Out Through Community Service,* no. 14. San Francisco: Jossey-Bass, 1976.

Tatham, E. L. "A Five-Year Perspective on Job Placement for JCCC Career Students (Classes of 1973-1977)." Unpublished paper, Johnson County Community College (Overland Park, Kans.), 1978. 64 pp. (ED 161 508)

Temple, R. J. "Reverse Articulation and 4 + 2." *Community and Junior College Journal,* 1978, *49* (1), 10-12.

Texas Education Agency. *State Follow-Up Reporting (State Analysis), Data Summary—Fall 1976 Occupational/Technical Graduates. Tex-SIS Follow-Up; Postsecondary Student Follow-Up Management Information System.* Monograph No. 4. Austin: Department of Occupational Education and Technology, Texas Education Agency, 1977. 173 pp. (ED 145 883)

Thompson, F. A. *TIPS (Teaching Information Processing Systems) Implementation at Riverside City College, 1976-77: An Experiment in Educational Innovation.* Final Report, Riverside, Calif.: Riverside City College, 1977. 44 pp. (ED 142 248)

Thornton, J. W., Jr. *The Community Junior College.* (2nd ed.) New York: Wiley, 1966.

Thornton, J. W., Jr. *The Community Junior College.* (3rd ed.) New York: Wiley, 1972.

Tighe, D. J. (Ed.). *Poet on the Moon: A Dialogue on Liberal Education in the Community College.* Washington, D.C.: Association of American Colleges, 1977. 21 pp. (ED 145 870)

Tinto, V. "College Proximity and Rates of College Attendance." *American Educational Research Journal,* 1973, *10* (4), 277-293.

Tolbert, P. S. "Survey of Attitudes Toward a Student Activities Program for Johnson County Community College, Shawnee Mission, Kansas." Paper prepared in conjunction with the EPDA Institute for Advanced Study in Student Personnel Work, University of Missouri—Columbia, September 8, 1970, through May 31, 1971. 38 pp. (ED 051 793)

Trent, J. W. *The Study of Junior Colleges.* Vol. 1: *Roles and Reality of Community Colleges: An Analysis of the Literature.* Los Angeles: Center for the Study of Evaluation, University of California, 1972. 306 pp. (ED 077 507)

Trivett, D. A. "The Ph.D. Job Crisis." *College and University Bulletin,* 1977, *30* (2), 3-6.

Trow, M. *Problems in the Transition from Elite to Mass Higher Education.* New York: McGraw-Hill, 1973.

Tschechtelin, J. D. *Black and White Students in Maryland Community Colleges.* Annapolis: Maryland State Board for Community Colleges, 1979. 20 pp. (ED 175 513)

Tucker, L. G. "Freshman English Programs at Public Two-Year Colleges in Texas." Unpublished master's thesis, School of Education, East Texas State University, 1969.

"Twenty-Year Trends in Higher Education."Fact-File. *Chronicle of Higher Education,* November 13, 1978, p. 13.

U.S. Department of Education, National Center for Education Statistics. *Bulletin.* Washington, D.C.: U.S. Government Printing Office, September 2, 1981.

U.S. Department of Health, Education and Welfare. *Opening (Fall) Enrollments in Higher Education.* (Annual.) Washington, D.C.: National Center for Education Statistics, U.S. Department of Health, Education and Welfare, 1963-1975.

U.S. Department of Health, Education and Welfare. *Digest of Higher Education.* (Annual.) Washington, D.C.: National Center for Education Statistics, U.S. Department of Health, Education and Welfare, 1970-1980.

U.S. Department of Health, Education and Welfare. *Condition of Education.* (Annual.) Washington, D.C.: National Center for Education Statistics, U.S. Department of Health, Education and Welfare, 1970-1980.

U.S. President's Commission on Higher Education. *Higher Education for American Democracy.* Washington, D.C.: U.S. Government Printing Office, 1947. (6 vols. in 1.)

University of Hawaii. *Survey of 1975-76 Graduates: Community Colleges.* Student Flow Project, Report No. 22. Honolulu: Community College System, University of Hawaii, 1977. 90 pp. (ED 135 448)

University of Hawaii. *Survey of 1976-77 Graduates, Community Colleges.* Student Flow Project, Report No. 35. Honolulu: Community College System, University of Hawaii, 1978. 134 pp. (ED 149 836)

University of Hawaii. *Survey of 1977-78 Graduates: Community Colleges.* Honolulu: Community College System, University of Hawaii, 1979. 27 pp. (ED 165 847)

Vaughan, G. B. (Ed.). *New Directions for Community Colleges: Questioning the Community College Role,* no. 32. San Francisco: Jossey-Bass, 1980.

Veblen, T. *The Higher Learning in America: A Memorandum on the Conduct of Universities by Business Men.* New York: B. W. Huebsch, 1918.

Walker, D. E. *The Effective Administrator: A Practical Approach to Problem Solving, Decision Making, and Campus Leadership.* San Francisco: Jossey-Bass, 1979.

Wallace, A. "Competency Evaluation and Expectations of the Public Comprehensive Community College Librarian: A National Survey of Chief Instructional Officers." Unpublished doctoral dissertation, School of Education, University of Toledo, 1977.

Ward, P. "Development of the Junior College Movement." In

J. P. Bogue (Ed.), *American Junior Colleges*. (2nd ed.) Washington, D.C.: American Council on Education, 1948.

Warford, A. R. *Handbook for Community College/Community School Cooperative Relationships: A Case Study of Cooperation in Clackamas County, Oregon.* Washington, D.C.: National Center for Community Education, American Association of Community and Junior Colleges, 1978. 97 pp. (ED 169 960)

Warner, W. L., and others. *Who Shall Be Educated? The Challenge of Unequal Opportunities.* New York: Harper & Row, 1944.

Wattenbarger, J. L. "Articulation with High Schools and Four Year Colleges and Universities." In T. O'Banion and A. Thurston (Eds.), *Student Development Programs in the Community Junior College.* Englewood Cliffs, N.J.: Prentice-Hall, 1972.

Wattenbarger, J. L. "The Dilemma of Reduced Resources: Action or Reaction." In R. L. Alfred (Ed.), *New Directions for Community Colleges: Coping with Reduced Resources,* no. 22. San Francisco: Jossey-Bass, 1978.

Wattenbarger, J. L., and Starnes, P. M. *Financial Support Patterns for Community Colleges 1976.* Gainesville: University of Florida, 1976. 127 pp. (ED 132 994)

Weiser, I. *The Los Angeles Community College District Student: Who, Where, Why, and How.* Research Report No. 77-01. Los Angeles: Division of Educational Planning and Development, Los Angeles Community College District, 1977. 64 pp. (ED 139 480)

Welch, T. "Cabrillo Serves an Exceptional Town." In H. M. Holcomb (Ed.), *New Directions for Community Colleges: Reaching Out Through Community Service,* no. 14. San Francisco: Jossey-Bass, 1976.

Wenckowski, C., and others. *Montgomery College Student Follow-Up Study: First-Time Students, Fall 1974.* Rockville, Md.: Office of Institutional Research, Montgomery College, 1979. 88 pp. (ED 172 871)

White, J. F. "Honors in North Central Association Community Colleges." Paper presented at annual meeting of the American Association of Community and Junior Colleges, Seattle, April 13-16, 1975. 8 pp. (ED 112 995)

Wilms, W., and Hansell, S. "The Unfulfilled Promise of Post-secondary Vocational Education: Graduates and Dropouts in the Labor Market." Unpublished paper, Los Angeles, 1980.

Winkler, B. J. "Graduation, Not Admissions, Urged on Desegregation Laws." *Chronicle of Higher Education,* March 21, 1977, p. 8.

Worthen, D. "Our Own True Watergate." Unpublished paper, Pleasant Hill, Calif., 1979. 8 pp. (ED 184 617)

Worthen, R. J. "Junior College English and the Discipline." Paper presented to the Modern Language Association Workshop on Junior College English at meeting of the National Council of Teachers of English, Milwaukee, December 1968. 11 pp. (ED 025 540)

Wozniak, L. C. "A Study of the Relationship of Selected Variables and the Job Satisfaction/Dissatisfaction of Music Faculty in Two-Year Colleges." Unpublished doctoral dissertation, School of Education, Catholic University of America, 1973.

Yarrington, R. "Finding the Funds." In H. M. Holcomb (Ed.), *New Directions for Community Colleges: Reaching Out Through Community Service,* no. 14. San Francisco: Jossey-Bass, 1976.

Young, R., and others. *Directions for the Future: An Analysis of the Community Services Dimension of Community Colleges.* Community Colleges, Community Education Monograph No. 2. Washington, D.C.: Center for Community Education, American Association of Community and Junior Colleges; Ann Arbor: Office of Community Education, University of Michigan, 1978. 70 pp. (ED 158 787)

Zigerell, J. J., and others. *A Contemporary Course in the Humanities for Community College Students.* Chicago: Chicago City Colleges; Costa Mesa, Calif.: Coast Community College District; Miami, Fla.: Miami-Dade Community College, 1977. 369 pp. (ED 140 892)

Zwerling, L. S. *Second Best: The Crisis of the Community College.* New York: McGraw-Hill, 1976.

Index

425